T0293032

Explainable AI in Healthcare

This book combines technology and the medical domain. It covers advances in computer vision (CV) and machine learning (ML) that facilitate automation in diagnostics and therapeutic and preventive health care. The special focus on eXplainable Artificial Intelligence (XAI) uncovers the black box of ML and bridges the semantic gap between the technologists and the medical fraternity. *Explainable AI in Healthcare: Unboxing Machine Learning for Biomedicine* intends to be a premier reference for practitioners, researchers, and students at basic, intermediary levels and expert levels in computer science, electronics and communications, information technology, instrumentation and control, and electrical engineering.

This book will benefit readers in the following ways:

- Explores state of art in computer vision and deep learning in tandem to develop autonomous or semi-autonomous algorithms for diagnosis in health care
- Investigates bridges between computer scientists and physicians being built with XAI
- Focuses on how data analysis provides the rationale to deal with the challenges of healthcare and making decision-making more transparent
- Initiates discussions on human-AI relationships in health care
- Unites learning for privacy preservation in health care

Analytics and AI for Healthcare Series

Artificial Intelligence (AI) and analytics are increasingly applied to various healthcare settings. AI and analytics are salient to facilitate better understanding and identifying key insights from healthcare data in many areas of practice and inquiry in healthcare including at the genomic, individual, hospital, community and/or population levels. The Chapman & Hall/CRC Press Analytics and AI in Healthcare Series aims to help professionals upskill and leverage analytics and AI techniques, tools, technologies, and tactics to achieve better healthcare delivery, access and outcomes. The series covers all areas of analytics and AI as applied to healthcare. It will examine critical areas, including prevention, prediction, diagnosis, treatment, monitoring, rehabilitation and survivorship.

About the Series Editor

Nilmini Wickramasinghe is Professor of Digital Health and the Deputy Director of the Iverson Health Innovation Research Institute at Swinburne University of Technology, Australia, and is Inaugural Professor – Director Health Informatics Management at Epworth HealthCare, Victoria, Australia. She also holds honorary research professor positions at the Peter MacCallum Cancer Centre, Murdoch Children's Research Institute and Northern Health. For over 20 years, Professor Wickramasinghe has been researching and teaching within the health informatics/digital health domain. She was awarded the prestigious Alexander von Humboldt Award in recognition of her outstanding contribution to digital health.

Explainable AI in Healthcare
Unboxing Machine Learning for Biomedicine
Edited by Mehul S Raval, Mohendra Roy, Tolga Kaya, and Rupal Kapdi

For more information about this series please visit: www.routledge.com/analytics-and-ai-for-healthcare/book-series/Aforhealth

Explainable AI in Healthcare

Unboxing Machine Learning for Biomedicine

Edited by Mehul S Raval, Mohendra Roy, Tolga Kaya, and Rupal Kapdi

CRC Press is an imprint of the
Taylor & Francis Group, an **informa** business
A CHAPMAN & HALL BOOK

Designed cover image: Getty

First edition published 2024
by CRC Press
2385 Executive Center Drive, Suite 320, Boca Raton, FL 33431

and by CRC Press
4 Park Square, Milton Park, Abingdon, Oxon, OX14 4RN

CRC Press is an imprint of Taylor & Francis Group, LLC

First edition published by Routledge 2024

ISBN: 978-1-032-36711-8 (hbk)
ISBN: 978-1-032-36712-5 (pbk)
ISBN: 978-1-003-33342-5 (ebk)

DOI: 10.1201/9781003333425

Typeset in Bembo
by Apex CoVantage, LLC

In dedication to my wife– Hemal, son– Hetav, and in memory of my mother– Charu, and father, Shirish, for their constant encouragement and support through thick and thin.
By Mehul S Raval

In dedication to my mother and my mentors.
By Mohendra Roy

In dedication to my children– Ela and Edward, my wife– Carolyn, Kaya and Baltazar Families, and in memory of my grandfather– Izzet and father-in-law– Dr. Amado Sr.
By Tolga Kaya

In dedication to my parents– Padma and Rashmikant, my husband– Amit, and my son– Nihit for their unconditional continuous support and encouragement.
By Rupal Kapdi

Contents

Foreword

Healthcare has been identified as one of the most significant industries that will be transformed by AI in future. Diverse applications of AI in healthcare include drug discovery and pharmacogenomics, pharmacovigilance, clinical text understanding (natural language processing and understanding applied to electronic medical records); medical image analysis; personalized digital care (including use of healthcare devices, mobile apps, and chatbots); and robots. With around $10 billion as the market value of AI in healthcare at the start of this decade, it is expected to grow at over 40% annually, exceeding $200 billion by 2030. Despite this prediction, the adoption and application of AI are likely to have unique and significant challenges in healthcare.

Two of the most important challenges that can slow the process of adoption of AI in healthcare are explainability and safety. Let me share the underlying reasons. AI has been particularly successful in focused or narrow and well-defined tasks, such as the ones that involve classification, prediction, and recommendation. Some AI applications, such as medical image classification, belong to this category. But many other healthcare tasks are broad-spectrum tasks involving attention to human behavior and involving higher levels of human-like intelligence that encompass broad, complex, and multifaceted activities related to making decisions and taking action. These include contextualization (e.g., utilizing specific medical knowledge), personalization (to support a specific patient), causality, abstraction, and analogy. AI is still at an early stage of meeting these requirements. The second is the clinician's role (and medical expertise) and clinicians' use of or adherence to specific medical guidelines or protocols that cannot be replaced. The clinician cannot rely on an AI algorithm purely or largely driven by data, as today's deep learning algorithms do. It is necessary that the clinician can explain how a particular decision (e.g., reaching a diagnosis) is made and that the relevant clinical guideline or protocol is followed (which typically involves following a process that would require ensuring certain tests/labs have been done, certain contributing factors are ruled in or ruled out, and the decision-making has followed a stepwise process in the clinical guideline). Despite some appealing applications of large data-driven systems like language models, AI systems have shown spectacular failures in ensuring patient safety (e.g., giving dangerous advice or concurring on obviously undesirable options). The AI systems bring many risks related to biases and ethics that must be avoided or ruled out.

This book comes at an opportune time as it is critical for us to assess what is the need to understand what we cannot do without explainability in healthcare. The chapters provide a set of use cases that involve a broad variety of health conditions and real-world healthcare data. Specifically, three types of healthcare data are well covered – clinical text, patient-generated data, and medical images. Finally, the chapters cover a variety of state-of-the-art techniques and methods for achieving explainability. I compliment the editors for bringing an excellent collection of contributions authored by researchers doing interdisciplinary work that fits the theme of this book.

Amit Sheth
Founding Director
Artificial Intelligence Institute
University of South Carolina
Columbia, South Carolina, USA

Preface

Explainable AI in Healthcare combines technology with the medical domain. The advances in computer vision (CV) and machine learning (ML) enable automation in diagnostics and therapeutic and preventive healthcare. The book provides a guide on combining CV and ML and shows the development of algorithms and the architecture for health care. The book is meant for technologists and researchers ranging from novices to experts, as well as to entrepreneurs and practitioners who would like to dive into the domain. The special focus on eXplainable Artificial Intelligence (XAI) will uncover the black box of ML and help find the reasons behind the decisions of automated algorithms. XAI is believed to bridge the *semantic gap* between the technologists and the medical fraternity.

The book will focus on the following two broad sections: Section I – Introduction and Preprocessing and Section II – Use Cases of XAI in Healthcare. The book commences with a chapter on "Human–AI Relationship in Healthcare." It discusses the hurdles in adopting AI algorithms in the field of medicine even though AI algorithms are better or match human capabilities. It highlights the need to better understand human–AI relationships and interactions. It suggests viewing AI as an assistant from whom humans can seek and give feedback over time. The second chapter "Deep Learning in Medical Image Analysis: Recent Models and Explainability" lays the foundation and reviews recent Deep Learning (DL) algorithms for medical image analysis. It showcases implementations in critical applications. It then introduces XAI techniques for DL methods and discusses the challenges in this domain. Imaging techniques provide a wealth of information in clinical applications. Chapter 3, "An Overview of Functional Near-Infrared Spectroscopy (fNIRS) and Explainable Artificial Intelligence (XAI) in fNIRS," discusses the noninvasive neuroimaging technology and shows favorable trade-offs in spatial/temporal resolutions compared to fMRI (functional Magnetic Resonance Imaging) and EEG (electroencephalogram). The image hypercubes need image registration – a process of aligning two or more images. Chapter 4, "An Explainable Method for Point Feature-Based Medical Image Registration," overviews the techniques of image registration and presents some new techniques on the basis of combinatorial and information-theoretic methods.

After laying the foundation in Section I, Section II initiates the journey into use cases of XAI in healthcare. Chapter 5, "State-of-the-Art Deep Learning Methods and Its Explainability for Computerized Tomography Image Segmentation," discusses the foundations of image segmentation. It provides structural information to clinicians for diagnosis and treatment. The DL methods are discussed using CT images, and XAI tools and techniques are introduced. The next chapter "Interpretability of Segmentation and Overall Survival for Brain Tumors" discusses segmentation and survival prediction techniques for glioblastoma patients. It uses MRI images for segmentation and OS prediction and explores the interpretability of ML models used in brain tumor segmentation. It is crucial to characterize the brain tissue to determine the low-grade or high-grade glioma. The MR image biomarkers can noninvasively determine the grades of gliomas. Chapter 7, "Identification of MR Image Biomarkers in Brain Tumor Patients Using Machine Learning and Radiomics Features," provides insights into the use of biomarkers and its validation for tumor grade classification using gene expressions. Chapter 8, "Explainable Artificial Intelligence (XAI) in Breast Cancer Identification," discusses an interesting use case of XAI for breast cancer detection. It introduces various stages and the taxonomy of XAI and discusses various frameworks for breast cancer detection. Usually, a medical dataset is small and noisy, and high-quality medical annotations are difficult to generate. Self-supervised learning (SSL) approach can help to overcome such challenges. Chapter 9, "Interpretability of Self-Supervised Learning for Breast Cancer Image Analysis" covers SSL in screening mammograms. The chapter covers a range of experiments and statistical evaluation and shows that it attains a high accuracy on unlabeled datasets. Moreover, the chapter also discusses the interpretability of the SSL methods.

Reducing hospital readmissions is always the goal of the healthcare system. It will reduce the burden on the system and improve patient care at a reduced cost. Prediction of readmission allows hospitals to plan and improve the quality of care. Using diabetes as an example, Chapter 10, "Predictive Analytics in Hospital Readmission for Diabetes Risk Patients," discusses issues of rehospitalization risk. Since the model is interpretable, clinicians will be able to derive insights into the predictions. The model uses healthcare domain knowledge and risk stratification for making readmission predictions for diabetic patients. Continuing with diabetes as a disease, Chapter 11, "Continuous Blood Glucose Monitoring Using Explainable AI Techniques," covers continuous glucose monitoring. The ML algorithm predicts the future blood glucose level and suggests appropriate insulin dosage. Chapter 12, "Decision Support System for Facial Emotion-Based Progression Detection of Parkinson's Patients," highlights a movement disease – Parkinson's Disease (PD). The decision support system (DSS) can provide optimal care for patients with PD. The DSS detects and grades the facial expression and uses speech classifiers to classify the Hoehn–Yahr (H-Y) stage. Sports data analytics is widely used for performance measurement and injury risk prediction. Chapter 13, "Interpretable Machine Learning in Athletics for Injury Risk Prediction," articulates the use of Decision Tree (DT) classifiers for injury risk prediction of Division I women's basketball team. The data is collected from wearable sensors, the cognitive states of athletes are collected through surveys, and training data is available from coaches. The use of DT and feature engineering provides interpretable ML methods for injury risk prediction. Chapter 14 (the last chapter), "Federated Learning and Explainable AI in Healthcare," highlights risks to patients' data privacy and security. Federated learning provides a distributed computing approach where models are trained across multiple systems. Without sharing data, models and parameters are shared which build the needed trust across the health care community.

Acknowledgements

Writing or editing a book with excellence is an asymptotic process toward perfection – there is always a scope to improvise. The editors are eternally grateful to all the authors of the book – N. Sertac Artan, Jayendra M. Bhalodiya, Jignesh S. Bhatt, Pooja Bidwai, Komal Borisagar, Jacob T. Browne, Anca Bucur, Wing Keung Cheung, Srikrishnan Divakaran, Shilpa Gite, Smita Khairnar, Gitika Jha, Manashree Jhawar, Maulin Joshi, Mukta Joshi, Rupal Kapdi, Tolga Kaya, Radhika Kotecha, Ketan K. Lad, Vedant Manelkar, Mousami Munot, Sarat Kumar Patra, Nicola Pezzotti, Ashish Phophalia, Swati Rai, Snehal Rajput, Mehul S Raval, Mohendra Roy, Kaustubh V. Sakhare, Priyanka Sharma, Srishti Sharma, Bhakti Sonawane, Vibha Vyas, Francesca Manni, Aleksandr Bukharev, Shiva Moorthy, Nancy Irisarri Mendez, and Anshul Jain. The book would not have seen a timely outcome without their expert contribution and real-time responses to reviewers' comments.

Big thanks to Professor Amit Sheth for penning the Foreword and words of advice.

The editors express their gratitude to all associated with IEEE Gujarat section's organized National Seminar on Computer Vision and Image Processing (NaS-CoVIP 2020) where the seeds of the book were sown.

The editors would like to thank leadership at their parent organizations – Ahmedabad University, Ahmedabad, India; Pandit Deendayal Energy University, Gandhinagar, India; Sacred Heart University, Fairfield, Connecticut, USA; and Nirma University, Ahmedabad, India, for providing time and freedom to work on this book project.

The editors also acknowledge the support from Professor Nilmini Wickramasinghe, Series Editor, Analytics and AI in Healthcare, of Chapman and Hall/CRC; George Knott, Commissioning Editor, CRC Press; and Nivedita Menon, Editorial Assistant, CRC Press, and finally Jayachandran R, Project Manager, for helping us through the production phase and for project coordination of the book.

Mehul S Raval, Ahmedabad, India
Mohendra Roy, Gandhinagar, India
Tolga Kaya, Fairfield, Connecticut, USA
Rupal Kapdi, Ahmedabad, India
24th April 2023

Acronyms and Abbreviations

AA	Ascending Aorta
ACA	Affordable Care Act
AD	Alzheimer's Disease
ADC	Analog-To-Digital Converter
ADFES-BIV	The Amsterdam Dynamic Facial Expression Set-Bath Intensity Variation
ADL	Activities of Daily Living
AI	Artificial Intelligence
AL	Active Learning
ALS	Amyotrophic Lateral Sclerosis
AMI	Acute Myocardial Infarction
ANN	Artificial Neural Networks
ARIMA	Autoregressive Integrated Moving Average
ASB11	Ankyrin Repeat and Socs Box Containing 11
AUC	Area Under Curve
BCE	Binary Cross Entropy
BCI	Brain–Computer Interface
BDL	Bayesian Deep Learning
BG	Blood Glucose
BLL	Beer–Lambert Law
BN	Batch Normalization
BraTS	Brain Tumor Segmentation
BRCA1	Breast Cancer Gene 1
BRCA2	Breast Cancer Gene 2
BYOL	Bootstrap Your Own Latent
CAD	Computer-Aided Diagnosis
CARTPT	Cocaine and Amphetamine-Regulated Transcript Prepropeptide
CDX4	Caudal Type Homeobox 4
CE	Conformitè Europëenne
CEGA	Clarke Error Grid Analysis
ceT1	Contrast-Enhanced T1-Weighted
ceT1wMRI	Contrast-Enhanced T1-Weighted Magnetic Resonance Imaging
CFD	Computational Fluid Dynamics

CGM	Continuous Glucose Monitoring
CMMD	Chinese Mammography Database
CMS	Center For Medicare and Medicaid Services
CNN	Convolution Neural Network
COVID-19	Coronavirus Disease
CPD	Coherent Point Drift
CRNN	Convolutional Recurrent Neural Network
CT	Computerized Tomography
CTCA	Computerized Tomography Coronary Angiography
CV	Computer Vision
CVML	Computer Vision and Machine Learning
CW	Continuous Wave
CXR	Chest X-Ray
DBT	Digital Breast Tomosynthesis
DCN	Developmental Cognitive Neuroscience
DDSM	Digital Database for Screening Mammography
DES	Diethylstilbestrol
DICOM	Digital Imaging and Communications in Medicine
DL	Deep Learning
DM	Digital Mammography
DNN	Deep Neural Network
DR	Diabetic Retinopathy
DRN	Deep Residual Network
DSC	Dice Similarity Coefficient
DSS	Decision Support System
DVF	Displacement Vector Field
ECoG	Electrocorticography
ED	Emergency Department
EDA	Exploratory Data Analysis
EDNN	Explainable Deep Neural Network
EEG	Electroencephalography
ENTPD7	Ectonucleoside Triphosphate Diphosphohydrolase 7
FC	Fully Connected
FCN	Fully Connected Network
FDA	U.S Food and Drug Administration
FER	Facial Expression Recognition
FFDM	Full-Field Digital Mammography
FFR	Fractional Flow Reserve
FIR	Finite Impulse Response Filters
FL	Federated Learning
FLAIR	Fluid-Attenuated Inversion Recovery
fMRI	Functional Magnetic Resonance Imaging
fNIRS	Functional Near-Infrared Spectroscopy
FSCB	Fibrous Sheath CABYR Binding Protein
GAN	Generative Adversarial Network

GBM	Glioblastoma Multiforme
GGO	Ground Glass Opacity
GLCM	Grey Level Cooccurrence Matrix
GLDM	Grey Level Dependence Matrix
GLNU	Grey Level Non-Uniformity
GLRLM	Grey Level Run Length Matrix
GLSZM	Grey Level Size Zone Matrix
GLV	Grey Level Variance
GM	Graph Matching
GMM	Gaussian Mixture Models
GPU	Graphics Processing Unit
GradCAM	Gradient-Weighted Class Activation Mapping
GRU	Gated Recurrent Unit
GT	Ground Truth
H & Y	Hoehn and Yahr
HbA1c	Glycosylated Hemoglobin
HbO	Oxygenated Hemoglobin
HbR	De-Oxygenated Hemoglobin
HbT	Total Hemoglobin
HCI	Human–Computer Interaction
HGG	High-Grade Glioma
HGL	High Grey Level
HGLE	High Grey Level Emphasis
HNRNPA3P1	Heterogeneous Nuclear Ribonucleoprotein A3 Pseudogene 1
HOG	Histogram of Oriented Gradients
HPC	High Performance Computing
hPod	Hemoglobin Phase of Oxygenation and Deoxygenation
HRCT	High-Resolution Computerized Tomography
HRRP	Hospital Readmission Reduction Program
HSNE	Hierarchical Stochastic Neighbor Embedding
ICC	Intraclass Correlation Coefficient
ICD9	International Statistical Classification of Diseases (9th Revision)
ICU	Intensive Care Unit
ID	Inverse Difference
IDM	Inverse Difference Moment
iGLU	Intelligent Glucometer
IIR	Infinite Impulse Response
IMC	Informational Measure of Correlation
IMF	Intrinsic Mode Function
IPF	Idiopathic Pulmonary Fibrosis
IR	Image Registration
IRT	Infrared Thermography
KDEF	The Karolinska Directed Emotional Faces
KNN	K-Nearest Neighbor
LCA	Left Coronary Artery

LCX	Left Circumflex Artery
LD	Large Dependence
LDCT	Low-Dose Ct
LGG	Low-Grade Glioma
LGL	Low Grey Level
LGLE	Low Grey Level Emphasis
LIME	Local Interpretable Model-Agnostic Explanations
LIPC	Lipschitz Constant
LIS	Locked-In State
LLM	Logic Learning Machine
LNS	Local Neighborhood Structures
LRP	Layer-Wise Relevance Propagation
LR-ULDCT	Low-Resolution ULDCT
LSTM	Long-Short Term Memory
LTMMC & GH	Lokmanya Tilak Municipal Medical College and Government Hospital
MAD	Mean Absolute Deviation
MARD	Mean Absolute Relative Difference
MBLL	Modified Beer–Lambert Law
MDS	Movement Disorder Society
MEG	Magneto Electroencephalography
MFCC	Mel-Frequency Cepstral Coefficients
MIA	Mammography Intelligent Assessment
MIAS	Mammographic Image Analysis Society
ML	Machine Learning
MLP	Multi-Layer Perceptron
MRI	Magnetic Resonance Imaging
MSE	Mean-Squared Error
MSFDE	Montreal Set of Facial Displays of Emotion
MVPA	Multivariate Pattern Analysis
NGTDM	Neighboring Grey Tone Difference Matrix
NHR	Noise-to-Harmonic Ratio
NIfTI	Neuroimaging Informatics Technology Initiative
NIR	Near Infrared Spectroscopy
NLP	Natural Language Processing
NN	Neural Network
PA	Predictive Analysis
PAIR	People + AI Research
PCA	Principal Component Analysis
PD	Parkinson's Disease
PDL	Patch-Based Dictionary Learning
PDP	Partial Dependence Plot
PEIPA	Pilot European Image Processing Archive
PET	Positron-Emission Tomography
PIQE	Perception-Based Image Quality Evaluator

PMS2P2	Postmeiotic Segregation Increased 1 Homolog 2 Pseudogene 2
PNG	Portable Network Graphics
PSM	Point Set Matching
PSNR	Peak Signal-to-Noise Ratio
PSO	Particle Swarm Optimization
RCA	Right Coronary Artery
ReLU	Rectified Linear Activation Unit
RF	Radio Frequency
RMS	Root Mean Square
RMSE	Root Mean-Squared Error
RNN	Recurrent Neural Network
RPM	Robust Point Matching
$rScO_2$	Regional Cerebral Oxygen Saturation
SD	Small Dependence
SHAP	Shapley Additive Explanations
SIFT	Scale Invariant Feature Transform
SPECT	Single-Photon Emission Computed Tomography
SR	Success Rate
SR	Super-Resolution
SSIM	Structural Similarity Index
SSL	Self-Supervised Learning
SUMO1P3	Small Ubiquitin-Like Modifier 1 Pseudogene 3
SURF	Speed Up Robust Features
SVM	Support Vector Machine
T1	T1-Weighted
T1D	Type-1 Diabetes
T2D	Type-2 Diabetes
T1wMRI	T1-Weighted Magnetic Resonance Imaging
TA2	Tcga Assembler2
TAMI	Taiwan Aging and Mental Illness
TCGA	The Cancer Genome Atlas
TE	Time For Echo
TPS-RPM	Thin Plate Spline Robust Point Matching
TR	Time For Repetition
TRE	Target Registration Error
TRPS	Topology Preserving Robust Point Matching
tSNE	Geometric T Distributed Stochastic Neighbor Embedding
UCI	University of California at Irvine
UKCA	United Kingdom Conformity Assessed
ULDCT	Ultra-LDCT
UMAP	Uniform Manifold Approximation and Projection
UPDRS	Unified Parkinson's Disease Rating Scale
US	Ultrasound
USFDA	United States Food and Drug Administration
VMD	Various Mode Decomposition

WFDC10A	WAP Four-Disulfide Core Domain 10a
WHO	World Health Organization
WIT	What-If-Tool
XAI	Explainable Artificial Intelligence
XED	Explainable Emotion Detection
XFR	Explainable Face Recognition
ZED	Explainable Emotion Detection
ZFR	Explainable Face Recognition

Editors

Mehul S Raval, PhD, is an educationist, mentor, advisor, and researcher with expertise in computer vision. As a Professor at Ahmedabad University he teaches undergraduate and post graduate students of computer science and engineering.

Mohendra Roy, PhD, is an assistant professor in the Department of Information and Communication Technology at Pandit Deendayal Energy University, India. His areas of interest include quantum computing, artificial intelligence, and bio-inspired systems.

Tolga Kaya, PhD, joined Sacred Heart University in the fall of 2017 as an associate professor and program director of the computer engineering program in the School of Computer Science and Engineering. His teaches undergraduate engineering and graduate computer science courses and conducts research in these fields.

Rupal Kapdi, PhD, is an assistant professor in the Computer Science and Engineering Department at the Institute of Technology, Nirma University, India. Her areas of interest include machine learning, deep learning, image processing, and medical imaging.

Contributors

N. Sertac Artan
New York Institute of Technology
Old Westbury, New York, USA

Jayendra M. Bhalodiya
School of Engineering and Applied Science
Ahmedabad University
Ahmedabad, Gujarat, India

Jignesh S. Bhatt
Indian Institute of Information Technology Vadodara
Gandhinagar, Gujarat, India

Pooja Bidwai
Symbiosis Institute of Technology
Symbiosis International University
Pune, Maharashtra, India

Komal Borisagar
GTU Graduate School of Engineering and Technology
Ahmedabad, Gujarat, India

Jacob T. Browne
Philips Experience Design
Delft University of Technology
Delft, South Holland, Netherlands

Anca Bucur
Philips Research Europe
AI Data Science and Digital Twin
Eindhoven, Netherlands

Aleksandr Bukharev
Philips Research Europe
AI Data Science and Digital Twin
Eindhoven, Netherlands

Wing Keung Cheung
University College London
London, United Kingdom

Srikrishnan Divakaran
School of Interwoven Arts and Sciences
Krea University
Sricity, Andhra Pradesh, India

Shilpa Gite
Symbiosis Institute of Technology
Symbiosis Centre for Applied AI (SCAAI)
Symbiosis International University
Pune, Maharashtra, India

Anshul Jain
Philips Research India
Research Digital-Data and AI_CoE
Bengaluru, India

Gitika Jha
K. J. Somaiya Institute of Engineering and Information Technology
Mumbai, Maharashtra, India

Manashree Jhawar
K. J. Somaiya Institute of Engineering and Information Technology
Mumbai, Maharashtra, India

Maulin Joshi
Sarvajanik College of Engineering and Technology
Surat, Gujarat, India

Mukta Joshi
Philips Healthcare
Andover, Massachusetts, USA

Rupal Kapdi
Institute of Technology
Nirma University
Ahmedabad, Gujarat, India

Tolga Kaya
Sacred Heart University
Fairfield, Connecticut, USA

Smita Khairnar
Symbiosis Institute of Technology
Symbiosis International University
and
Pimpri Chinchwad College of Engineering
Savitribai Phule Pune University
Pune, Maharashtra, India

Radhika Kotecha
K. J. Somaiya Institute of Engineering and Information Technology
Mumbai, Maharashtra, India

Ketan K. Lad
GIDC Degree Engineering College
Navsari, Gujarat, India

Vedant Manelkar
K. J. Somaiya Institute of Engineering and Information Technology
Mumbai, Maharashtra, India

Francesca Manni
Philips Research Europe
AI Data Science and Digital Twin
Eindhoven, Netherlands

Nancy Irisarri Mendez
Philips Research Europe
AI Data Science and Digital Twin
Eindhoven, Netherlands

Shiva Moorthy
Philips Research India
Research Digital-Data and AI_CoE
India

Mousami Munot
Pune Institute of Computer Technology
Pune, Maharashtra, India

Sarat Kumar Patra
Indian Institute of Information Technology Vadodara
Gandhinagar, Gujarat, India

Nicola Pezzotti
Eindhoven University of Technology
Eindhoven, Netherlands

Ashish Phophalia
Indian Institute of Information Technology Vadodara
Gandhinagar, Gujarat, India

Swati Rai
Indian Institute of Information Technology Vadodara
Gandhinagar, Gujarat, India

Snehal Rajput
Pandit Deendayal Energy University
Gandhinagar, Gujarat, India

Mehul S Raval
School of Engineering and Applied Science
Ahmedabad University
Ahmedabad, Gujarat, India

Mohendra Roy
Pandit Deendayal Energy University
Gandhinagar, Gujarat, India

Kaustubh V. Sakhare
Lear Corporation
Baroda, Gujarat, India

Priyanka Sharma
Samyak InfoTech
Ahmedabad, Gujarat, India

Srishti Sharma
School of Engineering and Applied Science
Ahmedabad University
Ahmedabad, Gujarat, India

Bhakti Sonawane
Institute of Technology
Nirma University
Ahmedabad, Gujarat, India

Vibha Vyas
College of Engineering
Pune, Maharashtra, India

1 Human–AI Relationship in Healthcare

Mukta Joshi, Nicola Pezzotti, and Jacob T. Browne

Contents

1.1 Introduction

Integrating AI into clinical practice is a difficult, complex process, and we have yet to see widespread adoption (Bedoya et al., 2019; He et al., 2019; Chen and Asch, 2017; Rajpurkar et al., 2022). One hindering factor prominent in prior work is the lack of transparency in AI recommendations. As AI increases in complexity, often the ability of the AI to explain its decisions becomes more difficult. This is purported to have negative effects on clinician–AI team performance: miscalibration of trust, risk of disuse, risk of automation bias, and so on (Bussone et al., 2015; Suresh et al., 2021). For instance, a radiologist encountering a high workload might

DOI: 10.1201/9781003333425-1

over-rely on an AI that detects tumors despite having low accuracy, resulting in misdiagnosed and undiagnosed patients. This lack of model interpretability has been called a "missing piece" in AI for medicine (Gilvary et al., 2019). Given that clinical decisions can have severe consequences and are prone to interpretation errors, clinical explainable AI (XAI) is seemingly crucial for the success of the adoption of clinical AI (Reyes et al., 2020).

1.2 How Trust Is Built

Trust plays a crucial role in almost all human relationships. Trust is a critical element in virtually all forms of interactions, including those between humans and machines (Lee and See, 2004). It is widely recognized that trust is a precondition to (successful) human–machine interactions (Kaplan et al., 2021; Vereschak et al., 2021).

An important factor in human relationships is communication and how each party treats the other. In human interactions, we hypothesize that there are three main elements that create a "good" experience: active listening, mutual respect, and not insulting the other's intelligence. People tend to have more pleasant interactions with one another when these elements are upheld. Justification describing the rationale and the data that influenced one's choice, together with the level of certainty, gives transparency, which builds trust.

Humility is often viewed as a crucial component in trustworthiness, according to Nielsen, Marrone, and Slay (2010). High humility in the trustee allows the trustor to have a greater sense that an unknown trustee is trustworthy. This is because the display of humility garners trust efficacy ("Trustworthiness, Humility, and Empathy in Business by Lead2Goals" n.d.). This is especially important in the clinical setting where crucial decisions have long-lasting impact and to avoid overreliance on AI. Humility can be described as an accurate and realistic view of self-knowledge and the communication of that knowledge to others. Humility can manifest in many ways, including acknowledgment of one's mistakes and limitations.

1.3 How Experts Interact with Apprentices

An apprentice is knowledgeable in their domain and needs an apprenticeship for practical application of their knowledge, to learn by watching the experts make decisions in real-world scenarios.

Over time the apprentice is tested by the expert and asked to give their opinion or choice before the expert acts. The expert then decides whether to accept, modify, or reject the apprentice's input. When the apprentice presents their opinion, they give more than a simple A or B, yes or no answer. They explain the factors they considered and any impediments or obstructions and qualify their answer with a level of confidence.

This allows the expert to fully understand the apprentice's point of view and to weigh the input. The expert can give feedback and teach the apprentice where the flaw in their logic may be or adjust the influence of certain factors. The apprentice brings a different point of view and may see things the expert misses. This creates a team, and the apprentice can, at times, augment the expert's skills and make for a stronger combination.

1.4 Expectations of Human–AI Interactions

Understanding how humans build trust, the elements of good communication, and what meaningful interactions look like in an expert–apprentice setting helps to guide what humans might expect when interacting with AI agents.

Highly skilled individuals, such as medical professionals, expect high performance relevant to the task being performed from an AI agent. At the same time, it is known that neither human nor machine can be perfectly right all the time. Hence, most interactions are related to the fact that neither is perfect, and therefore a more involved interaction is required. For a task that can be performed with perfection, such as a calculation, the interaction expectations are minimal and simple. The interaction, the dialogue, becomes crucial when the performance cannot be perfect. An algorithm that claims to have 99% accuracy gets it wrong 1 in 100 times. The issue is not that it may get it wrong 1 in 100 times; the issue is which 1 of the 100 did it get wrong? How does the user find out? So far, in many computer vision and classification algorithms, metrics such as rate of false positives or sensitivity and specificity are documented. However, these algorithms cannot indicate when specific cases had a likelihood of failing. This created a very cumbersome user experience where each case had to be checked by the user, diminishing the value of the automation.

The inherent complexity of technological systems invariably leads to a state of "epistemic vulnerability," whereby the internal dynamics of the system are hidden to the user and, crucially, must be inferred by the observer via the behavior of the system. By epistemic vulnerability here, we mean that the user relies on inference to understand the machine–what the machine does, how it does it, how its actions change given context, and so on (Kaplan et al., 2021; Schoeller et al., 2021). Enter explanation. "Explain" is defined in the Cambridge Dictionary as: *to make something clear or easy to understand by describing or giving information about it* (n.d.). It is a shared meaning-making process that occurs between the explainer and the explainee (Ehsan et al., 2021).

As we have outlined so far, humans need specific characteristics in their interactions, that is, high performance, trustworthy behavior, and meaningful communication.

For AI to be useful in practice, in the near term, it needs to assist doctors as a second reader or a second opinion (not replace them) (Evans et al., 2022). In these scenarios, human–AI interaction should be modeled after interactions between doctors and their peers or doctors and residents, such as the expert–apprentice model.

The human intellect needs feedback and explanation, or else it can be easily frustrated and angered, especially in stressful and high-stakes environments such as healthcare. Communication that allows the user to take action to improve the algorithm's performance or confidence creates a sense of dialogue. For example, communication that the image quality of the input may be suboptimal due to metal in the field of view, causing performance degradation, can give actionable feedback. This kind of communication reduces the feeling of helplessness when an algorithm shows obvious failure and in turn contributes to building trust.

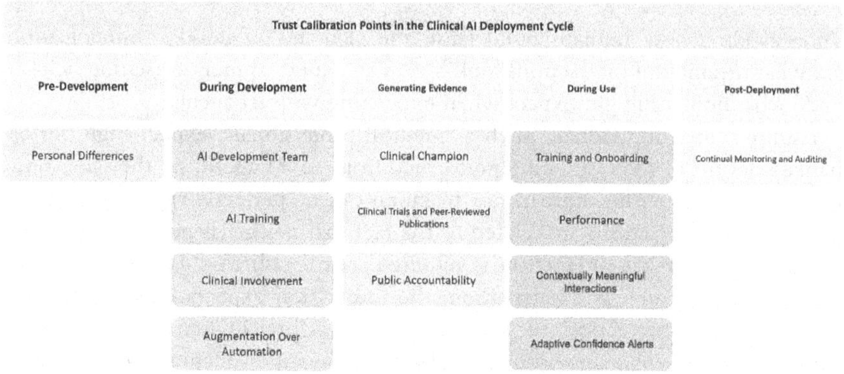

Trust Calibration Points in the Clinical AI Deployment Cycle				
Pre-Development	**During Development**	**Generating Evidence**	**During Use**	**Post-Deployment**
Personal Differences	AI Development Team	Clinical Champion	Training and Onboarding	Continual Monitoring and Auditing
	AI Training	Clinical Trials and Peer-Reviewed Publications	Performance	
	Clinical Involvement	Public Accountability	Contextually Meaningful Interactions	
	Augmentation Over Automation		Adaptive Confidence Alerts	

Figure 1.1 Diagram depicting different trust calibration points within the development of clinical AI deployment cycle extending the concept from Browne et al. with elements important during use.

On the rare occasion that the AI agent encounters input that it has not been trained on, it should be able to say the equivalent of "I don't know." The AI agent should be able to state the certainty of its answer like in the expert–apprentice model. With such communication, the agent would display humility and garner trust.

Within clinical AI, trust generation between clinicians and AI systems expands throughout the development and deployment cycle (Browne et al., 2022). Building on Browne et al.'s model, we focus on AI behavior during use to emphasize the points we wish to make (see Figure 1.1) (2022). Cultivating relationships over time to successfully calibrate trust at each point in the deployment cycle requires practicing humility, whether through human–human or human–AI interactions.

1.5 The Human–Machine Combination – A Stronger Team

The expert–apprentice model is what we envision for the human–AI partnership: a team that works to complement each other and increase the combined success rate (see Figure 1.2). This is especially relevant in a complex field like healthcare, where a multitude of factors can influence a situation.

The attending doctor in this case would be the expert and the final authority in making decisions and choices about the patient's diagnosis or treatment. For the AI input to be helpful to the human expert, there needs to be a meaningful engagement. For instance, the expert expects to be given contextual information that has influenced the suggestion or detection. In a review of what makes human–agent collaborations robust and pleasant, Cila presents 11 collaboration qualities for designers (2022). Among these qualities, Cila emphasizes several key points relevant to explainable AI in healthcare: that the intentions and protocols of the agent are visible, augmenting rather than replacing; that there is intelligibility in how an agent works and why it behaves a certain way; and that the agent establishes common

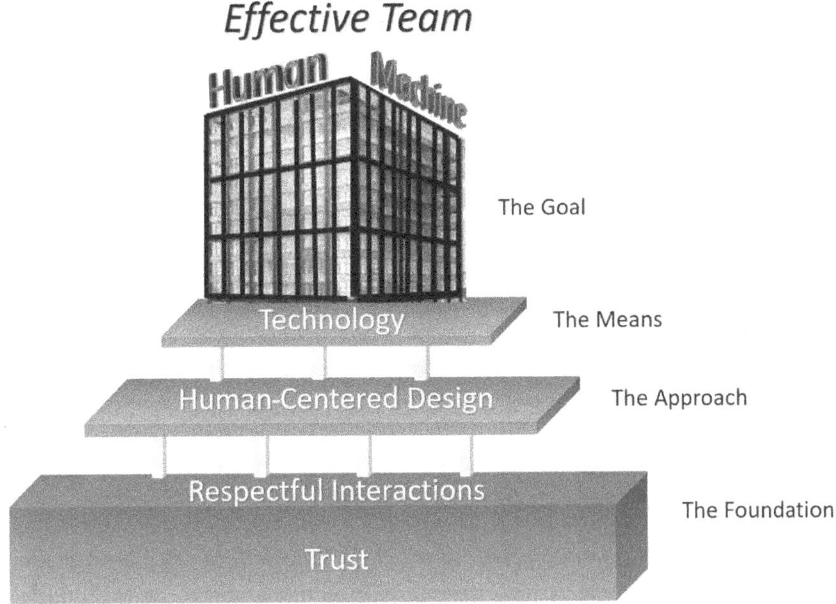

Figure 1.2 Pyramid model for considering the importance of trust and respectful interactions as foundations for effective human–machine teams.

ground with the user (2022). In this light, XAI is seen as a crucial component of creating effective human–agent collaboration: generating conditions of joint activity and mutual responsiveness (Cila, 2022).

1.6 Technical Developments

The field of human–computer interaction, or HCI in short, is focused on understanding the principles behind the interplay of human and computer actors. More specifically, it focuses on the design, development, and use of computer technology through interfaces between people (users) and computers. While the term HCI was popularized by the book *The Psychology of Human-Computer Interaction* by Card, Moran, and Newell (Huesmann et al., 1984), the field has seen extreme development in the last three decades, with several seminal works such as *Designing the User Interface, Strategies for Effective Human-Computer Interaction* from Ben Shneiderman (1987).

Aspects of HCI in the field of artificial intelligence have been addressed and developed for many years. For example, visualization and interaction have been extensively used to understand models such as logistic regression (Royston and Altman, 2010; Mitchell, 2012; Chatzimparmpas et al., 2020), support vector machines (Jakulin et al., 2005; Van Belle et al., 2016; Cervantes et al., 2020), decision trees, and random forests (Elzen and Van Wijk, 2011; Zhao et al., 2019; Tam et al., 2017). Such approaches focus on understanding which input features are provided as input to the model and the relative importance for the prediction at hand. Many algorithms for feature importance estimation have been developed over the years (Lipovetsky and Conklin, 2001; Hancer et al., 2020; Kumar et al., 2020), but they often tend to provide insights on how the presence or corruption of a given feature, that is, a specific aspect of the data, affects the corresponding prediction. Specialized systems have been developed to support the exploration of model predictions and their corresponding features in an interactive manner (Chatzimparmpas et al., 2020; Muhlbacher et al., 2014). Such systems require a good understanding of the models and features.

In the last ten years, a dramatic shift happened in the field of artificial intelligence and machine learning. A class of algorithms and models, known as deep-neural-networks (DNNs) (Lecun et al., 2015), demonstrated an unprecedented ability to tackle complex problems for which clear features are not defined. Despite being known for decades, neural networks have proven difficult to optimize and often too computationally complex to train. Thanks to the availability of cheap parallel processing engines, in the form of GPUs, and novel optimization approaches, deep neural networks have taken the world by storm, providing an unprecedented ability to address previously unapproachable problems (Litjens et al., 2017; L. Liu et al., 2020; Zhang et al., 2022; Kamilaris and Prenafeta-Boldú, 2018). In the field of medical imaging, DNN and a specific architecture known as UNets (Ronneberger et al., n.d.) have become the de facto standard for problems like semantic segmentation, disease detection (Litjens et al., 2017), and image reconstruction (Pezzotti et al., 2020).

Deep neural networks pose a problem for a human-centric approach to AI. Where traditional models rely on interpretable features, DNNs derive features directly from the data. Such "learned" features are not easily identifiable in the model and often do not match the intuition of a subject matter expert concerning their meaning. Therefore, linked to the development of DNNs, a new field developed focused on the interpretability and expandability of such models. Interpretability refers to the ability of a human to have a broad understanding of the computations that the model performs. For example, is the model affected by biases? Are the classes of the models properly defined? Which kind of patterns has the model learned from the dataset? On the other hand, explainability refers to the ability to pinpoint exactly which part of the input is responsible for a given decision, and it is often referred in literature as eXplainable AI or XAI. While explainability is desired, it is often hard to achieve; hence, many systems are verified and tested by a mix of sound validation metrics and a set of insights derived from interpretability methods.

We now present a broad categorization of the methodologies that can be employed to achieve interpretable or explainable models, with a specific focus on deep-learning models. We refer the interested reader to surveys that provide a more extensive categorization and description of the methods (Dosilovic et al., 2018; Hohman et al., 2019; Tjoa and Guan, 2021).

A first approach taken by the community was to inspect which kind of patterns are learned by a network. Such methods are known as feature-visualization techniques and rely on optimization methods to extract a visual representation of the learned patterns. Several evolutions exist, which nowadays allow a good understanding of what a network sees in the data (Szegedy et al., 2014; Mordvintsev et al., 2015; Erhan et al., 2009). Notably, the algorithms evolved to be used beyond providing explanations, for example, for image style transfer (Jing et al., 2020; Gatys et al., 2016; Mordvintsev et al., 2018). A well-known drawback of such methods is that they often provide a hard-to-interpret motivation of how the network comes to a decision, a problem made worse in the healthcare context by the difficulty of distinguishing relevant features in the original data (it is much easier to understand the concept of a "dog" in a natural image dataset than a faint lesion in an MRI dataset).

A different approach to understanding deep-learning models is to treat them as high-dimensional transformation engines and try to understand the geometric operations they perform. A deep-neural network takes as input high-dimensional data, for example, an image where each pixel is considered a dimension. By applying non-linear transformations in such a space, the data are moved into a space which, for example, can be linearly separated for classification purposes. A similar approach is taken for segmentation, where, rather than the complete image, a patch can be considered. Understanding high-dimensional spaces is not an easy task, but in recent years several methods have been developed to facilitate this task. Algorithms such as tSNE (Pezzotti et al., 2020), HSNE (Pezzotti et al., 2016), UMAP (McInnes et al., 2018), and other variants are routinely used in systems to facilitate the understanding of what is globally learned by the models (Pezzotti et al., 2017; Kahng et al., 2018).

Note that, for both previous classes of methods, only a global understanding of the model can be achieved, that is, understanding either the features that were learned or how the model treats the training or validation set in its entirety. For specific input data, and for explaining why a prediction is given on it, other methods must be employed. Many of these rely on the concept of attribution: the idea of identifying which pixels are responsible for a given classification or segmentation output. GradCAM (Selvaraju et al., 2020) is one of the most widely used approaches and relies on backpropagating through the network information related to the activation of the class of interest. The "attribution" is often represented as a heatmap drawn on top of the image, which can then be easily interpreted by the user. Several evolutions of the method exist (Chattopadhyay et al., 2018; Desai and Ramaswamy, 2020; Wang et al., 2020). Other methods, such as LIME (Ribeiro et al., 2016), rely on a more local explanation of the classification boundary, estimating in which "directions" an image can be changed in order to modify the expected classification.

In recent years, many different variants of these categories have been introduced. The vast majority of methods are aimed at model developers, providing insights on the robustness of the models and how they can be improved to achieve better performance and robustness with respect to outlier and out-of-distribution data. On the other hand, techniques aimed at explaining decisions made by the models to the user of the models have found limited applications due to the complexity and the difficulty of implementing them effectively in end-to-end systems. However, the awareness of having a human-centered approach to artificial intelligence is constantly increasing (Shneiderman, 2020), and we expect that an increasing number of systems will embrace this philosophy, providing tools to assess the predictions in a reliable manner. Human-centered AI is achieved not by directly explaining a prediction of a classifier but by devising strategies for deployment that can provide reliable control-points for the user, who can then override the decision when trust is not high. Such trust is achieved by informing the user about the confidence on a given prediction or how "different" given data are with respect to the dataset used for training. After the user is informed about this, a decision can be made to override or refine the user AI decision, potentially providing new training data that are used to refine the model performance using a continual learning paradigm (B. Liu, 2017; Pianykh et al., 2020; Deasy and Stetson, 2021).

Many different approaches can be taken to assess the confidence of an AI model. An extremely simple approach is to leverage the prediction of the model: if the prediction probabilities for a classification task are not above a certain threshold, the prediction is discarded, a strategy that also works for segmentation models. This can be further augmented to show when the prediction is in a so-called "gray zone," that is, just below or above the threshold. In these cases, we can flag the algorithm output as uncertain and bring these cases to the expert's attention. However, this approach has the limitation of not being able to capture the intrinsic uncertainty in the model and data. For example, a model can come with an extremely high probability solution just because it does not generalize well on the data at hand, a behavior that is explored in the literature around adversarial examples (Goodfellow et al., 2015). To address this, several methods have been developed to model uncertainty so that the model can provide an assessment of its confidence in the prediction while potentially improving the performance of such models (Kendall and Gal, 2017; Hu et al., 2021; Malinin and Gales, 2018; Cipolla et al., 2018). Quantifying predictive uncertainty is an area of active research. Bayesian neural networks (NNs) require significant modifications to the training procedure and are computationally expensive compared to standard non-Bayesian NNs. Alternatives to Bayesian NNs have been proposed, such as by Lakshminarayanan et al. (n.d.).

Finally, another topic of interest is the detection of outliers and out-of-distribution samples. This category of methods is aimed at detecting input data that are so different from the training set that not even confidence estimation will provide reliable results (Ren et al., 2019; W. Liu et al., 2020; Liang et al., 2018; Vyas et al., 2018). The ability to detect out-of-distribution samples brings an awareness that the input is a case that the network has not seen before, and this can be leveraged to communicate to the user and offer this indication along with any result that is shown.

A successful solution will need to incorporate many different components that will enable a human-centered workflow. The next section will heavily focus on such aspects and how they can be implemented in a clinical context.

1.7 Human-Centered Clinical XAI

Clinicians often lack the technical knowledge to understand developer-centric XAI and can have varying needs for XAI depending on context, making this a challenging design space. To address this need, recent research in human-centered XAI offers some paths forward (Pazzani et al., 2022; Ehsan and Riedl, 2020; Schoonderwoerd et al., 2021). For instance, human-centered XAI development processes have been explored in post-treatment of patients with atrial fibrillation and chest X-ray analysis (Xie et al., 2020; She et al., 2022).

In this section, we will illuminate some recent trends towards building human-centered XAI. Our goal here is to uplift the recent turn in XAI research: the turn to XAI as a sociotechnical problem rather than a technical problem (Ehsan and Riedl, 2020). To illuminate our points, we will use CheXplain to provide an example to help ground readers (Xie et al., 2020). CheXplain is a proof-of-concept prototype built by Xie et al. to enable clinicians to explore AI-enabled chest X-ray (CXR) analysis (2020). CheXplain takes in single CXR images and outputs labels made up of a list of observations (findings from the radiograph).

1.8 Recommendations for Designing Human-Centered Clinical XAI

This review primarily looks at work where XAI was evaluated by actual users, ideally clinicians, rather than formalizations of the ideal XAI. This review also incorporates papers that have reviewed the literature (e.g., systematic review) of XAI guidelines or offered a framework for developing XAI. While not intended to be exhaustive, we hope this offers a well-rounded survey of current trends. In Figure 1.3, we build on the process outlined by Browne et al. for recommendations over the clinical AI deployment cycle (2022), with added focus on design for the "during use" phase.

1.8.1 Start with an Interdisciplinary Team

To craft effective XAI, we will need to work across disciplines: AI engineers, designers, clinicians, and so on (Vaughan and Wallach, 2021; Reyes et al., 2020; Cutillo et al., 2020). One domain cannot control the entire development of XAI: it requires a thorough understanding of technical, social, and clinical factors that go into

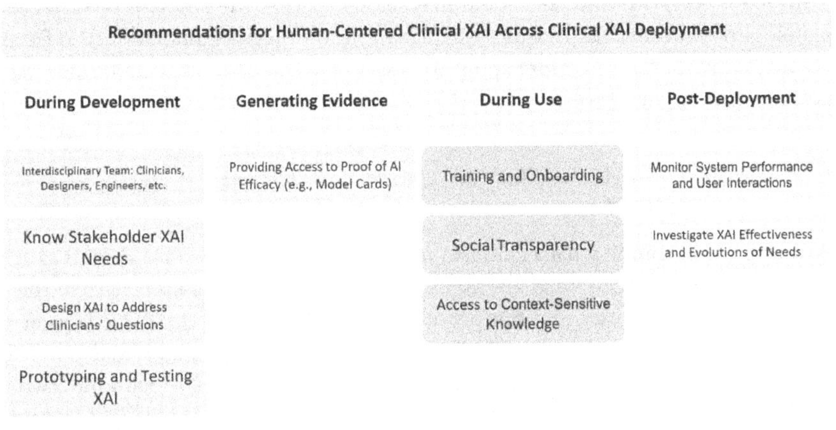

Figure 1.3 Diagram depicting our recommendations for human-centered clinical XAI across clinical XAI deployment.

the design. Clinicians must be involved in every step of the development process through participatory means to bridge the sociotechnical gap between development and implementation (Antoniadi et al., 2021; Matthiesen et al., 2021). For instance, developing CheXplain would require cross-collaboration between AI engineers, clinicians, designers, and other stakeholders to iteratively prototype designs based on AI capabilities and user needs.

1.8.2 Know Different Stakeholder XAI Needs

Different stakeholders in the AI development and deployment process will have different XAI needs (Bhatt et al., 2020; Vaughan and Wallach, 2021; Ehsan and Riedl, 2020; Arbelaez Ossa et al., 2022; Suresh et al., 2021; Gerlings et al., 2022). The design of XAI varies by a user's domain expertise and task types (e.g., differences in need on confidence scores, counterfactuals, saliency maps, etc.) (X. Wang and Yin, 2021; Ehsan and Riedl, 2020; Evans et al., 2022; Suresh et al., 2021; Gerlings et al., 2022; Liao et al., 2020; Xie et al., 2020). Clinical user needs are different from what a developer needs to test the model for bias (Gerlings et al., 2022). Clinical solutions are often multi-user systems, and XAI ought to accommodate the needs of these users (Jacobs et al., 2021).

Different clinical contexts will have different XAI needs and tolerances (e.g., identifying nail fungus vs. pneumothorax detection), which may require a change in model choice (Antoniadi et al., 2021; Arbelaez Ossa et al., 2022). Findings from user studies can then inform model selection after understanding user XAI needs (Jin et al., 2021; Antoniadi et al., 2021). Cognitive resources and time can vary by context: consider intensive care units (ICUs) or emergency departments (EDs) where time resources are at a minimum (Tonekaboni et al., 2019; Arbelaez Ossa et al., 2022). As Ossa et al. note, XAI development "should respond to the specific need and potential risks of each clinical scenario for a responsible and ethical implementation of artificial intelligence" (2022).

In the CheXplain case, we would need to understand the different XAI needs of radiologists (who may expect more explanations on specific annotations), referring physicians (who may care more about the validity of the AI results), and other stakeholders who might use or be affected by the system (Xie et al., 2020).

1.8.3 Design XAI to Address Clinicians' Questions and Integrate into Their Workflow

Rather than imagining what a clinician might need, it should be investigated early in the development process what questions and expectations actual users have of the AI through exploratory user research processes (Arbelaez Ossa et al., 2022; Liao et al., 2020; Doshi-Velez and Kim, 2017; Bhatt et al., 2020; Vaughan and Wallach, 2021; Reyes et al., 2020; Sokol and Flach, 2020; Barda et al., 2020; Schoonderwoerd et al., 2021). We should know what it is clinicians might need explained and what that explanation should look like (Liao et al., 2020).

XAI should accommodate the clinical workflow: providing the right information, at the right time, in the right way (e.g., progressive disclosure and interactive explanations) (Sokol KSokol and Flach, 2020; X. Wang and Yin, 2021; Evans et al., 2022; Springer et al., 2020). Explanations need to be understandable by the clinician without having technical knowledge about AI (Jin et al., 2022; Jin et al., 2022; Matthiesen et al., 2021). As mentioned earlier, think about drawing parallels to the expert–apprentice analogy or doctor–trainee interactions. Clinicians should be able to validate model output through their own clinical knowledge (Tonekaboni et al., 2019). Explanations should fit into and support a clinician's existing clinical reasoning practice or be "clinically sound" explanations (e.g., visualizing important parameters that led to the decision so clinicians can compare their own reasoning process) (Jin et al., 2022; Jin et al., 2022; Sokol KSokol and Flach, 2020; Matthiesen et al., 2021; Tonekaboni et al., 2019; Evans et al., 2022; Wang et al., 2019). The AI should give them a "second opinion" based on similar reasoning to their own (Evans et al., 2022) For instance, a radiologist examining a CXR with the help of an AI system may want a second opinion by using XAI to see what the AI is "seeing" and why it came to that recommendation (Xie et al., 2020).

Conversely, user studies with clinicians could indicate the unimportance of XAI in a clinical workflow. Henry et al. found that XAI was not a primary driver of the use of an ML-based clinical system (2022). Some researchers advocate interrogating the widespread requirement of XAI for clinical use, instead vouching that trust should be generated via other means (e.g., rigorous validation across contexts and involvement of clinical team during development) (Sendak et al., 2020; Ghassemi et al., 2021; Jacobs et al., 2021). Clinicians routinely use information in clinical decision making without a thorough understanding of the mechanisms which created that information (e.g., acetaminophen) (Sendak et al., 2020; Kirkpatrick, 2005). Clinicians may not have the time to even look at an XAI after adopting the AI into their workflow (Jacobs et al., 2021). Sendak et al. note how XAI could negatively orient clinicians away from patients and towards technology and even confuse them (Sendak et al., 2020; Ghassemi et al., 2021). As London puts it, "when the demand for explanations of how interventions work is elevated above careful, empirical validation, patients suffer, resources are wasted, and progress is delayed" (2019).

With these opposing views, there is no one-size-fits-all approach to clinical XAI (Amann et al., 2022). Taking the varying views into account, a development team must understand the intended use for which they are designing: what explanations clinicians need and how those effectively fit into the workflow, keeping a focus on human-centered explainability and not only on technology-centered explainability as some of the previous studies did.

In the CheXplain case, we would need to conduct user research with clinicians early in the development process. How do they explain their own reasoning between clinicians, when do these explanations surface in their workflow, and how can XAI integrate into and augment that process? In showing clinician's prototypes of the potential system, what questions do they actually want answered by the XAI?

1.8.4 Investigate XAI Effectiveness throughout the Development and Deployment Process

It is crucial to know how XAI will inform clinical practice (Bhatt et al., 2020; Vaughan and Wallach, 2021). Pre-deployment, teams can craft prototypes to test different XAI methods the team is considering (explanation forms, onboarding flows, etc.) (Jin et al., 2021; Browne, 2019; Cai et al., 2019; Schoonderwoerd et al., 2021). Different contexts might call for multiple different types of XAI to be present depending on user needs (Ehsan and Riedl, 2020; Tonekaboni et al., 2019). Designs may need to support providing counterfactuals, confidence scores, indicating if the input data fits the training distribution, allowing exploration of source data, allowing users to explore alternative recommendations, why a model is diverging from common practice, and testing other hypotheses (Buçinca and Gajos, 2021; X. Wang and Yin, 2021; Miller, 2019; Bussone et al., 2015; Jacobs et al., 2021).

Testing XAI prototypes emphasizes that situational context matters more than technically explaining the machine (Ehsan et al., 2021). Using these prototypes, teams can test the impact the XAI has on the clinical workflow (e.g., if participants might skip, misuse, or misunderstand the explanation). Further, teams need to investigate how providing XAI affects decision making, where clinicians can blindly trust the XAI even though the model could be wrong or biased (Bansal et al., 2021; Buçinca and Gajos, 2021). We often assume that people will interact with explanations analytically, when instead people tend to over-rely on AI, even with explanations (Buçinca and Gajos, 2021). Just the mere presence of XAI leads to an increase in trust (Bansal et al., 2021). Timing the explanation is also crucial; whether the user sees a recommendation before forming their own can have an impact on performance (Bansal et al., 2021; Wang et al., 2019; Fogliato et al., 2022).

This investigation should expand throughout the development process and even once the AI is deployed (Davis et al., 2020; Doshi-Velez and Kim, 2017) As people use the system, their mental model and trust evolves, and their needs for explanation will change (Liao et al., 2020). Often, task performance with XAI varies from context to context, depending on human factors beyond the XAI (e.g., cognitive motivation) (Buçinca and Gajos, 2021). The clinical context is one of social, team-oriented decision making. Investigations need to keep in mind the wider interactions with different team members and their needs (Ehsan and Riedl, 2020). Development teams can investigate how their XAIs fit into this wider clinical team (Lage et al., 2019).

While we would like to propose metrics for XAI, there is a lack of research in concrete metrics to evaluate XAI (Doshi-Velez and Kim, 2017; Lage et al., 2019). This is partly due to different contexts needing different metrics, making a generalizable framework for measuring the effectiveness for AI difficult (Mohseni et al., 2021). We encourage developers to make XAI metrics that matter to their context and users. Regardless, the efficacy of the XAI should be evaluated throughout development and deployment cycles.

In the CheXplain case, we would design prototypes of varying fidelities with clinical stakeholders to test how it impacts the workflow and whether the XAI works for them. After deploying into a real clinical workflow, we would need similar studies investigating how it has affected the workflow and how usage of XAI changes over time (e.g., over-reliance on the system). Their needs may have altered as the human-AI trust relationship evolves.

1.9 New Directions in Human-Centered Clinical XAI

1.9.1 Exploring Cognitive Differences in How Humans and AI Explain

A good starting point for developing clinical XAI is often understanding how users currently give explanations to other users and stakeholders on such a decision (Liao et al., 2020; Wang et al., 2019; Xie et al., 2020). Kaufman and Kirsh conducted an observation and ethnographic study looking at how radiologists explain findings to other radiologists (2022). They note three ways current XAI methods differ from actual explanations. XAI does not give adequate, direct attention to visual features in a way that explains why they see what they see in a way that establishes proper temporal sequence. XAI also does not attend to the needs of radiologists of different expertise levels. Last, XAI does not hedge qualitatively like a radiologist does. If we want to create human-centered AI, we need to understand how clinicians make explanations and take care to reflect how they create this common ground with each other. In our CheXplain case, we would investigate how clinicians offer explanations to each different stakeholders (to novices, senior members, patients, etc.) prior to developing an AI model to better understand how we could integrate into this workflow.

1.9.2 Socially Transparent XAI

Another promising direction known as socially transparent XAI expands the epistemic boundary of XAI. Explanations are socially situated in human–human interactions, a shared sense-making process (Ehsan et al., 2021). Why do we limit XAI where the algorithm ends? AI is embedded in sociotechnical contexts, where people are working with this system to make informed decisions. Socially transparent XAI goes beyond the confines of the algorithm to incorporate "social-organizational contexts to facilitate explainability of AI's recommendations" (Ehsan et al., 2021). This is to include other people's interactions with the AI system in XAI. Clinicians would be able to see what decisions and reasons other clinicians used when interacting with the AI in similar scenarios. This has immense potential for benefits in cross-training, peer-review, and building trust (Ehsan et al., 2021). In our CheXplain case, we would show how other radiologists interacted with the AI given a similar CXR.

1.10 Conclusions

Current trends point towards a human-centered XAI: away from formalisms, solutionism, and technology-centered implementations, towards realizing XAI as a sociotechnical problem (Ehsan et al., 2021). There is no one-size-fits-all approach to knowing how to develop XAI in clinical practice (Amann et al., 2022). There are many different technical tools that were outlined here that can be leveraged to fit the clinical workflow and task at hand. Whether an XAI is useful or crucial depends on the user and context (Amann et al., 2022). As Amann et al. state, "we need to individually analyze implemented systems and their specific needs with regards to technology, displayed information, user groups, and the intended use of the system in decision making to draw conclusions about explainability requirements" (2022). While more case studies are showing up, we need more work that directly examines the challenges of real-world integration into clinical practice, and how XAI plays a role (or detractor) from that integration (Sendak et al., 2020; Jacobs et al., 2021). The purpose of this chapter was to bring a perspective to technical readers as well as clinicians that highlights the human side of the problem, the complexity of the topic, and the challenges of the technology. Developers should keep the users and intended use in mind as well as understanding the explainability requirements when designing, engaging with clinicians and users throughout the development process and beyond into post-deployment.

Acknowledgments

We would like to thank the reviewers for the helpful comments and suggestions to enrich the chapter.

This work is part of the DCODE project that has received funding from the European Union's Horizon 2020 research and innovation program under the Marie Skłodowska-Curie grant agreement No. 955990.

References

Amann, Julia, Dennis Vetter, Stig Nikolaj Blomberg, Helle Collatz Christensen, Megan Coffee, Sara Gerke, Thomas K. Gilbert, et al., 2022. "To Explain or Not to Explain? – Artificial Intelligence Explainability in Clinical Decision Support Systems." *PLOS Digital Health* 1 (2): e0000016. https://doi.org/10.1371/JOURNAL.PDIG.0000016.

Antoniadi, Anna Markella, Yuhan Du, Yasmine Guendouz, Lan Wei, Claudia Mazo, Brett A. Becker, and Catherine Mooney. 2021. "Current Challenges and Future Opportunities for XAI in Machine Learning-Based Clinical Decision Support Systems: A Systematic Review." *Applied Sciences* 11 (11): 5088. https://doi.org/10.3390/APP11115088.

Arbelaez Ossa, Laura, Georg Starke, Giorgia Lorenzini, Julia E. Vogt, David M. Shaw, and Bernice Simone Elger. 2022. "Re-Focusing Explainability in Medicine." *Digital Health* 8. https://doi.org/10.1177/20552076221074488.

Bansal, Gagan, Raymond Fok, Marco Tulio Ribeiro, Tongshuang Wu, Joyce Zhou, Ece Kamar, Daniel S. Weld, and Besmira Nushi. 2021. "Does the Whole Exceed Its Parts? The Effect of AI Explanations on Complementary Team Performance." *Proceedings of the 2021 CHI Conference on Human Factors in Computing Systems* 16. https://doi.org/10.1145/3411764.

Barda, Amie J., Christopher M. Horvat, and Harry Hochheiser. 2020. "A Qualitative Research Framework for the Design of User-Centered Displays of Explanations for Machine Learning Model Predictions in Healthcare." *BMC Medical Informatics and Decision Making* 20 (1): 1–16. https://doi.org/10.1186/S12911-020-01276-X/FIGURES/6.

Bedoya, Armando D., Meredith E. Clement, Matthew Phelan, Rebecca C. Steorts, Cara O'Brien, and Benjamin A. Goldstein. 2019. "Minimal Impact of Implemented Early Warning Score and Best Practice Alert for Patient Deterioration." *Critical Care Medicine* 47 (1): 49–55. https://doi.org/10.1097/CCM.0000000000003439.

Belle, Vanya Van, Ben Van Calster, Sabine Van Huffel, Johan A.K. Suykens, and Paulo Lisboa. 2016. "Explaining Support Vector Machines: A Color Based Nomogram." *PLoS ONE* 11 (10). https://doi.org/10.1371/journal.pone.0164568.

Bhatt, Umang, Alice Xiang, Shubham Sharma, Adrian Weller, Ankur Taly, Yunhan Jia, Joydeep Ghosh, Ruchir Puri, José MF. Moura, and Peter Eckersley. 2020. "Explainable Machine Learning in Deployment." *Proceedings of the 2020 Conference on Fairness, Accountability, and Transparency*, 648–657. https://doi.org/10.1145/3351095.

Browne, Jacob T. 2019. "Wizard of Oz Prototyping for Machine Learning Experiences." *Conference on Human Factors in Computing Systems – Proceedings*, 1–6. https://doi.org/10.1145/3290607.3312877.

Browne, Jacob T., Saskia Bakker, Bin Yu, Peter Lloyd, and Somaya ben Allouch. 2022. "Trust in Clinical AI: Expanding the Unit of Analysis." *First International Conference on Hybrid Human-Artificial Intelligence*. www.hhai-conference.org/wp-content/uploads/2022/06/hhai-2022_paper_30.pdf.

Buçinca, Zana, and Krzysztof Z. Gajos. 2021. "To Trust or to Think: Cognitive Forcing Functions Can Reduce Overreliance on AI in AI-Assisted Decision-Making." *Proceedings of the ACM on Human-Computer Interaction* 5: 21. https://doi.org/10.1145/3449287.

Bussone, Adrian, Simone Stumpf, and Dympna O'Sullivan. 2015. "The Role of Explanations on Trust and Reliance in Clinical Decision Support Systems." *Proceedings – 2015 IEEE International Conference on Healthcare Informatics, ICHI 2015*, December, 160–169 https://doi.org/10.1109/ICHI.2015.26.

Cai, Carrie J., Google Research, Brain Team, Usa Samantha Winter, Google Health, Usa David Steiner, Usa Lauren Wilcox, et al., 2019. "'Hello AI': Uncovering the Onboarding Needs of Medical Practitioners for Human-AI Collaborative Decision-Making." *Proceedings of the ACM on Human-Computer Interaction* 3 (CSCW). https://doi.org/10.1145/3359206.

Cervantes, Jair, Farid Garcia-Lamont, Lisbeth Rodríguez-Mazahua, and Asdrubal Lopez. 2020. "A Comprehensive Survey on Support Vector Machine Classification: Applications, Challenges and Trends." *Neurocomputing* 408: 189–215. https://doi.org/10.1016/j.neucom.2019.10.118.

Chattopadhyay, Aditya, Anirban Sarkar, and Prantik Howlader. 2018. "Grad-CAM ++ : Improved Visual Explanations for Deep Convolutional Networks." *IEEE Winter Conference on Applications of Computer Vision (WACV)*, 839–847. https://doi.org/10.1109/WACV.2018.00097

Chatzimparmpas, Angelos, Rafael M. Martins, Ilir Jusufi, and Andreas Kerren. 2020. "A Survey of Surveys on the Use of Visualization for Interpreting Machine Learning Models." *Information Visualization* 19 (3). https://doi.org/10.1177/1473871620904671.

Chen, Jonathan H., and Steven M. Asch. 2017. "Machine Learning and Prediction in Medicine – Beyond the Peak of Inflated Expectations." *The New England Journal of Medicine* 376 (26): 2507. https://doi.org/10.1056/NEJMP1702071.

Cila, Nazli. 2022. "Designing Human-Agent Collaborations: Commitment, Responsiveness, and Support." *CHI Conference on Human Factors in Computing Systems*, 1–18. https://doi.org/10.1145/3491102.

Cipolla, Roberto, Yarin Gal, and Alex Kendall. 2018. "Multi-Task Learning Using Uncertainty to Weigh Losses for Scene Geometry and Semantics." *Proceedings of the IEEE*

Computer Society Conference on Computer Vision and Pattern Recognition, 7482–7491. https://doi.org/10.1109/CVPR.2018.00781.

Cutillo, Christine M., Karlie R. Sharma, Luca Foschini, Shinjini Kundu, Maxine Mackintosh, Kenneth D. Mandl, Tyler Beck, et al., 2020. "Machine Intelligence in Healthcare – Perspectives on Trustworthiness, Explainability, Usability, and Transparency." *NPJ Digital Medicine* 3 (1): 1–5. https://doi.org/10.1038/s41746-020-0254-2.

Davis, Brittany, Maria Glenski, William Sealy, and Dustin Arendt. 2020. "Measure Utility, Gain Trust: Practical Advice for XAI Researchers." *Proceedings – 2020 IEEE Workshop on TRust and EXpertise in Visual Analytics, TREX 2020,* October, 1–8. https://doi.org/10.1109/TREX51495.2020.00005.

Deasy, Joseph O., and Peter D. Stetson. 2021. "A Platform for Continuous Learning in Oncology." *Nature Cancer* 2 (7): 675–676. https://doi.org/10.1038/s43018-021-00239-z.

Doshi-Velez, Finale, and Been Kim. 2017. "Towards A Rigorous Science of Interpretable Machine Learning." February, 1–16. arXiv:1702.08608. https://doi.org/10.48550/arxiv.1702.08608.

Dosilovic, Filip Karlo, Mario Brcic, and Nikica Hlupic. 2018. "Explainable Artificial Intelligence: A Survey." 2018 41st International Convention on Information and Communication Technology, Electronics and Microelectronics, MIPRO 2018 – Proceedings, 0210–0215. https://doi.org/10.23919/MIPRO.2018.8400040.

Ehsan, Upol, and Mark O. Riedl. 2020. "Human-Centered Explainable AI: Towards a Reflective Sociotechnical Approach." *Lecture Notes in Computer Science (Including Subseries Lecture Notes in Artificial Intelligence and Lecture Notes in Bioinformatics)* 12424 (LNCS): 449–466. https://doi.org/10.1007/978-3-030-60117-1_33/TABLES/3.

Ehsan, Upol, Q. Vera Liao, Michael Muller, Mark O. Riedl, and Justin D. Weisz. 2021. "Expanding Explainability: Towards Social Transparency in AI Systems." *Proceedings of the 2021 CHI Conference on Human Factors in Computing Systems* 19: 1–19. https://doi.org/10.1145/3411764.

Elzen, Stef Van Den, and Jarke J. Van Wijk. 2011. "BaobabView: Interactive Construction and Analysis of Decision Trees." *VAST 2011 – IEEE Conference on Visual Analytics Science and Technology 2011, Proceedings,* 151–160. https://doi.org/10.1109/VAST.2011.6102453.

Erhan, Dumitru, Yoshua Bengio, Aaron Courville, and Pascal Vincent. 2009. "Visualizing Higher-Layer Features of a Deep Network." *Bernoulli* 1341.

Evans, Theodore, Carl Orge Retzlaff, Christian Geißler, Michaela Kargl, Markus Plass, Heimo Müller, Tim Rasmus Kiehl, Norman Zerbe, and Andreas Holzinger. 2022. "The Explainability Paradox: Challenges for XAI in Digital Pathology." *Future Generation Computer Systems* 133: 281–96. https://doi.org/10.1016/J.FUTURE.2022.03.009.

Fogliato, Riccardo, Shreya Chappidi, Matthew Lungren, Michael Fitzke, Mark Parkinson, Diane Wilson, Paul Fisher, Eric Horvitz, Kori Inkpen, and Besmira Nushi. 2022. "Who Goes First? Influences of Human-AI Workflow on Decision Making in Clinical Imaging." *ACM Conference on Fairness, Accountability, and Transparency,* 22. https://doi.org/10.1145/3531146.

Gatys, Leon, Alexander Ecker, and Matthias Bethge. 2016. "A Neural Algorithm of Artistic Style." *Journal of Vision* 16 (12). https://doi.org/10.1167/16.12.326.

Gerlings, Julie, Millie Søndergaard Jensen, and Arisa Shollo. 2022. "Explainable AI, But Explainable to Whom? An Exploratory Case Study of XAI in Healthcare." *Intelligent Systems Reference Library* 212: 169–198. https://doi.org/10.1007/978-3-030-83620-7_7.

Ghassemi, Marzyeh, Luke Oakden-Rayner, and Andrew L. Beam. 2021. "The False Hope of Current Approaches to Explainable Artificial Intelligence in Health Care." *The Lancet Digital Health* 3 (11): e745–750. https://doi.org/10.1016/S2589-7500(21)00208-9/ATTACHMENT/F419A161-CE0C-4D86-8197–39B3190CA57B/MMC1.PDF.

Gilvary, Coryandar, Neel Madhukar, J. Elkhader, and Olivier Elemento. 2019. "The Missing Pieces of Artificial Intelligence in Medicine." *Trends in Pharmacological Sciences* 40 (8): 555–564. https://doi.org/10.1016/J.TIPS.2019.06.001.

Goodfellow, Ian J., Jonathon Shlens, and Christian Szegedy. 2015. "Explaining and Harnessing Adversarial Examples." *3rd International Conference on Learning Representations, ICLR 2015 – Conference Track Proceedings*, 1–12, arXiv preprint arXiv:1412.6572.

Hancer, Emrah, Bing Xue, and Mengjie Zhang. 2020. "A Survey on Feature Selection Approaches for Clustering." *Artificial Intelligence Review* 53 (6). https://doi.org/10.1007/s10462-019-09800-w.

He, Jianxing, Sally L. Baxter, Jie Xu, Jiming Xu, Xingtao Zhou, and Kang Zhang. 2019. "The Practical Implementation of Artificial Intelligence Technologies in Medicine." *Nature Medicine* 25 (1): 30–36. https://doi.org/10.1038/s41591-018-0307-0.

Henry, Katharine E., Rachel Kornfield, Anirudh Sridharan, Robert C. Linton, Catherine Groh, Tony Wang, Albert Wu, Bilge Mutlu, and Suchi Saria. 2022. "Human–Machine Teaming Is Key to AI Adoption: Clinicians' Experiences with a Deployed Machine Learning System." *Npj Digital Medicine 2022 5:1* 5 (1): 1–6. https://doi.org/10.1038/s41746-022-00597-7.

Hohman, Fred, Minsuk Kahng, Robert Pienta, and Duen Horng Chau. 2019. "Visual Analytics in Deep Learning: An Interrogative Survey for the Next Frontiers." *IEEE Transactions on Visualization and Computer Graphics* 25 (8). https://doi.org/10.1109/TVCG.2018.2843369.

Hu, Shi, Nicola Pezzotti, and Max Welling. 2021. "Learning to Predict Error for MRI Reconstruction." *Lecture Notes in Computer Science (Including Subseries Lecture Notes in Artificial Intelligence and Lecture Notes in Bioinformatics)* 12903 (LNCS). https://doi.org/10.1007/978-3-030-87199-4_57.

Huesmann, Rowell L., Stuart K. Card, Thomas P. Moran, and Allen Newell. 1984. "The Psychology of Human-Computer Interaction." *The American Journal of Psychology* 97 (4). https://doi.org/10.2307/1422176.

Jacobs, Maia, Jeffrey He, and Melanie F. Pradier. 2021. "Designing AI for Trust and Collaboration in Time-Constrained Medical Decisions: A Sociotechnical Lens." *Conference on Human Factors in Computing Systems – Proceedings*, May, 1–14. https://doi.org/10.1145/3411764.3445385.

Jakulin, Aleks, Martin Možina, Janez Demšar, Ivan Bratko, and Blaž Zupan. 2005. "Nomograms for Visualizing Support Vector Machines." *Proceedings of the ACM SIGKDD International Conference on Knowledge Discovery and Data Mining,* 108–117. https://doi.org/10.1145/1081870.1081886.

Jin, Weina, Xiaoxiao Li, and Ghassan Hamarneh. 2022. Evaluating Explainable AI on a Multi-Modal Medical Imaging Task: Can Existing Algorithms Fulfill Clinical Requirements? www.aaai.org.

Jin, Weina, Xiaoxiao Li, Mostafa Fatehi, and Ghassan Hamarneh. 2022. *Guidelines and Evaluation for Clinical Explainable AI on Medical Image Analysis*. https://doi.org/10.1016/j.media.2022.102684

Jing, Yongcheng, Yezhou Yang, Zunlei Feng, Jingwen Ye, Yizhou Yu, and Mingli Song. 2020. "Neural Style Transfer: A Review." *IEEE Transactions on Visualization and Computer Graphics* 26 (11). https://doi.org/10.1109/TVCG.2019.2921336.

Kahng, Minsuk, Pierre Y. Andrews, Aditya Kalro, and Duen Horng Polo Chau. 2018. "ActiVis: Visual Exploration of Industry-Scale Deep Neural Network Models." *IEEE Transactions on Visualization and Computer Graphics* 24 (1). https://doi.org/10.1109/TVCG.2017.2744718.

Kamilaris, Andreas, and Francesc X. Prenafeta-Boldú. 2018. "Deep Learning in Agriculture: A Survey." *Computers and Electronics in Agriculture* 147: 70–90. https://doi.org/10.1016/j.compag.2018.02.016.

Kaplan, A.D., T.T. Kessler, and P.A. Hancock. 2021. "How Trust Is Defined and Its Use in Human–Human and Human–Machine Interaction." *SAGE Journals* 64 (1): 1150–1154. https://doi.org/10.1177/1071181320641275.

Kaufman, Robert A., and David J. Kirsh. 2022. "Cognitive Differences in Human and AI Explanation." *Proceedings of the Annual Meeting of the Cognitive Science Society* 44: 2694–2700. https://escholarship.org/uc/item/9p24077n.

Kelly, Christopher J., Alan Karthikesalingam, Mustafa Suleyman, Greg Corrado, and Dominic King. 2019. "Key Challenges for Delivering Clinical Impact with Artificial Intelligence." *BMC Medicine* 17 (1): 1–9. https://doi.org/10.1186/S12916-019-1426-2/PEER-REVIEW.

Kendall, Alex, and Yarin Gal. 2017. "What Uncertainties Do We Need in Bayesian Deep Learning for Computer Vision?" *Advances in Neural Information Processing Systems* 2017.

Kirkpatrick, Peter. 2005. "New Clues in the Acetaminophen Mystery." *Nature Reviews Drug Discovery* 4 (11): 883–883. https://doi.org/10.1038/nrd1887.

Kumar, Elizabeth I., Suresh Venkatasubramanian, Carlos Scheidegger, and Sorelle A. Friedler. 2020. "Problems with Shapley-Value-Based Explanations as Feature Importance Measures." *37th International Conference on Machine Learning, ICML 2020* PartF168147–8.

Lage, Isaac, Emily Chen, Jeffrey He, Menaka Narayanan, Been Kim, Samuel J. Gershman, and Finale Doshi-Velez. 2019. "Human Evaluation of Models Built for Interpretability." *Proceedings of the AAAI Conference on Human Computation and Crowdsourcing*, 59–67. https://ojs.aaai.org/index.php/HCOMP/article/view/5280.

Lakshminarayanan, Balaji, Alexander Pritzel, and Charles Blundell Deepmind. n.d. *Simple and Scalable Predictive Uncertainty Estimation Using Deep Ensembles*. Accessed September 2, 2022. https://proceedings.neurips.cc/paper/2017/file/9ef2ed4b7fd2c810847ffa5fa85bce38-Paper.pdf.

Lecun, Y., Y. Bengio, and G. Hinton. 2015. "Deep Learning." *Nature* 521 (7553): 436–444. https://doi.org/10.1038/nature14539.

Lee, John D., and Katrina A. See. 2004. "Trust in Automation: Designing for Appropriate Reliance." *Human Factors* 46 (1): 50–80. https://doi.org/10.1518/hfes.46.1.50_30392.

Liang, Shiyu, Yixuan Li, and R. Srikant. 2018. "Enhancing the Reliability of Out-of-Distribution Image Detection in Neural Networks." *6th International Conference on Learning Representations, ICLR 2018 – Conference Track Proceedings.* https://doi.org/10.48550/arXiv.1706.02690

Liao, Vera Q., Daniel Gruen, and Sarah Miller. 2020. "Questioning the AI: Informing Design Practices for Explainable AI User Experiences." *Proceedings of the 2020 CHI Conference on Human Factors in Computing Systems,* 1–15. https://doi.org/10.1145/3313831.

Lipovetsky, Stan, and Michael Conklin. 2001. "Analysis of Regression in Game Theory Approach." *Applied Stochastic Models in Business and Industry* 17 (4). https://doi.org/10.1002/asmb.446.

Litjens, Geert, Thijs Kooi, Babak Ehteshami Bejnordi, Arnaud Arindra Adiyoso Setio, Francesco Ciompi, Mohsen Ghafoorian, Jeroen AWM. van der Laak, Bram van Ginneken, and Clara I. Sánchez. 2017. "A Survey on Deep Learning in Medical Image Analysis." *Medical Image Analysis* 42: 60–88. https://doi.org/10.1016/j.media.2017.07.005.

Liu, Bing. 2017. "Lifelong Machine Learning: A Paradigm for Continuous Learning." *Frontiers of Computer Science* 11 (3). https://doi.org/10.1007/s11704-016-6903-6.

Liu, Li, Wanli Ouyang, Xiaogang Wang, Paul Fieguth, Jie Chen, Xinwang Liu, and Matti Pietikäinen. 2020. "Deep Learning for Generic Object Detection: A Survey." *International Journal of Computer Vision* 128 (2). https://doi.org/10.1007/s11263-019-01247-4.

Liu, Weitang, Xiaoyun Wang, John D. Owens, and Yixuan Li. 2020. "Energy-Based Out-of-Distribution Detection." *Advances in Neural Information Processing Systems* 33, 21464–21475.

London, Alex John. 2019. "Artificial Intelligence and Black-Box Medical Decisions: Accuracy versus Explainability." *The Hastings Center Report* 49 (1): 15–21. https://doi.org/10.1002/HAST.973.

Malinin, Andrey, and Mark Gales. 2018. "Predictive Uncertainty Estimation via Prior Networks." *Advances in Neural Information Processing Systems* 2018.

Matthiesen, Stina, Søren Zöga Diederichsen, Mikkel Klitzing Hartmann Hansen, Christina Villumsen, Mats Christian Højbjerg Lassen, Peter Karl Jacobsen, Niels Risum, et al., 2021. "Clinician Preimplementation Perspectives of a Decision-Support Tool for the Prediction of Cardiac Arrhythmia Based on Machine Learning: Near-Live Feasibility and Qualitative Study." *JMIR Human Factors* 8 (4). https://doi.org/10.2196/26964.

McInnes, Leland, John Healy, Nathaniel Saul, and Lukas Großberger. 2018. "UMAP: Uniform Manifold Approximation and Projection." *Journal of Open Source Software* 3 (29). https://doi.org/10.21105/joss.00861.

Miller, Tim. 2019. "Explanation in Artificial Intelligence: Insights from the Social Sciences." *Artificial Intelligence* 267: 1–38. https://doi.org/10.1016/J.ARTINT.2018.07.007.

Mitchell, MN. 2012. *Interpreting and Visualizing Regression Models Using Stata*. Stata Press Books, May, 558.

Mohseni, Sina, Niloofar Zarei, Eric D Ragan, and; E D Ragan. 2021. "A Multidisciplinary Survey and Framework for Design and Evaluation of Explainable AI Systems." *ACM Transactions on Interactive Intelligent Systems (TiiS)* 11 (3–4): 1–45. https://doi.org/10.1145/3387166.

Mordvintsev, Alexander, Christopher Olah, and Mike Tyka. 2015. "Inceptionism: Going Deeper into Neural Networks." *Research Blog*.

Mordvintsev, Alexander, Nicola Pezzotti, Ludwig Schubert, and Chris Olah. 2018. "Differentiable Image Parameterizations." *Distill* 3 (7). https://doi.org/10.23915/distill.00012.

Muhlbacher, Thomas, Harald Piringer, Samuel Gratzl, Michael Sedlmair, and Marc Streit. 2014. "Opening the Black Box: Strategies for Increased User Involvement in Existing Algorithm Implementations." *IEEE Transactions on Visualization and Computer Graphics* 20 (12): 1643–52. https://doi.org/10.1109/TVCG.2014.2346578.

Nielsen, Rob, Jennifer A. Marrone, and Holly S. Slay. 2010. "A New Look at Humility: Exploring the Humility Concept and Its Role in Socialized Charismatic Leadership." *Journal of Leadership and Organizational Studies* 17 (1): 33–43. https://doi.org/10.1177/1548051809350892.

Pazzani, Michael, Severine Soltani, Robert Kaufman, Samson Qian, and Albert Hsiao. 2022. "Expert-Informed, User-Centric Explanations for Machine Learning." *Proceedings of the AAAI Conference on Artificial Intelligence* 36 (11): 12280–12286. https://doi.org/10.1609/AAAI.V36I11.21491.

Pezzotti, N., S. Yousefi, MS. Elmahdy, J. van Gemert, C. Schülke, M. Doneva, T. Nielsen, et al., 2020. "An Adaptive Intelligence Algorithm for Undersampled Knee MRI Reconstruction: Application to the 2019 FastMRI Challenge." *ArXiv*.

Pezzotti, N., T. Höllt, B. Lelieveldt, E. Eisemann, and A. Vilanova. 2016. "Hierarchical Stochastic Neighbor Embedding." *Computer Graphics Forum* 35 (3). https://doi.org/10.1111/cgf.12878.

Pezzotti, N., T. Hollt, JV. Gemert, BP. Lelieveldt, E. Eisemann, and A. Vilanova. 2017. "DeepEyes: Progressive Visual Analytics for Designing Deep Neural Networks." *IEEE Transactions on Visualization and Computer Graphics*, 98–108. https://doi.org/10.1109/TVCG.2017.2744358.

Pianykh, Oleg S., Georg Langs, Marc Dewey, Dieter R. Enzmann, Christian J. Herold, Stefan O. Schoenberg, and James A. Brink. 2020. "Continuous Learning AI in Radiology: Implementation Principles and Early Applications." *Radiology* 297: 6–14. https://doi.org/10.1148/radiol.2020200038.

Rajpurkar, Pranav, Emma Chen, Oishi Banerjee, and Eric J. Topol. 2022. "AI in Health and Medicine." *Nature Medicine* 28 (1): 31–38. https://doi.org/10.1038/s41591-021-01614-0.

Ramaswamy, H.G. 2020. "Ablation-cam: Visual Explanations for Deep Convolutional Network Via Gradient-Free Localization." *Proceedings of the IEEE/CVF Winter Conference on Applications of Computer Vision*, 983–991. https://doi.org/10.1109/WACV45572.2020.9093360.

Ren, Jie, Peter J. Liu, Emily Fertig, Jasper Snoek, Ryan Poplin, Mark A. DePristo, Joshua V. Dillon, and Balaji Lakshminarayanan. 2019. "Likelihood Ratios for Out-of-Distribution Detection." *Advances in Neural Information Processing Systems* 32.

Reyes, Mauricio, Raphael Meier, Sérgio Pereira, Carlos A. Silva, Fried Michael Dahlweid, Hendrik von Tengg-Kobligk, Ronald M. Summers, and Roland Wiest. 2020. "On the Interpretability of Artificial Intelligence in Radiology: Challenges and Opportunities." *Radiology: Artificial Intelligence* 2 (3). https://doi.org/10.1148/RYAI.2020190043/ASSET/IMAGES/LARGE/RYAI.2020190043.FIG5.JPEG.

Ribeiro, Marco Tulio, Sameer Singh, and Carlos Guestrin. 2016. "'Why Should I Trust You?' Explaining the Predictions of Any Classifier." *NAACL-HLT 2016–2016 Conference of the North American Chapter of the Association for Computational Linguistics: Human Language Technologies, Proceedings of the Demonstrations Session*, 1135–1144. https://doi.org/10.18653/v1/n16-3020.

Ronneberger, Olaf, Philipp Fischer, and Thomas Brox. n.d. "U-Net: Convolutional Networks for Biomedical Image Segmentation." *MICCAI – 2015*, 1–8.

Royston, Patrick, and Douglas G. Altman. 2010. "Visualizing and Assessing Discrimination in the Logistic Regression Model." *Statistics in Medicine* 29 (24). https://doi.org/10.1002/sim.3994.

Schoeller, Felix, Mark Miller, Roy Salomon, and Karl J. Friston. 2021. "Trust as Extended Control: Human-Machine Interactions as Active Inference." *Frontiers in Systems Neuroscience* 15. https://doi.org/10.3389/FNSYS.2021.669810.

Schoonderwoerd, Tjeerd A.J., Wiard Jorritsma, Mark A. Neerincx, and Karel van den Bosch. 2021. "Human-Centered XAI: Developing Design Patterns for Explanations of Clinical Decision Support Systems." *International Journal of Human-Computer Studies* 154: 102684. https://doi.org/10.1016/J.IJHCS.2021.102684.

Selvaraju, Ramprasaath R., Michael Cogswell, Abhishek Das, Ramakrishna Vedantam, Devi Parikh, and Dhruv Batra. 2020. "Grad-CAM: Visual Explanations from Deep Networks via Gradient-Based Localization." *International Journal of Computer Vision* 128 (2). https://doi.org/10.1007/s11263-019-01228-7.

Sendak, Mark, Madeleine Clare Elish, Michael Gao, Joseph Futoma, William Ratliff, Marshall Nichols, Armando Bedoya, Suresh Balu, and Cara O'Brien. 2020. "'The Human Body Is a Black Box': Supporting Clinical Decision-Making with Deep Learning." *FAT* 2020 – Proceedings of the 2020 Conference on Fairness, Accountability, and Transparency*, January, 99–109. https://doi.org/10.1145/3351095.3372827.

She, Wan Jou, Keitaro Senoo, Hibiki Iwakoshi, Noriaki Kuwahara, and Panote Siriaraya. 2022. "AF'fective Design: Supporting Atrial Fibrillation Post-Treatment with Explainable AI." *27th International Conference on Intelligent User Interfaces* 22: 22–25. https://doi.org/10.1145/3490100.

Shneiderman, Ben. 1987. "Designing the User Interface Strategies for Effective Human-Computer Interaction." *ACM SIGBIO Newsletter* 9 (1). https://doi.org/10.1145/25065.950626.

Shneiderman, Ben. 2020. "Bridging the Gap between Ethics and Practice: Guidelines for Reliable, Safe, and Trustworthy Human-Centered AI Systems." *ACM Transactions on Interactive Intelligent Systems* 10 (4). https://doi.org/10.1145/3419764.

Sokol KSokol, Kacper, and Peter Flach. 2020. "Explainability Fact Sheets: A Framework for Systematic Assessment of Explainable Approaches." *Proceedings of the 2020 Conference on Fairness, Accountability, and Transparency*, 252–260. https://doi.org/10.1145/3351095.

Springer, Aaron, Steve Whittaker, A. Springer, and S Whittaker. 2020. "Progressive Disclosure: When, Why, and How Do Users Want Algorithmic Transparency Information?" *ACM Transactions on Interactive Intelligent Systems (TiiS)* 10 (4). https://doi.org/10.1145/3374218.

Suresh, Harini, Steven R. Gomez, Kevin K. Nam, and Arvind Satyanarayan. 2021. "Beyond Expertise and Roles: A Framework to Characterize the Stakeholders of Interpretable Machine Learning and Their Needs." *Conference on Human Factors in Computing Systems – Proceedings* 16 (21). https://doi.org/10.1145/3411764.3445088.

Szegedy, Christian, Wojciech Zaremba, Ilya Sutskever, Joan Bruna, Dumitru Erhan, Ian Goodfellow, and Rob Fergus. 2014. "Intriguing Properties of Neural Networks." *2nd International Conference on Learning Representations, ICLR 2014 – Conference Track Proceedings*, arXiv preprint arXiv:1312.6199.

Tam, Gary K.L., Vivek Kothari, and Min Chen. 2017. "An Analysis of Machine- and Human-Analytics in Classification." *IEEE Transactions on Visualization and Computer Graphics* 23 (1). https://doi.org/10.1109/TVCG.2016.2598829.

Tjoa, Erico, and Cuntai Guan. 2021. "A Survey on Explainable Artificial Intelligence (XAI): Toward Medical XAI." *IEEE Transactions on Neural Networks and Learning Systems* 32 (11). https://doi.org/10.1109/TNNLS.2020.3027314.

Tonekaboni, Sana, Shalmali Joshi, Melissa D Mccradden, Anna Goldenberg, and Anna Goldenberg@vectorinstitute Ai. 2019. "What Clinicians Want: Contextualizing Explainable Machine Learning for Clinical End Use." *Proceedings of Machine Learning Research*, 259–280.

Trustworthiness, Humility, and Empathy in Business by Lead2Goals. n.d. *Trustworthiness, Humility, and Empathy in Business by Lead2Goals*. Accessed August 4, 2022. https://lead2goals.com/understanding-trust-and-trustworthiness-part-1/.

Vaughan, Jennifer Wortman, and Hanna Wallach. 2021. "A Human-Centered Agenda for Intelligible Machine Learning." *Machines We Trust*, August. https://doi.org/10.7551/MITPRESS/12186.003.0014.

Vereschak, Oleksandra, Gilles Bailly, and Baptiste Caramiaux. 2021. "How to Evaluate Trust in AI-Assisted Decision Making? A Survey of Empirical Methodologies." *Proceedings of the ACM on Human-Computer Interaction* 5 (CSCW2). https://doi.org/10.1145/3476068.

Vyas, Apoorv, Nataraj Jammalamadaka, Xia Zhu, Dipankar Das, Bharat Kaul, and Theodore L. Willke. 2018. "Out-of-Distribution Detection Using an Ensemble of Self Supervised Leave-out Classifiers." *Lecture Notes in Computer Science (Including Subseries Lecture Notes in Artificial Intelligence and Lecture Notes in Bioinformatics)* 11212 (LNCS). https://doi.org/10.1007/978-3-030-01237-3_34.

Wang, D., Q. Yang, A. Abdul, and B.Y. Lim. 2019. "Designing Theory-Driven User-Centric Explainable AI." *Proceedings of the 2019 CHI Conference on Human Factors in Computing Systems*, 1–15. https://doi.org/10.1145/3290605.3300831.

Wang, Haofan, Zifan Wang, Mengnan Du, Fan Yang, Zijian Zhang, Sirui Ding, Piotr Mardziel, and Xia Hu. 2020. "Score-CAM: Score-Weighted Visual Explanations for Convolutional Neural Networks." *IEEE Computer Society Conference on Computer Vision and Pattern Recognition Workshops* 2020. https://doi.org/10.1109/CVPRW50498.2020.00020.

Wang, Xinru, and Ming Yin. 2021. "Are Explanations Helpful? A Comparative Study of the Effects of Explanations in AI-Assisted Decision-Making." *26th International Conference on Intelligent User Interfaces*, 1–15. https://doi.org/10.1145/3397481.

Weina Jin, Jianyu Fan, Diane Gromala, Philippe Pasquier, Ghassan Hamarneh. 2021. "EUCA: The End-User-Centered Explainable AI Framework." *arXiv preprint arXiv:2102.02437*, 1–15.

Xie, Yao, Melody Chen, David Kao, Ge Gao, and Xiang Anthony Chen. 2020. "CheXplain: Enabling Physicians to Explore and Understand Data-Driven, AI-Enabled Medical Imaging Analysis." *Conference on Human Factors in Computing Systems – Proceedings* 20. https://doi.org/10.1145/3313831.3376807.

Zhang, Ziwei, Peng Cui, and Wenwu Zhu. 2022. "Deep Learning on Graphs: A Survey." *IEEE Transactions on Knowledge and Data Engineering* 34 (1). https://doi.org/10.1109/TKDE.2020.2981333.

Zhao, Xun, Yanhong Wu, Dik Lun Lee, and Weiwei Cui. 2019. "IForest: Interpreting Random Forests via Visual Analytics." *IEEE Transactions on Visualization and Computer Graphics* 25 (1). https://doi.org/10.1109/TVCG.2018.2864475.

2 Deep Learning in Medical Image Analysis

Recent Models and Explainability

Swati Rai, Jignesh S. Bhatt, and Sarat Kumar Patra

Contents

2.1 Introduction

Medical imaging refers to a process of creating visual representation of internal human structures in order to analyze and help diagnose diseases by healthcare practitioners (Suetens, 2017). There are various types of medical imaging, as shown in Figure 2.1: X-ray, computed tomography (CT), magnetic resonance imaging (MRI), positron-emission tomography (PET), and ultrasound. They are variedly captured by scanning specified human body parts for specific purposes. Now, each modality is quickly reviewed along with the use of deep learning (DL) in order to assist in creating various models for computer-assisted diagnosis.

DOI: 10.1201/9781003333425-2

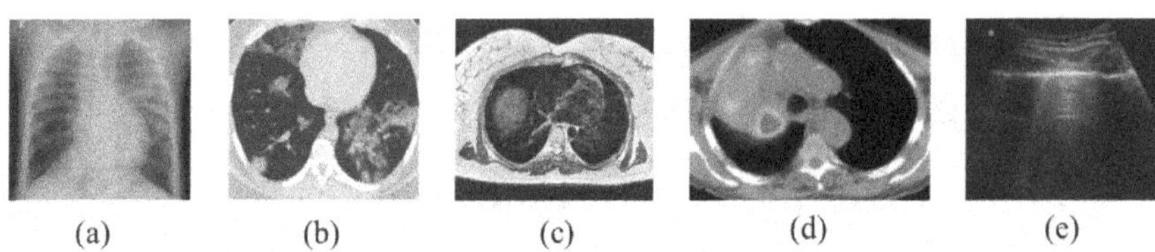

Figure 2.1 Medical imaging modalities: (a) X-ray, (b) CT, (c) MRI, (d) PET, and (e) Ultrasound. Illustration reproduced from (Saha et al., 2021; Vasilev et al., 2020; Chen et al., 2021; Oliveira et al., 2020).

X-ray (Bushberg et al., 2003) is the oldest form of medical imaging and uses a small amount of X-ray radiation through a required part of the human body. The interior structures either absorb this radiation or scatter it, which results in formation of an X-ray scan. A typical wavelength range identified for the ionizing dose is 10 picometers to 10 nanometers, with an energy range from 124 electron-volts (eV) to 124 kiloelectron-volts (KeV). It is generally used for checking bone fractures and also can spot pneumonia. CT (Bushberg et al., 2003) is an advancement in X-ray imaging and is formed by the combination of X-rays and a computer. Here, multiple X-rays are passed from different angles around the human body to capture a series of images that are further given to a computer to create cross-sectional slices. Different types of CT scans are available on the basis of radiation dose: high-resolution CT (HRCT), normal-dose CT, low-dose CT (LDCT), and ultra-LDCT (ULDCT). Note that normal-dose CT uses 10 millisieverts (mSv); HRCT uses ten times the normal dose, 100 mSv; LDCT uses less than one-tenth the normal dose, <1 mSv; and ULDCT uses less than 1/3 of LDCT, <0.3 mSv. The CT technology is popularly used to detect bone tumors, fractures, infections, or blood clots in the human body.

MRI (Bushberg et al., 2003) is another revolution in imaging modality that captures finer details from different parts of the human body. An MRI is acquired by passing strong magnetic and radio waves (1 to 300 megahertz [MHz]) through the human body. An MRI scan is based on the fact that the human body consists of water molecules that are combinations of hydrogen and oxygen atoms. Since protons are present at the center of hydrogen atoms, the protons act as tiny magnets in the presence of strong magnetic fields and align themselves in same direction as the magnetic field. Then radio waves are sent briefly to specific areas, which makes the protons misaligned. Then the radio wave is turned off, which realigns the protons and sends out radio signals collected by receivers. This type of scan helps to capture detailed information of interior structures, as each tissue has a different hydrogen content. MRI scans are extremely useful to detect cancer; find causes of dementia, including many more neurological diseases; and examine the spinal cord.

A positron-emission tomography (Bushberg et al., 2003) scan is done by detecting the photons emitted by a radionuclide inserted into the human body. In this case, the range of energy used is from 0.5 to 5 megaelectron-volts (MeV). A PET scan is typically used to evaluate organs and/or tissues for the presence of disease or to evaluate the functionality of organs, such as the heart or brain, and is also commonly used in the detection of cancer and its treatment. Ultrasound imaging (Bushberg et al., 2003) is developed on concept of echoes. Here, a transducer is present to send small pulses of high-frequency sound waves and receive the echoes produced by the sound to know whether a structure is solid, filled with fluid, moving, or stationary, since each tissue will respond to the sound wave differently. It involves a frequency range from 3 to 10 MHz. Ultrasound is used to diagnose gallbladder disease, view the uterus and ovaries during pregnancy, and guide a needle for biopsy or tumor treatment and is popular in monitoring the health of a developing baby.

2.2 A Standard Chain of Processing for Medical Image Analysis

A series of operations is performed in order to acquire and process medical images for analysis and treatment purposes by healthcare practitioners. A standard medical image processing chain begins with scanning the human body and ends with reconstructing modified images of the body part, as shown in Figure 2.2.

As shown in Figure 2.2, first a human body is scanned through an appropriate scanning machine depending on the type of imaging modality required. The data are imported using different acquisition tools and stored mostly in digital imaging and communications in medicine (DICOM) format. This is the standard format that groups multiple attributes of data, such as patient ID, name, and gender. The acquired image is further analyzed and processed using medical imaging analysis models. First, denoising is performed on the data, as noise often intervenes in medical images during image acquisition, transmission, or reconstruction, as multiple detectors are involved in the process. Therefore, many post-processing challenges arise to reduce the noise content without affecting the information content in the images. This is important since doctors and radiologists rely on these processed images to diagnose/treat patients. Special attention has to be given that denoising not remove any critical information content, making denoising a challenging problem. Generally, multiple sensors or machines are used at different time intervals or different

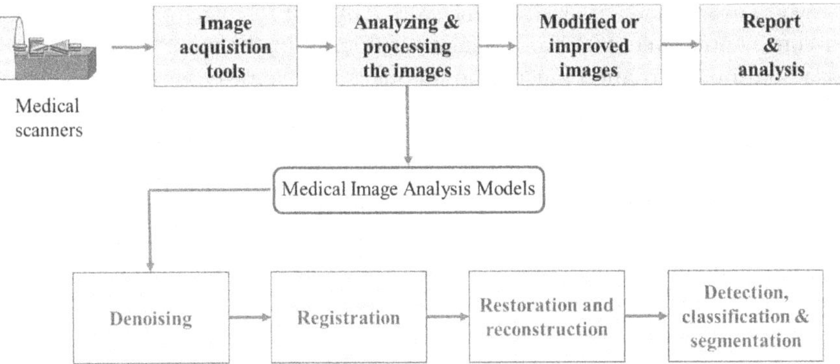

Figure 2.2 A typical chain of processing for computer-assisted medical image diagnosis.

angles to capture the desired body part. Therefore, the next issue is image registration, in which two or more images are aligned, typically called moving images, with respect to reference image coordinates or human anatomy. Further restoration has to be carried out, as the acquired images might be degraded due to movement of patients during scanning, temperature variation in the scanning room, a fault in the machine, or an error in post-processing methods. Many times, the internal structures scanned are in low resolution, hence super-resolution (SR) reconstruction is yet another challenge in order to improve the resolution and enhance the visual quality of images. Then the obtained images are used for detecting any tumor or infection present in the human body with the help of classification and segmentation models. All these post-processed images are suitably modified and reported for analysis purposes by healthcare practitioners.

2.2.1 Deep Learning in Medical Image Analysis

DL and artificial intelligence (AI) have been extensively used by researchers in medical image analysis for various applications, including denoising (Rai et al., 2021a; 2021b), registration (Deshpande et al., 2019; Balakrishnan et al., 2019), restoration (Rai et al., 2022; Thakkar et al., 2022), super-resolution (Kennedy et al., 2006; Robinson et al., 2017), classification (Sharma et al., 2018; Challa et al., 2019), and segmentation (Chen et al., 2018; Guo et al., 2019). However, there are various challenges associated with medical imaging using DL, including restricted access to data for training that involves overfitting of data, variations in input images, quality of data, understanding the context, and high volume of data. Challenges are also related to limited availability of ground truth (GT) information and a higher risk of getting inaccurate results, and in many cases, human intervention is required to validate results.

Using DL for medical image analysis or diagnosis purposes should meet certain constraints; that is, the edges of the image should be preserved, and visual information in the resultant image must be improved. Therefore, both low- and high-frequency content should be maintained. DL models designed to do this can be in the form of deep convolution neural networks (CNNs), an autoencoder-based network, or a generative adversarial network (GAN). Each type of network consists of convolution layers to learn the inherent features in the input images followed by a non-linear activation function to introduce non-linearity into the framework, like a rectified linear activation unit (ReLU). The hidden layers are often followed by batch normalization (BN) to train the model for higher learning rates and bring stability to the training process. Dropout layers with a certain probability are introduced in between these layers to avoid overfitting phenomena. Many times, skip connections are also employed to avoid the vanishing gradient problem that commonly occurs in training a deep network. Such neural models require rigorous training and validation to perform the task assigned well. Then they are tested with qualitative and quantitative analysis.

In this chapter, we shall discuss different models related to various applications of DL in medical image analysis. First, we will discuss the denoising problem depicted in an augmented learning denoising model (Rai et al., 2021a), followed by a Bayesian DL model for registration (Deshpande et al., 2019). Then we will present a restoration and SR reconstruction model for COVID-19 detection (Rai et al., 2022), accompanied by a classification process in which the designed DL framework is trained to perform binary classification on lung CT images to detect lung cancer (Sharma et al., 2018). Further, we discuss detection of diabetic retinopathy (DR) in retinal fundus image using a multi-class classification model (Challa et al., 2019). Segmentation is yet another process that is widely used to get the desired portion from images and make decisions on infection present in the human body via segmented images, as used in roughly all the models. Finally, we shall discuss the explainability of such a model (Mallat, 2016; Manaswini et al., 2021) with the CNNs as a baseline example in a lung cancer detection case.

2.2.2 Dataset and Machine Specifications

In this chapter, the synthetic MRI dataset is used from Blystad et al. (2012), and the synthetic CT/low-resolution ULDCT (LR-ULDCT) Shepp-Logan image is considered from in MATLAB R2020a. The real MRI, CT/LDCT/ULDCT data considered are available from Clark et al. (2013), Andreopoulos et al. (2008), Castillo et al. (2009), Armato et al. (2011), Moen et al. (2021), and Parnian (20210. The retinal fundus images are downloaded from the Kaggle dataset ("www.Kaggle.Com/c/Diabetic-Retinopathy-Detection/Data" 2017). All the images are in DICOM format. The models are executed on a high-performance computing (HPC) system: a PARAM Shavak Supercomputer comprising 96 GB RAM and an NVIDIA GP100 accelerator card. Along with HPC, the models are also tested on a Nvidia Geforce GTX 1050 4GB with 24 GB RAM, including a GTX TITANX machine and Intel core i5. The programming language used is Python, along with some of the important libraries, including pytorch, pydicom, tensorflow, matplotlib, numpy, scipy, and keras.

2.3 Recent Deep Learning Models for Medical Image Analysis

2.3.1 Denoising Model: Image Denoising Using Augmented Noise Learning on MRI/CT/LDCT of Brain and Abdomen

Denoising is an *ill-posed* problem that is very challenging, as reducing noise should not affect the information characteristics of the medical images. Here, researchers present an augmented noise learning neural network (Rai et al., 2021a) model to reduce the noise content present in the given MRI/CT/LDCT (2D/3D), keeping the information content as is. The constraints are that edges in the image should be preserved, and visual information in the resultant image should improve. The assumption is that MRI and CT images are degraded by Rician and Poisson noise, respectively (Nowak, 1999; Thanh et al., 2019).

As shown in Figure 2.3, the augmented noise learning model (Rai et al., 2021a) comprises patch-based dictionary learning (PDL) along with a deep residual network (DRN). For 3D volumetric processing, a block of image cube $Y^{l}_{i(i=1)}$ is considered,

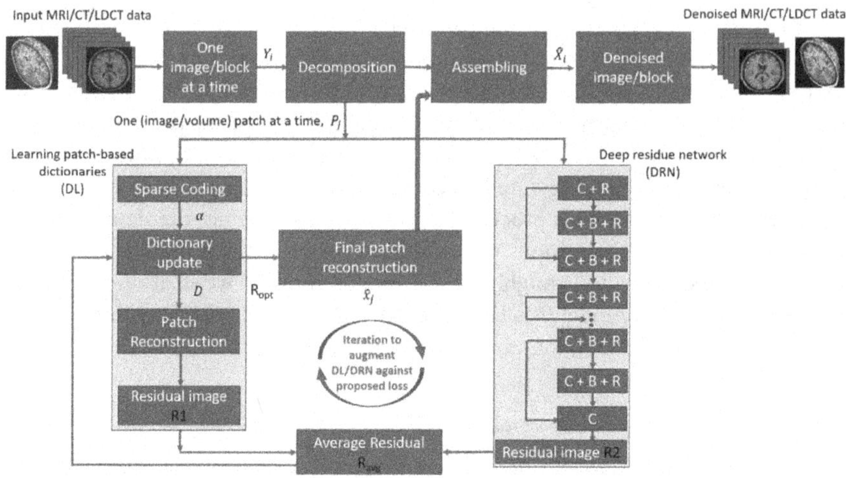

Figure 2.3 Augmented noise learning model for denoising MRI/CT/LDCT volume/image. Illustration reproduced from Rai et al. (2021a).

where l is the total image cubes comprising voxels. The image cubes are given to the decomposition stage, where they are split into overlapping volumetric patches $\{P_j\}_{j=1}^{r}$, where r is the total volume of patches. These volumetric patches are gradually given to the PDL and DRN parts for processing. For 2D processing, slices are decomposed in overlapping patches, and one patch at a time is forwarded to the PDL and DRN parts.

The PDL part consists of three steps: sparse coding, dictionary update, and patch reconstruction. An initial dictionary of discrete cosine transform D_{init} and P_j is used to obtain the sparse coefficient α_j. The sparse representation of P_j is considered:

$$P_j \approx D_{init}\alpha_j. \tag{1}$$

α_j and dictionary D of a patch are computed and updated using standard orthogonal matching pursuit and the K-singular value decomposition algorithm. The denoised image/volume patch $\hat{X}_j$ is reconstructed via the updated D and a_j as:

$$\hat{X}_j = Da_j. \tag{2}$$

The $R1_j$, that is, the residual patch, is extracted by:

$$R1_j := \left|P_j - \hat{X}_j\right|, \forall j. \tag{3}$$

Now, P_j is passed through the DRN part of the augmented learning model shown in Figure 2.3 comprising ten layers. The first layer comprises 84 filters of kernel size 3 × 3 that perform convolution (C) between the patch and a filter to generate feature maps from the extracted features. Then ReLU (R) layer is also added to introduce non-linearity. The first layer is followed by eight layers that include BN (B) to act as regularizer term between C and R. Here, 128 filters of size 3 × 3 are considered. The last convolution layer gives the output residue $R2_j$ (noise) part that is averaged with $R1_j$ to construct $R_{avg\ j}$ to preserve noise characteristics learned indirectly and directly by the PDL and DRN, respectively. $R_{avg\ j}$ is fed to the PDL subnetwork to upgrade D:

$$D = arg\,arg\,\lambda \sum_{j=1}^{r} \left\| \mathrm{P_j} - \mathrm{D}a_j \right\|_2^2 + \mu \left\| a_j \right\|_0 + \frac{1}{r} \left\| R_{avg_j} - R1_j \right\|^2 \tag{4}$$

where λ and μ are regularization parameters. Now the optimum residue R_{optj} is generated from the upgraded D for the final denoised patch $\hat{X}_{opt_j}$ estimated from PDL as:

$$\hat{X}_{opt_j} := \left| P_j - R_{opt_j} \right|, \forall j. \tag{5}$$

The entire process is repeated for all patches of Y_i. In the end, the denoised patches obtained are put together to form an entire denoised volume/image. Note that the voxels/pixels in overlapping regions are calculated using local patch-level averaging.

For 3D denoising: 400 slices of 3D MRI and 350 slices of CT images are used with 256 × 256 voxels. Each voxel has 1 × 1 × 1 mm resolution. The model is tested using 50 and 45 slices of 3D MRI and CT real datasets, respectively. For 2D denoising: 1500 slices of MRI and 1000 slices of CT images are used with dimensions of 512 × 512 pixels. The model is tested using 442 and 250 image slices for real 2D datasets of MRI and CT images, respectively. The LDCT data library consists of a total of 10,112,591 scans that include low-dose non-contrast CT scans of head, chest, and abdomen.

Three different levels, 5%, 10%, and 15%, of Rician/Poisson noise are added in the GT MRI/CT image to generate synthetic data. A result of adding 5% Rician noise to a synthetic 3D MRI is displayed in Figure 2.4. Figure 2.4(a) shows a GT image, and a denoised image through other existing approaches along with the augmented learning framework is shown in Figure 2.4(b–f). One can observe that the image denoised through the augmented approach meets all the constraints. Similarly, Figure 2.5 displays the results of the synthetic 3D CT image. Figures 2.6 and 2.7 show the results obtained using the augmented noise learning model on real 3D MRI and CT, respectively. A signal leakage phenomena usually occurs when a part of the information content is considered noise. The results of signal leakage are shown in Figure 2.8, which indicates the designed augmented model shows the least signal leakage as compared to other existing approaches. Figure 2.9 presents the denoising result on low-dose CT (Mayo Clinic) scans on the abdomen of a 32-year-old male with id L033 by different algorithms. Ablation analysis on a 2D CT brain scan is displayed in Figure 2.10.

Considering both a 2D and 3D image/voxel as input, medical image denoising is effectively enhanced using an augmented noise learning model. It handles the Rician noise present in MRI images and the Poisson noise in CT/LDCT images. The

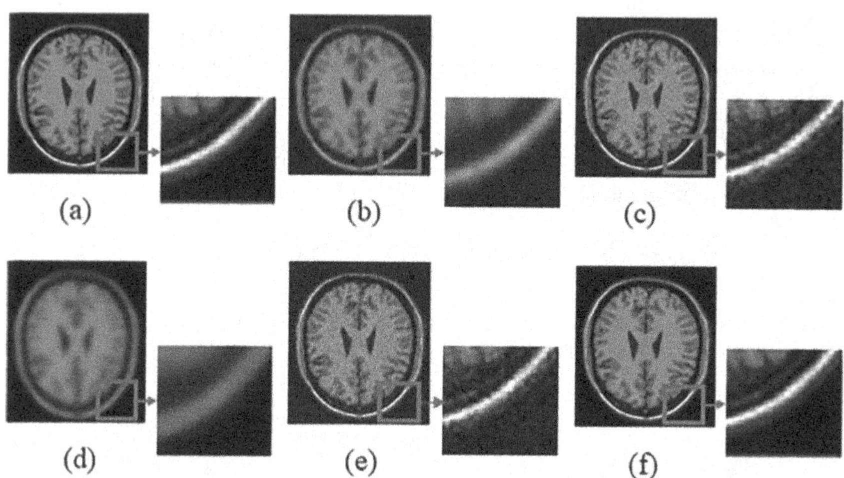

Figure 2.4 Qualitative denoising performance on synthetic 3D MRI by adding 5% Rician noise: (a) GT, (b) TV (Ben Said et al., 2019), (c) NLM (Manjón et al., 2008), (d) ADF (Krissian and Aja-Fernández, 2009), (e) RED-WGAN (Ran et al., 2019), and (f) augmented 3D (Rai et al., 2021a). Illustration reproduced from (Rai et al., 2021a).

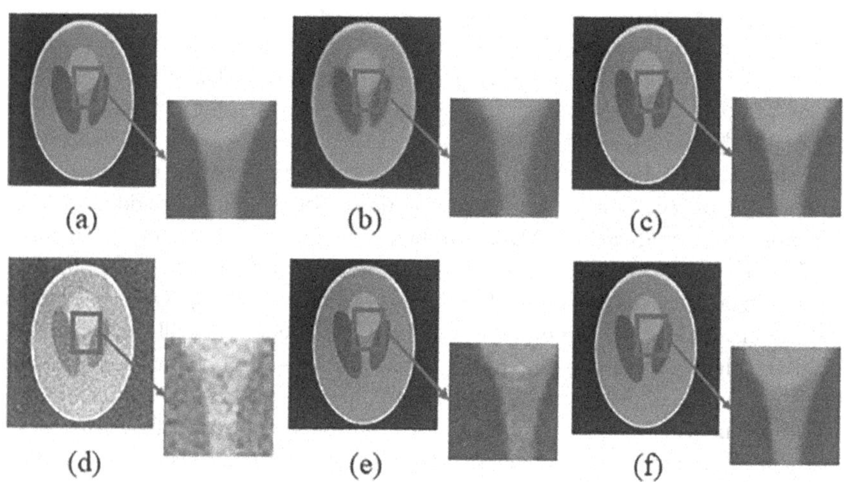

Figure 2.5 Qualitative denoising performance on synthetic 3D CT by adding 5% Poisson noise: (a) GT, (b) TV (Ben Said et al., 2019), (c) NLM (Manjón et al., 2008), (d) ADF (Krissian and Aja-Fernández, 2009), (e) RED-WGAN (Ran et al., 2019), and (f) augmented 3D (Rai et al., 2021a). Illustration reproduced from (Rai et al., 2021a).

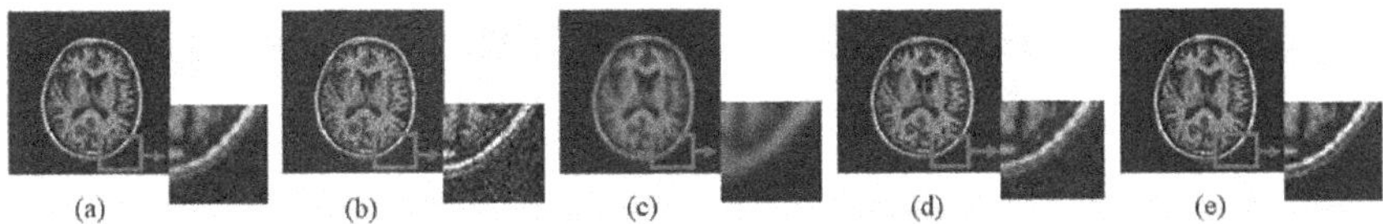

Figure 2.6 Qualitative denoising performance on real 3D MRI brain scans: (a) TV (Ben Said et al., 2019), (b) NLM (Manjón et al., 2008), (c) ADF (Krissian and Aja-Fernández, 2009), (d) RED-WGAN (Ran et al., 2019), and (e) augmented 3D (Rai et al., 2021a). Illustration reproduced from (Rai et al., 2021a).

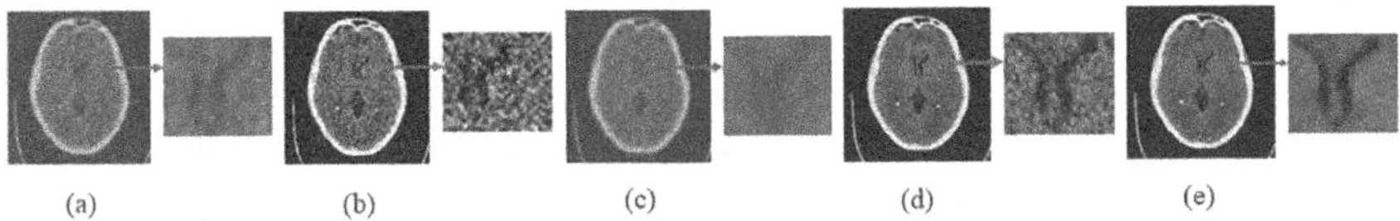

Figure 2.7 Qualitative denoising performance on real 3D CT brain scans: (a) TV (Ben Said et al., 2019), (b) NLM (Manjón et al., 2008), (c) ADF (Krissian and Aja-Fernández, 2009), (d) RED-WGAN (Ran et al., 2019), and (e) augmented 3D (Rai et al., 2021a). Illustration reproduced from (Rai et al., 2021a).

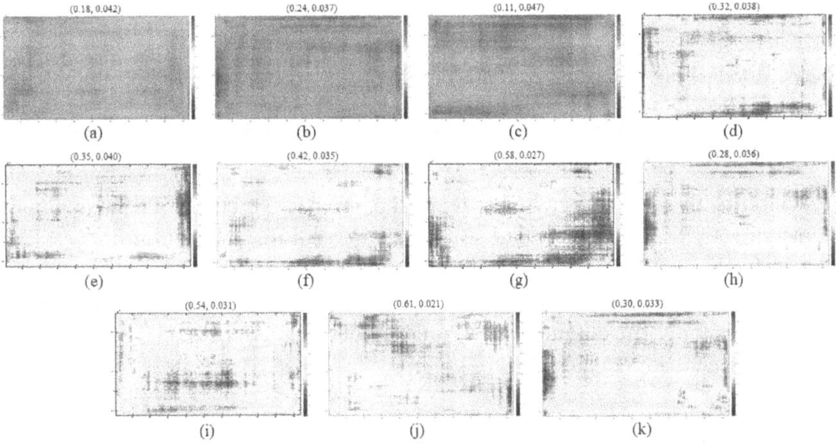

Figure 2.8 Signal leakage phenomena by different algorithms after denoising MRI/CT datasets: (a) only DRN, (b) only PDL, (c) augmented noise learning framework (Rai et al., 2021a), (d) CNN-RL (Jifara et al., 2019), (e) RED-CNN (Chen et al., 2017), (f) K-SVD (Aharon et al., 2006), (g) TV (Ben Said et al., 2019), (h) BM3D (Dabov et al., 2007), (i) NLM (Manjón et al., 2008), (j) ADF (Krissian and Aja-Fernández, 2009), and (k) RED-WGAN (Ran et al., 2019). Illustration reproduced from (Rai et al., 2021a).

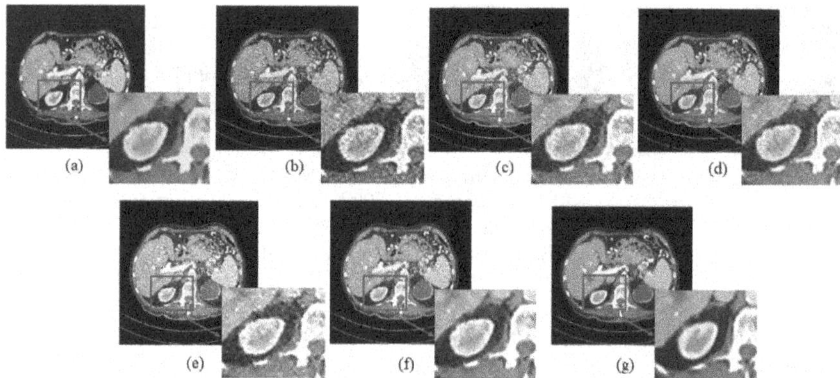

Figure 2.9 Denoising performance on abdomen part of a 32-year-old male with id L033 from low-dose CT (Mayo Clinic) using different algorithms: (a) normal dose image, (b) corresponding LDCT, (c) PURE (Kim et al., 2020), (d) MAP-NN (Shan et al., 2019), (e) CPCE (Shan et al., 2018), (f) AdaIN CycleGAN (Gu and Ye, 2021), and (g) augmented (Rai et al., 2021a). Illustration reproduced from (Rai et al., 2021a).

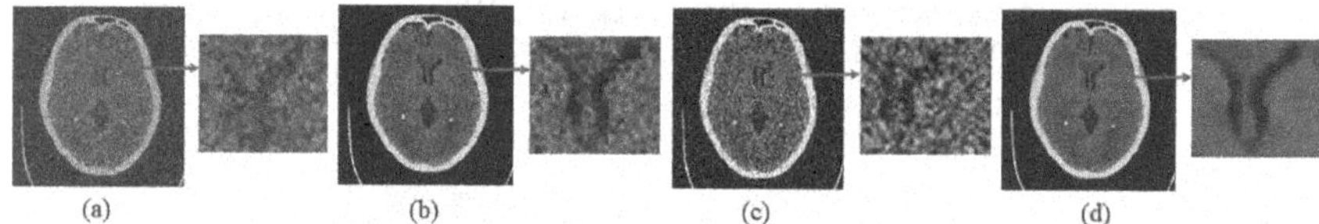

Figure 2.10 A result of ablation experiment on 2D CT brain image data: (a) available image, (b) using DRN subnetwork, (c) using PDL subnetwork, and (d) using augmented neural network (Rai et al., 2021a). Illustration reproduced from (Rai et al., 2021a).

model indirectly learns the noise content via patch-based dictionaries and augments it with directly learning the residue (noise) contents using DRN from the available images. In this way, the PDL part takes care of the signal leakage from DRN, and DRN avoids the Gibbs/ringing artifact of PDL. Note that clean images are not required for training the augmented learning model (Rai et al., 2021a), unlike many DL-based recent approaches.

2.3.2 *Registration Model: Deformable Registration Using Bayesian Deep Learning on CT/MRI of Lungs and Heart*

Image registration is a crucial task in medical image analysis, as any misalignment of images may lead to misjudgment of infection present in the human body. Here, given a set of reference and acquired moving medical images, the researchers develop a Bayesian deep learning (BDL) model to register a moving image on the reference image coordinates. It is assumed that the images are corrupted by random nonlinear geometric distortions. Note that it preserves the pixel (statistical) distribution of the moving image over the reference image. The BDL uses backpropagation to learn

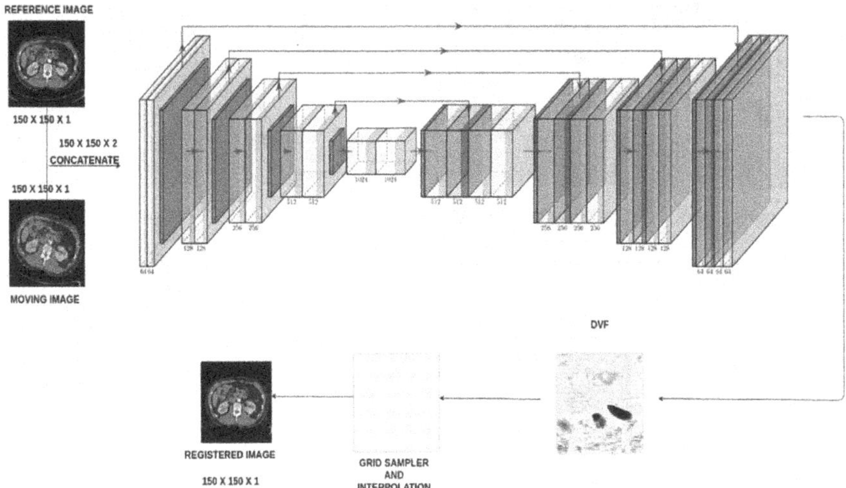

Figure 2.11 Block diagram of medical image registration using Bayesian deep learning. Illustration reproduced from (Deshpande et al., 2019).

posterior distribution over the weights. The block diagram of BDL for registration (Deshpande et al., 2019) of CT/MRI is shown in Figure 2.11.

As shown in Figure 2.11, it is an autoencoder-type structure in which a pair of reference and moving images is concatenated into a two-channel 2D image with five downsampling and four upsampling layers. Moving images are generated with different degrees of elastic, deformable, or geometric distortions of order 0.8 leading to generation of distorted images for a single slice. The estimated displacement vector field (DVF) by the network along with bilinear interpolation and grid resampling of the moving image generates the final registered image. The autoencoder structure of BDL is trained in supervised way with the combination of mean-squared error (MSE) and structural similarity index (SSIM). Backpropagation is used to update the weight of each layer. After every convolution layer, a BN layer with learning rate of 0.001 is added, and batch size is 1 throughout the training process.

The result obtained from BDL on the CT dataset is shown in Figure 2.12. The estimated DVF is presented in Figure 2.12(c), from which registered images are obtained through BDL, as shown in Figure 2.12(d). Figure 2.13 presents the results on a cardiac MRI using BDL. For further analysis and details, readers are encouraged to refer to Deshpande et al. (2019).

2.3.3 Restoration and Super-Resolution Reconstruction Model: COVID-19 Detection Using Deep Cascade Network on LDCT/ULDCT of Lungs

Image reconstruction using DL without the knowledge of ground truth data is a challenging research problem. Here, researchers work on the recent widespread life-threatening pandemic COVID-19 caused by the SARS-CoV-2 virus. People

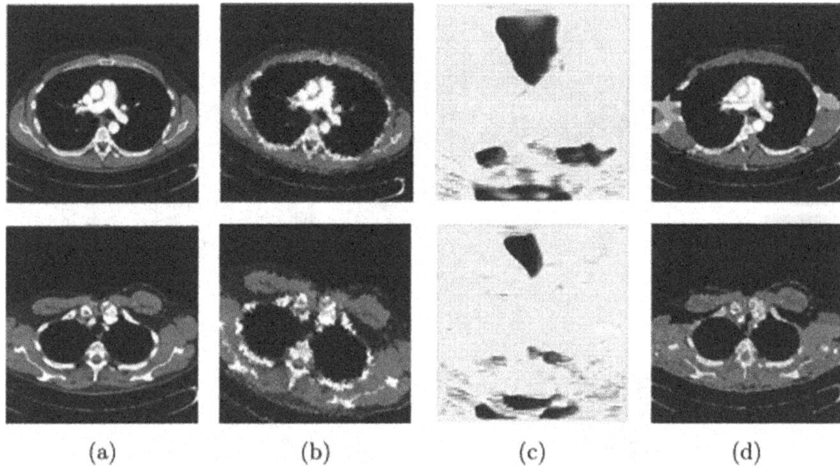

Figure 2.12 A few results on lung CT image registration: (a) reference images, (b) moving images, (c) learned DVF, and (d) output registered images using proposed BDL. Illustration reproduced from Deshpande et al. (2019).

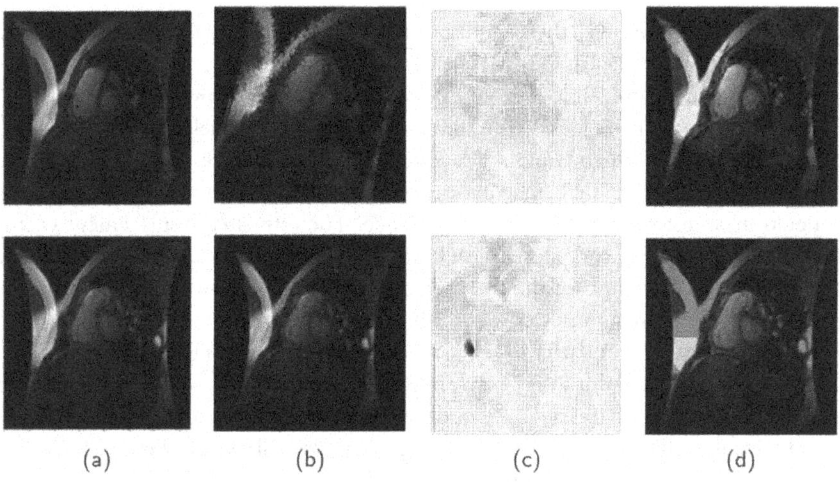

Figure 2.13 A few results on cardiac MRI image registration: (a) reference images, (b) moving images, (c) learned DVF, and (d) output registered images using proposed BDL. Illustration reproduced from Deshpande et al. (2019).

suffering from COVID-19 show the presence of a misty gray region in CT scans called ground glass opacity (GGO). Mostly, HRCT scans of lungs are taken to evaluate the spread of GGO; however, the radiation dose used and the cost required to take a single HRCT is high, while such a facility may not be readily available in all places. Considering these practical issues, researchers developed a deep cascade network that uses LR-ULDCT scans to detect the presence of COVID-19 infection in lungs, making it less risky, as the radiation dose is very low, and economical as well. Also, this type of scanning facility is available nearly everywhere. The assumption is that LR-ULDCTs are corrupted by the Poisson noise typically found in CT data and degraded by motion blur using different kernel sizes of the Gaussian point spread function. A block diagram of a deep cascade network is shown in Figure 2.14.

A deep cascade network consists of three subnetworks: restoration, SR, and segmentation. The restoration subnetwork learns the degradation function in the available degraded LR-ULDCT data using an upgraded augmented noise learning framework for restoration. Patch-based dictionary learning is augmented with a DRN that consists of 12 convolution layers to learn degradation directly. The convolution layer is followed by Leaky-ReLU since it speeds up the learning process and avoids the vanishing gradient problem. Further, BN layers are added to improve the restoration process and have high learning rates along with an additional dropout layer to avoid possible overfitting phenomena. The obtained restored LR-ULDCT image is fed to the SR subnetwork. Here, GAN is employed to upscale the spatial resolution of the restored LR-ULDCT to SR-ULDCT. The generator of this subnetwork consists of 16 convolution layers along with alternate layer skip connections to form a residual neural network. To overcome the dying ReLU issue, Leaky-ReLU layers are added, and to improve image quality and spatial resolution, BN is added. The other part of this subnetwork, the discriminator, is influenced by visual geometry group (VGG) with a sigmoid function employed to differentiate between LR-ULDCT and SR-ULDCT. This SR-ULDCT is given to the third subnetwork, that is, segmentation that employs a modified U-Net architecture with 24 convolution layers as well as Leaky-ReLU and BN layers to segment the GGOs present in the chest portion. Now, to avoid overfitting and to better segment the chest portion from the restored SR-ULDCT, dropout layers are added alternately. At the end, to perform colorization, an extra block of convolution followed by BN and Leaky-ReLU is added on the obtained segmented chest portion: yellow for background,

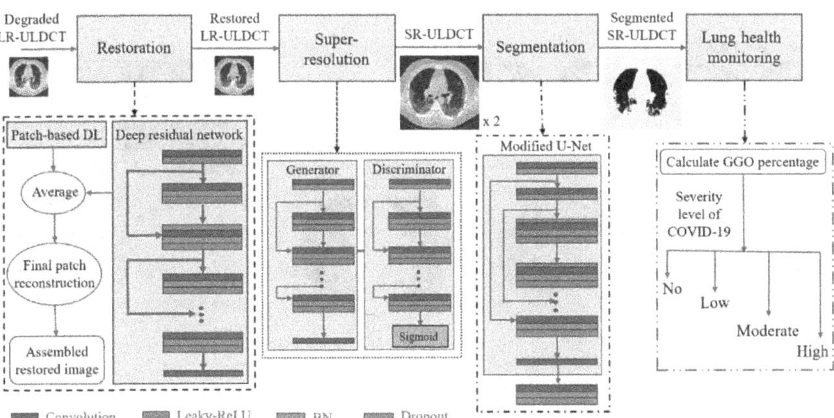

Figure 2.14 Deep cascade neural network to detect COVID-19 lung infection using degraded LR-ULDCT images. Illustration reproduced from Rai et al. (2022).

black for the chest, and white for GGOs. Finally, the GGO percentage is calculated from the colorized segmented SR-ULDCT using Rai et al. (2022):

$$GGO\% = \frac{\#\,white\ pixels}{\#\left(white + black\right)pixels} \times 100 \tag{6}$$

where # indicates cardinality. In the end, the severity of lung contamination under COVID-19 infection is finally classified depending on the value obtained: No (0%−≤5%), Low (5%−≤30%), Moderate (30%−≤60%), and High (60%−≤100%). Note that all the subnetworks are trained individually. The first subnetwork, restoration, is trained with 3500 LR-ULDCTs and tested with 800 images, where each patch is of size 64 × 64 pixels. In order to train the second subnetwork, downsampling by a factor of 2 is performed on the 3000 available ULDCT images, and it is tested with 500 images. For COVID-19 detection, a segmentation subnetwork is trained separately with 4000 ULDCTs together with normal-dose CT scans and tested with 650 ULDCTs.

The real COVID-19 ULDCT dataset consists of 1000 LDCT and 5000 ULDCT positive cases as well as 100 normal cases. Ablation study results on real COVID-19 data along with a confusion matrix are shown in Figure 2.15. Figure 2.15(d) presents the result of detecting infection without using a SR subnetwork, and Figure 2.15(g) shows the result obtained using SR on the given LR-ULDCT. Perception-based image quality evaluator (PIQE) is a no-reference quality score, where low values indicate good quality of images. High values of peak signal-to-noise ratio (PSNR) and low values of root-MSE (RMSE) indicate high-quality images. Similarly, another result on real data is presented in Figure 2.16. Quantitative analysis is displayed in Table 2.1 that shows high accuracy, precision, and F1-score for the deep cascade network.

The deep cascade network effectively detects GGO coverage in lungs by restoring the available degraded LR-ULDCT images and super-resolving them by a factor of 2. The SR successfully upgrades the resolution of images as it is applied on degraded images after restoration. COVID-19 detection with and without SR is approximately the same; however, the quality of images is enhanced by super-resolving

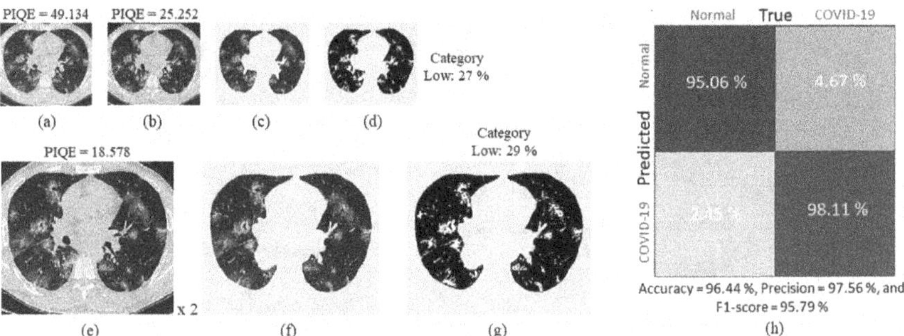

Figure 2.15 A result of the ablation experiment using a deep cascade neural network with and without SR on real COVID-19 lung images: (a) available degraded LR-ULDCT, (b) restored (a), (c) segmented (b), (d) GGO from (c), (e) SR-ULDCT of (b), (f) segmentation on (e), (g) GGO from (f), and (h) confusion matrix using real (1000 infected + 100 normal) COVID-19 cases. Illustration reproduced from Rai et al. (2022).

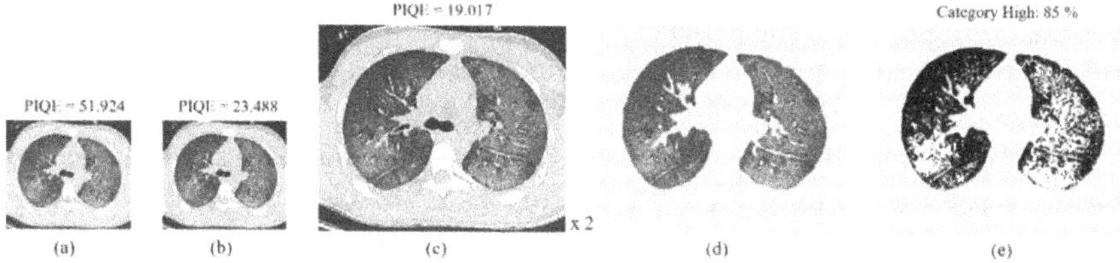

Figure 2.16 A result with deep cascade neural network after SR of real COVID-19 images: (a) available LR-ULDCT, (b) restored version of (a), (c) SR-ULDCT of (b), (d) colorized and segmented (c), and (e) estimated GGO from (d). Illustration reproduced from Rai et al. (2022).

Table 2.1 Average Errors and Performance Indices by Different Neural Networks at 5% of Poisson Noise along with Moderate Motion Blur Distortions in 250 Synthetic LR-ULDCT Images. Illustration reproduced from Rai et al. (2022).

Subnetworks	*Models*	*RMSE*	*PSNR*	*SSIM*
Restoration	StatNet (Choi et al., 2020)	17.112	39.924	0.881
	Autoencoder (Liu and Zhang, 2018)	18.035	38.457	0.823
	Cascade network (Rai et al., 2022)	14.119	44.577	0.901
Super-resolution (SR)	Multi-window (Qiu et al., 2021)	16.748	40.611	0.832
	DL (Jiang et al., 2018)	19.553	39.094	0.779
	Cascade network (Rai et al., 2022)	12.329	45.487	0.927
		Accuracy	**Precision**	**F1-Score**
COVID-19 detection	WS-CNN (Hu et al., 2020)	0.8891	0.795	0.779
	DenseNet (Wang et al., 2020)	0.902	0.823	0.796
	ResNet (Rahimzadeh et al., 2021)	0.919	0.809	0.801
	Cascade network without SR (Rai et al., 2022)	0.909	0.828	0.813
	Cascade network with SR (Rai et al., 2022)	0.921	0.869	0.832

them. In this way, the proposed deep cascade neural network can serve as a low-risk, economical, and accessible system for detecting COVID-19 or other similar lung diseases.

2.3.4 Classification Model: Early Detection of Lung Cancer Using CNN on CT Images

Cancer appears in the human body when undesirable cells grow and spread in body parts, causing the formation of cancerous or non-cancerous tumors. It is one of the major life-threatening diseases and the risk is expected to rise with the passage of time (Sung et al., 2021). Hence, early detection of cancer can help to bring down abnormal cell growth in the patient's body and help to cure them. Here, researchers have developed a model to detect lung cancer from given CT images at an early stage. A two-step algorithm approach (Sharma et al., 2018) is designed first to extract the patch through which a lung nodule is segmented, and then binary classification is carried out using a PDL network, as shown in Figure 2.17. Unlike other models, this early detection model performs segmentation without using the complete information of contour. The CNN architecture with three convolution layers comprising 64 filters of size 3×3 and two fully connected layers is constructed to classify the extracted patches as malignant and benign and is presented in Figure 2.18.

Training is performed in a supervised manner with a batch size of 250 for 300 epochs. Optimization is performed using an Adam optimizer to minimize the dissimilarity between the favorable and obtained outputs of the network. Cross entropy is used as the loss in the objective function along with the backpropagation method to update the weights in all the convolution layers. A total of 6306 images, with 2607 benign and 3699 malignant, were randomly divided into three sets: training, validation, and test. Here, malignancy <3 is considered benign and ≥ 3 malignant.

The results obtained through the deep CNN architecture (Figure 2.18) on the given CT images from the LIDC-IDRI database for some challenging cases are shown in Figure 2.19. Quantitative results in classification of lung nodule tumors with several state-of-the-art approaches are displayed in Table 2.2. One can observe

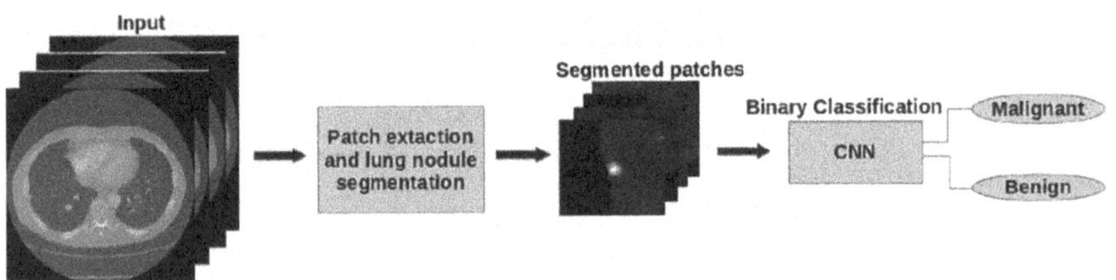

Figure 2.17 Block diagram of early detection of lung cancer. Illustration reproduced from Sharma et al. (2018).

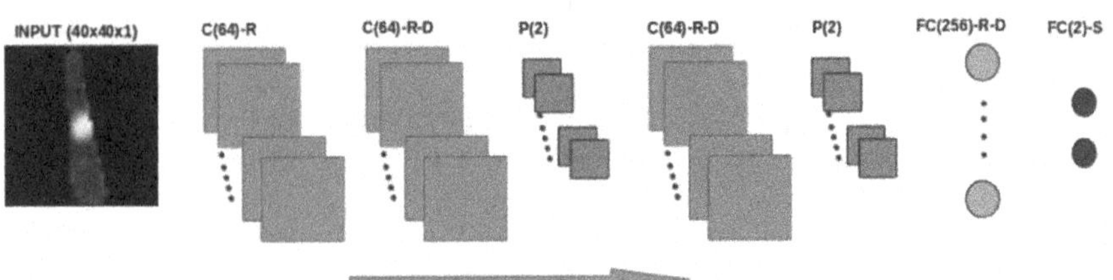

Figure 2.18 Proposed CNN-based neural architecture for early detection of lung cancer using binary classification of segmented patches. Illustration reproduced from Sharma et al. (2018).

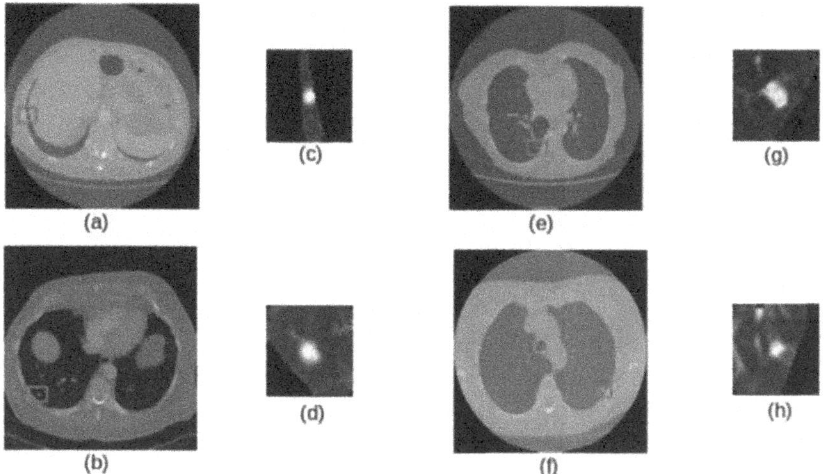

Figure 2.19 A few results in difficult scenarios for early detection of lung cancer: (a), (b), (e), and (f) are the available input CT images, and (c), (d), (g), and (h) are corresponding extracted and segmented patches. Illustration reproduced from Sharma et al. (2018).

Table 2.2 Quantitative Results on Classification of Extracted Lung Nodules. Illustration reproduced from Sharma et al. (2018).

Algorithms	*Database (Samples)*	*Accuracy (%)*	*Sensitivity (%)*	*Specificity (%)*
(Nascimento et al., 2012)	LIDC (73)	92.78	85.64	97.89
(Orozco et al., 2012)	NBIA-ELCAP (113)	–	96.15	52.17
(Krewer et al., 2013)	LIDC-IDRI (33)	90.91	85.71	94.74
(Kuruvilla and Gunavathi, 2014)	Private (128)	93.30	91.40	100
(Dandil et al., 2014)	Private (128)	90.63	92.30	89.47
(Hua et al., 2015)	LIDC (2,545)	–	73.30	78.70
(Kumar et al., 2015)	LIDC (4,323)	75.01	83.35	–
(Xiuli et al., 2017)	LIDC (2,620)	83.03	–	–
(Sharma et al., 2018)	LIDC-IDRI (6,306)	84.13	91.69	73.16

from the table that the deep CNN architecture (Figure 2.18) achieves an accuracy of 84.13%, sensitivity of 91.69%, and specificity of 73.16%, which is comparable to or better than other approaches. More details on binary classification may be found in Sharma et al. (2018).

This binary classifier first performs accurate segmentation with image processing techniques followed by improved classification performance using the proposed deep CNN architecture that helps in detecting lung cancer at an early stage. Hence it could help further increase the survival rate. The results show that this binary classifier effectively classifies nodular tumors as malignant or benign.

2.3.5 Multi-Class Classification Model: Diabetic Retinopathy Using All-CNN in Retinal Fundus Images of the Eyes

Diabetes is a long-term disease caused if the insulin level is not balanced, leading to sugar imbalance in the human body. The rate of diabetic patients is continuously increasing, and 422 million people throughout the world currently have diabetes (Sun et al., 2022). Importantly, diabetes harms the blood vessels of the eyes, leading to vision problems called diabetic retinopathy (DR). This condition is seen in people suffering from Type 1 (insulin deficiency) and Type 2 (ineffective usage of insulin) diabetes. Retinal fundus (fundoscopy) images are used to see the spread of infection in blood vessels at the back side of the eye, that is, the retina. Here, researchers have developed a deep all-CNN model to detect DR in a multi-class manner using retinal fundus images, as shown in Figure 2.20.

The all-CNN model (Challa et al., 2019) performs five-class classification of the given fundoscopy images after preprocessing. The retinal fundus images are first preprocessed in three steps: data augmentation, corrections against sensor parameters,

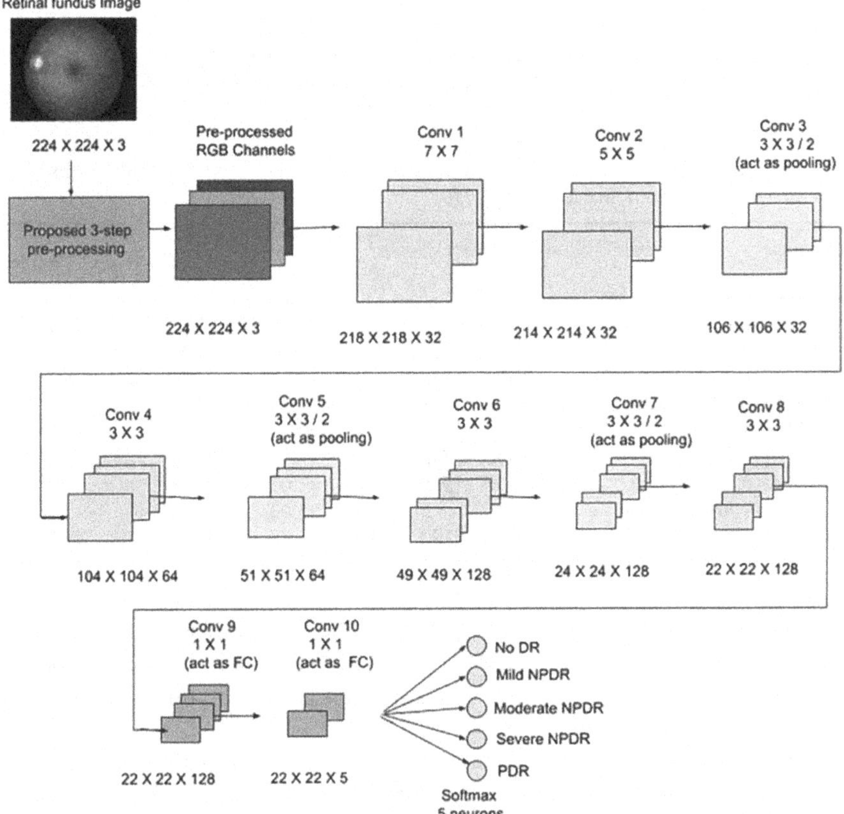

Figure 2.20 An all-CNN model for five-class detection of DR. Illustration reproduced from Challa et al. (2019).

and removal of boundaries. After preprocessing, 224 × 224–pixel colored images are given for five-class classification. The model comprises ten convolution layers, with three layers acting as pooling layers, as shown in Figure 2.20. After every convolutional layer, a BN layer is added to increase the stability of the network. A dropout layer is added after the BN at each convolutional layer with probability 0.5 to avoid overfitting phenomena. The all-CNN is trained in supervised way on the given preprocessed DR images, with 3000 images utilized for both training and testing purposes. The all-CNN is run with a batch size of 32 for 200 epochs. Cross entropy is used as loss in the objective function. Note that to minimize the dissimilarity between the required and obtained output of the network, stochastic gradient descent optimization is used. A backpropagation algorithm is used to update the weights at all convolution layers in the all-CNN network.

Saliency maps are displayed in Figure 2.21. The maps indicate how an image is processed at each convolution layer of the network. Table 2.3 displays the accuracy obtained by the all-CNN model as compared to other existing models for DR under binary and multi-level classification. For more details, readers can refer to Challa et al. (2019).

The proposed novel deep all-CNN neural network is presented here to detect DR at multi-severity scales, that is, five scales. The preprocessing performed before all-CNN helps to extract intrinsic features that lead to major insights for discrete stages in the disease. Hence, a simpler and effective architecture is presented here that is useful for practical applications in medical imaging.

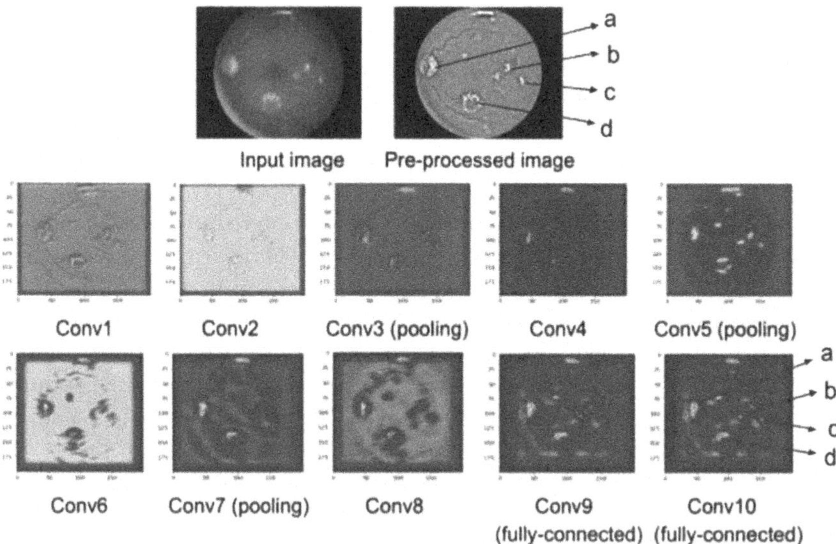

Figure 2.21 Saliency maps of a fundoscopy image using the proposed all-CNN: (a) optic disc, (b) hard exudates, (c) soft exudates, and (d) microaneurysms. Illustration reproduced from Challa et al. (2019).

Table 2.3 Comparative Performance for DR Classification. Illustration reproduced from Challa et al. (2019).

Neural Network	*Output Class*	*Model*	*Sampled Data*	*Accuracy*
(Ghosh et al., 2017)	Two-class, five-class	CNN	Kaggle (30,000)	95%; claimed up to 85%
(Pratt et al., 2016)	Five-class	CNN	Kaggle (80,000)	75%
(Alban and Gilligan, 2016)	Two-class, three-class, five-class	GoogLeNet	Kaggle	77%, 58%, 45%
(Lam et al., 2018)	Two-class, three-class	GoogLeNet	Kaggle (35,000), Messidor-1 (1200)	95%, 75%
(Masood et al., 2017)	Five-class	Inception-v3	Kaggle	48.2%
(Challa et al., 2019)	Five-class	All-CNN	Kaggle (33,000)	86.64%

All the models discussed use a deep convolutional neural architecture to perform the required tasks of denoising, registration, restoration, reconstruction, super-resolution, and segmentation. All of these models are trained on huge amounts of data in order to learn the features and set the parameters to produce the desired output. Now, let's discuss what happens inside the layers of a deep CNN model.

2.4 On the Explainability of Deep Neural Models for Medical Image Analysis

Explainability of neural networks for medical image analysis helps us better understand them in detail by describing the function of each layer and the analytical reasoning to reach a decision by the artificial intelligence (AI) model (Zhao et al., 2018; Tonekaboni et al., 2019; Holzinger et al., 2019). Explainable AI (XAI) is now a trending research topic, as it helps new researchers in the machine learning field to appreciate the functionality of a deep model while providing more confidence to users, especially by healthcare practitioners. XAI can better elucidate the contribution of each layer and unwrap pattern formation in the intermittent steps of a learning algorithm. Interpretability of a deep neural network can be classified into three broad categories: perceptive, mathematical, and data-driven methods (Tjoa and Guan, 2020). The perceptive method describes how a human recognizes the results generated by the given neural model. Perceptive interpretability can be explained by taking saliency maps at layers to see through their effect in the result. Ablation studies would further assist to understand the importance of layers in the feature extraction process in the given deep neural models. On the other hand, mathematical models and structures can be used to describe the underlying feature extraction process and interpretability of inherent layers in the given predefined model. To this end, linearity-based methods and sensitivity analysis are explored to add mathematical tractable interpretability in a neural model. Furthermore, layerwise relevance propagation, guided backpropagation, deconvolution and case-based reasoning are explored under data-driven interpretability to have a clear understanding regarding the deep learning models with respect to medical applications. Additionally, to build the theoretical foundation of XAI, one explores Shapley values, Taylor decomposition, deep Taylor decomposition, and heatmaps to discover the individual contributions of series of layers in a deep model (Samek et al., 2021).

Let us consider a case in medical image analysis for mathematical interpretability. An image is high-dimensional data with structural information that is better handled by a CNN, as it consists of many filters along with pooling and fully connected layers that considers each pixel of the image a feature. For image processing tasks, including medical images, the CNN is often used as black-box architecture where one performs trial and error to set the parameters and re-train the model to learn inherent features in order to produce the desired output (Mallat, 2016; Manaswini and Bhatt, 2021). Therefore, we consider the CNN a baseline neural model and present a brief mathematical understanding of CNN for early detection of lung cancer (refer to classification model in section 2.3.5, Figure 2.18).

As shown in Figure 2.22, CNN takes a medical image as an input vector, x. This is passed through j layers in the CNN to obtain x_j given by $x_j = \rho W_j x_{j-1}$. Here, ρ is the pointwise non-linearity, W_j is the weight matrix referred to as a linear operator, and x_{j-1} is the output from the previous layer. Usually ρ is taken to be a max function or sigmoid depending upon the application. These layers help the neural network to learn functions for the required task, such as early detection of lung cancer in a binary classification model (Figure 2.18). The neural network learns the classification function to decide whether the detected tumor is malignant or benign. Since most of the functions $f(x)$ learned by CNN are invariant or covariant to translations, the filters used to learn W_j are also covariant to translations. As W_j is linear, it can be described as a summation of convolutions. The ρW_j operator generates x_j from the input X.

Referring to the binary classification CNN model for early detection of lung cancer, as shown in Figure 2.18, it can be explained as the composition of a large-scale function estimation problem where all layers estimate an integral function that is applied forward, that is, $f(f(f(f(...))))$, where $f(.)$ is a linear/non-linear function. Let us consider a set of all CT images used for lung cancer detection a subset of $R^{n\times n}$ in which each CT image $x \in R^{d\times d}$. The x is mapped to its class label, that is, malignant/benign, via a function $f(x)$, which is learned along this binary

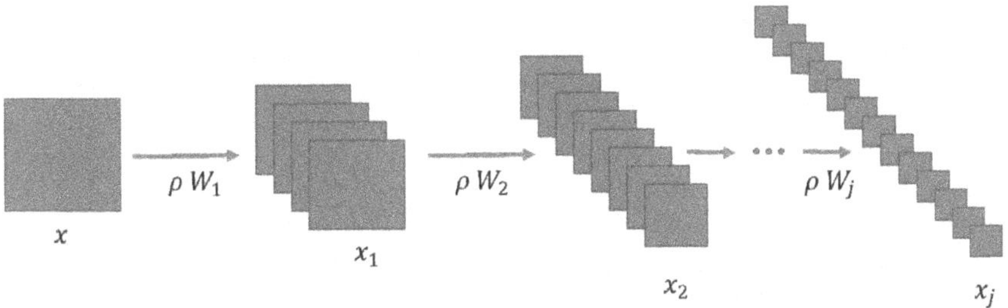

Figure 2.22 General CNN architecture.

classification CNN architecture, $f(x): x \rightarrow D$, where $D \in R$ is a set of the two class labels. Now, for interpretability, one can consider $\Phi = \varphi(x)$ the internal representation of CT data in the CNN. It would further help explain the generalization ability of a CNN. To this end, $g \in G$ may be considered a group of symmetries acting on the *f*; then $g(x)$ is the transformed image obtained after applying *g*. In turn, f^1 maps $\varphi(x)$ to the class label, that is, $f^1(x): \Phi(x) \rightarrow D$. Note that CNNs solve this mapping problem by finding a wide range of representations of the image x in their internal representation Φ. It is evident that this mapping Φ in the CNNs constitutes high-dimensional representation. Often we use linearization for dimensionality reduction using linear projections in dictionary learning. One can linearize the high-dimensional domain and find a low-dimensional linear projection of x, that is, $\Phi(x)$. In this way, a CNN can be explained for binary classification problems in general as well as in medical image analysis tasks.

2.5 Concluding Remarks

DL models are successfully applied in various medical imaging applications. We sincerely hope they will help assisting healthcare practitioners in deep analysis of intrinsic features in the acquired images. We have presented useful insights on how modern researchers are constructing learning algorithms for medical image denoising, registration, restoration, super-resolution, classification, and segmentation. We have observed that with rigorous training, DL models can achieve higher accuracies, precisions, and F1 scores over conventional approaches for targeted applications in medical imaging. However, the models can only be used for the specified data on which they are trained. Also, plenty of datasets are generally required to train such models to extract the inherent features present in medical images. Models have to be trained on multiple datasets and cross-validated to make them more robust and practically acceptable by medical practitioners. Though researchers have partly attempted it, an unsupervised learning paradigm is still a challenge for life-critical applications in medical imaging.

References

Aharon, Michal, Michael Elad, and Alfred Bruckstein. 2006. "K-SVD: An Algorithm for Designing Overcomplete Dictionaries for Sparse Representation." *IEEE Transactions on Signal Processing* 54 (11). https://doi.org/10.1109/TSP.2006.881199.

Alban, Marco, and Tanner Gilligan. 2016. "Automated Detection of Diabetic Retinopathy Using Fluorescein Angiography Photographs." *Report of Standard Education*, pp. 1–8.

Andreopoulos, Alexander, and John K. Tsotsos. 2008. "Efficient and Generalizable Statistical Models of Shape and Appearance for Analysis of Cardiac MRI." *Medical Image Analysis* 12 (3). https://doi.org/10.1016/j.media.2007.12.003.

Armato, Samuel G., Geoffrey McLennan, Luc Bidaut, Michael F. McNitt-Gray, Charles R. Meyer, Anthony P. Reeves, Binsheng Zhao, et al., 2011. "The Lung Image Database Consortium (LIDC) and Image Database Resource Initiative (IDRI): A Completed Reference Database of Lung Nodules on CT Scans." *Medical Physics* 38 (2). https://doi.org/10.1118/1.3528204.

Balakrishnan, Guha, Amy Zhao, Mert R. Sabuncu, John Guttag, and Adrian v. Dalca. 2019. "VoxelMorph: A Learning Framework for Deformable Medical Image Registration." *IEEE Transactions on Medical Imaging* 38 (8). https://doi.org/10.1109/TMI.2019.2897538.

Ben Said, Ahmed, Rachid Hadjidj, and Sebti Foufou. 2019. "Total Variation for Image Denoising Based on a Novel Smart Edge Detector: An Application to Medical Images." *Journal of Mathematical Imaging and Vision* 61 (1). https://doi.org/10.1007/s10851-018-0829-6.

Blystad, I., JBM. Warntjes, O. Smedby, AM. Landtblom, P. Lundberg, and EM. Larsson. 2012. "Synthetic MRI of the Brain in a Clinical Setting." *Acta Radiologica* 53 (10). https://doi.org/10.1258/ar.2012.120195.

Bushberg, Jerrold T., J. Anthony Seibert, Edwin M. Leidholdt, John M. Boone, and Edward J. Goldschmidt. 2003. "The Essential Physics of Medical Imaging." *Medical Physics* 30 (7). https://doi.org/10.1118/1.1585033.

Castillo, Richard, Edward Castillo, Rudy Guerra, Valen E. Johnson, Travis McPhail, Amit K. Garg, and Thomas Guerrero. 2009. "A Framework for Evaluation of Deformable Image Registration Spatial Accuracy Using Large Landmark Point Sets." *Physics in Medicine and Biology* 54 (7). https://doi.org/10.1088/0031-9155/54/7/001.

Challa, Uday Kiran, Pavankumar Yellamraju, and Jignesh S. Bhatt. 2019. "A Multi-Class Deep All-CNN for Detection of Diabetic Retinopathy Using Retinal Fundus Images." In *Lecture Notes in Computer Science (Including Subseries Lecture Notes in Artificial Intelligence and Lecture Notes in Bioinformatics)*, 11941 LNCS, pp. 191–199. Berlin: Springer (https://doi.org/10.1007/978-3-030-34869-4_21).

Chen, Hu, Yi Zhang, Mannudeep K. Kalra, Feng Lin, Yang Chen, Peixi Liao, Jiliu Zhou, and Ge Wang. 2017. "Low-Dose CT with a Residual Encoder-Decoder Convolutional Neural Network." *IEEE Transactions on Medical Imaging* 36 (12). https://doi.org/10.1109/TMI.2017.2715284.

Chen, Liang, Paul Bentley, Kensaku Mori, Kazunari Misawa, Michitaka Fujiwara, and Daniel Rueckert. 2018. "DRINet for Medical Image Segmentation." *IEEE Transactions on Medical Imaging* 37 (11). https://doi.org/10.1109/TMI.2018.2835303.

Chen, Weixiang, Jianfu Zhao, Zhenhui Dai, Mingyue Lv, Zhenhua Yang, and Yuqin Zhang. 2021. "Application of CT Image Technology Based on Nearest Neighbor Propagation Clustering Segmentation Algorithm in Lung Cancer Radiotherapy." *Scientific Programming* 2021.

Choi, Kihwan, Joon Seok Lim, and Sungwon Kim Kim. 2020. "StatNet: Statistical Image Restoration for Low-Dose CT Using Deep Learning." *IEEE Journal on Selected Topics in Signal Processing* 14 (6). https://doi.org/10.1109/JSTSP.2020.2998413.

Clark, Kenneth, Bruce Vendt, Kirk Smith, John Freymann, Justin Kirby, Paul Koppel, Stephen Moore, et al., 2013. "The Cancer Imaging Archive (TCIA): Maintaining and Operating a Public Information Repository." *Journal of Digital Imaging* 26 (6). https://doi.org/10.1007/s10278-013-9622-7.

Dabov, Kostadin, Alessandro Foi, Vladimir Katkovnik, and Karen Egiazarian. 2007. "Image Denoising by Sparse 3-D Transform-Domain Collaborative Filtering." *IEEE Transactions on Image Processing* 16 (8). https://doi.org/10.1109/TIP.2007.901238.

Dandil, Emre, Murat Cakiroglu, Ziya Eksi, Murat Ozkan, Ozlem Kar Kurt, and Arzu Canan. 2014. "Artificial Neural Network-Based Classification System for Lung Nodules on Computed Tomography Scans." *6th International Conference on Soft Computing and Pattern Recognition, SoCPaR 2014*, pp. 382–386. https://doi.org/10.1109/SOCPAR.2014.7008037.

Deshpande, Vijay S., and Jignesh S. Bhatt. 2019. "Bayesian Deep Learning for Deformable Medical Image Registration." In *Lecture Notes in Computer Science (Including Subseries Lecture Notes in Artificial Intelligence and Lecture Notes in Bioinformatics)*, 11942 LNCS, pp. 41–49. Berlin: Springer (https://doi.org/10.1007/978-3-030-34872-4_5).

Ghosh, Ratul, Kuntal Ghosh, and Sanjit Maitra. 2017. "Automatic Detection and Classification of Diabetic Retinopathy Stages Using CNN." *4th International Conference on Signal Processing and Integrated Networks, SPIN 2017*, pp. 550–554. https://doi.org/10.1109/SPIN.2017.8050011.

Graham, B., 2015. *Kaggle diabetic retinopathy detection competition report. University of Warwick*, 24–26. Online: https://www.Kaggle.Com/c/Diabetic-Retinopathy-Detection/Data. 2017.

Gu, Jawook, and Jong Chul Ye. 2021. "AdaIN-Based Tunable CycleGAN for Efficient Unsupervised Low-Dose CT Denoising." *IEEE Transactions on Computational Imaging* 7. https://doi.org/10.1109/TCI.2021.3050266.

Guo, Zhe, Xiang Li, Heng Huang, Ning Guo, and Quanzheng Li. 2019. "Deep Learning-Based Image Segmentation on Multimodal Medical Imaging." *IEEE Transactions on Radiation and Plasma Medical Sciences* 3 (2). https://doi.org/10.1109/TRPMS.2018.2890359.

Holzinger, Andreas, Georg Langs, Helmut Denk, Kurt Zatloukal, and Heimo Müller. 2019. "Causability and explainability of artificial intelligence in medicine." *Wiley Interdisciplinary Reviews: Data Mining and Knowledge Discovery* 9 (4): e1312.

Hu, Shaoping, Yuan Gao, Zhangming Niu, Yinghui Jiang, Lao Li, Xianglu Xiao, Minhao Wang, et al., 2020. "Weakly Supervised Deep Learning for COVID-19 Infection Detection and Classification from CT Images." *IEEE Access* 8. https://doi.org/10.1109/ACCESS.2020.3005510.

Hua, Kai Lung, Che Hao Hsu, Shintami Chusnul Hidayati, Wen Huang Cheng, and Yu Jen Chen. 2015. "Computer-Aided Classification of Lung Nodules on Computed Tomography Images via Deep Learning Technique." *OncoTargets and Therapy* 8. https://doi.org/10.2147/OTT.S80733.

Jiang, Changhui, Qiyang Zhang, Rui Fan, and Zhanli Hu. 2018. "Super-Resolution CT Image Reconstruction Based on Dictionary Learning and Sparse Representation." *Scientific Reports* 8 (1). https://doi.org/10.1038/s41598-018-27261-z.

Jifara, Worku, Feng Jiang, Seungmin Rho, Maowei Cheng, and Shaohui Liu. 2019. "Medical Image Denoising Using Convolutional Neural Network: A Residual Learning Approach." *Journal of Supercomputing* 75 (2). https://doi.org/10.1007/s11227-017-2080-0.

Kennedy, John A., Ora Israel, Alex Frenkel, Rachel Bar-Shalom, and Haim Azhari. 2006. "Super-Resolution in PET Imaging." *IEEE Transactions on Medical Imaging* 25 (2). https://doi.org/10.1109/TMI.2005.861705.

Kim, Kwanyoung, Shakarim Soltanayev, and Se Young Chun. 2020. "Unsupervised Training Of Denoisers For Low-Dose CT Reconstruction Without Full-Dose Ground Truth." *IEEE Journal on Selected Topics in Signal Processing* 14 (6): 1112–1125. https://doi.org/10.1109/JSTSP.2020.3007326.

Krewer, Carmen, Katrin Rieß, Jeannine Bergmann, Friedemann Müller, Klaus Jahn, and Eberhard Koenig. 2013. "Immediate Effectiveness of Single-Session Therapeutic Interventions in Pusher Behaviour." *Gait and Posture* 37 (2). https://doi.org/10.1016/j.gaitpost.2012.07.014.

Krissian, Karl, and Santiago Aja-Fernández. 2009. "Noise-Driven Anisotropic Diffusion Filtering of MRI." *IEEE Transactions on Image Processing* 18 (10). https://doi.org/10.1109/TIP.2009.2025553.

Kumar, Devinder, Alexander Wong, and David A. Clausi. 2015. "Lung Nodule Classification Using Deep Features in CT Images." *Proceedings – 2015 12th Conference on Computer and Robot Vision, CRV 2015*, pp. 133–138. https://doi.org/10.1109/CRV.2015.25.

Kuruvilla, Jinsa, and K. Gunavathi. 2014. "Lung Cancer Classification Using Neural Networks for CT Images." *Computer Methods and Programs in Biomedicine* 113 (1). https://doi.org/10.1016/j.cmpb.2013.10.011.

Lam, Carson, Darvin Yi, and Margaret Guo. 2018. "Automated Detection of Diabetic Retinopathy Using Deep Learning." *AMIA Summits on Translational Science Proceedings* 147.

Li, Xiuli, Yueying Kao, Wei Shen, Xiang Li, and Guotong Xie. 2017. "Lung Nodule Malignancy Prediction Using Multi-Task Convolutional Neural Network." *Medical Imaging 2017: Computer-Aided Diagnosis* 10134. https://doi.org/10.1117/12.2253836.

Liu, Yan, and Yi Zhang. 2018. "Low-Dose CT Restoration via Stacked Sparse Denoising Autoencoders." *Neurocomputing* 284. https://doi.org/10.1016/j.neucom.2018.01.015.

Mallat, Stéphane. 2016. "Understanding Deep Convolutional Networks." *Philosophical Transactions of the Royal Society A: Mathematical, Physical and Engineering Sciences* 374: 1–16. https://doi.org/10.1098/rsta.2015.0203.

Manaswini, Piduguralla, and Jignesh S. Bhatt. 2021. *Towards Glass-Box CNNs*, January. http://arxiv.org/abs/2101.10443.

Manjón, José v., José Carbonell-Caballero, Juan J. Lull, Gracián García-Martí, Luís Martí-Bonmatí, and Montserrat Robles. 2008. "MRI Denoising Using Non-Local Means." *Medical Image Analysis* 12 (4). https://doi.org/10.1016/j.media.2008.02.004.

Masood, Sarfaraz, Tarun Luthra, Himanshu Sundriyal, and Mumtaz Ahmed. 2017. "Identification of Diabetic Retinopathy in Eye Images Using Transfer Learning." *Proceeding – IEEE International Conference on Computing, Communication and Automation, ICCCA* 2017. https://doi.org/10.1109/CCAA.2017.8229977.

Moen, Taylor R., Baiyu Chen, David R. Holmes, Xinhui Duan, Zhicong Yu, Lifeng Yu, Shuai Leng, Joel G. Fletcher, and Cynthia H. McCollough. 2021. "Low-Dose CT Image and Projection Dataset." *Medical Physics* 48 (2). https://doi.org/10.1002/mp.14594.

Nascimento, Leonardo Barros, Anselmo Cardoso de Paiva, and Aristófanes Corrêa Silva. 2012. "Lung Nodules Classification in CT Images Using Shannon and Simpson Diversity Indices and SVM." *Lecture Notes in Computer Science (Including Subseries Lecture Notes in Artificial Intelligence and Lecture Notes in Bioinformatics)* 7376 (LNAI). https://doi.org/10.1007/978-3-642-31537-4_36.

Nowak, Robert D. 1999. "Wavelet-Based Rician Noise Removal for Magnetic Resonance Imaging." *IEEE Transactions on Image Processing* 8 (10). https://doi.org/10.1109/83.791966.

Oliveira, Rodrigo Ribeiro de, Thiago Potrich Rodrigues, Paulo Savoia Dias da Silva, Andrea Cavalanti Gomes, and Maria Cristina Chammas. 2020. "Lung Ultrasound: An Additional Tool in COVID-19." *Radiologia Brasileira* 53: 241–251.

Orozco, Hiram Madero, Osslan Osiris Vergara Villegas, Leticia Ortega Maynez, Vianey Guadalupe Cruz Sanchez, and Humberto De Jesus Ochoa Dominguez. 2012. "Lung Nodule Classification in Frequency Domain Using Support Vector Machines." *2012 11th International Conference on Information Science, Signal Processing and Their Applications, ISSPA 2012*, pp. 870–875. https://doi.org/10.1109/ISSPA.2012.6310676.

Parnian, Afshar and Others. 2021. "COVID-19 Low-Dose and Ultra-Low-Dose CT Scans." *IEEE Dataport*. https://dx.doi.org/10.21227/sed8-6r15.

Pratt, Harry, Frans Coenen, Deborah M. Broadbent, Simon P. Harding, and Yalin Zheng. 2016. "Convolutional Neural Networks for Diabetic Retinopathy." *Procedia Computer Science* 31: 1420–1431. https://doi.org/10.1016/j.procs.2016.07.014.

Qiu, Defu, Yuhu Cheng, Xuesong Wang, and Xiaoqiang Zhang. 2021. "Multi-Window Back-Projection Residual Networks for Reconstructing COVID-19 CT Super-Resolution Images." *Computer Methods and Programs in Biomedicine* 200. https://doi.org/10.1016/j.cmpb.2021.105934.

Rahimzadeh, Mohammad, Abolfazl Attar, and Seyed Mohammad Sakhaei. 2021. "A Fully Automated Deep Learning-Based Network for Detecting COVID-19 from a New and

Large Lung CT Scan Dataset." *Biomedical Signal Processing and Control* 68. https://doi.org/10.1016/j.bspc.2021.102588.

Rai, Swati, Jignesh S. Bhatt, and Sarat Kumar Patra. 2021a. "Augmented Noise Learning Framework for Enhancing Medical Image Denoising." *IEEE Access* 9: 117153–117168. https://doi.org/10.1109/ACCESS.2021.3106707.

Rai, Swati, Jignesh S. Bhatt, and Sarat Kumar Patra. 2021b. *An Unsupervised Deep Learning Framework for Medical Image Denoising*, March. http://arxiv.org/abs/2103.06575.

Rai, Swati, Jignesh S. Bhatt, and Sarat Kumar Patra. 2022. "Accessible, Affordable and Low-Risk Lungs Health Monitoring in Covid-19: Deep Cascade Reconstruction from Degraded LR-ULDCT." *2022 IEEE 19th International Symposium on Biomedical Imaging (ISBI)*: 1–5. https://doi.org/10.1109/ISBI52829.2022.9761566.

Ran, Maosong, Jinrong Hu, Yang Chen, Hu Chen, Huaiqiang Sun, Jiliu Zhou, and Yi Zhang. 2019. "Denoising of 3D Magnetic Resonance Images Using a Residual Encoder–Decoder Wasserstein Generative Adversarial Network." *Medical Image Analysis* 55. https://doi.org/10.1016/j.media.2019.05.001.

Robinson, Dirk M., Stephanie J. Chiu, Cynthia A. Toth, Joseph A. Izatt, Joseph Y. Lo, and Sina Farsiu. 2017. "New Applications of Super-Resolution in Medical Imaging." *Super-Resolution Imaging* 383–412. https://doi.org/10.1201/9781439819319.

Saha, Pritam, Debadyuti Mukherjee, Pawan Kumar Singh, Ali Ahmadian, Massimiliano Ferrara, and Ram Sarkar. 2021. "Retracted article: GraphCovidNet: A Graph Neural Network Based Model for Detecting COVID-19 from CT Scans and X-rays of Chest." *Scientific Reports* 11 (1): 1–16.

Samek, Wojciech, Grégoire Montavon, Sebastian Lapuschkin, Christopher J. Anders, and Klaus-Robert Müller. 2021. "Explaining deep neural networks and beyond: A review of methods and applications." *Proceedings of the IEEE* 109 (3): 247–278.

Shan, Hongming, Atul Padole, Fatemeh Homayounieh, Uwe Kruger, Ruhani Doda Khera, Chayanin Nitiwarangkul, Mannudeep K. Kalra, and Ge Wang. 2019. "Competitive Performance of a Modularized Deep Neural Network Compared to Commercial Algorithms for Low-Dose CT Image Reconstruction." *Nature Machine Intelligence* 1 (6). https://doi.org/10.1038/s42256-019-0057-9.

Shan, Hongming, Yi Zhang, Qingsong Yang, Uwe Kruger, Mannudeep K. Kalra, Ling Sun, Wenxiang Cong, and Ge Wang. 2018. "3-D Convolutional Encoder-Decoder Network for Low-Dose CT via Transfer Learning From a 2-D Trained Network." *IEEE Transactions on Medical Imaging* 37 (6). https://doi.org/10.1109/TMI.2018.2832217.

Sharma, Manu, Jignesh Bhatt, and Manjunath Joshi. 2018. "Early Detection of Lung Cancer from CT Images: Nodule Segmentation and Classification Using Deep Learning." *Tenth International Conference on Machine Vision (ICMV 2017)* 10696: 226–233. https://doi.org/10.1117/12.2309530.

Suetens, Paul. 2017. *Fundamentals of Medical Imaging*. Belgium: Cambridge University Press. https://doi.org/10.1017/9781316671849.

Sun, Hong, Pouya Saeedi, Suvi Karuranga, Moritz Pinkepank, Katherine Ogurtsova, Bruce B. Duncan, Caroline Stein, et al., 2022. "IDF Diabetes Atlas: Global, Regional and Country-Level Diabetes Prevalence Estimates for 2021 and Projections for 2045." *Diabetes Research and Clinical Practice* 183. https://doi.org/10.1016/j.diabres.2021.109119.

Sung, Hyuna, Jacques Ferlay, Rebecca L. Siegel, Mathieu Laversanne, Isabelle Soerjomataram, Ahmedin Jemal, and Freddie Bray. 2021. "Global Cancer Statistics 2020: GLOBOCAN Estimates of Incidence and Mortality Worldwide for 36 Cancers in 185 Countries." *CA: A Cancer Journal for Clinicians* 71 (3). https://doi.org/10.3322/caac.21660.

Thakkar, Jay D, Jignesh S Bhatt, and Sarat Kumar Patra. 2022. "Self-Supervised Learning for Medical Image Restoration: Investigation and Finding." *4th International Conference on Machine Intelligence and Signal Processing (MISP 2022)*, Lecture Notes in Electrical Engineering (LNEE), Springer Nature.

Thanh, Dang NH., VB. Surya Prasath, and Le Minh Hieu. 2019. "A Review on CT and X-Ray Images Denoising Methods." *Informatica (Slovenia)* 43 (2): 151–159. https://doi.org/10.31449/inf.v43i2.2179.

Tjoa, Erico, and Cuntai Guan. 2020. "A Survey on Explainable Artificial Intelligence (Xai): Toward Medical Xai." *IEEE Transactions on Neural Networks and Learning Systems* 32 (11): 4793–4813.

Tonekaboni, Sana, Shalmali Joshi, Melissa D. McCradden, and Anna Goldenberg. 2019. "What Clinicians Want: Contextualizing Explainable Machine Learning for Clinical End Use." *Machine Learning for Healthcare Conference*, 359–380. PMLR.

Vasilev, Yuriy A., Alexander V. Bazhin, Amir G. Masri, Yulia N. Vasileva, Olga Yu Panina, and Valentin E. Sinitsyn. 2020. "Chest MRI of a Pregnant Woman with COVID-19 Pneumonia." *Digital Diagnostics* 1 (1): 61–68.

Wang, Shuo, Yunfei Zha, Weimin Li, Qingxia Wu, Xiaohu Li, Meng Niu, Meiyun Wang, et al., 2020. "A Fully Automatic Deep Learning System for COVID-19 Diagnostic and Prognostic Analysis." *European Respiratory Journal* 56 (2). https://doi.org/10.1183/13993003.00775-2020.

Zhao, Guannan, Bo Zhou, Kaiwen Wang, Rui Jiang, and Min Xu. 2018. "Respond-Cam: Analyzing Deep Models for 3d Imaging Data by Visualizations." In *International Conference on Medical Image Computing and Computer-Assisted Intervention*, pp. 485–492. Cham: Springer.

3 An Overview of Functional Near-Infrared Spectroscopy and Explainable Artificial Intelligence in fNIRS

N. Sertac Artan

Contents

3.1 Introduction

Neuroimaging – producing images of the brain by non-invasive techniques – revolutionized our understanding of brain structures and functions. There are various neuroimaging technologies such as functional magnetic resonance imaging (fMRI), positron emission tomography (PET), magnetoelectroencephalography (MEG), single-photon emission computed tomography (SPECT), and electroencephalography (EEG), with different advantages and disadvantages for different applications.

Functional near-infrared spectroscopy (fNIRS) is a non-invasive neuroimaging technology, which saw significant growth in the last few decades (Ferrari and Quaresima, 2012; Yücel et al., 2021). Frans F. Jöbsis discovered near-infrared spectroscopy (Jöbsis, 1977; Delpy et al., 2007) and showed that oxygenated hemoglobin (HbO) and de-oxygenated hemoglobin (HbR) concentrations in the brain can be monitored noninvasively using near-infrared (NIR) light. He showed that, unlike visible light, tissue absorption of NIR light is small (Delpy et al., 1988; Scholkman,

DOI: 10.1201/9781003333425-3

2014). Living tissue is mostly transparent to NIR light (between 700 and 900 nm), and NIR light can penetrate through the scalp and skull. fNIRS infers relative oxygen use in each superficial brain region to determine regional activation patterns. This is achieved by measuring the hemoglobin concentration in these regions. Hemoglobin is an oxygen carrier in the blood. Neuronal activity via neurovascular coupling causes an increase in the HbO concentration due to an increase in blood flow and a decrease in the HbR concentration as HbR leaves the veins. During this process, the total hemoglobin (HbT) concentration usually increases as the increase in HbO concentration is higher than the decrease in HbR concentration (Lloyd-Fox et al., 2010). These concentrations are measured via optical sensors built into headbands or inside caps placed noninvasively on the scalp. The distance between the light source and the sensor determines the imaging depth. The first commercial fNIRS system (NIRO-1000) was developed by Hamamatsu Photonics K.K. in 1986 (Ferrari and Quaresima, 2012). An example waveform showing changes in HbO and HbR concentrations is shown in Figure 3.1.

Neuroimaging technologies have different advantages and disadvantages, making each suitable for certain applications and use cases. These technologies differ in their spatial and temporal resolutions, cost, and patient comfort, among other properties. fNIRS shows favorable trade-offs in spatial/temporal resolutions compared to fMRI and EEG while being the most convenient among the three. fNIRS has various advantages over other neuroimaging technologies. The main advantages of fNIRS as a neuroimaging technology are summarized in the following:

- fNIRS provides higher temporal resolution (0.01–0.5 s) compared to fMRI,
- fNIRS has higher spatial resolution (1–2 cm) compared to EEG,
- fNIRS requires minimal patient preparation,

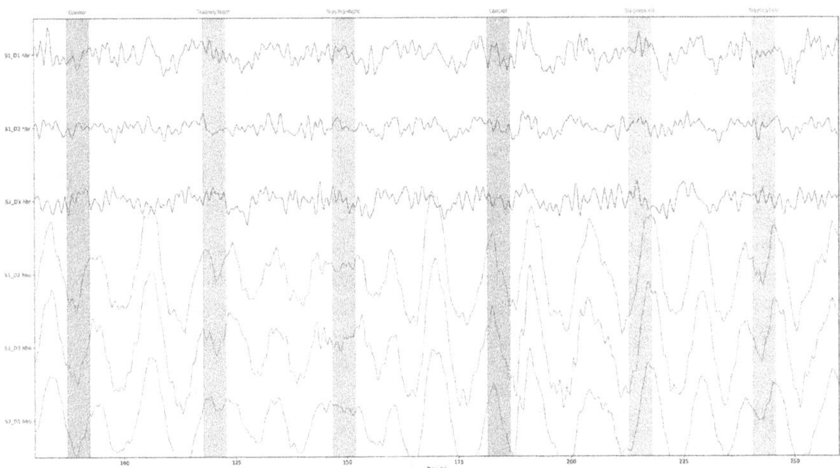

Figure 3.1 The change in HbO and HbR concentrations during a finger tapping task on three representative HbO and HbR channels measured with fNIRS. The data are from the publicly available fNIRS finger tapping dataset (Luke et al., 2021a).

- fNIRS needs modest to no infrastructure, and
- fNIRS has relatively low initial investment and maintenance cost.

These attractive properties of fNIRS make it a popular choice for a wide range of studies on cognitive function. fNIRS also has limitations. In addition to comparatively low temporal resolution compared to EEG and low spatial resolution compared to fMRI, unlike both, NIR light penetration depth in the brain is limited, making fNIRS unsuitable for studying deep brain regions. Thus fNIRS studies are primarily limited to superficial brain structures. Other aspects of fNIRS that currently limit its applicability are its poor within- and intersubject reproducibility (Novi et al., 2020), lack of standards for co-registration with structural images (Chen et al., 2017), and variations in still-evolving experiment protocols (Yücel et al., 2021).

fNIRS has a growing list of clinical applications (Chen et al., 2020). In particular, fNIRS is used extensively in developmental cognitive neuroscience (Lloyd-Fox et al., 2010) (Section 3.2.1). fNIRS also has the potential to be used for brain–computer interface applications (Li et al., 2020) (Section 3.2.2). Non-clinical applications of fNIRS span a broad range of fields, including neuromarketing, where neuroimaging along with other methods are used to better understand consumer behavior and optimize marketing strategies (Ramirez et al., 2022; Sandoe-Pedersen et al., 2022). Another non-clinical application example for fNIRS is security, where researchers use fNIRS for detecting the legitimacy of speakers to avoid voice impersonation to steal personal data over the phone (Neupane et al., 2019).

As the capabilities and applications of fNIRS grow, the signal processing algorithms used to process and analyze the fNIRS data also become more complicated. In particular, deep learning algorithms have recently become popular for processing and analyzing fNIRS data (Eastmond et al., 2022). Adding this to the inherent complexities of the brain, it is becoming hard to draw conclusions from the fNIRS studies that are interpretable and explainable. Explainable artificial intelligence (XAI) aims to make the behavior and outcomes of AI methods more accessible to humans. Recently, XAI in fNIRS has started to emerge as a new field. In this chapter, we briefly review these efforts as well.

In this chapter, we review different aspects of fNIRS starting with some representative applications in Section 3.2. In Section 3.3, fundamental concepts in fNIRS are covered. Section 3.4 gives examples of machine learning (ML) and deep learning (DL) approaches as they are applied to fNIRS data processing and analysis. After a brief introduction to explainable artificial intelligence in healthcare in Section 3.5, the state of explainable artificial intelligence in fNIRS is outlined in Section 3.6. Section 3.7 concludes the chapter.

3.2 Applications of fNIRS

Before we delve into the details of the fNIRS technology, it will be informative to first introduce applications of fNIRS. It is not practical to cover all of the numerous applications of fNIRS in this chapter. Nevertheless, in this section, we summarize some representative applications. Readers are referred to various excellent recent and comprehensive reviews such as Chen et al. (2020), Hong et al. (2020), Pinti et al. (2020), and Rahman et al. (2020).

3.2.1 fNIRS in Developmental Cognitive Neuroscience

It is a challenge to study functional brain development in infancy through adolescence with standard clinical neuroimaging techniques. fMRI and MEG restrict the movement of the subjects; thus use of fMRI and MEG in infants is mostly limited to studies where the infants are sleeping or sedated. In contrast, EEG can be used in awake infants but with the disadvantage of low spatial resolution. fNIRS is suitable for this task due to its low cost, easy preparation, reasonable spatial resolution, relatively high resilience to motion artifacts, quiet operation, and portability (Lloyd-Fox et al., 2010; Yeung, 2021). Thus, subjects can be awake and free to move. Furthermore, they can be monitored in natural environments. Thus, fNIRS has been extensively used in DCN, since its early days starting with the work of Meek et al. (1998) to study regional hemodynamics (changes in blood flow) in neonates.

Brain injury in pre-term infants can cause various complications, including behavioral and cognitive issues. Brain injury can be caused by a lack of cerebral perfusion and oxygenation. As the number of preterm infants increases, monitoring cerebral oxygenation with timely measurements becomes more critical in neonatal care (Dix et al., 2017; Peng and Hou, 2021). Regional cerebral oxygen saturation ($rScO_2$), which is the ratio of HbO to HbR, can be monitored for long periods with NIRS.

One challenge of using fNIRS in developmental cognitive neuroscience is that the skull and brain change through development. These changes affect the distance traveled by the NIR light, which determines measured concentration levels of HbO and HbR. Thus, the measured data should be corrected to take into account age-related effects. Most fNIRS analysis frameworks are tailored toward adults, exacerbating these challenges. The frameworks make assumptions that the underlying structure and hemodynamic responses are static, which limits their applicability to the developing brain (Andreu-Perez et al. (2021). Further studies are needed to expand these frameworks to take into account the developing brain.

The hemoglobin phase of oxygenation and deoxygenation (hPod), which is the phase difference between low-frequency oscillations in changes in HbO and HbR concentrations in fNIRS, can identify developmental stages of certain functions in neonate and infant brains (Watanabe et al., 2017). Liang et al. (2021) characterized the phase difference between changes (hPod) and showed that the phase difference is highest for children and lower for adults. Furthermore, there is a significant drop in phase difference in infants and the elderly.

3.2.2 fNIRS as Brain–Computer Interfaces

Brain–computer interfaces (BCIs) infer user intent by monitoring their brain signals and use these signals to aid rehabilitation, to actuate objects, or to assist the user in communicating with the outside world without any muscle movement. BCI can help monitor the progress of patients going through rehabilitation and offer neurofeedback to these patients to improve rehabilitation outcomes.

Prosthetic devices for patients with motor disorders and injuries such as amyotrophic lateral sclerosis (ALS) and spinal cord injury can also incorporate BCI for regaining partial motor function via control of the prosthetic devices. In addition to controlling prosthetic devices, patients in a locked-in state (LIS) also use BCI for communication. Finally, BCI is also used in non-clinical settings as a way of interacting with computers, for instance, as game controllers. Figure 3.2 shows an overview of the fNIRS used for BCI.

For BCI applications, well-characterized cortical activations are used as a control output from the brain, which can then be interpreted by a BCI system to actuate virtual objects (e.g., a computer cursor) or physical objects (e.g., a prosthetic arm). In fNIRS-based BCI, the regions of interest are primarily the motor cortex and prefrontal cortex (Naseer and Hong, 2015). Activations due to motor execution or motor imagery tasks in the motor cortex are interpreted as control signals, whereas activations in the prefrontal cortex are due to mental tasks such as mental arithmetic, music imagery, or emotion-inducing tasks.

Motor execution tasks involve actually moving a body part and are subject to proprioceptive feedback. Conversely, in motor imagery, a subject only imagines physical movement rather than executing the movement. Yet motor imagery results in similar neural activation patterns as the actual movement. In BCI, by imagining different movements, the subjects can generate distinct control outputs. A variety of imagined movements have been evaluated for BCI, for instance, imagining hand grasping, finger/foot tapping, wrist flexion, and finger folding. For BCI applications, motor imagery is preferable to motor execution, especially when the subject cannot execute the actual movement in the first place. Furthermore, as no muscular activity is involved in motor imagery, it is free from proprioceptive feedback. Tasks leading to the prefrontal cortex are also good candidates for BCI, as they are free from motion artifacts. However, for some applications such as neurorehabilitation, motor execution is required.

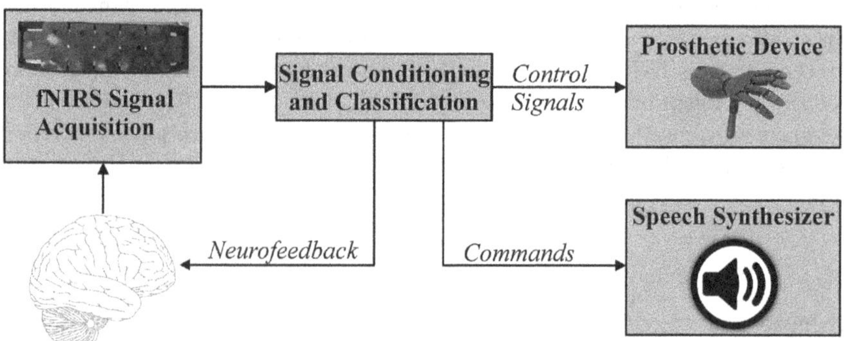

Figure 3.2 Overview of the use of fNIRS for BCI.

Coyle et al. (2004) were the first who used fNIRS for BCI successfully (Naseer and Hong, 2015). They used motor imagery as a control input where the subjects were asked to either clench a rubber ball or imagine they were executing the same task while monitoring blood oxygenation via fNIRS at the side of the brain opposite to the hand used.

An important aspect of BCI is the requirement for real timeliness, as signal processing, classification, and any resulting activation and feedback should be completed within a limited time frame. The low information rate of the hemodynamic response in fNIRS makes real-time BCI applications a challenge. Studies looking into the phenomenon called initial dip, that is, the reduction in HbO after initial neural activity, led to promising results for faster BCI with fNIRS (Hong and Zafar, 2018; Zafar et al., 2018). However, further research is required to reduce classification latency, especially for closed-loop applications (such as actuation of prosthetic devices and neurofeedback) to make fNIRS a practical BCI modality.

3.2.3 fNIRS in Epilepsy

Epilepsy is a highly prevalent (0.5–1%) chronic neurological disorder (Fattorusso et al., 2021). Patients whose seizures can be controlled by anti-epileptic drugs may still have seizures, albeit at a lower frequency of occurrence. These patients can benefit from automatic seizure detection methods for keeping track of the frequency and severity of their seizures to determine or adjust their drug therapy regimens (Kim et al., 2013). Patients with intractable (drug-resistant) epilepsy may need to go under resective surgery so that the area of the brain (seizure focus) causing seizures can be removed. For these patients, neuroimaging techniques are used to localize the seizure focus. Rizki et al. (2015) evaluated whether fNIRS can be used to determine seizure locus. They showed that time-averaged HbO concentration following EEG seizure onset or clinical seizure onset is higher on the side of the brain where the seizure originated compared to the contralateral side.

A major goal of epilepsy research for all patients is to predict a seizure so that patients or their caregivers can be informed before the seizure occurs. In response, the patients and their caregivers can take precautions. For instance, a patient can take her medication to prevent the seizure altogether or to better prepare for an upcoming seizure, or a driver with epilepsy may pull over and avoid an accident if she receives a warning that a seizure is imminent. Neuroimaging, especially with EEG (Rasheed et al., 2020) or electrocorticography (ECoG), along with a variety of non-imaging approaches, has long been studied for predicting and detecting seizures.

One advantage of fNIRS in epilepsy monitoring is that it can be used for a long period of time for recording cerebral hemodynamics, unlike fMRI. EEG is the standard modality for evaluating and monitoring epilepsy patients. Yet, if used along with EEG, fNIRS is shown to improve seizure detection performance (Peng et al., 2016). Sirpal et al. (2019) reported that a combined fNIRS-EEG system improves seizure detection performance compared to using EEG only. Furthermore, Guevara et al. (2020) evaluated seizure prediction and showed that fNIRS outperforms EEG in seizure prediction, albeit using a small patient cohort (five patients). The multimodal approaches using EEG and fNIRS in epilepsy research is exciting. However, larger studies with more patients and longitudinal studies are needed for translating these approaches to clinical practice.

3.3 Fundamental Concepts in fNIRS

In this section, we review the fundamental concepts used in fNIRS. Starting with the modified Beer-Lambert law, which governs the absorbance of light in biological tissue, we cover the different methods in instrumentation for fNIRS, options for study design, and required preprocessing steps. These topics will not only allow us to better understand the underlying mechanisms of the fNIRS technology but also serve as a basis for later sections where we discuss ML and DL in the context of fNIRS.

3.3.1 Modified Beer-Lambert Law

When light goes through a medium, it is attenuated as it is absorbed by the medium. The Beer-Lambert law (BLL) quantifies the *absorbance*, that is, the amount of light absorbed by the medium in relation to the properties of the medium. These properties are the molar absorption coefficient (ε), molar concentration (c), and optical path length (l). The optical path length is the distance between the light source and the detector. The BLL states that absorbance is linearly proportional to ε, c, and l (Almajidy et al., 2019). However, the BLL is not readily applicable to biological tissue, as it does not take into account the scattering of light through the tissue, and biological tissue is a scattering medium. Delpy et al. (1988) developed the modified Beer-Lambert law (MBLL) to extend the BLL to scattering media, including biological tissue (Scholkman, 2014). The MBLL defines the absorbance, A as

$$A = \varepsilon \times c \times l \times DBF + G \tag{3.1}$$

where DBF stands for the differential path length factor, which is a correction factor added to the optical path length to take into account the random path photons travel due to scattering. This is different from the path of photons in a non-scattering medium, where the photons follow a straight line instead. The G term takes into consideration the uncertainty due to the geometry. The MBLL is used to estimate the changes in molar concentrations of chromophores (i.e., molecules, which absorb particular wavelengths of light) and thus gives color to materials such as HbO and HbR (Millington, 2009). For this estimation, it is assumed that the uncertainty term G does not change during an experiment, and thus its impact can be canceled by taking the difference between two absorbance measurements (Kocsis et al., 2006). It should also be noted that G cannot be exactly calculated, so the calculation of the absolute value of chromophore concentrations using the MBLL is not possible in a scattering medium.

3.3.2 fNIRS Instrument Design

fNIRS instruments are built primarily on one of these three techniques:

1. Time-domain fNIRS
2. Frequency-domain fNIRS, and
3. Continuous wave (CW) fNIRS.

Time-domain fNIRS uses extremely short pulses and can deduce tissue scattering and absorbance information from the distribution of response in time. In frequency-domain fNIRS, the light signal is modulated before it is directed to the tissue, and the decay and phase shift of the detected signal are then compared with the source signal (Izzetoglu et al., 2005). Both time-domain and frequency-domain fNIRS are complex to implement (Scholkmann et al., 2014). fNIRS instruments based on the continuous wave technique are the most common, and most of the current commercial systems are based on CW; thus, the CW technique will be the focus of this chapter. In the CW technique, a light source generates a constant intensity light (constant amplitude), which is directed towards the biological tissue. A detector detects the intensity of the light after it passes through the tissue. The difference in the light intensity is used to determine chromophore concentrations. Figure 3.3 illustrates the CW technique. CW is a relatively low-cost and simple technique and thus allows affordable mobile fNIRS devices (von Lühmann et al., 2015). Nevertheless, the accuracy of CW is low compared to the other two techniques.

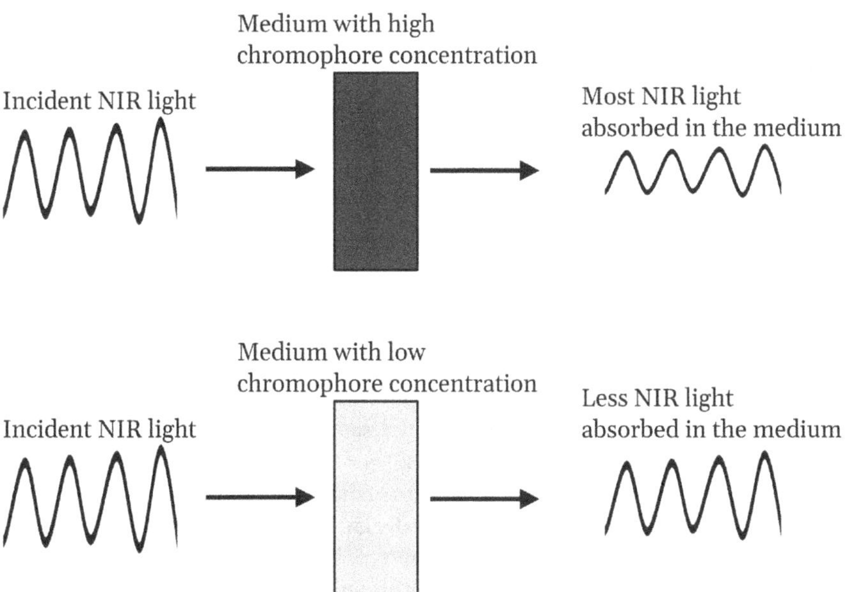

Figure 3.3 Using the CW technique, the relative chromophore concentration in a medium can be determined by measuring the absorption of the NIR light in the medium. For higher chromophore concentrations, the intensity for the outgoing NIR light wave will be lower at wavelengths where the particular chromophore's absorption is high.

The raw light intensity signal is collected and digitized with an fNIRS device. The raw light intensity should be converted into the changes in chromophore concentrations to extract useful information corresponding to the neurovascular activity. More specifically, raw light intensity should be converted into changes in HbO, that is, ΔHbO, and changes in HbR, that is, ΔHbR. Following the fNIRS data acquisition, the raw light intensity data are first converted into optical density data. Then the optical density data are converted into changes in chromophore concentrations (ΔHbO and ΔHbR) using the modified Beer-Lambert law. In some studies, the total change in chromophore concentrations ($\Delta HbT = \Delta HbO + \Delta HbR$) is also reported.

In fNIRS, a detector is placed approximately 3 cm away from a light source. The NIR light from the source follows a banana shape through the brain tissue to the detector. As HbO and HbR absorb different wavelengths of light, the dip in the light in frequencies absorbed by HbO and HbR indicates the level of HbO and HbR. NIR light at two different frequencies is used concurrently to detect both chromophore concentrations. The isosbestic point for HbO and HbR, where they have the same absorption coefficient, is around 800 nm. Thus, an fNIRS device will typically have at least two wavelengths of NIR light, one below and one above the isosbestic point. The resulting data provide a system of two equations (one per wavelength) in the form of MBLL. Solving these equations reveals the chromophore concentration changes.

3.3.3 fNIRS Study Design

fNIRS studies can be classified as one of these three types:

1. Block design,
2. Event-related design, and
3. Resting-state

In block design, the same stimulus is presented continuously or repeatedly as a *block*, with brief intervals between each presentation if repetition is used. Then, the subject rests for a period of time, and another block of stimulus condition is applied. The experiments usually consist of multiple blocks of alternating stimuli. When analyzing results from an experiment with block design, the hemodynamic responses to each of the presentations of the stimulus are considered in aggregate and compared with other blocks. The aggregation of responses to individual stimulus presentations increases the statistical power of the analysis (Tie et al., 2009). Event-related design is similar to block design. Unlike block design, in event-related design, different brief events are presented consecutively, and the presentation order is random. Due to this random ordering, event-related design has lower statistical power compared to block design; however, event-related design also allows the detection of transient effects and prevents habituation.

In resting-state fNIRS studies, no explicit stimulus is presented, no task is carried out, and the hemodynamic response of the brain is recorded while the subject is resting. Resting-state studies are particularly useful for populations unable to carry out tasks such as pediatric subjects and patients with psychiatric conditions (Lv et al., 2018).

3.3.4 *fNIRS Data Preprocessing*

Before analyzing fNIRS data, the collected data should be inspected to make sure that optical coupling is strong. This can be verified by the presence of the heartbeat in the signal. Additionally, during the inspection, noisy channels should be identified. Channels with poor optical coupling and channels with visible noise are usually not considered for analysis. There are various artifacts in data collected with the fNIRS device. These include motion artifacts due to head movements, cardiovascular effects due to respiration, heartbeat, and Mayer waves (Luke et al., 2021a, 2021b).

Frequency filters are most commonly used to remove artifacts. Butterworth infinite impulse response (IIR) filters, moving average filters, and finite impulse response (FIR) filters are the most common filters used (Pinti et al., 2019). Yet a rich variety of other filters and signal processing techniques are reported in the literature to be used for preprocessing of fNIRS data, such as wavelet minimum description length detrending, Savitzky-Golay filter, and discrete cosine transform (DCT), to name a few.

After the artifacts are removed, for block design and event-related studies, data are divided into epochs based on the timings of the stimuli-task timings. For resting state studies, data are divided into overlapping segments by applying a sliding window. Traditionally, the effects are tested against hemodynamic responses in different brain regions via statistical analysis of regional changes in chromophore concentrations.

3.4 Machine Learning and Deep Learning for fNIRS

Due to the recent progress in machine learning and deep learning coupled with the increasing complexity of experimental protocols and advances in instrumentation, more fNIRS studies are opting for ML and DL flows for analyzing fNIRS data. Furthermore, ML and DL are also being employed to optimize or eliminate preprocessing steps. In ML, statistical features such as mean, variance, skewness, and kurtosis are extracted from changes in chromophore concentrations and evaluated with ML algorithms such as support vector machines (SVMs), the *k*-nearest neighbor algorithm (*k*-NN), and artificial neural networks (ANNs). In DL, spatial maps or time-series data are applied directly to DL networks such as convolutional neural networks (CNNs) or long-short term memory (LSTM) networks (Eastmond et al., 2022).

As introduced previously, Guevara et al. (2020) evaluated seizure prediction using EEG, fNIRS, and ML. They compared different combinations of EEG and fNIRS signals as feature vectors to two different classifiers, an SVM classifier with a fine Gaussian kernel function and a multi-layer perceptron (MLP). Instantaneous samples from the time series for each channel of each modality are used to create a feature vector for each time instance. These feature vectors are fed into one of the two classifiers (SVM or MLP). They reported better seizure prediction (pre-ictal period detection) performance is achieved using fNIRS, where seizures are predicted up to 15 minutes prior to seizure onset.

Asgher et al. (2020) applied ML and DL to a passive brain–computer interface (pBCI). They compared traditional ML (SVMs, k-NN, and ANNs) with DL (CNN and LSTM) to classify four different classes of cognitive and mental workload using fNIRS. Their results show higher average accuracies for DL over traditional ML (87.45% for CNN, 89.31% for LSTM versus 54.33% for SVM, 54.31% for *k*-NN, and 69.36 for ANN). For traditional ML, optimal features are identified as signal mean, slope, variance, skewness, kurtosis, and signal peak. The authors cited the ability of DL to automatically learn features and the curse of dimensionality for ML algorithms as main reasons DL outperforms ML.

Bandara et al. (2019) used DL with a network consisting of a CNN and LSTM to determine the level of valence on fNIRS data, using self-reported valance levels as the ground truth, and achieved 77.89% accuracy on classifying the results into three classes, low valence, neutral, and high valence. With CNN and a dense fNIRS sensor array, the authors were able to explore spatial relations in the data and showed that accuracy drops significantly when sensor data are shuffled row-wise but not significantly when the data are shuffled column-wise. They speculated that this result indicates the uniqueness of left and right brain activity is lost when rows are shuffled. By varying the timestep, they were able to show that the accuracy is highest at a timestep of 1 second.

Early diagnosis of Alzheimer's disease (AD) can save $7 trillion by reducing medical and long-term care costs (Porsteinsson, 2021). fNIRS studies showed that AD patients have lower activation in various brain regions during cognitive tasks compared to healthy controls (Arai et al., 2006). Ho et al. (2022) carried out a comprehensive study to evaluate fNIRS in diagnosing AD using DL. They achieved the highest multi-class classification (cognitively normal individuals, asymptomatic AD, prodromal AD, and AD dementia) performance using convolutional neural network-long short-term memory (CNN-LSTM).

Recently, DL approaches focusing on end-to-end processing of fNIRS data started to appear (Dargazany et al., 2019; Wang et al., 2022). Dargazany et al. (2019) proposed a truly end-to-end DL approach for human activity recognition from multi-modal data (including fNIRS) without any pre- or post-processing. Raw fNIRS data are used to train a four-layered MLP and achieved 77–80% classification task accuracy using only fNIRS data. However, the training cost of this approach is significant, and there is a potential for overfitting. Wang et al. (2022) combined two networks for end-to-end processing of fNIRS data. The first network consists of a one-dimensional average pooling and layer normalization for preprocessing of fNIRS data and a transformer for classification. It should be noted that this work still has some preprocessing (Beer-Lambert law calculations and filtering); however, these are standard operations without any decision making (with the exception of selecting filter bands). They evaluated the performance of their proposed approach on three publicly available fNIRS datasets (Bauernfeind et al., 2011; Pfurtscheller et al., 2010; Shin et al., 2016; Bak et al., 2019). Their results show superior performance over traditional machine learning (k-NN, ANN, and SVM), as well as deep learning (CNN, LSTM) methods. However, these improvements also came at a high computational cost. Further research is required to optimize these techniques for efficient preprocessing.

Table 3.1 Some Representative, Publicly Available fNIRS Datasets

Source	*Emphasis*
(Yücel et al., 2014)	Motion artifacts
(Shin et al., 2018)	Multimodal (EEG + fNIRS)
(von Lühmann et al., 2020)	Resting state
(Luke et al., 2021c)	Comparison of analysis techniques

Datasets are crucial for improving and objectively comparing ML/DL techniques in any domain, and fNIRS is no exception. There are publicly accessible fNIRS datasets, which can be used for developing ML/DL methods for fNIRS. Some example datasets are given in Table 3.1. However, these datasets are usually limited in size. More comprehensive, public fNIRS datasets are needed to promote rapid progress in ML/DL techniques for fNIRS.

3.5 Explainable AI in Healthcare

ML and DL have been revolutionizing many distinct disciplines, bringing about very significant advances in a short period of time. This rapid change, however, also brings in an uneasy transition: These new ML/DL-based methods usually lack rigorous domain-specific explanations of the processes and their results, leading to umbrella terms such as black-box models or opaque methods when describing these ML/DL techniques (Gunning et al., 2019). It is vital to have explanations for justifying the outputs produced by AI. XAI can help increase the trust in a model by quantifying and improving the model's reliability and fairness (Kamath and Liu, 2021).

XAI is especially important for mission-critical applications, for instance, in medicine and security. According to a recent systematic review of XAI, the highest number of domain-specific XAI articles are in the healthcare domain (Islam et al., 2022). A key question, which is particularly critical in the healthcare setting, is the trade-off between accuracy and explainability, which are usually at odds with each other (Ghassemi et al., 2021). Finding the right balance between an accurate cancer diagnosis and explaining the decision process leading to this decision is challenging. Furthermore, different stakeholders will have different expectations when it comes to the explainability of the processes and their results. In the healthcare domain, an explanation of a diagnosis to a patient will look very different from an explanation of the same diagnosis to a healthcare professional.

There is an ongoing debate about the use of XAI in medical decision-making. Relying on black-box models for decision-making is not a welcome approach for many clinicians. London (2019) suggested these clinicians likened "ceding medical decision-making to black box systems" to "contravening the profound moral responsibilities of clinicians." On the other hand, Ghassemi et al. (2021) argued that in patient-level AI decision-making, current XAI methods are not expected to bring more transparency and trust.

3.6 State of XAI in fNIRS

fNIRS research traditionally relied on purely statistical models. As more sophisticated ML and DL models have become more prevalent in fNIRS in recent years, the explainability of these models is also becoming more prevalent. Yet work in fNIRS research explicitly addressing XAI concerns is just starting to appear, in particular from Dr. Andreu-Perez's group at the University of Essex in the United Kingdom and their collaborators in the area of developmental cognitive neuroscience.

Andreu-Perez et al. (2021) developed an XAI-based analysis for explaining infant fNIRS data in developmental cognitive neuroscience. They proposed the multivariate pattern analysis (xMVPA) method for fNIRS data based on XAI principles. In their work, fNIRS data from 6-month-old infants are analyzed for explaining the infants' visual and auditory processing. A publicly available dataset for processing visual and auditory stimuli is used. (Emberson and Zinszer, 2016). Multivariate pattern analysis (MVPA) allows analyzing multiple fNIRS channels concurrently. MVPA provides a richer set of data compared to simple statistical models. Yet MVPA does not require large datasets, which are typical for deep learning but may not be practical in many experimental settings. As MVPA spans multiple (or all available) channels, it can potentially show interactions between different brain regions via activation patterns under a given experimental setting. For each of the ten fNIRS channels, first, the time average of HbO concentrations in response to a stimulus is calculated. This average is then classified into one of three classes, *inactive, active*, and *very active*, to represent the state of that channel in response to the stimulus. It is argued in the paper that having these three coarse conceptual classes will allow incorporating intersubject variability into the results. Furthermore, keeping the number of classes small will make the results comprehensive and easily interpretable. The average values used to delineate these classes are learned via an evolutionary algorithm. Their results indicated six distinct patterns of activation.

Kiani et al. (2022) reviewed XAI in functional brain development studies and highlighted non-explainable or partially explainable approaches in fNIRS along with other modalities. They argued that ML techniques such as ridge regression are not suitable to explain the association between inputs and cortical networks using fNIRS data, although they provide statistically significant results for functional connectivity analysis (Duan et al., 2020). Kiani et al. (2022) also pointed out that as research on brain development moves toward analyzing multiple areas at once (multivariate analysis), AI techniques used do not readily explain the relations between these different areas.

3.7 Conclusions

In this chapter, we reviewed functional near-infrared spectroscopy, a non-invasive neuroimaging technology using near-infrared light to evaluate brain oxygenation at different locations in the brain, a proxy for regional brain activity. In addition to the fundamental concepts and representative applications in fNIRS, we also summarized recent ML/DL approaches used in fNIRS. Finally, we also introduced the emerging field of explainable AI in fNIRS.

XAI in fNIRS is a new area of research and can help us better understand the underlying mechanisms leading to fNIRS results. An open problem hindering the expansion of DL and XAI in fNIRS is the lack of more comprehensive publicly available datasets. XAI solutions to better link theories in understanding of various diseases to underlying fNIRS mechanisms can help improve acceptance of fNIRS in clinical practice.

References

Almajidy, Rand K., Kunal Mankodiya, Mohammadreza Abtahi, and Ulrich G. Hofmann. "A newcomer's guide to functional near infrared spectroscopy experiments." *IEEE Reviews in Biomedical Engineering* 13 (2019): 292–308.

Andreu-Perez, Javier, Lauren L. Emberson, Mehrin Kiani, Maria Laura Filippetti, Hani Hagras, and Silvia Rigato. "Explainable artificial intelligence based analysis for interpreting infant fNIRS data in developmental cognitive neuroscience." *Communications Biology* 4, no. 1 (2021): 1–13.

Arai, Heii, Maki Takano, Koichi Miyakawa, Tsuneyoshi Ota, Tadashi Takahashi, Hirokazu Asaka, and Tsuneaki Kawaguchi. "A quantitative near-infrared spectroscopy study: A decrease in cerebral hemoglobin oxygenation in Alzheimer's disease and mild cognitive impairment." *Brain and Cognition* 61, no. 2 (2006): 189–194.

Asgher, Umer, Khurram Khalil, Muhammad Jawad Khan, Riaz Ahmad, Shahid Ikramullah Butt, Yasar Ayaz, Noman Naseer, and Salman Nazir. "Enhanced accuracy for multiclass mental workload detection using long short-term memory for brain–computer interface." *Frontiers in Neuroscience* 14 (2020): 584.

Bak, SuJin, Jinwoo Park, Jaeyoung Shin, and Jichai Jeong. "Open-access fNIRS dataset for classification of unilateral finger-and foot-tapping." *Electronics* 8, no. 12 (2019): 1486.

Bandara, Danushka, Leanne Hirshfield, and Senem Velipasalar. "Classification of affect using deep learning on brain blood flow data." *Journal of Near Infrared Spectroscopy* 27, no. 3 (2019): 206–219.

Bauernfeind, Günther, Reinhold Scherer, Gert Pfurtscheller, and Christa Neuper. "Single-trial classification of antagonistic oxyhemoglobin responses during mental arithmetic." *Medical & Biological Engineering & Computing* 49, no. 9 (2011): 979–984.

Chen, Michelle, Helena M. Blumen, Meltem Izzetoglu, and Roee Holtzer. "Spatial coregistration of functional near-infrared spectroscopy to brain MRI." *Journal of Neuroimaging* 27, no. 5 (2017): 453–460.

Chen, Wei-Liang, Julie Wagner, Nicholas Heugel, Jeffrey Sugar, Yu-Wen Lee, Lisa Conant, Marsha Malloy, et al. "Functional near-infrared spectroscopy and its clinical application in the field of neuroscience: advances and future directions." *Frontiers in Neuroscience* 14 (2020): 724.

Coyle, Shirley, Tomás Ward, Charles Markham, and Gary McDarby. "On the suitability of near-infrared (NIR) systems for next-generation brain–computer interfaces." *Physiological Measurement* 25, no. 4 (2004): 815.

Dargazany, Aras R., Mohammadreza Abtahi, and Kunal Mankodiya. "An end-to-end (deep) neural network applied to raw EEG, fNIRs and body motion data for data fusion and BCI classification task without any pre-/post-processing." *arxiv Preprint arXiv:1907.09523* (2019), pp. 1–6.

Delpy, David T., Marco Ferrari, Claude A. Piantadosi, and Mamoru Tamura. "Pioneers in biomedical optics: Special section honoring professor Frans F. Jöbsis of Duke University." *Journal of Biomedical Optics* 12, no. 6 (2007): 062101.

Delpy, David T., Mark Cope, Pieter van der Zee, Simon Arridge, Susan Wray, and JS. Wyatt. "Estimation of optical pathlength through tissue from direct time of flight measurement." *Physics in Medicine & Biology* 33, no. 12 (1988): 1433.

Dix, Laura Marie Louise, Frank Van Bel, and Petra Maria Anna Lemmers. "Monitoring cerebral oxygenation in neonates: an update." *Frontiers in Pediatrics* 5 (2017): 46.

Duan, Lian, Nicholas T. Van Dam, Hui Ai, and Pengfei Xu. "Intrinsic organization of cortical networks predicts state anxiety: An functional near-infrared spectroscopy (fNIRS) study." *Translational Psychiatry* 10, no. 1 (2020): 1–9.

Eastmond, Condell, Aseem Subedi, Suvranu De, and Xavier Intes. "Deep learning in fNIRS: A review." *arXiv Preprint arXiv:2201.13371* (2022), pp. 1–41.

Emberson, Lauren, and Benjamin Zinszer. "Multichannel pattern analysis: Correlation-based decoding with fNIRS." (2016). http://arks.princeton.edu/ark:/88435/dsp01xs55mf543.

Fattorusso, Antonella, Sara Matricardi, Elisabetta Mencaroni, Giovanni Battista Dell'Isola, Giuseppe Di Cara, Pasquale Striano, and Alberto Verrotti. "The pharmacoresistant epilepsy: An overview on existent and new emerging therapies." *Frontiers in Neurology* 12 (2021): 1030.

Ferrari, Marco, and Valentina Quaresima. "A brief review on the history of human functional near-infrared spectroscopy (fNIRS) development and fields of application." *Neuroimage* 63, no. 2 (2012): 921–935.

Ghassemi, Marzyeh, Luke Oakden-Rayner, and Andrew L. Beam. "The false hope of current approaches to explainable artificial intelligence in health care." *The Lancet Digital Health* 3, no. 11 (2021): e745–e750.

Guevara, Edgar, Jorge-Arturo Flores-Castro, Ke Peng, Dang Khoa Nguyen, Frédéric Lesage, Philippe Pouliot, and Roberto Rosas-Romero. "Prediction of epileptic seizures using fNIRS and machine learning." *Journal of Intelligent & Fuzzy Systems* 38, no. 2 (2020): 2055–2068.

Gunning, David, Mark Stefik, Jaesik Choi, Timothy Miller, Simone Stumpf, and Guang-Zhong Yang. "XAI – Explainable artificial intelligence." *Science Robotics* 4, no. 37 (2019): eaay7120.

Ho, Thi Kieu Khanh, Minhee Kim, Younghun Jeon, Byeong C. Kim, Jae Gwan Kim, Kun Ho Lee, Jong-In Song, and Jeonghwan Gwak. "Deep learning-based multilevel classification of Alzheimer's disease using non-invasive functional near-infrared spectroscopy." *Frontiers in Aging Neuroscience* 14 (2022).

Hong, Keum-Shik, and Amad Zafar. "Existence of initial dip for BCI: an illusion or reality." *Frontiers in Neurorobotics* 12 (2018): 69.

Hong, Keum-Shik, Usman Ghafoor, and M. Jawad Khan. "Brain–machine interfaces using functional near-infrared spectroscopy: a review." *Artificial Life and Robotics* 25, no. 2 (2020): 204–218.

Islam, Mir Riyanul, Mobyen Uddin Ahmed, Shaibal Barua, and Shahina Begum. "A systematic review of explainable artificial intelligence in terms of different application domains and tasks." *Applied Sciences* 12, no. 3 (2022): 1353.

Izzetoglu, Meltem, Kurtulus Izzetoglu, Scott Bunce, Hasan Ayaz, Ajit Devaraj, Banu Onaral, and Kambiz Pourrezaei. "Functional near-infrared neuroimaging." *IEEE Transactions on Neural Systems and Rehabilitation Engineering* 13, no. 2 (2005): 153–159.

Jöbsis, Frans F. "Noninvasive, infrared monitoring of cerebral and myocardial oxygen sufficiency and circulatory parameters." *Science* 198, no. 4323 (1977): 1264–1267.

Kamath, Uday, and John Liu. *Explainable Artificial Intelligence: An Introduction to Interpretable Machine Learning*. Berlin: Springer, 2021.

Kiani, Mehrin, Javier Andreu-Perez, Hani Hagras, Silvia Rigato, and Maria Laura Filippetti. "Towards understanding human functional brain development with explainable artificial intelligence: Challenges and perspectives." *IEEE Computational Intelligence Magazine* 17, no. 1 (2022): 16–33.

Kim, Taehoon, N. Sertac Artan, Ivan W. Selesnick, and H. Jonathan Chao. "Seizure detection methods using a cascade architecture for real-time implantable devices." In *2013 35th Annual International Conference of the IEEE Engineering in Medicine and Biology Society (EMBC)*, pp. 1005–1008. New York: IEEE, 2013.

Kocsis, Laszlo, Peter Herman, and Andras Eke. "The modified Beer–Lambert law revisited." *Physics in Medicine & Biology* 51, no. 5 (2006): N91.

Li, Chunguang, Jiacheng Xu, Yufei Zhu, Shaolong Kuang, Wei Qu, and Lining Sun. "Detecting self-paced walking intention based on fNIRS technology for the development of BCI." *Medical & Biological Engineering & Computing* 58, no. 5 (2020): 933–941.

Liang, Zhenhu, Hao Tian, Ho-ching Shawn Yang, Takeshi Arimitsu, Takao Takahashi, Angelo Sassaroli, Sergio Fantini, Haijing Niu, Yasuyo Minagawa, and Yunjie Tong. "Tracking brain development from neonates to the elderly by hemoglobin phase measurement using functional near-infrared spectroscopy." *IEEE Journal of Biomedical and Health Informatics* 25, no. 7 (2021): 2497–2509.

Lloyd-Fox, Sarah, Anna Blasi, and CE. Elwell. "Illuminating the developing brain: the past, present and future of functional near infrared spectroscopy." *Neuroscience & Biobehavioral Reviews* 34, no. 3 (2010): 269–284.

London, Alex John. "Artificial intelligence and black-box medical decisions: accuracy versus explainability." *Hastings Center Report* 49, no. 1 (2019): 15–21.

Luke, Robert, Maureen J. Shader, and David McAlpine. "Characterization of Mayer-wave oscillations in functional near-infrared spectroscopy using a physiologically informed model of the neural power spectra." *Neurophotonics* 8, no. 4 (2021a): 041001.

Luke, Robert, and McAlpine, David. "FNIRS finger tapping data in BIDS format." *Zenodo* (2021b). https://doi.org/10.5281/zenodo.6575155.

Luke, Robert, Eric D. Larson, Maureen J. Shader, Hamish Innes-Brown, Lindsey Van Yper, Adrian KC Lee, Paul F. Sowman, and David McAlpine. "Analysis methods for measuring passive auditory fNIRS responses generated by a block-design paradigm." *Neurophotonics* 8, no. 2 (2021c): 025008.

Lv, Han, Zhenchang Wang, Elizabeth Tong, Leanne M. Williams, Greg Zaharchuk, Michael Zeineh, Andrea N. Goldstein-Piekarski, Tali M. Ball, Chengde Liao, and Max Wintermark. "Resting-state functional MRI: everything that nonexperts have always wanted to know." *American Journal of Neuroradiology* 39, no. 8 (2018): 1390–1399.

Meek, Judith H., Michael Firbank, Clare E. Elwell, Janette Atkinson, Oliver Braddick, and John S. Wyatt. "Regional hemodynamic responses to visual stimulation in awake infants." *Pediatric Research* 43, no. 6 (1998): 840–843.

Millington, KR. "Improving the whiteness and photostability of wool." In *Advances in Wool Technology*, pp. 217–247. Cambridge: Woodhead Publishing, 2009.

Naseer, Noman, and Keum-Shik Hong. "fNIRS-based brain-computer interfaces: A review." *Frontiers in Human Neuroscience* 9 (2015): 3.

Neupane, Ajaya, Nitesh Saxena, Leanne M. Hirshfield, and Sarah E. Bratt. "The crux of voice (In) security: A brain study of speaker legitimacy detection." In *Network and Distributed Systems Security (NDSS) Symposium,* pp. 1–41. San Diego, CA, 2019.

Novi, Sergio Luiz, Edwin Johan Forero, Jose Angel Ivan Rubianes Silva, Nicolas Gabriel SR De Souza, Giovani Grisotti Martins, Andres Quiroga, Shin-Ting Wu, and Rickson C. Mesquita. "Integration of spatial information increases reproducibility in functional near-infrared spectroscopy." *Frontiers in Neuroscience* 14 (2020): 746.

Peng, Cheng, and Xinlin Hou. "Applications of functional near-infrared spectroscopy (fNIRS) in neonates." *Neuroscience Research* 170 (2021): 18–23.

Peng, Ke, Dang Khoa Nguyen, Phetsamone Vannasing, Julie Tremblay, Frédéric Lesage, and Philippe Pouliot. "Using patient-specific hemodynamic response function in epileptic spike analysis of human epilepsy: a study based on EEG–fNIRS." *NeuroImage* 126 (2016): 239–255.

Pfurtscheller, Gert, Günther Bauernfeind, Selina Christin Wriessnegger, and Christa Neuper. "Focal frontal (de) oxyhemoglobin responses during simple arithmetic." *International Journal of Psychophysiology* 76, no. 3 (2010): 186–192.

Pinti, Paola, Felix Scholkmann, Antonia Hamilton, Paul Burgess, and Ilias Tachtsidis. "Current status and issues regarding pre-processing of fNIRS neuroimaging data: an investigation of diverse signal filtering methods within a general linear model framework." *Frontiers in Human Neuroscience* 12 (2019): 505.

Pinti, Paola, Ilias Tachtsidis, Antonia Hamilton, Joy Hirsch, Clarisse Aichelburg, Sam Gilbert, and Paul W. Burgess. "The present and future use of functional near-infrared spectroscopy (fNIRS) for cognitive neuroscience." *Annals of the New York Academy of Sciences* 1464, no. 1 (2020): 5–29.

Porsteinsson, AP., RS. Isaacson, Sean Knox, MN. Sabbagh, and I. Rubino. "Diagnosis of early Alzheimer's disease: Clinical practice in 2021." *The Journal of Prevention of Alzheimer's Disease* 8, no. 3 (2021): 371–386.

Rahman, Md, Abu Bakar Siddik, Tarun Kanti Ghosh, Farzana Khanam, and Mohiuddin Ahmad. "A narrative review on clinical applications of fNIRS." *Journal of Digital Imaging* 33, no. 5 (2020): 1167–1184.

Ramirez, Maria, Shima Kaheh, Mohammad Affan Khalil, and Kiran George. "Application of convolutional neural network for classification of consumer preference from hybrid EEG and FNIRS signals." In *2022 IEEE 12th Annual Computing and Communication Workshop and Conference (CCWC)*, pp. 1024–1028. New York: IEEE, 2022.

Rasheed, Khansa, Adnan Qayyum, Junaid Qadir, Shobi Sivathamboo, Patrick Kwan, Levin Kuhlmann, Terence O'Brien, and Adeel Razi. "Machine learning for predicting epileptic seizures using EEG signals: A review." *IEEE Reviews in Biomedical Engineering* 14 (2020): 139–155.

Rizki, Edmi Edison, Minako Uga, Ippeita Dan, Haruka Dan, Daisuke Tsuzuki, Hidenori Yokota, Keiji Oguro, and Eiju Watanabe. "Determination of epileptic focus side in mesial temporal lobe epilepsy using long-term noninvasive fNIRS/EEG monitoring for presurgical evaluation." *Neurophotonics* 2, no. 2 (2015): 025003.

Sandoe-Pedersen, Lisbeth, Kirk, Colleen, and Artan, N. Sertac. *fNIRS Applied in Neuromarketing*. New York: New York Institute of Technology, The Symposium of University Research and Creative Expression (SOURCE), 2022.

Scholkmann, Felix, Stefan Kleiser, Andreas Jaakko Metz, Raphael Zimmermann, Juan Mata Pavia, Ursula Wolf, and Martin Wolf. "A review on continuous wave functional near-infrared spectroscopy and imaging instrumentation and methodology." *Neuroimage* 85 (2014): 6–27.

Shin, Jaeyoung, Alexander von Lühmann, Benjamin Blankertz, Do-Won Kim, Jichai Jeong, Han-Jeong Hwang, and Klaus-Robert Müller. "Open access dataset for EEG+ NIRS single-trial classification." *IEEE Transactions on Neural Systems and Rehabilitation Engineering* 25, no. 10 (2016): 1735–1745.

Shin, Jaeyoung, Alexander von Lühmann, Do-Won Kim, Jan Mehnert, Han-Jeong Hwang, and Klaus-Robert Müller. "Simultaneous acquisition of EEG and NIRS during cognitive tasks for an open access dataset." *Scientific data* 5, no. 1 (2018): 1–16.

Sirpal, Parikshat, Ali Kassab, Philippe Pouliot, Dang Khoa Nguyen, and Frédéric Lesage. "fNIRS improves seizure detection in multimodal EEG-fNIRS recordings." *Journal of Biomedical Optics* 24, no. 5 (2019): 051408.

Tie, Yanmei, Ralph O. Suarez, Stephen Whalen, Alireza Radmanesh, Isaiah H. Norton, and Alexandra J. Golby. "Comparison of blocked and event-related fMRI designs for pre-surgical language mapping." *Neuroimage* 47 (2009): T107–T115.

von Lühmann, Alexander, Christian Herff, Dominic Heger, and Tanja Schultz. "Toward a wireless open source instrument: functional near-infrared spectroscopy in mobile neuroergonomics and BCI applications." *Frontiers in Human Neuroscience* 9 (2015): 617.

von Lühmann, Alexander, Xinge Li, Natalie Gilmore, David A. Boas, and Meryem A. Yücel. "Open access multimodal fNIRS resting state dataset with and without synthetic hemodynamic responses." *Frontiers in Neuroscience* 14 (2020): 579353.

Wang, Zenghui, Jun Zhang, Xiaochu Zhang, Peng Chen, and Bing Wang. "Transformer model for functional near-infrared spectroscopy classification." *IEEE Journal of Biomedical and Health Informatics* 26, no. 6 (2022): 2559–2569.

Watanabe, Hama, Yoshihiko Shitara, Yoshinori Aoki, Takanobu Inoue, Shinya Tsuchida, Naoto Takahashi, and Gentaro Taga. "Hemoglobin phase of oxygenation and deoxygenation in early brain development measured using fNIRS." *Proceedings of the National Academy of Sciences* 114, no. 9 (2017): E1737–E1744.

Yeung, Michael K. "An optical window into brain function in children and adolescents: A systematic review of functional near-infrared spectroscopy studies." *Neuroimage* 227 (2021): 117672.

Yücel, Meryem A., Alexander V. Lühmann, Felix Scholkmann, Judit Gervain, Ippeita Dan, Hasan Ayaz, David Boas, et al. "Best practices for fNIRS publications." *Neurophotonics* 8, no. 1 (2021): 012101.

Yücel, Meryem A., Juliette Selb, David A. Boas, Sydney S. Cash, and Robert J. Cooper. "Reducing motion artifacts for long-term clinical NIRS monitoring using collodion-fixed prism-based optical fibers." Neuroimage 85 (2014): 192–201.

Zafar, Amad, Muhammad Jawad Khan, Jongseo Park, and Keum-Shik Hong. "Initial-dip based quadcopter control: Application to fNIRS-BCI." *IFAC-PapersOnLine* 51, no. 15 (2018): 945–950.

4 An Explainable Method for Image Registration with Applications in Medical Imaging

Srikrishnan Divakaran

Contents

4.1 Introduction

Image registration (IR) (Antoine et al., 1996; Crum et al., 2004; Fatma et al., 2016; Hill et al., 2001) involves determining a mapping between the points of a given input image and a reference image. The reference image is constructed from either a single image or by integrating features from multiple images, where a feature is characterized based on user interest to be either an anatomical structure, functionally active region, or something that relates an anatomical structure to a functional region. The goal of IR is to construct a mapping that helps to bring the input and reference image into a common coordinate system. The nature of this mapping varies based on the application the user is interested in: (i) structural mapping – mapping of an anatomical structure before and after the treatment, (ii) functional mapping – mapping the functionally equivalent regions, and (iii) structural-functional

DOI: 10.1201/9781003333425-4

mapping – mapping the functional information onto the relevant anatomical structure. IR plays a key role in the analysis of medical images by enabling the integration of structural and functional information from scans done at different times and/or by employing different modalities (magnetic resonance imaging [MRI], computer tomography [CT], and positron emission tomography [PET]). This has helped in the development of analytical tools for disease diagnosis and progression by enabling the evaluation of structural and functional variations of medical images in a population.

4.1.1 *Categorization of Image Registration Problems*

IR problems can be categorized across various factors, including spatial dimensions, the use of external markers, nature, and scope of transformations that relates to the input and the reference image, nature of medical modality, and the nature of the subject.

The spatial dimension of the input and target images can be either two- or three-dimensional (2D or 3D). Accordingly, based on the spatial dimensions of the input and the reference images, IR is categorized into (i) 2D to 2D, (ii) 3D to 3D, and (iii) 2D to 3D. If we attach clinical instruments to patients as external markers and thereby constrain the mapping between the input and the reference image, this type of IR that employs external markers is referred to as extrinsic IR. However, if instead the geometric or structural features in images (edges, contours, outlines of bones, and the centerline of vessels) are used to implicitly constrain the mapping between the input and reference image, this type of IR is referred to as intrinsic IR. Extrinsic registration methods are simpler and computationally more efficient when compared to intrinsic registration. However, the constraints placed by external markers limit the flexibility of the nature of image transformations IR can consider while determining the mapping between the input and the reference image. This has restricted the applicability of extrinsic IR to mainly brain and orthopedic imaging. If the input and the reference images are related by affine transformations (rotation, shearing, and translation), then we refer to the IR as rigid. However, if the images are related by transformations that involve localized stretching for which affine transformations do not suffice, then we refer to the IR as non-rigid. The registering of medical images of the brain/skull where there is little change in the images between short periods of scans can be adequately addressed as a rigid IR problem. However, for images involving non-rigid objects that are subject to some deformation during imaging, we need to use non-rigid IR methods. If the construction of IR requires considering almost all the points in the input and reference images, then we will have to construct a global IR; otherwise, mapping that considers a subset of points would suffice. In this case, local IR would be sufficient. If the input image and the reference image both employ the same medical modality, then the IR is mono-modal; otherwise, it is multi-modal. Furthermore, if the images correspond to a single patient, then the IR is intrasubject IR, and intersubject IR is otherwise. Intrasubject-based registration methods help in achieving considerable clinical benefits through accurate alignment of the images gathered from the same subject using the same modality at different times. They are mostly used in the alignment of serial MRIs of the brain. Intersubject-based registration methods are used in registering images belonging to different patients.

4.1.2 IR Methods

IR methods can be broadly categorized into geometry-based approaches (Sprawls, 2020; Zheng and Doermann, 2006) and intensity-based approaches (Antoine et al., 1996; Fatma et al., 2016, Guan et al., 2018). Geometry-based approaches first identify anatomical features within each image that are informative and then interpolate this mapping to infer the mapping between the input and reference images. These features typically include functionally important surfaces, curves, and point landmarks that have biological validity (relevance to underlying anatomy) and help in the development of interpretative methods. For these geometry-based methods to be effective, we rely either on being able to reliably identify anatomical features from these images or being provided images with anatomical features annotated. Intensity-based approaches identify salient features based on intensity patterns that satisfy some statistical, combinatorial, or information-theoretic properties. Then a mapping between salient features of the input and the reference image is determined by maximizing a similarity score defined as a function of these statistical, combinatorial, or information-theoretic properties. Some commonly used measures of similarity include the sum of squared differences, correlation coefficient, measures based on optical flow, and information-theoretic measures such as mutual information.

4.1.3 Related Work

In this chapter, our focus is only on the development of methods/algorithms for non-rigid IR that exploit point features because they are the most commonly used features in clinical applications. However, for a comprehensive overview of medical image registration, we refer the readers to Crum et al. (2004), Fatma et al. (2016), and Hill et al. (2001).

Point feature-based IR (Gold et al., 1998; Guan et al., 2018) means that we need to first identify a set of points (point set) corresponding to each informative point feature in both the input and reference images, then determine a point set matching (PSM) between these point sets in the input and the reference image, and then interpolate this point set matching to establish a mapping between the input and the reference images. In point feature-based IR, there are many standard tools and techniques for identifying point sets and the key challenge that we are focusing on is in designing methods for the construction of PSM.

In point feature-based IR, we can define a point set matching algorithm in terms of a transformation defined in terms of parameters. In the case of non-rigid registration, characterizing and determining such a function is extremely hard, and hence the focus of existing methods is on determining a transformation based on approximate characterizations. Given the point sets corresponding to the point features of both the input and the reference images, we now summarize some of the related work in developing non-rigid IR methods for PSM.

Robust point matching-based methods (RPM) (Guan et al., 2018): These methods use a coordinate descent approach for computing the transformation parameters and a soft-assign algorithm for determining the mapping between the two-point sets. There are variants like thin plate spline robust point matching (TPS-RPM) (Rangarajan et al., 1997) that make use of thin splines for interpolation (used in the context of non-rigid registration), robust point matching by preserving local neighborhood structures (RPM-LNS) (Zheng and Doermann, 2006), and topology preserving robust point matching (TRPM) (Zheng and Doermann, 2006) that uses a simple graph to exploit the neighborhood structure of point sets. These methods work well when there are small deformations, the signal-to-noise ratio of the image is high, and there are not many outliers. Furthermore, computing these transformation parameters is very hard, and their results are difficult to interpret.

Graph matching (GM) (Deng et al., 2010; Knoll et al., 2002)*-based approaches*: These approaches treat point sets as graphs, where the nodes represent the correspondence between points and the weights stand for the pairwise similarity between potential correspondences and use graph matching to establish PSM by essentially exploiting topological structures in point sets. The graph shift (GS) (Liu and Yan, 2010) method was proposed to make the GM approach robust. However, these methods are effective only if there are clearly identifiable topological structures in the medical images.

Energy method (MEF) (Timoshenko and Woinowsky-Krieger, 1959): This method incorporates deformation information into an energy function that is minimized while trying to establish a PSM with minimum error.

Gaussian mixture model (GMM): This algorithm by Jian and Vemuri (2011) describes the two-point sets in terms of a Gaussian mixture model and constructs a PSM by aligning two Gaussian mixtures so as to minimize their L2 distance.

Coherent point drift (CPD) (Baka et al., 2013; Rangarajan et al., 1997) *algorithm*: This is a probabilistic method extended from the GMM for both rigid and non-rigid registration that considers the registration of point sets as a maximum likelihood estimation problem.

4.1.4 Chapter Outline

In this chapter, our focus is on the development of point feature-based methods for IR. In particular, our focus is restricted to methods for intrinsic non-rigid local registration of two-dimensional magnetic resonance imaging brain images of a single subject (intrasubject) taken over time. These algorithms have applications that include (i) correction of MRI images for a small amount of subject motion during imaging and (ii) spatial normalization – integrating several images of a subject into a single image. Our IR methods exploit combinatorial and information-theoretic techniques to partition the input and the reference images into informative regions and establish a mapping between these informative regions. We also provide a statistical guarantee on the quality of IR in terms of a p-value, a probability of obtaining an IR better than our method by random chance. The rest of this chapter is organized as follows: In Section 4.2, we present a new point matching algorithm for IR that make use of combinatorial and information-theoretic techniques. In

Section 4.3, we present the performance of a new measure for IR and illustrate how this can in explaining the IR results. In Section 4.4, we present some preliminary empirical analysis of our point matching method for IR.

4.2 A Point Set Matching Algorithm for IR

IR algorithms construct a mapping between the points of a given input and the reference image. For different clinical applications, the user may be interested in different aspects of the subject (i.e., structural, functional, or structural-functional features of the imaged organ) and exploits MRI modes/parameters to capture the feature of interest. In this chapter, our focus is on IR methods that exploit point features (i.e., features that are the basis of lines, surfaces, and bodies) to identify informative features. More precisely, we present a method that exploits point features within images by first identifying a point set (PS) corresponding to each informative point feature in both the input and the reference image. Then, we construct a point set matching between a subset of these point sets in the input and the reference image and use it for constructing an IR between the input and the reference image. For a detailed review of point feature-based IR, we refer the readers to Guan et al. (2018).

Our method is a hybrid approach (i.e., a mix of both geometric and intensity-based approaches) that exploits point features for intrinsic non-rigid local registration of two-dimensional MRI images. Our algorithm can be described in terms of the following four major components.

4.2.1 Data Acquisition

MRI (Drissi, 2018; Dempster et al., 1977; Kostelec and Periaswamy, 2002) is based on using a powerful external magnetic field to align randomly oriented protons within the water nuclei of tissues. Then the aligned protons are perturbed by applying an external radio frequency (RF) pulse. The perturbed protons, while returning to their resting alignment (through relaxation processes), emit RF signals. These RF signals contain information about the properties of nuclear magnetic spin specific to the tissue to which the proton belongs. The measured RF signals are localized to a small block of tissue referred to as a voxel. The size of the voxel can vary between 1 and 5 mm, and the scanner will measure each two-dimensional layer of voxels, called slices, and then combine all the slices into a three-dimensional image (called volume). These RF signals from each slice are stored in a configuration commonly known as K-space. The K-space consists of lines of data that are filled one at a time. The K-space data are then transformed using Fourier transforms into images (i.e., intensity levels in the spatial domain). Different types of images are created by varying the sequence of RF pulses applied (MRI parameters).

4.2.1.1 MR Image Control through Parameter Settings

Repetition time (TR) is the amount of time between successive pulse sequences applied to the same slice. Time to echo (TE) is the time between the delivery of

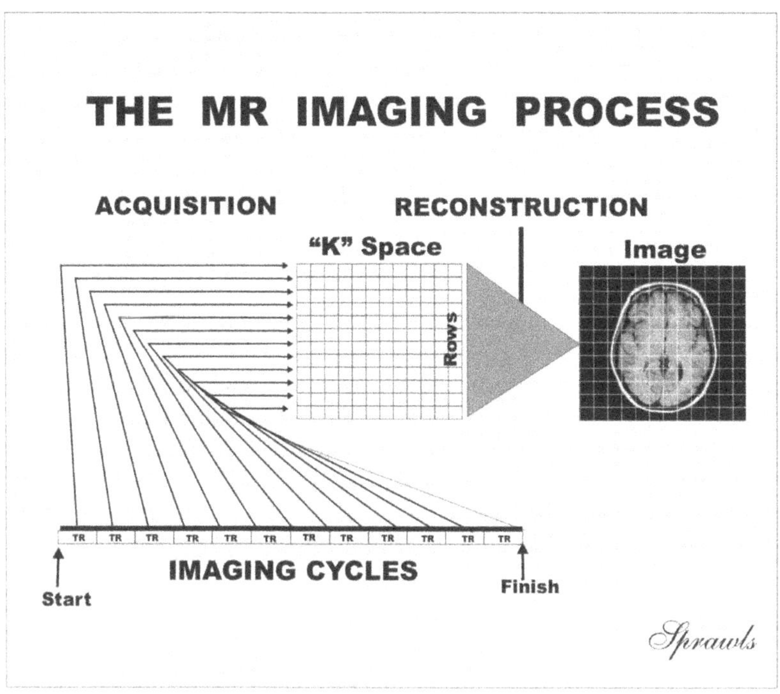

Figure 4.1 MR imaging process (from Sprawls, 2020).

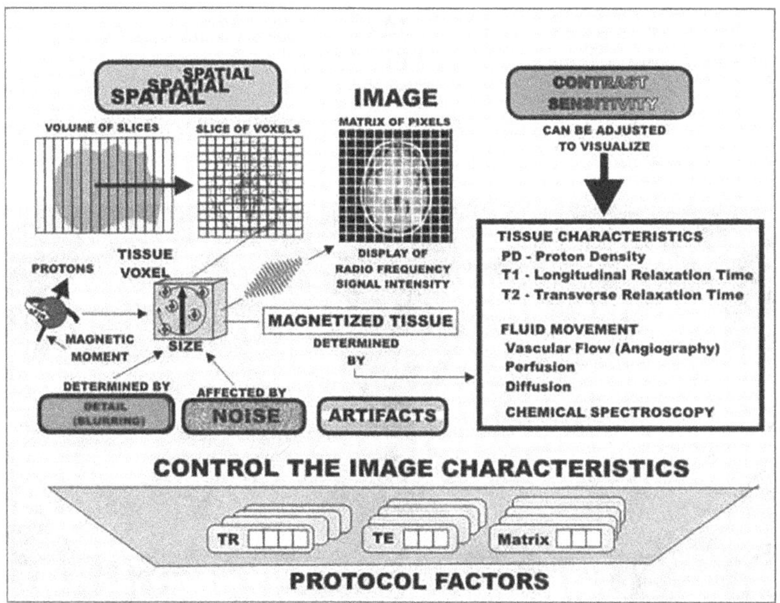

Figure 4.2 MR image control through parameter settings (from Sprawls, 2020).

the RF pulse and the receipt of the echo signal. Tissue can be characterized by two different relaxation times, T1 and T2. T1 (longitudinal relaxation time) is the time constant that determines the rate at which excited protons return to equilibrium. It is a measure of the time taken for spinning protons to realign with the external magnetic field. T2 (transverse relaxation time) is the time constant that determines the time taken for spinning protons to lose phase coherence among the nuclei spinning in the transverse plane (i.e., perpendicular to the external magnetic field).

4.2.1.2 MRI Sequences

The most common MRI sequences are T1-weighted and T2-weighted scans. T1-weighted images are produced by using short TE and TR times. The contrast and brightness of the image are predominantly determined by the T1 properties of tissue. Conversely, T2-weighted images are produced by using longer TE and TR times. In these images, the contrast and brightness are predominantly determined by the T2 properties of tissue. T1-weighted imaging can also be performed while infusing gadolinium (Gad). Gad is a paramagnetic contrast enhancement agent. When injected during the scan, Gad changes signal intensities by shortening T1.

4.2.2 Pre-Processing

For the IR problem, the input image is a slice of an MRI volume of a subject obtained using one of the standard modes (i.e., T1-weighted, T2-weighted, or T1-weighted with gadolinium) for a specified TE, TR, and magnetic field strength. The reference image is constructed from MRI volumes of the subject (i.e., patient) taken over a period of time using different MRI modes for different parameter settings (i.e., TE, TR, and magnetic field strength):

1. We can view the MRI reference volume as consisting of $5n$ slices $S1$, $S2$, ..., $S5n$ for some integer $n > 0$, and it is partitioned in n groups $G_1, G_2,$& $,G_n$,where

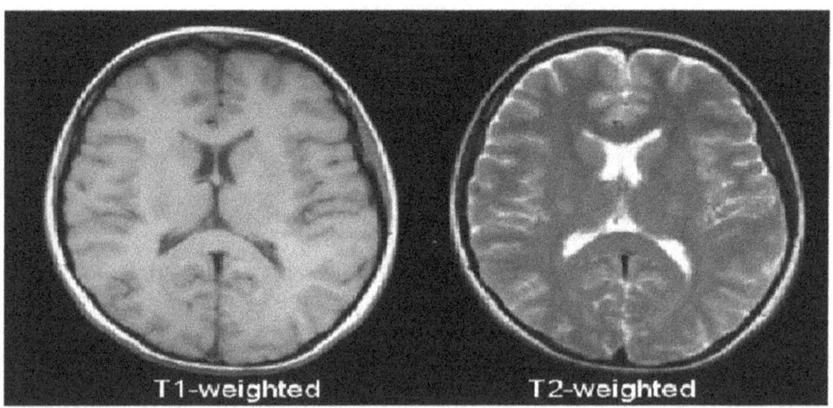

Figure 4.3 T1-weighted and T2-weighted images (from Preston, 2019).

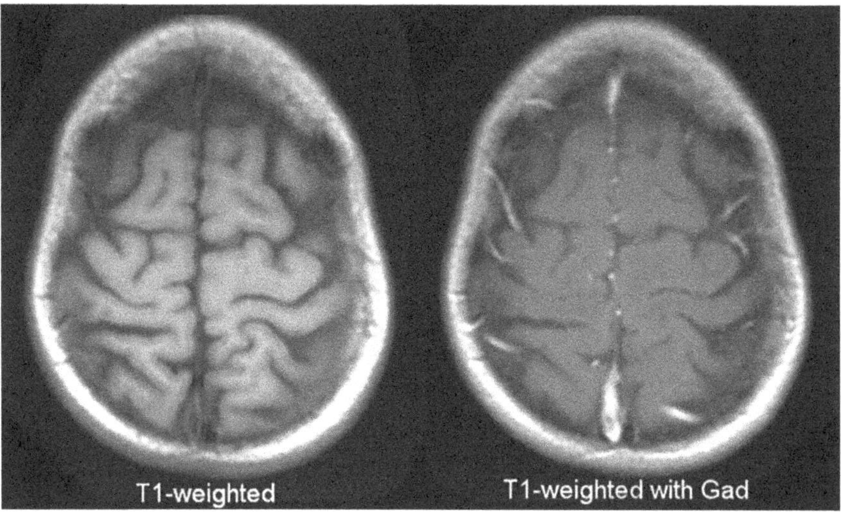

Figure 4.4 T1-weighted and T1-weighted with Gad images (from Preston, 2019).

Group $G_i, i \in [1..5]$ consists of five consecutive slices $S_{5(i-1)+1}, \ldots, S_{5i-1}$, where each group is a set of related slices that were taken over a period of time with the same MRI mode and parameter settings.

2. From each slice *Si* for $i \in [1..n]$, we identify the set $IRi = \{Ri1, Ri2, \ldots, Ril\}$ of at most l informative regions (circled regions in Figure 4.6 with information content above a threshold determined based on parameter l) by extracting edges, corners, speed-up robust feature (SURF) points, and scale-invariant feature transform (SIFT) points from *Si*. Each informative region Rij is characterized by its (i) $c(x, y)$: center coordinates, (ii) *r*: radius, (iii) *o*: orientation, (iv) *w*: information content (i.e., importance computed based on image contrast), and (v) *f*: an eight-bit field vector summarizing the intensity distribution of the pixels in Rij.
3. For each group *Gi*, construct a consensus slice *cSi* as follows:

    a. Characterize an informative region in terms of an eight-dimensional *feature vector* defined in terms of the normalized weighted histogram values of the intensity distribution associated with that region. The weighting helps the feature vector capture image contrast independent of the intensity range, and normalization helps in relating the components of the feature vector in a scale-invariant manner.
    b. Partition the informative regions in *Gi* into *l* clusters by hierarchically clustering them based on the similarity between pairs of informative regions. The similarity between a pair of informative regions is computed based on the relative entropy between their corresponding feature vectors. Let $CCSi = \{Ci1, Ci2, \ldots, Cil\}$ be these l clusters.

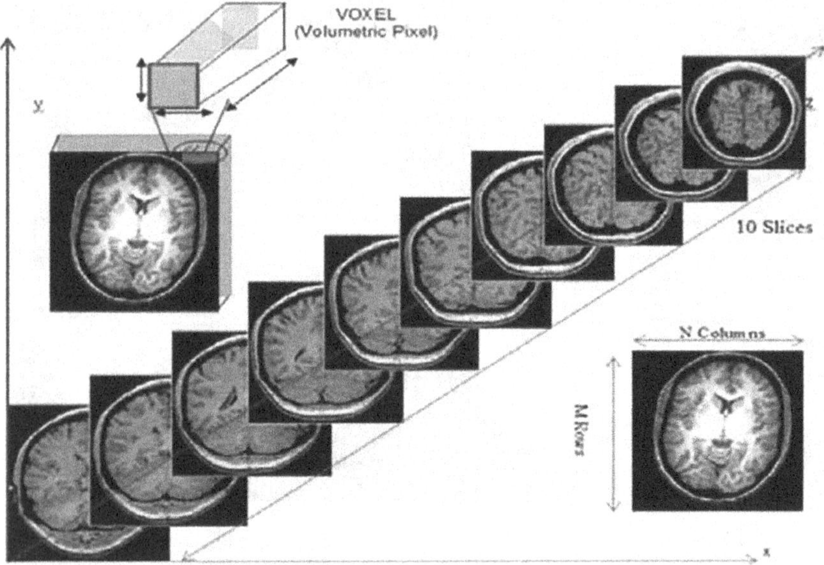

Figure 4.5 An MRI volume consisting of a sequence of slices (from Joseph et al., 2019).

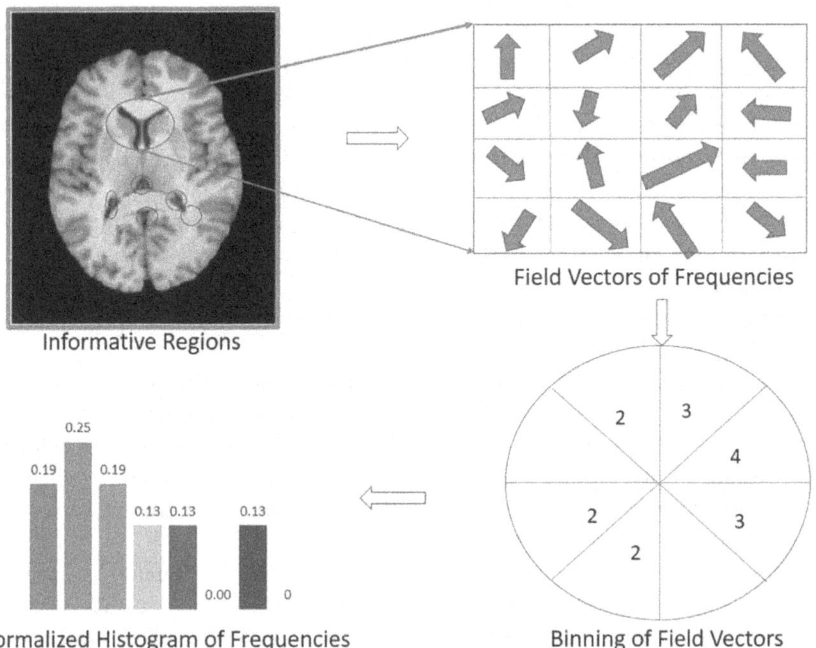

Figure 4.6 Identifying and characterizing informative segments.

c. Construct the set *CCSimax* of l representative informative regions of G_i by choosing from each cluster in *ccsi* an informative region with maximum weight.

d. Let PIR be the collection of *l* sets where each set is a collection of pixel locations corresponding to the informative region in *ccsi* and *PNIR* be the pixel locations not belonging to any informative region in *ccsi*. Construct the consensus slice *csi* by setting the pixel intensities for locations in PIR from the corresponding region in CCS_i and for locations in PNIR by interpolation using the average pixel intensity of the corresponding locations from the five slices in Gl.

4.2.3 Extraction of Informative Regions from Input and Reference Volume

Given the input image Inp, the following is a description of how we extract the informative regions from the input image and also identify for each region the informative region within a consensus slice in the reference volume with high similarity.

1. From the input image Inp, we identify the set $InpR = \{InpR1, InR2, \ldots, InpRl\}$ of at most l informative regions with information content above a threshold (determined based on parameter l) by extracting edges, corners, speed-up robust feature points, and scale-invariant feature transform points from Inp. Each informative region *inpRi* is characterized by its (i) $c(x,y)$: center coordinates, (ii) *r*: radius, (iii) *o*: orientation, (iv) *w*: information content (i.e., importance computed based on image contrast), and (v) *f*: an eight-bit field vector summarizing the intensity distribution of the pixels in *inpRi*.
2. For each informative region $InpRi \in InpR$,

   a. Find the consensus slice in the reference volume that contains an informative region with the highest similarity to *inpRi*. Let $Refmaxi$ be the informative region in *csj* for some $j \varepsilon [1..n]$ with the maximum similarity to *inpRi*. Recall that the similarity between a pair of informative regions is computed based on the relative entropy between their corresponding feature vectors.

   b. Rotate *inpRi* about its center so that both *inpRi* and *Refmaxi* are oriented in the same direction. Now using bi-cubic spline interpolation, rescale *inpRi* to bring it to the same scale as *Refmaxi*.

   c. Now construct a local alignment between *inpRi* and *Refmaxi* of maximum similarity, where relative entropy between their feature vectors of their respective scaled regions is used as the weight/similarity score associated with that alignment.

Notice the feature vector is an eight-dimensional vector defined in terms of the normalized weighted histogram values of the intensity distribution associated with that region. The weighting helps the feature vector capture image contrast independent of the intensity range, and normalization helps in relating the components of the feature vector in a scale-invariant manner.

4.2.4 Construction of IR

We establish the mapping between the pixels in the informative regions in the input image and the informative regions from the slices in the reference volume as follows:

1. Construct a bi-partite graph $G = (U \cup V, E)$, where U is the set of informative regions from the input image, V is the set of informative regions from the reference volume that are similar to one or more informative regions in U, and E is the set of edges between a vertex in U and a vertex in V with an associated weight equal to the similarity score of the local alignment between the corresponding regions.
2. Construct BM, a maximal weighted bi-partite matching, under the constraint that no two regions overlap as follows: Iteratively augment the existing matching by introducing an edge at a time by checking whether the regions corresponding to the newly introduced edge do not overlap in either the x and y direction with any of the existing regions.
3. Now, for each edge in BM, construct a maximum point set matching between the pixels corresponding to the respective matched informative regions in BM. Now, define the IR to be the union of these point set matchings and its match score to be the sum of the scores of the maximum point set matching of the corresponding matched informative regions in BM.

4.3 Performance Measures and Explainability

The quality of a point matching algorithm for IR is usually evaluated in terms of its speed, precision, accuracy, and statistical guarantees it provides on its precision and accuracy. In many medical imaging problems, it is difficult to evaluate the accuracy and precision of IR due to (i) the inability to obtain image registration datasets [23] for which ground truth data are available, (ii) inherent complexity in the measurement context/processes, (iii) lack of comparable measures due to inconsistent application of MRI protocols, and (iv) inherent randomness in the underlying physical processes involved in data acquisition and image reconstruction.

In the context of point set matching, the accuracy of IR is usually expressed in terms of an error function that evaluates the dissimilarity between the point sets of the input and reference image as specified by the PSM. The commonly used error functions that are applicable in our registration context are the root mean square (RMS)/mean square error (MSE), target registration error (TRE), and success rate (SR). RMS explicitly takes advantage of the distance measures to evaluate dissimilarity between points. However, if the distance measure is not chosen properly, then RMS may not accurately reflect the accuracy of IR. The target registration error uses some markers based on ground truths about surgically targeted tissues as a reference to calculate the distance between the corresponding points in the mapped point sets. SR counts the number of successfully registered point pairs. This has been successfully applied in retinal image registrations where they count the number of centerline points that have been successfully registered.

We analyze the accuracy of our method in terms of a match score that reflects how well the informative regions of the input image match the corresponding informative regions in the reference image. This match score is computed by evaluating the information content of the local alignment between the matched informative regions. Notice that our score makes use of local matching and exploits the information content using both image contrast and image structure. Our method first gives a segment map that indicates the most informative regions in both images enclosed in a circle along with a mapping between similar informative regions indicated by an edge (line segment) connecting the corresponding regions. The weight associated with the edge indicates the extent of similarity (information content) and is shown visually by the thickness of the connecting line segment.

4.3.1 Example

We show the segment map in Figure 4.7 constructed by our method while determining an IR between the given input and reference images. In addition, we show in Table 4.1 the weights indicating the information content of locally aligning the corresponding informative segments as specified by the segment map.

We analyze the accuracy and precision of our method by providing statistical guarantees in terms of a p-value determined by comparing the IR score with the IR score of 1000 synthetic input images generated by randomly perturbing the points within the informative segments in the input image. We then compute what percentage of the 1000 IR scores are better than the IR score generated by our method. A p-value of 0.05 means that fewer than 5 out of 1000 randomly generated IRs are better than the IR generated by our method. A p-value of less than 0.05 indicates that that method is robust.

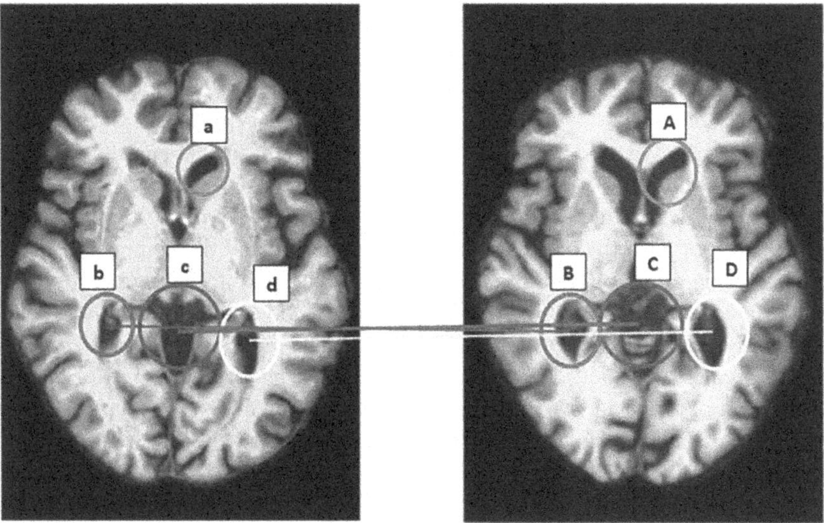

Figure 4.7 IR showing the informative segments and their segment map.

Table 4.1 Weight of the Pairwise Matches of Informative Segments

Informative Segments	*A*	*B*	*C*	*D*
A	3	0.8	0.6	0.8
B	0.8	1.3	0.5	0.9
C	0.6	0.5	2.5	0.4
D	0.8	0.9	0.4	2

4.4 A Preliminary Empirical Analysis of Our Method

We analyzed the accuracy of our method in terms of a match score computed by evaluating the information content of the local alignment between the matched informative regions. Notice that our score makes use of local matching and exploits the information content using both image contrast and image structure. In addition, we provide statistical guarantees on the precision of the results generated by our method by providing statistical guarantees in terms of a *p*-value determined by comparing the IR score with the IR score of 1000 synthetic input images generated by randomly perturbing the points within the informative segments in the input image

For our experiments, we used the Brain MRI from the fastMRI dataset (Knoll et al., 2002). We used 12 datasets from 6970 fully sampled brain MRIs obtained on 3- and 1.5-Tesla magnets. We made use of the raw dataset of T1 weighted, T2 weighted and T1 weighted contrast axial brain images. Some of the T1 weighted acquisitions included admissions of contrast agents. This dataset consisted of k-space data as well as DICOM data that were transformed into MRI using simple Python scripts as well as K-Space Explorer (Gergely, 2011), an open-source educational tool. We selected 10 nearly similar slices of an axial brain MRI from one subject, and from each one of these slices, we created 15 synthetic images by first segmenting the image and identifying 5 rectangular regions that contained either visually identifiable informative anatomical structures or had a lot of intensity variations. Then, we randomly perturbed 1%, 3%, and 5% of voxels in that image to obtain a total of 150 synthetic images. We used these synthetic images as input images and the ten slices as the MRI volume from which we constructed the reference image. For each of the 150 image registrations we performed, we did the following: (i) extracted the segmentation of both the input and the reference image and the mapping between these segments, (ii) computed the match score by computing the mutual information of the local alignment of the matched segments, and (iii) computed the *p*-value of our IR by comparing the matched score of our algorithm with the matched score of 1000 segmentations of the input image generated by randomly perturbing the classification of points in the input image. From these preliminary experiments, we evaluated our IR accuracy both in terms of SR as well as the *p*-value. We were able to achieve a success rate between 80 and 92% (i.e., we only compared the points in the informative segments) and a *p*-value of 0.04. However, we need to extend the scope of our experiments by including more MRI modes and more subjects as well as using annotated MRI data where the ground truth is available.

4.5 Conclusions and Future Work

In this chapter, we present a new point matching method for IR that makes use of combinatorial and information-theoretic techniques. Our method's result can be easily explained in terms of the segmentation of the input and reference image and the mapping that relates the corresponding matched informative segments. In addition, we describe how we provide a statistical guarantee in terms of computing a p-value associated with the match score of our method. This method, however, needs to be fine tuned, and our experimental setup needs to be extended. We need to test our method against annotated data in various settings in order to analyze it rigorously and objectively.

References

Anand, R., Haili C., Eric M., Suguna P., Lila D., Goldman-Rakic, P., and James D. 1997. A robust point-matching algorithm for autoradiograph alignment. *Medical Image Analysis* 1(4): 379–398. https://doi.org/10.1016/S1361-8415(97)85008-6.

Antoine Maintz, JB., and Viergever MA. 1996. An overview of medical image registration methods. In *Symposium of the Belgian Hospital Physicists Association (SBPH-BVZF)*, the Netherlands, 12, No. V, pp. 1–22.

Baka, N., Metz CT., Schultz C., Neefjes L., van Geuns RJ., Lelieveldt BP., Niessen WJ., van Walsum T., and de Bruijne M. 2013. Statistical coronary motion models for 2D+t/3D registration of X-ray coronary angiography and CTA. *Medical Image Analysis* 17(6): 698–709. https://doi.org10.1016/j.media.2013.03.003.

Crum, WR., Hartkens T., and Hill DL. 2004. Non-rigid image registration: Theory and practice. *The British Journal of Radiology* 77(2): S140–S153. doi: 10.1259/bjr/25329214. PMID: 15677356.

Dempster, AP., Laird NM., and Rubin DB. 1977. Maximum likelihood from incomplete data via the EM Algorithm. *Journal of the Royal Statistical Society* (Methodological) 39(1): 1–38. www.jstor.org/stable/2984875.

Deng, K., Tian J., Zheng J., Zhang X., Dai X., and Xu M. 2010. Retinal fundus image registration via vascular structure graph matching. *International Journal of Biomedical Imaging* 2010: 906067. doi: 10.1155/2010/906067. Epub 2010 Sep 7. PMID: 20871853; PMCID: PMC2943092.

Drissi, NM. 2018. *Brain Networks and Dynamics in Narcolepsy*. PhD dissertation, Linköping: Linköping University Electronic Press (https://doi.org/10.3384/diss.diva-153629).

Fatma, E-Z, El-Gamal, A., Mohammed, E., and Ahmed, A. 2016. Current trends in medical image registration and fusion. *Egyptian Informatics Journal* 17(1): 99–124. https://doi.org/10.1016/j.eij.2015.09.002.

Gergely, B. 2011. *K-Space Explorer Online: An Open Source Educational Tool to Visualise k-Space in MR Imaging*. https://kspace.app.

Guan, SY., Wang TM., Meng C., et al., 2018. A review of point feature based medical image registration. *Chinese Journal of Mechanical Engineering* 31(76). https://doi.org/10.1186/s10033-018-0275-9

Hill, DL., Batchelor PG., Holden M., and Hawkes DJ. 2001. Medical image registration. *Physics in Medicine and Biology* 46(3): R1–R45. https://doi.org/10.1088/0031-9155/46/3/201. PMID: 11277237.

Jian, B., and Vemuri, BC. 2011. Robust point set registration using gaussian mixture models. *IEEE Transactions on Pattern Analysis and Machine Intelligence* 33(8): 1633–1645. https://doi.org/10.1109/TPAMI.2010.223.

Kostelec, P., and Periaswamy, S. 2002. Image registration for MRI. *Mod Signal Process* 46. https://doi.org/10.1.1.173.2671

Knoll, F., Zbontar J., Sriram A., Muckley MJ., Bruno M., Defazio A., Parente M., Geras KJ., Katsnelson J., Chandarana H., Zhang Z., Drozdzalv M., Romero A., Rabbat M., Vincent P., Pinkerton J., Wang D., Yakubova N., Owens E., Zitnick CL., Recht MP., Sodickson DK., and Lui YW. 2002. fastMRI: A publicly available raw k-space and DICOM dataset of knee images for accelerated MR image reconstruction using machine learning. *Radiology: Artificial Intelligence* 2(1): e190007. https://doi.org/10.1148/ryai.2020190007. PMID: 32076662; PMCID: PMC6996599.

Liu, H., and Yan S. 2010. Common visual pattern discovery via spatially coherent correspondences. *2010 IEEE Computer Society Conference on Computer Vision and Pattern Recognition* 1609–1616. https://doi.org/10.1109/CVPR.2010.5539780.

Michael, J., Jerrold J., and Erin D., eds. 2019. Data carpentry: Introduction to MRI data analysis. *Version 2019.11*, November. https://github.com/carpentries-incubator/SDC-BIDS-IntroMRI.

Preston, D. 2019. *Magnetic Resonance Imaging (MRI) of the Brain and Spine: Basics*. Department of Neurology, Case Western Reserve University. https://case.edu/med/neurology/NR/MRI%20Basics.htm.

Sprawls, P. 2020. Magnetic resonance imaging: Principles, methods, and techniques. *Emory University, Sprawls Educational Foundation*. www.sprawls.org/mripmt/MRI05/.

Steven, G., Anand, R., Chien-Ping, L., Suguna, P., and Eric, M. 1998. New algorithms for 2D and 3D point matching: Pose estimation and correspondence. *Pattern Recognition* 31(8): 1019–1031. https://doi.org/10.1016/S0031-3203(98)80010-1.

Timoshenko, S., and Woinowsky-Krieger S. 1959. Theory of plates and shells: Bending moments in a simply supported rectangular plate with a concentrated load. *No. Engineering Soc Monographs*.

Zheng, Y., and Doermann D. 2006. Robust point matching for nonrigid shapes by preserving local neighborhood structures. *IEEE Transactions on Pattern Analysis and Machine Intelligence* 28(4): 643–649. https://doi.org/10.1109/TPAMI.2006.81.

5 State-of-the-Art Deep Learning Method and Its Explainability for Computerized Tomography Image Segmentation

Wing Keung Cheung

Contents

DOI: 10.1201/9781003333425-5

5.1 Introduction

Medical image segmentation is an important research area that provides useful information on anatomical structures for clinical diagnosis and treatment. Traditionally, physicians perform visual assessment from images. This process is time consuming, and the judgment is subjective. The diagnostic accuracy depends on the physician's experience. The introduction of computerized image segmentation provides a more objective and robust approach to estimate and visualize the target structure. Techniques such as thresholding, edge-based filters, model-based segmentation, and atlas-based segmentation (Pham et al., 2000) are widely used. However, most techniques require parameter tuning to obtain optimal results, and tuning is performed manually. Research in soft computing (Cheung and Szeto, 2005; Sinha et al., 2020) provides numerical algorithms to estimate the optimal parameters automatically, yet it requires applying an appropriate optimizer for robust results.

Machine learning (ML) is used extensively in medical image segmentation. When the ML model is trained, it can provide a fast, robust, and fully automatic segmentation of the target structure. In particular, deep learning (DL) methods are receiving great attention and improve segmentation performance and computational efficiency for medical image segmentation.

Currently, the DL method is treated as a black box, and the mechanism of DL method is not fully understood. Explainable AI (XAI) is another important research area that provides explanation for the DL method. This can help in building trust and increasing confidence for end users. This is particularly important, as physicians are non-technical users. XAI can help them understand the mechanism of the DL method, and they can use DL tools reliably in the clinical environment.

This chapter is intended to provide a unique technical review of deep learning methods and their explainablility with minimal mathematics, relevant clinical case studies, and implementations for CT image segmentation. Furthermore, we will discuss the future of deep learning methods and XAI from a current practitioner's viewpoint. The chapter is organized as follows. Section 5.2 introduces the principles and workflow of DL. Section 5.3 describes the explainability of DL methods. Section 5.4 introduces the application of DL methods on clinical use cases. Section 5.5 addresses limitations and future opportunities. Finally, Section 5.6 concludes this chapter.

5.2 Machine Learning–Deep Learning Method's Principles and Workflow

In this section, the principles – mathematical theory (Roberts et al., 2022) – of DL and workflow – tasks required for developing DL methods – are discussed. The principles and workflow also constitute best practices.

5.2.1 Principles

A simple neural network is composed of input neurons, hidden layers, and output neurons. The input is denoted as x, the link between neurons as w, the value in each neuron (hidden layer) as z, and the output as $\hat{y}$. Mathematically, the neuron network is represented by the following equations (Eqs. 5.1 and 5.2).

$$z = \sum_i w_i \times x_i + b \tag{5.1}$$

$$\hat{y} = \varphi(z) \tag{5.2}$$

where w is the weight, b is the bias, and φ is the activation function.

The unknown weights and the bias terms are estimated by forward propagation and backpropagation. The activation function (e.g., sigmoid) is defined in the classification layer (output layer). The mathematical problem is formulated as an optimization problem. A loss function (Eq. 5.3) is defined in order to compute the optimal values of w and b. It should be noted that y is the ground-truth label. The choice of loss function is problem specific. Here, dice similarity coefficient (DSC) loss is chosen for medical image segmentation.

$$loss = 1 - DSC = 1 - \left(2 \times \frac{|y \cap \hat{y}|}{|y| + |\hat{y}|}\right) \tag{5.3}$$

The predicted output ($\hat{y}$) is calculated by forward propagation. The error is estimated by computing the loss function. Then backpropagation is used to compute the gradients of the loss function. Update of the gradients is performed by a numerical optimizer (e.g., gradient descent and adam). The optimal weights and bias are estimated when loss is minimized. An example of a neural network with two hidden layers is shown in Figure 5.1.

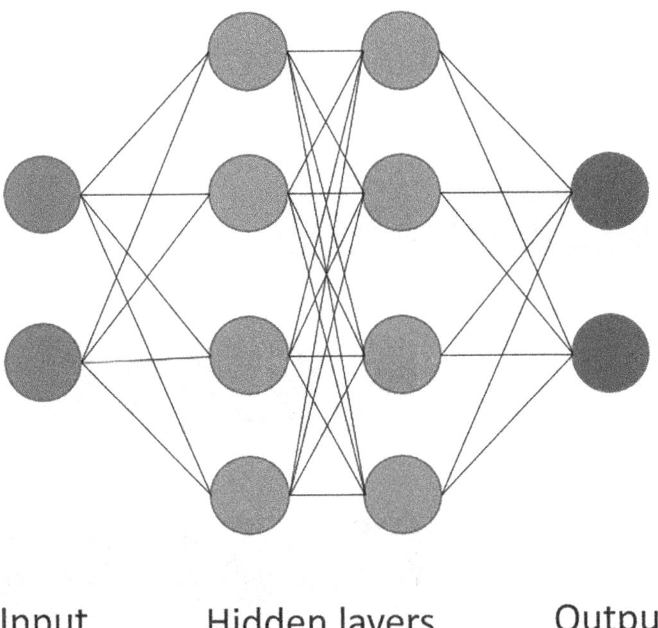

Figure 5.1 An example of neural network (input layer, two hidden layers, and output layer).

5.2.2 Workflow

Clear understanding of the development workflow is the key to successful delivery of the deep learning method. The workflow is composed of several tasks:

A. User (physician) requirement – the task is to define the functionality of the deep learning method (i.e., segmentation of aorta and coronary arteries). Physicians are involved in the consultation to ensure the defined requirements meet their expectations.
B. Data collection – the task is to collect the data (i.e., CT image in digital imaging and communications in medicine [DICOM] format) required.
C. Data preprocessing – the task is to select appropriate subject/patient cases for development. The annotation task is also performed at this stage.
D. Model development – the task is to build/adopt a DL model (e.g., U-Net).
E. Performance evaluation – the task is to evaluate the performance (segmentation) by using similarity measures (e.g., DSC).
F. Model fine-tuning – the task is to optimize the parameters in the model for optimal performance.
G. Acceptance test – the task is to evaluate the deep learning model by the user and ensure it meets industry, safety, health, and environmental protection requirements (e.g., United Kingdom Conformity Assessed [UKCA], Conformitè Europëenne [CE] and United States Food and Drug Administration [USFDA] marks).
H. Deployment – the task is to package the deep learning method as AI software and install it on the client site. Alternatively, it is also popular to deliver AI software as a service.
I. Maintenance – the task is to keep up with user needs by changing, modifying, and updating AI software. For example, regular updates of trained models (weights and biases).

The development workflow is shown in Figure 5.2.

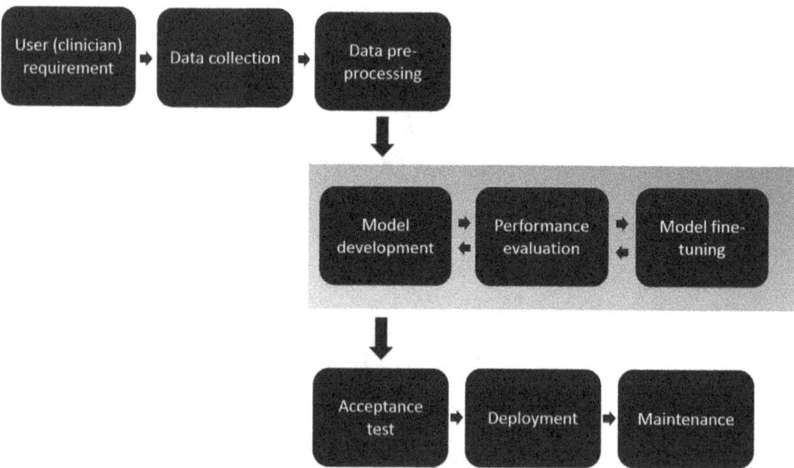

Figure 5.2 The development workflow of the deep learning method.

5.3 Explainability of Deep Learning Method

Post-hoc analysis is commonly used to interpret the deep learning model. This technique can provide an explanation of the mechanism of prediction performed by the deep learning model. In the context of medical image segmentation, post-hoc analysis is able to identify features from the input image, which are utilized by the deep learning model to generate segmented masks. Indirect and direct approaches are available for post-hoc analysis (Kenny et al., 2021; Horwath et al., 2020).

Indirect approach – It is an experimental method that alters features from the input images (one feature at a time) and checks if this change affects segmentation performance. The experimental procedures are as follows: The deep learning model is first trained by a set of reference images (i.e., CTCA images). In order to identify the feature used, one feature is altered intentionally in these images. For example, intensity is adjusted. Then the trained model is used to make a prediction on the altered images. One can expect the segmentation performance to be degraded significantly, as the altered feature is not learned from the trained model. Conversely, if the segmentation performance is maintained, this means that the feature is not used for segmentation.

Direct approach – It is a visualization method that examines the weights (gradients) in the deep learning model. Probability and saliency maps are commonly used. A probability map is a score distribution obtained from the classification layer after activation (e.g., sigmoid). This map is useful for confidence measures of the model on segmentation of target tissue. A saliency map (e.g., Grad-CAM [Selvaraju et al., 2020], Seg-Grad-CAM [Vinogradova et al., 2020] and a deep-learning toolkit for visualization and interpretation of segmented medical images [Ghosal and Shah, 2021]) uses the gradients in the model and highlights the regions that are important and relevant for the segmentation task. These approaches are demonstrated in the clinical application sections.

5.4 Clinical Applications

5.4.1 Aorta and Coronary Artery Segmentation

The first clinical application of the deep learning method is aorta and coronary artery segmentation on computed tomography coronary angiography (CTCA) images. Part of the contents are reproduced from Cheung et al. (2021) under the terms of the CC BY 4.0 license.

5.4.1.1 Background

Coronary artery disease (CAD) is a main cause of death in the United Kingdom. It is a vascular disease that results in the narrowing of heart blood vessels. Vessel stenosis is caused by the building up of plaque in the coronary artery. If severe, the unstable plaque can break off and result in a myocardial infarction. Timely detection and diagnosis of plaque and stenosis could probably minimize the chances of myocardial infarction. Currently, physicians can use various non-invasive imaging methods to visualize the geometry of coronary arteries and stenosis. These methods are stress echocardiography (Senior et al., 2005), cardiac magnetic resonance imaging (MRI) (Saeed et al., 2015), and computed tomography coronary angiography (Meyersohn et al., 2016). CTCA is preferable to other methods, as it provides highly sensitive and specific scans for detection and exclusion of critical coronary artery stenosis (Wallis et al., 2012). It can be used to detect calcified, mixed, and non-calcified coronary plaques. This clinical information is valuable for physicians to diagnose and formulate a treatment strategy.

One of the approaches to examining CAD severity is computational fluid dynamics (CFD). Given the segmentation masks of coronary arteries and the aorta as well as boundary conditions, the blood flow can be calculated by solving various partial differential equations numerically. CT-derived fractional flow reserve (FFR) can be calculated subsequently, and it provides objective measurement of severeness of artery stenosis. CT-derived FFR is desirable, as additional imaging steps are not needed. Yet solving a CFD model is computationally expensive and requires high-performance computing (HPC) facilities. HPC service is usually not available in the hospital, and the CFD simulation is performed off site. This approach is not practical to implement in real time.

An alternative approach is visual assessment. Physicians visually evaluate CTCA scans. The geometry of coronary arteries is used to assess stenosis. This approach, however, is not objective and is labor intensive. The relevant clinical experience of individual physicians (Pugliese et al., 2009; Saur et al., 2010) is an important factor for accurate examination of CAD. Experienced specialists can provide a significantly different diagnosis from newly trained physicians.

Artery segmentation is a procedure to obtain the geometry of the aorta and coronary arteries. Manually or semi-automatic segmentation methods are available. Manual segmentation is not objective and is labor intensive, while semi-automatic segmentation is relatively objective and fast, though it requires manual amendment for inaccurately segmented arteries.

In order to improve existing segmentation techniques, there is a need to develop fully automatic, robust, and efficient computer methods to assist physicians to segment arteries and detect CAD. This is especially applicable in hospitals, as CTCA reviews can be delayed due to the unavailability of specialists.

Advanced DL software that detects and classifies CAD is therefore in demand. Segmented masks of the coronary arteries with the aorta are obtained from raw images initially. Then CAD severity is classified using these images.

The relevant studies were reviewed in two papers (Chen et al., 2020; Lesage et al., 2009). Recently, more advanced deep learning models have been published. These include a 3D multi-channel U-Net (Chen et al., 2019), 3D attention CNN (Shen et al., 2019), a template transformer network (Lee et al., 2019), graph convolutional networks (GCNs) (Wolterink et al., 2019), and a two-stage 2D CNN approach (Mirunalini et al., 2019). The segmentation performance of deep learning method is further improved. However, some methods require high computational resources, such as high GPU memory.

In this section, a U-Net (Ronneberger et al., 2015) model with modification from deep learning is proposed, and its performance is evaluated for segmenting coronary arteries with the aorta in cardiac CT angiography automatically.

5.4.1.2 *Data Preprocessing*

Sixty-nine patients had chest pain, and cardiac CT angiography was performed for CAD assessment. Ethical approval was obtained from the Research Ethics Committee, and written informed consent was obtained from patients. Details can be found in Cheung et al. (2021).

A simple and quick preprocessing technique was proposed: 3D Slicer (Fedorov et al., 2012) was used to preprocess the raw digital imaging and communications in medicine data. The image brightness was altered by modifying the intensity (center = 40, width = 400), and the adjusted image was stored in a NIfTI data format. The height and width of the image were 512 pixels, and all images were then loaded into ImageJ (Schneider et al., 2012) for further processing. The pixel intensity of these images was rescaled in [0, 255]. They were exported as 8-bit portable network graphics (PNG) format and used for DL model training, validation, and testing.

5.4.1.3 *Model Development*

The proposed model was modified from 2D U-Net (Ronneberger et al., 2015). 2D U-Net is a deep CNN and has an encoder and decoder architecture. The encoder

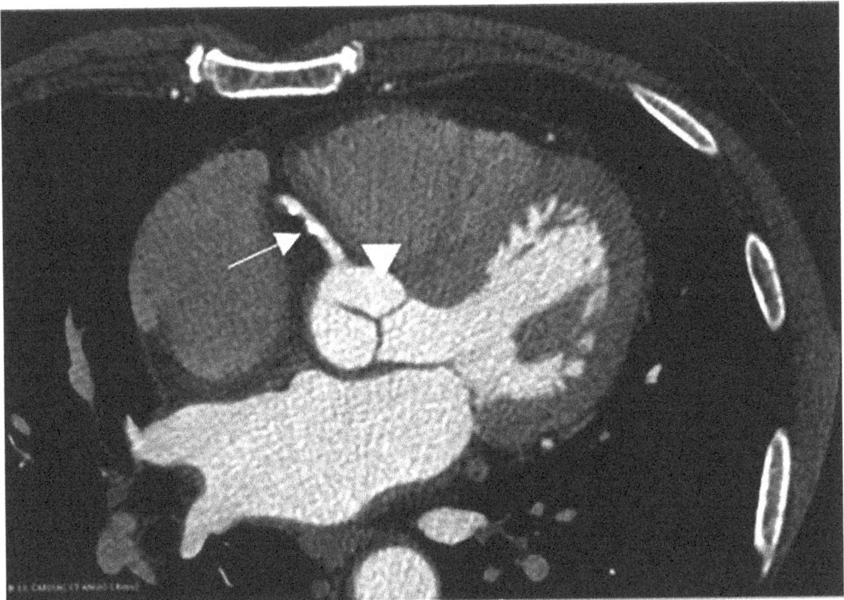

Figure 5.3 Cardiac CT angiography of a CAD patient. Arrow = right coronary artery; arrowhead = ascending aorta.

is used to extract spatial features and contexts, while the decoder is used to localize the extracted features by using deconvolution (transposed convolutions). The final background/foreground classification is performed by using a sigmoid function. The modification was done by (1) adding batch normalization to the convolution block and (2) adding dropout after each convolution block. Batch normalization can be used to stabilize the internal covariate shift during training. Furthermore, dropout can be used to fix the overfitting issue. The stability and performance of the modified U-Net model were improved by these additional techniques. The network architecture of the proposed model is shown in Figure 5.4.

5.4.1.4 *Implementation*

Fifty-five cases (13 cases without CAD, 42 cases with CAD) were split into two sets: training set (11,677 slices) and validation set (2920 slices). Fourteen cases (five cases with no CAD, nine cases with CAD) were held for the test set. Training with ground-truth masks was performed by sequential slice selection. The following scenarios were investigated: (1) aorta and coronary arteries and (2) coronary arteries only.

The proposed approach was developed using the following deep learning frameworks and HPC services: (1) Tensorflow (v2.1.0) and Keras (v2.3.1) on Linux (Rocks 7) and (2) high-performance computing machine (Intel Xeon Gold, 2.3GHz) with an Nvidia Tesla V100 32 GB card. The optimal models were obtained by adapting the Adam algorithm (learning rate = 10^{-3}, epochs = 200). The Keras function (*ReduceLROnPlateau*) was used to reduce the learning rate and speed up the training. The settings of this function were factor – 10^{-1}, patience – 3, and min_lr – 10^{-5}. Early stopping (patience – 10) was implemented when the training performance was not improved.

The prediction was implemented on these deep learning frameworks using a desktop (Intel i9 9960X, 3.1GHz) with an Nvidia Geforce RTX 2070 8 GB card: (1) Tensorflow (v2.1.0) and (2) Keras (v2.3.1) on Windows 10.

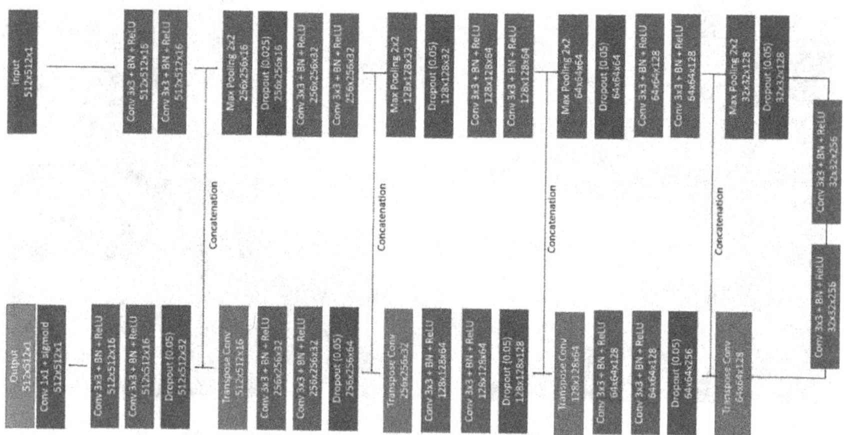

Figure 5.4 The network architecture of the proposed method.

The prediction time was also evaluated on a per-case basis. Two common similarity measures, dice similarity coefficient (DSC) and intersection over union (IoU), were employed to calculate the segmentation accuracy.

5.4.1.5 Training Strategy

5.4.1.5.1 GROUND-TRUTH MASK ANNOTATION

A good DL model requires a large amount of samples (CT images and their ground-truth masks). However, it is very time consuming to prepare ground-truth masks. A semi-automatic segmentation approach to this task is therefore introduced.

The initial segmentation mask was obtained using commercially available software, Simpleware ScanIP (Version 2018.12; Synopsys, Inc., Mountain View, CA). The workflow of segmenting the coronary arteries with aorta was: (1) thresholding, (2) floodfill, and (3) split. Thresholding was used to exclude non-contrast regions. Then, floodfill was used to obtain the mask containing the coronary arteries and cardiac chambers. Finally, the masks of the aorta and coronary arteries were obtained by adapting the split operation. This operation was repeated until no chambers were connected to either the aorta or coronary arteries. The procedure of these steps is shown in Figure 5.5.

The left circumflex artery (LCX), left coronary artery (LCA), right coronary artery (RCA), and ascending aorta (AA) were segmented initially. They were stored in a binary mask. At this step, this mask might contain an undersegmented/oversegmented vessels. It was then fixed manually using 3D Slicer (Fedorov et al., 2012). Additionally, the AA was excluded from the mask and the LCX, LCA, and RCA were kept. An example of these masks is shown in Figure 5.6. As the final step, it is critical to involve physicians for mask validation and quality assurance.

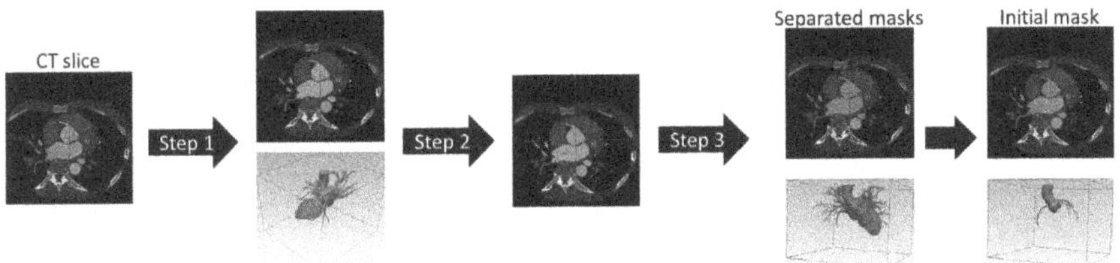

Figure 5.5 The initial segmentation mask was obtained using commercial available software, Simpleware-ScanIP: step 1 – thresholding and floodfill, step 2 – split selection and step 3 – split.

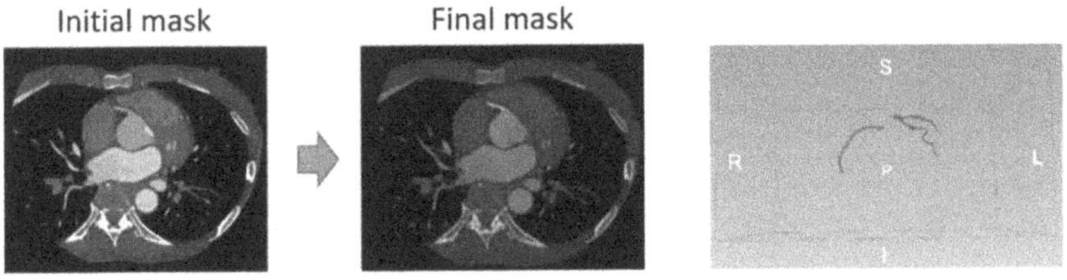

Figure 5.6 The postprocessed mask of the coronary artery using 3D Slicer.

5.4.1.5.2 LOSS FUNCTION

The loss function is composed of binary cross entropy (BCE) and DSC for training the DL model. BCE is used, as the segmentation task can be treated as binary classification. DSC is used to measure the similarity between predicted mask and the ground-truth mask. The combined loss utilized these two measures.

5.4.1.6 Results

5.4.1.6.1 TRAINING CURVE

The training curves of the proposed model are shown in Figure 5.7. The curves did not show signs of overfitting in the training. At the early stage of mini-batch training, the loss showed some fluctuation, and the training became smooth after about 30 epochs. It took 125 epochs to train the model containing the aorta and coronary arteries, while the training took only 51 epochs when only coronary arteries were used as the ground-truth masks. This reveals that distinct features can be found in the aorta and coronary arteries, and therefore the training took longer to complete.

The DSC of the training is displayed in Figure 5.8. It reveals that the model performance improved when more features were utilized by the model.

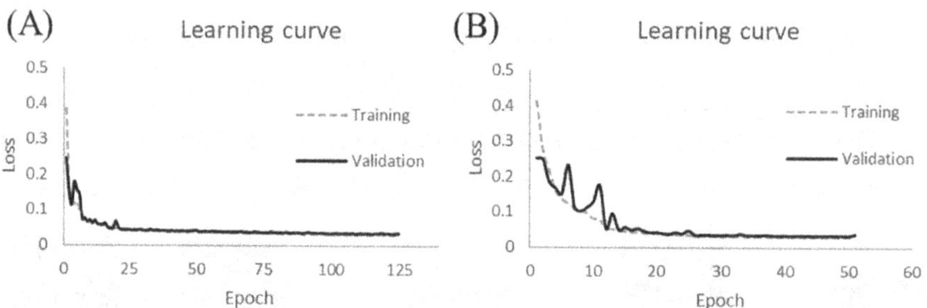

Figure 5.7 Training curves – loss: (A) coronary arteries with aorta (B) coronary arteries without aorta.

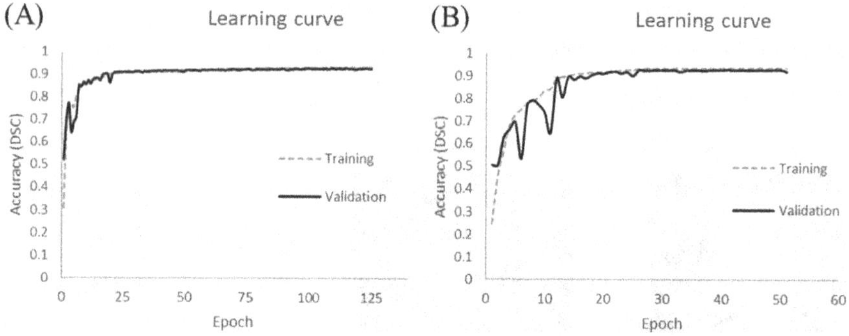

Figure 5.8 Training curves – accuracy (DSC): (A) coronary arteries with aorta (B) coronary arteries without aorta.

5.4.1.6.2 THE OPTIMAL NETWORK ARCHITECTURE

A shallow architecture can segment branch/narrow-diameter arteries, while a deeper architecture can segment main/larger-diameter arteries. An optimization study was conducted to determine the optimal network depth (see Table 5.1). The best test set results were obtained with a 4-skip connection layer network architecture.

5.4.1.6.3 PERFORMANCE OF SEGMENTING CORONARY ARTERIES WITH/WITHOUT AORTA

The performance of segmenting coronary arteries with/without the aorta is displayed in Table 5.2. The DSC of the proposed approach with/without the aorta were 91.20% and 88.80%, respectively. The better performance was obtained when segmenting the aorta and coronary arteries together. This can be explained by the fact that the aorta occupies most of the volume of the mask.

The segmentation result of a normal (no coronary disease) subject and a patient are displayed in Figures 5.9 and 5.10.

From Figure 5.9, it is shown that the coronary arteries with/without the aorta can be segmented, and the result is similar to the ground-truth.

For a case with CAD (Figure 5.10), the coronary arteries with/without the aorta can be segmented by the proposed method with good DSC, but the segmented mask contained a non-aorta/non-coronary artery segment (gray arrowhead). These segments can be excluded by keeping the largest connected components in the mask. Furthermore, the coronary arteries were undersegmented when a model with only coronary arteries was used for prediction.

5.4.1.6.4 TIME REQUIRED TO OBTAIN THE SEGMENTED MASKS

The time required to obtain the segmented masks is shown in Table 5.3 (aorta included) and Table 5.4 (aorta excluded). The proposed approach was fast: it only required about a few seconds to generate the segmented masks. When a CPU-only

Table 5.1 The Optimal Network Architecture of the Proposed Approach

DSC (average)	*Aorta and Coronary Arteries*			*Coronary Arteries Only*		
Number of skip connection layers	*Training*	*Validation*	*Test*	*Training*	*Validation*	*Test*
2	66.80%	67.13%	67.60%	66.46%	68.65%	73.34%
4	93.62%	93.33%	**91.20%**	93.82%	93.41%	**88.80%**
6	**95.37%**	**95.13%**	87.81%	**94.94%**	**94.55%**	88.22%
7	94.83%	94.99%	88.97%	94.56%	94.39%	87.58%

Table 5.2 Segmentation Performance of the Proposed Method

	DSC (average)	*IoU (average)*
Aorta and coronary arteries	91.20%	83.82%
Coronary arteries only	88.80%	79.85%

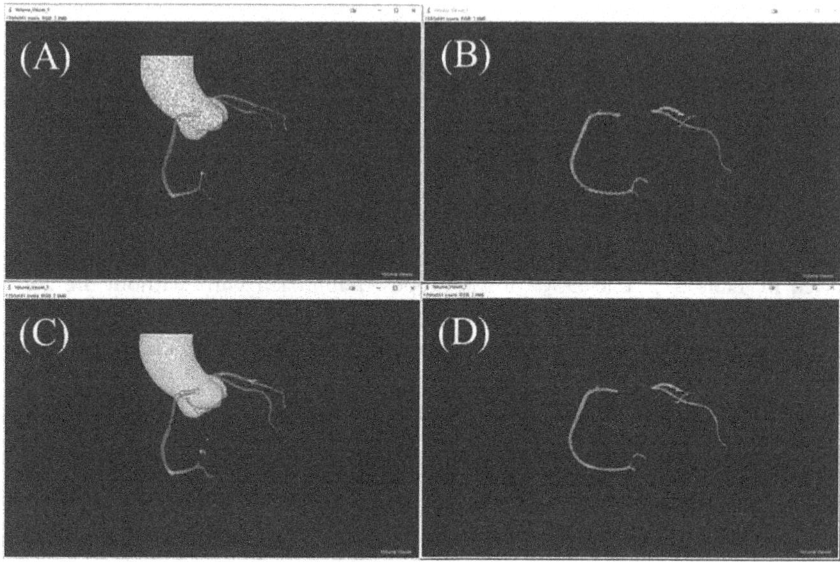

Figure 5.9 Segmentation results of a normal (no coronary disease) subject. Segmentation mask of aorta and coronary arteries: (A) ground-truth, (C) proposed approach. Segmentation mask of coronary arteries only: (B) ground-truth, (D) proposed approach.

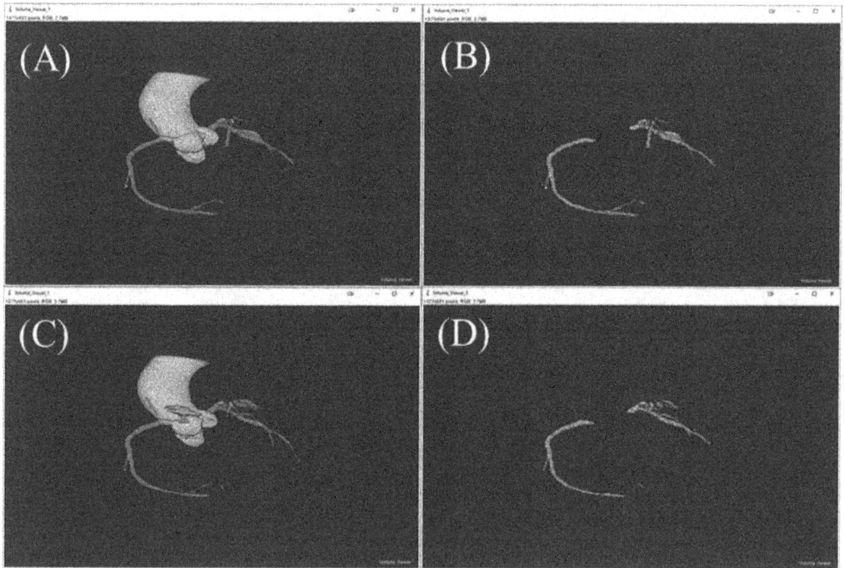

Figure 5.10 Segmentation results of a patient with coronary disease. Segmentation mask of aorta and coronary arteries: (A) ground-truth, (C) proposed approach. Segmentation mask of coronary arteries only: (B) ground-truth, (D) proposed approach.

Table 5.3 Segmentation Time – Mask Contains Aorta and Coronary Arteries

Aorta Included	*Average Time ± SD*
Proposed approach (Setting A)	3.29s ± 0.47s
Proposed approach (Setting B)	138.57s ± 15.74s
Proposed approach (Setting C)	40.93s ± 4.71s

Note: Setting A – GPU, Setting B – CPU alone with 2 cores, Setting C – CPU alone with 16 cores.

Table 5.4 Segmentation Time – Mask Contains Coronary Arteries Only

Aorta Excluded	*Average Time ± SD*
Proposed approach (Setting A)	3.36s ± 0.50s
Proposed approach (Setting B)	140.07s ± 16.90s
Proposed approach (Setting C)	40.93s ± 4.75s

Note: Setting A – GPU, Setting B – CPU alone with 2 cores, Setting C – CPU alone with 16 cores.

configuration was used, the time required was increased significantly. However, it is acceptable to physicians.

5.4.1.7 *Explainability*

The learning curves showed that unique image characteristics can be found in the aorta and coronary arteries. It is unclear what features from the input image were used for the segmentation task. A post-hoc analysis is used to provide insight on feature identification. In order to understand the behavior of the proposed neural network, an indirect approach is used to verify the features utilized by the proposed model.

5.4.1.7.1 INTENSITY

Figure 5.11 shows the CTCA images normalized by two different techniques. One is by applying a mediastinal window, and the other one is by linear stretching. It can be seen that the brightness is different for the same region (e.g., the aorta). The segmentation performance of the images normalized by linear stretching is very poor, when the model is trained by images normalized by a mediastinal window. It should be noted that if the image in Fig 5.11(A) is used for prediction, the segmentation performance is very good. It is concluded that intensity is a feature used by the deep learning model. Furthermore, histogram equalization can be used to rescale the intensity back to the original setting (normalized by a mediastinal window). This can avoid retraining the model by using the images normalized by linear stretching.

5.4.1.7.2 SHAPE

The reference image is a CTCA image normalized by a mediastinal window. In order to check the feature shape, the image is rotated by 180 degrees. These images are shown in Figure 5.12. Again, the segmentation performance is very poor when

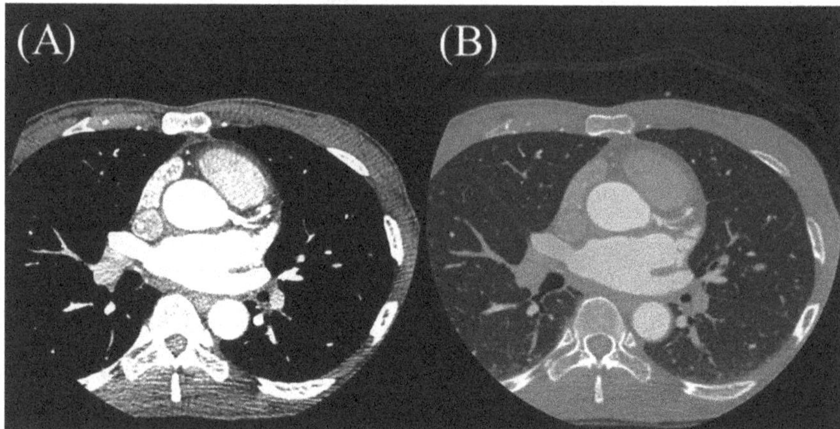

Figure 5.11 A CTCA image normalized by (A) mediastinal window, (B) linear stretching.

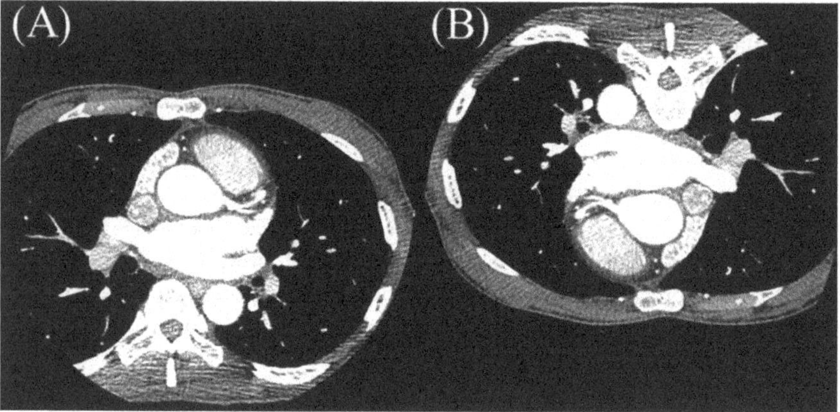

Figure 5.12 (A) CTCA image normalized by mediastinal window. (B) The same image rotated by 180 degrees.

the inverted image is used as the test image. This could be explained by the fact that convolution operation in the deep learning model is not rotation invariant, and it is confirmed that shape is a feature.

In order to understand the behavior of the proposed neural network, a direct approach is used to verify the features utilized by the proposed model.

5.4.1.7.3 PROBABILITY MAP

The probability map (Figure 5.13) is obtained by computing the weight in the classification layer after activation (sigmoid function). A threshold (0.5) is applied, and the final segmented mask is obtained. It can be seen that some pixels with low confidence are removed after thresholding. There is a high confidence score within the aorta, while the score is decreased for smaller coronary arteries and their artery walls.

5.4.1.7.4 GRAD-CAM (SALIENCY MAP)

Computing the Grad-CAM can be achieved by converting the binary segmentation to two-class semantic segmentation. SegGradCAM (Vinogradova et al., 2020) can be used to compute the saliency map accordingly. An example of aorta and coronary artery segmentation for CTCA images is shown in Figure 5.14. It is confirmed that the modified U-Net focused on the aorta and coronary arteries for segmentation. These regions have a high importance when compared with non-aorta and non–coronary artery regions.

5.4.2 Airway Segmentation

The second clinical application of the deep learning method is airway segmentation on HRCT images. Part of the contents are reproduced from Pakzad et al. (2021) with informed consent.

5.4.2.1 Background

Idiopathic pulmonary fibrosis (IPF) (Devaraj, 2014) is a disease that causes the lung tissue the be scarred and the lung airways dilated abnormally, for example, the increase of airway wall thickness (Miller et al., 2019). The thickening of scar tissue can slow down the oxygen flow from the lungs to blood. When the disease becomes severe, it can lead to respiratory failure and death.

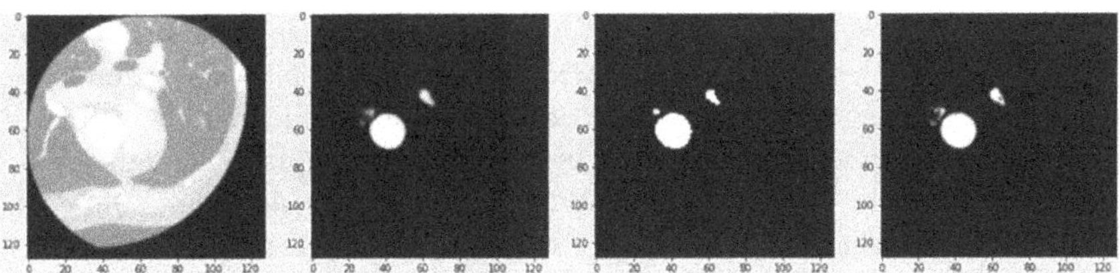

Figure 5.13 CTCA image and the corresponding probability map, predicted mask with thresholding, and ground-truth mask.

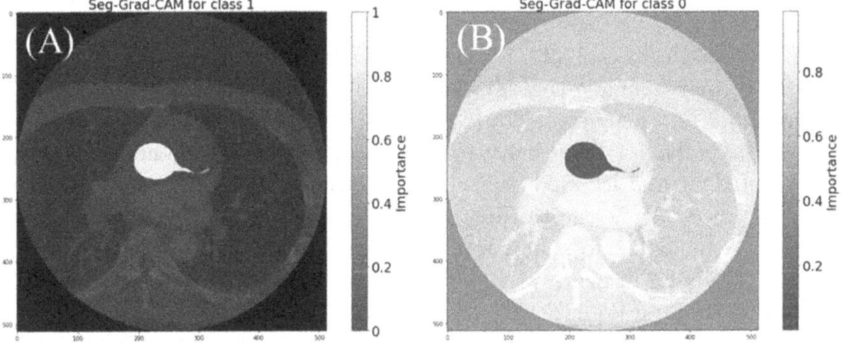

Figure 5.14 Saliency map for aorta and coronary artery segmentation: (A) aorta and coronary artery regions, (B) non-aorta and non-coronary artery regions.

Currently, the severity of this disease is diagnosed by visual assessment (Jacob et al., 2020). Visual analysis can (1) predict disease severity at baseline and (2) predict disease progression on longitudinal data. However, visual CT analysis is subjective and time consuming.

Airway tree analysis is a new approach to extract useful and clinical relevant information for diagnosis of IPF. Quantitative measurement can be performed on the segmented airway. Recently, an airway analysis tool (Pakzad et al., 2021) has been developed. It utilizes lung CT images and an airway tree and its skeletons and provides airway-related metrics for airway quantification, for example, segmental intertapering and segmental tortuosity. These parameters could be prognostic signals for severe IPF.

Accurate airway tree segmentation is an essential requirement for reliable quantitative airway measurement. Traditional techniques such as a Frangi filter (Jimenez-Carretero et al., 2013) and the region-growing method (Duan et al., 2020) have been used extensively to extract airway trees. They showed some promise but required manual parameters tuning for optimal performance. Segmentation performance could be degraded if the user is not familiar with these techniques.

The research community actively seeks a fully automatic method to resolve the issue mentioned previously. The advancement of GPU technology enables accelerated development of machine learning algorithms. In particular, the deep learning method is the most popular approach to this problem. A brief review of deep learning methods for airway segmentation is given in the next paragraph.

Charbonnier et al. (2017) presented convolution networks for leak detection in order to improve airway segmentation. Yun et al. (2019) developed a 2.5D convolutional network. The DSC of their approach is about 90%. Nadeem et al. (2019) proposed 3D U-Net with iterative topological leakage detection and branch augmentation for airway segmentation. This method relaxed the threshold on the probability map, and leaks were corrected by a freeze-and-growth algorithm. Qin et al. (2020) developed a simpler and effective deep learning approach for airway segmentation. A context scale fusion was used to improve the connectivity between airway segments. This approach achieved a DSC of 93% on a public dataset. Zhou et al. (2021) proposed a three-dimensional multi-scale feature aggregation network to deal with scale differences of substructures in airway tree segmentation. The proposed method achieved the best results, with DSC and TPR scores of 86.18% and 79.31%. Garcia-Uceda et al. (2021) presented a simpler and robust 3D U-Net with low GPU memory requirements. It can process large 3D image patches, and the approach is efficient. Zheng et al. (2021) proposed WingsNet with group supervision to tackle the problem of class imbalance between airway and non-airway regions. The proposed method achieved 80.5% branch detection rate. Guo et al. (2022) developed a coarse-to-fine segmentation framework to obtain a complete airway tree. It employed a multiple information fusion CNN (Mif-CNN) and a region growing within the CNN for main airway and small branch segmentation. The DSC of this work was 93.5% for private dataset.

In the next section, a deep learning method based on modified 2D dilated U-Net was proposed, and its performance was evaluated for automated segmentation of the airway on HRCT images.

5.4.2.2 Data Preprocessing

DICOM images (image size: 512 × 512) were converted to TIFF format by using ImageJ. Then the brightness of each image was normalized by using a lung window (W/L: 1500/−500). Finally, the intensity was rescaled to between 0 and 255. The ground-truth mask was annotated by using 3D Slicer. An example of an HRCT image of the lung is shown in Figure 5.15.

5.4.2.3 Model Development

A modified dilated U-Net (Piao and Liu, 2019) is employed to perform airway segmentation. It uses the architecture of U-Net as the base, which has contracting (down-sampling layers) and expanding (up-sampling layers) paths. The contracting path is to extract features, and the expanding path is to localize the features. The convolution in the bottleneck layer of U-Net is replaced by a sequential dilated convolution (Yu and Koltun, 2015) in dilated U-Net. This dilated convolution can improve global context capturing and maintain the resolution of the feature map. The architecture of dilated U-Net is shown in Figure 5.16. It should be noted that batch normalization and dropout are added to improve the model stability and performance.

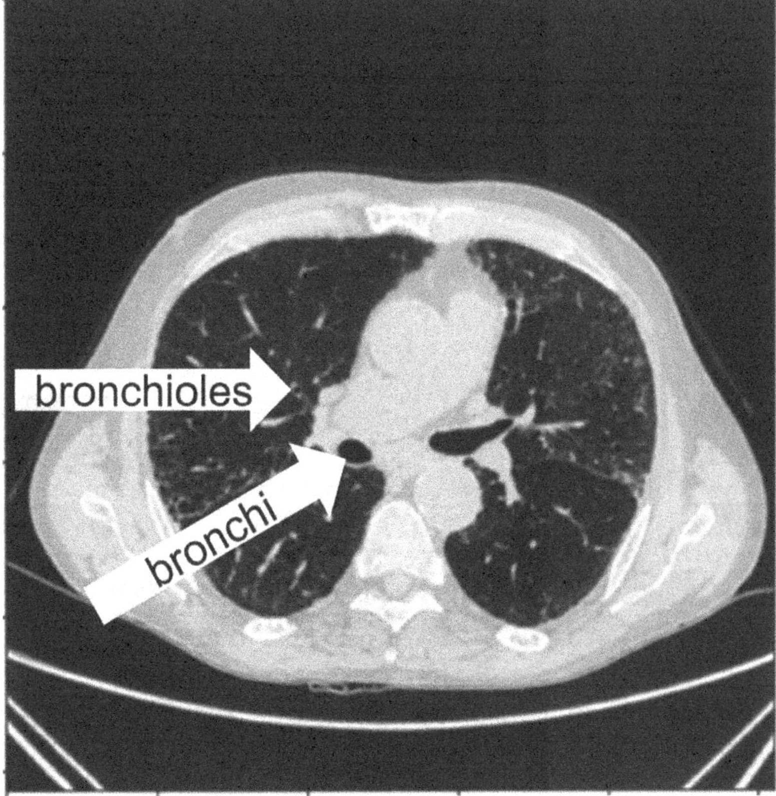

Figure 5.15 High-resolution CT image of lung.

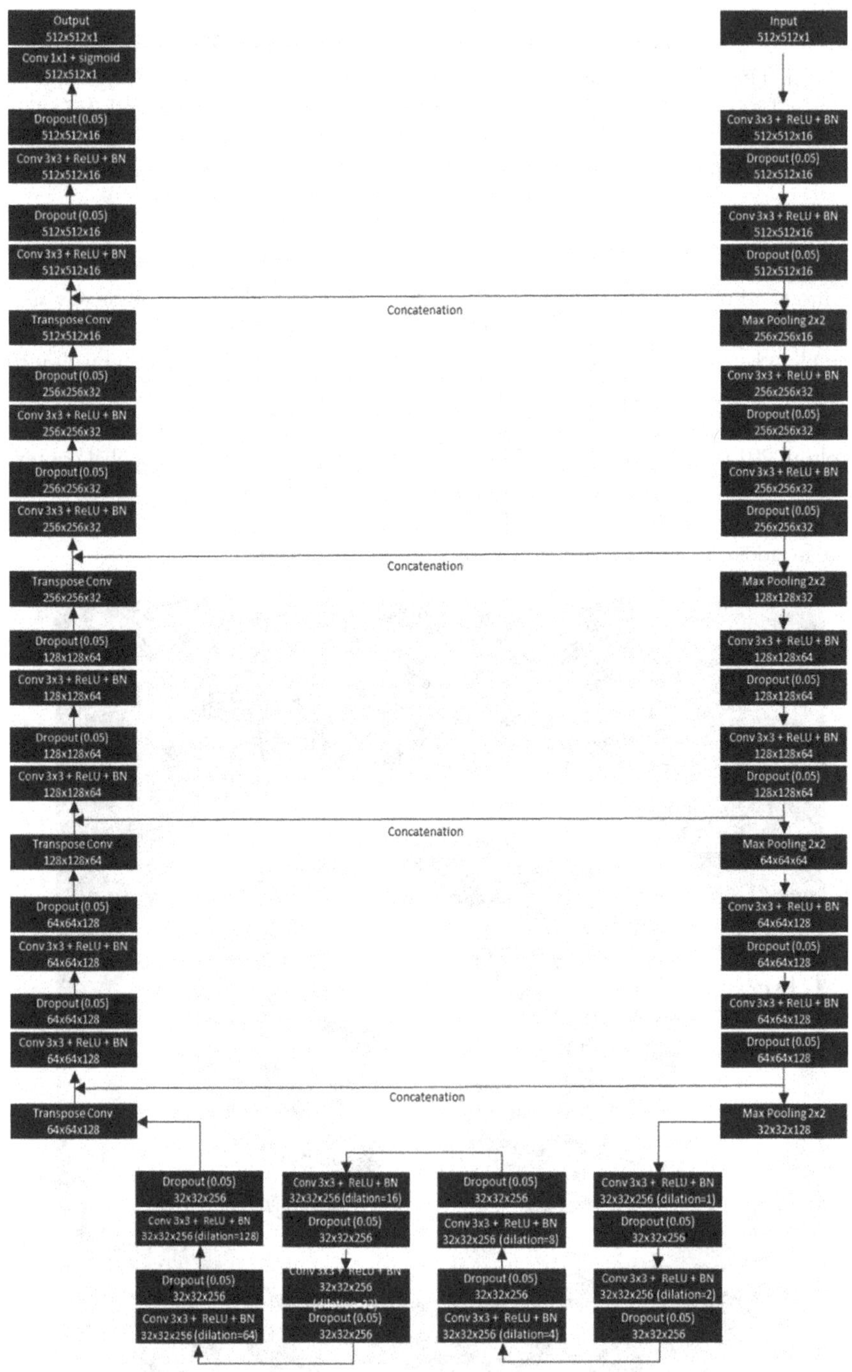

Figure 5.16 The network architecture of modified dilated U-Net.

5.4.2.4 Implementation

The model was trained and validated by using 25 manual segmented airway trees. The data contained 6 normal CTs in healthy never-smoker volunteers, 2 normal cases from the EXACT09 competition dataset (Lo et al., 2012), and 17 IPF cases. Eighty percent of CT images (7552 slices) were used for training, while 20% of CT images (1995 slices) were used for validation.

The proposed models were implemented using the following deep learning frameworks and HPC services: (1) Tensorflow (v1.1.4) and Keras (v2.2.4) on Linux (Rocks 7) and (2) high-performance computing machine (Intel Xeon Gold, 3GHz) with an Nvidia Quadro RTX 6000 24 GB GPU. The optimal models were obtained by adapting the Adam algorithm (learning rate = 10^{-3}, epochs = 200). The Keras function (*ReduceLROnPlateau*) was used to reduce the learning rate and speed up the training. The settings of this function were factor – 10^{-1}, patience – 3, and min_lr – 10^{-5}. Early stopping (patience – 10) was implemented when the training performance was not improved.

5.4.2.5 Training Strategy

5.4.2.5.1 ACTIVE LEARNING

Manual ground-truth annotation is very time consuming. Though the model was trained with manually segmented airways, the efficiency of the task can be improved by using active learning (AL). AL is a semi-supervised strategy that allows the user to interact with the DL model to complete data annotation. The initial DL model can be trained by using a few (e.g., five cases) manually annotated airway trees. Then the trained model was used to predict the airway for a new case. If the segmentation performance of this case is good, this airway tree will be kept. However, if the segmentation performance is unacceptable, it means that some features in this case are not learned by the model. Airway segmentation was subsequently corrected manually and was used for retraining the model. These steps were repeated until the desirable segmentation performance was reached (i.e., 25 cases were analyzed or DSC [training/test sets] => 85%). This strategy allows the performance of the model to be improved iteratively. It does not require complete ground-truth annotation and therefore reduces the effort of ground-truth preparation. The schematic diagram of the active learning strategy is shown in Figure 5.17.

5.4.2.5.2 LOSS FUNCTION

The loss function is composed of binary cross entropy and DSC for training the DL model. BCE is used because the segmentation task can be treated as binary classification. DSC is used to measure the similarity between the predicted mask and ground-truth mask. The combined loss utilized these two measures.

5.4.2.6 Results

The segmentation results of training and validation sets (without post-processing) are shown in Table 5.5. The average DSC for both sets was larger than 81%. No overfitting was seen.

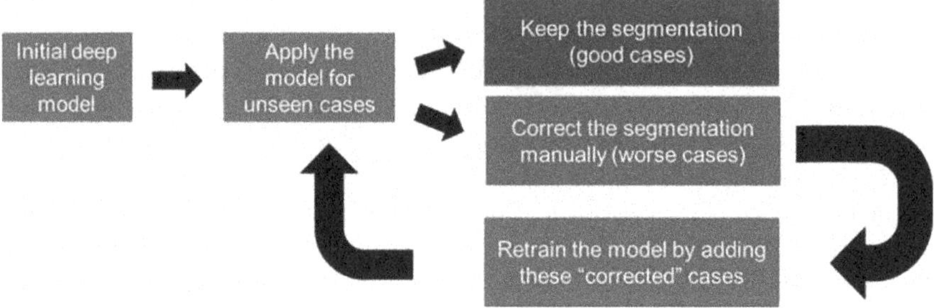

Figure 5.17 Active learning strategy.

Table 5.5 Training and Validation Performance of Proposed Deep Learning Model without Post-Processing

	DSC (average)
Training set	86.17%
Validation set	81.80%

Table 5.6 Segmentation Performance of a Normal Subject and an IPF Patient by the Proposed Deep Learning Model after Post-Processing

	DSC
Normal subject	85.27%
IPF patient	79.71%

The segmentation performance (with post-processing) of a normal subject and an IPF patient are shown in Table 5.6. The DSC of both cases exceeded 79%. The trachea, primary bronchi, and airway segments up to the sixth generations were reliably segmented. The segmented airway trees are shown in Figure 5.18. It should be noted that morphological closing and largest connected components were applied to improve the connectivity of airway segments and remove artifacts from the initial segmentation obtained by the proposed method.

5.4.2.7 Explainability

The indirect method mentioned in the previous section is used to examine features – intensity, shape, and scale.

5.4.2.7.1 INTENSITY

The reference images are HRCT images normalized by a lung window. The test image is produced by applying a mediastinal window (Figure 5.19). The segmentation performance of the test image is not good, and hence intensity is verified as a feature.

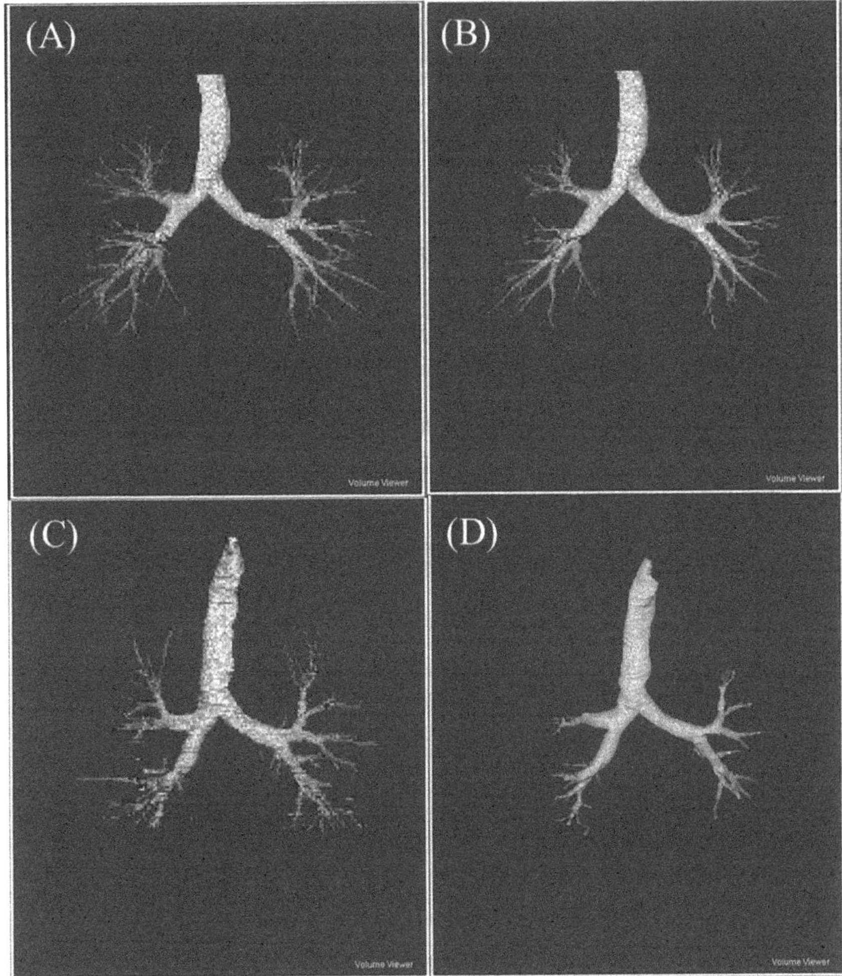

Figure 5.18 Airway segmentation results (proposed method with post-processing) and the optimal manual labels of (A, C) a normal subject and (B, D) an IPF patient.

5.4.2.7.2 SHAPE

The test image is produced by rotating the reference image by 180 degrees (Figure 5.20). The segmentation performance is again poor, and this implies the shape is a feature. It should be noted that orientation can also be used to describe the change on the test image. When the orientation is changed, the shape is also changed, as the shape of the tissue does not have rotational symmetry.

5.4.2.7.3 SCALE

Scale is examined by using zoom-in/zoom-out images (Figure 5.21). The zoom-in image is produced by using interpolation, while the zoom-out image is produced

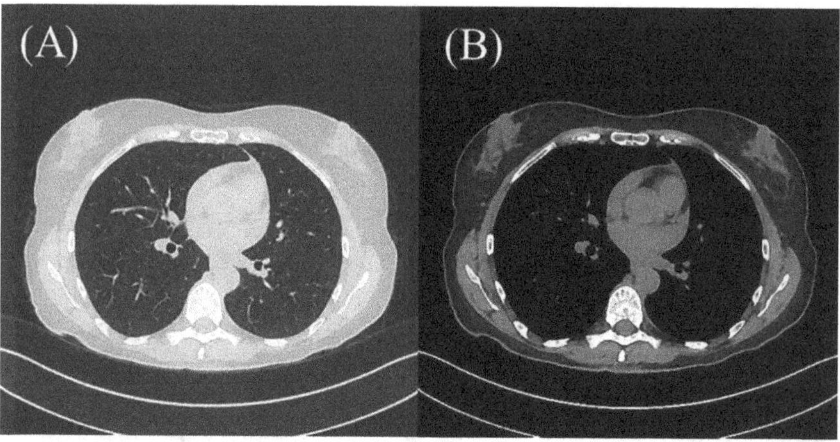

Figure 5.19 HRCT image normalized by (A) lung window, (B) mediastinal window.

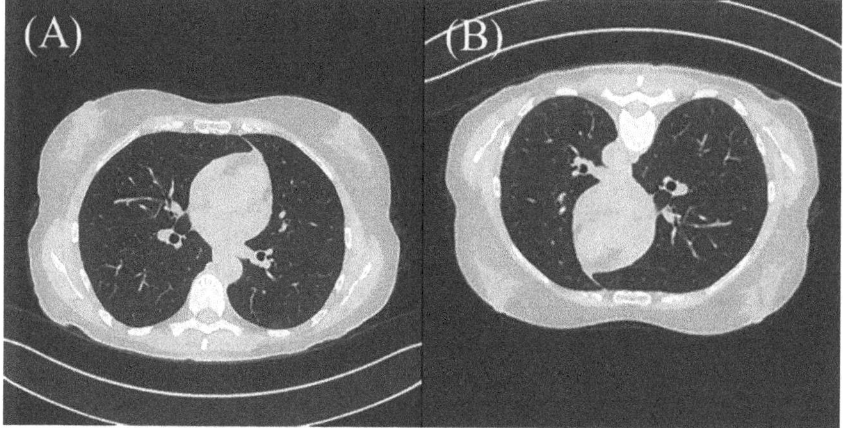

Figure 5.20 (A) HRCT image normalized by lung window. (B) The same image rotated by 180 degrees.

by downsampling the reference image. The segmentation performance is poor for zoom-in and zoom-out images. This indicates that scale is a feature for the deep learning model. It should be noted that size is an alternative term to describe the change on the test image. Changing the scale of the test image causes a change of tissue size. Additionally, the convolution is not scale invariant; this may explain the poor segmentation performance when the test image is rescaled.

In this section, a direct approach is used to verify the features utilized by the proposed model.

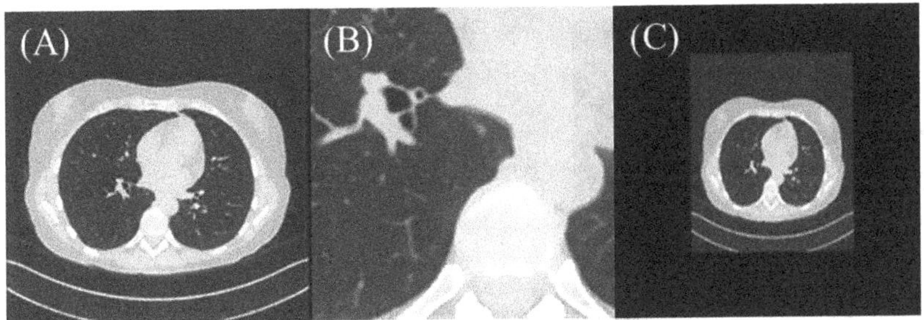

Figure 5.21 (A) HRCT image normalized by lung window. (B) The zoom-in image. (C) The zoom-out image.

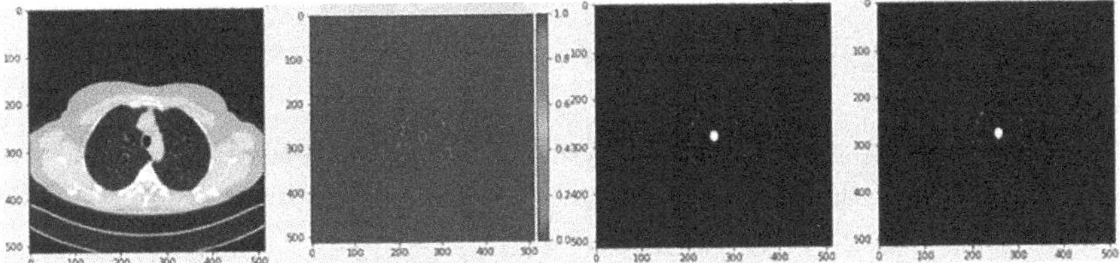

Figure 5.22 HRCT image and the corresponding probability map, predicted mask with thresholding, and ground-truth mask.

5.4.2.7.3.1 Probability map The probability map of an HRCT image is shown in Figure 5.22. There is a high confidence score within the trachea, while the score is lower for smaller airways and the airway walls. The predicted mask is obtained by applying a threshold (0.5). Some pixels with low confidence scores are removed after thresholding.

5.4.2.7.3.2 Grad-CAM (saliency map) Readers are referred to Section 5.4.1.7 for more details. An example of airway segmentation for HRCT images is shown in Figure 5.23. It is confirmed that the modified dilated U-Net focused on airways for segmentation. These regions have high importance when compared with non-airway regions.

5.5 Limitations and Future Opportunities

5.5.1 Limitations

5.5.1.1 Segmentation

5.5.1.1.1 COMMON ISSUES

First, bias in patient selection may exist, as the study was retrospective. Second, annotator bias may be present, as manual labeling was performed to obtain the

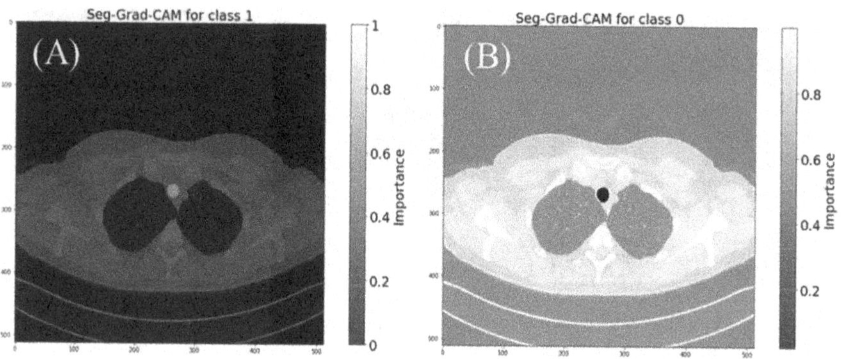

Figure 5.23 Saliency map for airway segmentation: (A) airway regions, (B) non-airway regions.

ground-truth. Last, the DSC evaluation may have been biased due to the co-existence of large and small tissues (e.g., aorta vs coronary arteries or trachea vs bronchioles).

5.5.1.1.2 Aorta- and coronary artery–specific issues

The proximal coronary artery is undersegmented when using the modified 2D U-Net model. This requires further investigation to improve the segmentation performance on these regions.

5.5.1.1 Airway-specific issues

The modified 2D dilated U-Net is able to segment airway trees from the trachea to about sixth-generation airway reliably. Higher-generation airway segments (i.e., 7th to 16th bronchioles) are not segmented well. It should be noted that CT scanner resolution (i.e., slice thickness) is also a factor that limits a scanner's ability to capture small bronchioles.

5.5.1.2 Explainability

5.5.1.2.1 Probability map

Though the probability is interpreted as a confidence score in the current status, it is still not well understood how this is linked to image features. For example, the geometry (shape and size) of the target tissue could influence the confidence score.

5.5.1.2.2 Grad-CAM (saliency map)

It can highlight important regions after the neural network analyzes the features at each layer. However, it does not explain how these features (from low-level to high-level) are processed throughout the whole network.

5.5.2 Future Opportunities

5.5.2.1 SEGMENTATION

The segmentation of smaller tissues (e.g., small coronary arteries or small bronchioles) can be further improved through the advancement of deep learning models (e.g., incorporating an attention mechanism into the DL model). Furthermore, a data-centric deep learning method is an emerging approach to improve segmentation performance while keeping the deep learning model fixed. In terms of DSC measurement, a more fair comparison can be performed on a per-tissue basis (e.g., per vessel or per airway segment).

5.5.2.2 EXPLAINABILITY

An ideal tool is to able to (1) identify the features used in the DL model, (2) trace the features throughout the whole network, (3) explain/visualize the mechanism of processing features (from low-level to high-level) by DL model, and (4) link these features to the final classification (segmentation).

5.6 Conclusions

This chapter reviews a state-of-the-art deep learning method and its explainability for computerized tomography image segmentation. Modified 2D U-Net and dilated U-Net deep learning models are proposed and discussed for CT image segmentation. Indirect and direct explainable methods are introduced. The future opportunities of deep learning methods and explainability are also highlighted.

References

Charbonnier, J. P., E. M. van Rikxoort, A. A. A. Setio, C. M. Schaefer-Prokop, B. van Ginneken, and F. Ciompi. 2017. "Improving airway segmentation in computed tomography using leak detection with convolutional networks." *Medical Image Analysis* 36:52–60. doi: 10.1016/j.media.2016.11.001.

Chen, C., C. Qin, H. Q. Qiu, G. Tarroni, J. M. Duan, W. J. Bai, and D. Rueckert. 2020. "Deep learning for cardiac image segmentation: A review." *Frontiers in Cardiovascular Medicine* 7. doi: 10.3389/fcvm.2020.00025.

Chen, Y.-C., Y.-C. Lin, C.-P. Wang, C.-Y. Lee, W.-J. Lee, T.-D. Wang, and C.-M. Chen. 2019. "Coronary artery segmentation in cardiac CT angiography using 3D multi-channel U-net." *MIDL* 2019.

Cheung, W. K., and K. Y. Szeto. 2005. "Optimal strategy for resource allocation of two-dimensional potts model using genetic algorithm." *8th International Work-Conference on Artificial Neural Networks, IWANN 2005, Vilanova i la Geltrú*, Barcelona, Spain.

Cheung, W. K., R. Bell, A. Nair, L. J. Menezes, R. Patel, S. Wan, K. Chou, J. Chen, R. Torii, R. H. Davies, J. C. Moon, D. C. Alexander, and J. Jacob. 2021. "A computationally efficient approach to segmentation of the aorta and coronary arteries using deep learning." *IEEE Access* 9: 108873–108888. doi: 10.1109/ACCESS.2021.3099030.

Devaraj, A. 2014. "Imaging: How to recognise idiopathic pulmonary fibrosis." *European Respiratory Review* 23 (132): 215–219. doi: 10.1183/09059180.00001514.

Duan, H. H., J. Gong, X. W. Sun, and S. D. Nie. 2020. "Region growing algorithm combined with morphology and skeleton analysis for segmenting airway tree in CT images." *Journal of X-Ray Science and Technology* 28 (2): 311–331. doi: 10.3233/Xst-190627.

Fedorov, A., R. Beichel, J. Kalpathy-Cramer, J. Finet, J. C. Fillion-Robin, S. Pujol, C. Bauer, D. Jennings, F. Fennessy, M. Sonka, J. Buatti, S. Aylward, J. V. Miller, S. Pieper, and R. Kikinis. 2012. "3D Slicer as an image computing platform for the quantitative imaging network." *Magnetic Resonance Imaging* 30 (9): 1323–1341. doi: 10.1016/j.mri.2012.05.001.

Garcia-Uceda, A., R. Selvan, Z. Saghir, H. A. W. M. Tiddens, and M. de Bruijne. 2021. "Automatic airway segmentation from computed tomography using robust and efficient 3-D convolutional neural networks." *Scientific Reports* 11 (1). doi: 10.1038/s41598-021-95364-1.

Ghosal, S., and P. Shah. 2021. "A deep-learning toolkit for visualization and interpretation of segmented medical images." *Cell Reports Methods* 1 (7): 100107. doi: 10.1016/j.crmeth.2021.100107.

Guo, J., R. Fu, L. Pan, S. Zheng, L. Huang, B. Zheng, and B. He. 2022. "Coarse-to-fine airway segmentation using multi information fusion network and CNN-based region growing." *Comput Methods Programs Biomed* 215: 106610. doi: 10.1016/j.cmpb.2021.106610.

Horwath, J. P., D. N. Zakharov, R. Megret, and E. A. Stach. 2020. "Understanding important features of deep learning models for segmentation of high-resolution transmission electron microscopy images." *NPJ Computational Materials* 6 (1). doi: 10.1038/s41524-020-00363-x.

Jacob, J., L. Aksman, N. Mogulkoc, A. J. Procter, B. Gholipour, G. Cross, J. Barnett, C. J. Brereton, M. G. Jones, C. H. van Moorsel, W. van Es, F. van Beek, M. Veltkamp, S. R. Desai, E. Judge, T. Burd, M. Kokosi, R. Savas, S. Bayraktaroglu, A. Altmann, and A. U. Wells. 2020. "Serial CT analysis in idiopathic pulmonary fibrosis: Comparison of visual features that determine patient outcome." *Thorax* 75 (8): 648–654. doi: 10.1136/thoraxjnl-2019-213865.

Jimenez-Carretero, D., A. Santos, S. Kerkstra, R. D. Rudyanto, and M. J. Ledesma-Carbayo. 2013. "3d Frangi-based lung vessel enhancement filter penalizing airways." *2013 IEEE 10th International Symposium on Biomedical Imaging (ISBI)*: 926–929.

Kenny, E. M., C. Ford, M. Quinn, and M. T. Keane. 2021. "Explaining black-box classifiers using post-hoc explanations-by-example: The effect of explanations and error-rates in XAI user studies." *Artificial Intelligence* 294: 103459. doi: 10.1016/j.artint.2021.103459.

Lee, M. C. H., K. Petersen, N. Pawlowski, B. Glocker, and M. Schaap. 2019. "TeTrIS: Template transformer networks for image segmentation with shape priors." *IEEE Transactions on Medical Imaging* 38 (11): 2596–2606. doi: 10.1109/Tmi.2019.2905990.

Lesage, D., E. D. Angelini, I. Bloch, and G. Funka-Lea. 2009. "A review of 3D vessel lumen segmentation techniques: Models, features and extraction schemes." *Medical Image Analysis* 13 (6): 819–845. doi: 10.1016/j.media.2009.07.011.

Lo, P., B. van Ginneken, J. M. Reinhardt, T. Yavarna, P. A. de Jong, B. Irving, C. Fetita, M. Ortner, R. Pinho, J. Sijbers, M. Feuerstein, A. Fabijanska, C. Bauer, R. Beichel, C. S. Mendoza, R. Wiemker, J. Lee, A. P. Reeves, S. Born, O. Weinheimer, E. M. van Rikxoort, J. Tschirren, K. Mori, B. Odry, D. P. Naidich, I. Hartmann, E. A. Hoffman, M. Prokop, J. H. Pedersen, and M. de Bruijne. 2012. "Extraction of airways From CT (EXACT'09)." *IEEE Transactions on Medical Imaging* 31 (11): 2093–2107. doi: 10.1109/Tmi.2012.2209674.

Meyersohn, N., S. Janjua, P. Staziaki, D. Bittner, R. Takx, R. Weiner, J. Wasfy, U. Hoffmann, and B. Ghoshhajra. 2016. "Medical management of non-obstructive coronary artery disease on coronary CT angiography: Insight from a modern emergency department clinical registry." *Journal of the American College of Cardiology* 67 (13): 1763–1763. doi: Doi 10.1016/S0735–1097(16)31764–8.

Miller, E. R., R. K. Putman, A. A. Diaz, H. Xu, R. San Jose Estepar, T. Araki, M. Nishino, S. Poli de Frias, T. Hida, J. Ross, H. Coxson, J. Dupuis, G. T. O'Connor, E. K. Silverman, I. O. Rosas, H. Hatabu, G. Washko, and G. M. Hunninghake. 2019. "Increased airway wall thickness in interstitial lung abnormalities and idiopathic pulmonary fibrosis." *Annals of the American Thoracic Society* 16 (4): 447–454. doi: 10.1513/AnnalsATS.201806-424OC.

Mirunalini, P., C. Aravindan, A. T. Nambi, S. Poorvaja, and V. P. Priya. 2019. "Segmentation of coronary arteries from CTA axial slices using deep learning techniques." *Proceedings of the 2019 IEEE Region 10 Conference (Tencon 2019): Technology, Knowledge, and Society*: 2074–2080.

Nadeem, S. A., E. A. Hoffman, and P. K. Saha. 2019. "A fully automated CT-based airway segmentation algorithm using deep learning and topological leakage detection and branch augmentation approaches." *Medical Imaging 2019: Image Processing* 10949. doi: 10.1117/12.2512286.

Pakzad, A., W. K. Cheung, K. Quan, N. Mogulkoc, C. H. M. Van Moorsel, B. J. Bartholmai, H. W. Van Es, A. Ezircan, F. Van Beek, and M. Veltkamp. 2021. "Evaluation of automated airway morphological quantification for assessing fibrosing lung disease." *arXiv Preprint arXiv:2111.10443*, pp. 1–15.

Pham, D. L., C. Xu, and J. L. Prince. 2000. "Current methods in medical image segmentation." *Annual Review of Biomedical Engineering* 2: 315–337. doi: 10.1146/annurev.bioeng.2.1.315.

Piao, S., and J. Liu. 2019. "Accuracy improvement of UNet based on dilated convolution." *Journal of Physics: Conference Series* 1345 (5): 052066. doi: 10.1088/1742-6596/1345/5/052066.

Pugliese, F., M. G. M. Hunink, K. Gruszczynska, F. Alberghina, R. Malago, N. van Pelt, N. R. Mollet, F. Cademartiri, A. C. Weustink, W. B. Meijboom, C. L. M. Witteman, P. J. de Feyter, and G. P. Krestin. 2009. "Learning curve for coronary CT angiography: What constitutes sufficient training?" *Radiology* 251 (2): 359–368. doi: 10.1148/radiol.2512080384.

Qin, Y. L., Y. Gu, H. Zheng, M. J. Chen, J. Yang, and Y. M. Zhu. 2020. "Airwaynet-Se: A simple-yet-effective approach to improve airway segmentation using context scale fusion." *2020 IEEE 17th International Symposium on Biomedical Imaging (Isbi 2020)*: 809–813.

Roberts, D. A., Yaida, S., and Hanin, B. 2022. *The Principles of Deep Learning Theory*. Cambridge, MA: Cambridge University Press.

Ronneberger, O., P. Fischer, and T. Brox. 2015. "U-Net: Convolutional networks for biomedical image segmentation." *Medical Image Computing and Computer-Assisted Intervention, Pt Iii* 9351: 234–241. doi: 10.1007/978-3-319-24574-4_28.

Saeed, M., T. A. Van, R. Krug, S. W. Hetts, and M. W. Wilson. 2015. "Cardiac MR imaging: Current status and future direction." *Cardiovascular Diagnosis and Therapy* 5 (4): 290–310. doi: 10.3978/j.issn.2223-3652.2015.06.07.

Saur, S. C., H. Alkadhi, P. Stolzmann, S. Baumuller, S. Leschka, H. Scheffel, L. Desbiolles, T. J. Fuchs, G. Szekely, and P. C. Cattin. 2010. "Effect of reader experience on variability, evaluation time and accuracy of coronary plaque detection with computed tomography coronary angiography." *European Radiology* 20 (7): 1599–1606. doi: 10.1007/s00330-009-1709-7.

Schneider, C. A., W. S. Rasband, and K. W. Eliceiri. 2012. "NIH image to imageJ: 25 years of image analysis." *Nat Methods* 9 (7): 671–675. doi: 10.1038/nmeth.2089.

Selvaraju, R. R., M. Cogswell, A. Das, R. Vedantam, D. Parikh, and D. Batra. 2020. "Grad-CAM: Visual explanations from deep networks via gradient-based localization." *International Journal of Computer Vision* 128 (2): 336–359. doi: 10.1007/s11263-019-01228-7.

Senior, R., M. Monaghan, H. Becher, J. Mayet, and P. Nihoyannopoulos. 2005. "Stress echocardiography for the diagnosis and risk stratification of patients with suspected or known coronary artery disease: A critical appraisal. Supported by the British Society of Echocardiography." *Heart* 91 (4): 427–436. doi: 10.1136/hrt.2004.044396.

Shen, Y., Z. J. Fang, Y. B. Gao, N. X. Xiong, C. S. Zhong, and X. H. Tang. 2019. "Coronary arteries segmentation based on 3D FCN with attention gate and level set function." *IEEE Access* 7: 42826–42835. doi: 10.1109/Access.2019.2908039.

Sinha, P., M. Tuteja, and S. Saxena. 2020. "Medical image segmentation: Hard and soft computing approaches." *Sn Applied Sciences* 2 (2). doi: 10.1007/s42452-020-1956-4.

Vinogradova, K., A. Dibrov, and G. Myers. 2020. "Towards interpretable semantic segmentation via gradient-weighted class activation mapping." *Thirty-Fourth Aaai Conference on Artificial Intelligence, the Thirty-Second Innovative Applications of Artificial Intelligence Conference and the Tenth Aaai Symposium on Educational Advances in Artificial Intelligence* 34: 13943–13944.

Wallis, A., N. Manghat, and M. Hamilton. 2012. "The role of coronary CT in the assessment and diagnosis of patients with chest pain." *Clinical Medicine* 12 (3): 222–229. doi: DOI 10.7861/clinmedicine.12–3–222.

Wolterink, J. M., T. Leiner, and I. Išgum. 2019. *Graph Convolutional Networks for Coronary Artery Segmentation in Cardiac CT Angiography*. Cham: Springer International Publishing.

Yu, F., and V. Koltun. 2015. "Multi-scale context aggregation by dilated convolutions." *arXiv preprint arXiv:1511.07122*. pp. 1–13.

Yun, J., J. Park, D. Yu, J. Yi, M. Lee, H. J. Park, J. G. Lee, J. B. Seo, and N. Kim. 2019. "Improvement of fully automated airway segmentation on volumetric computed tomographic images using a 2.5 dimensional convolutional neural net." *Medical Image Analysis* 51: 13–20. doi: 10.1016/j.media.2018.10.006.

Zheng, H., Y. Qin, Y. Gu, F. Xie, J. Yang, J. Sun, and G. Z. Yang. 2021. "Alleviating class-wise gradient imbalance for pulmonary airway segmentation." *IEEE Transactions on Medical Imaging* 40 (9): 2452–2462. doi: 10.1109/TMI.2021.3078828.

Zhou, K., N. Chen, X. Y. Xu, Z. H. Wang, J. X. Guo, L. X. Liu, and Z. Yi. 2021. "Automatic airway tree segmentation based on multi-scale context information." *International Journal of Computer Assisted Radiology and Surgery* 16 (2): 219–230. doi: 10.1007/s11548-020-02293-x.

6 Interpretability of Segmentation and Overall Survival for Brain Tumors

Rupal Kapdi, Snehal Rajput, Mohendra Roy, and Mehul S Raval

Contents

6.1 Introduction

Tumor detection is crucial in the medical domain, as tumors are one of the leading causes of cancer-related death. Early diagnosis helps medical professionals plan treatment and decision-making to improve a patient's life expectancy. It is even more complex for brain tumors, where overall survival (OS) prediction depends on the correct identification of tumor cells and their segmentation in magnetic resonance imaging (MRI) images (Fathi Kazerooni et al., 2022). Among all brain tumor types, glioblastoma multiforme (GBM), often known as glioblastoma, is the most commonly diagnosed brain tumor (Hanif et al., 2017, Ostrom et al., 2021). The World Health Organization (WHO) has classified it as a Type-4 tumor, the most aggressive tumor, due to its infiltrative and diffusive nature (Rindi et al., 2018). According to a 2021 Central Brain Tumor Registry of the United States (CBTRUS) report, a total

DOI: 10.1201/9781003333425-6

of 83,029 deaths occurred due to it between 2014 and 2018 in the United States alone (Ostrom et al., 2021).

In the last decade, artificial intelligence (AI) methods like deep neural networks (DNN)s have shown the potential to solve complex real-world problems with ground-breaking performance. If employed diligently, they can provide a solution to a wide range of real-time problems. To modulate these DNNs, we need to turn these black-box models into white-box models. DNNs help process massive amounts of data and do pattern recognition and decision making. There are four main reasons contributing to its success: 1) automatic feature learning, 2) faster process with parallel and distributed computing, 3) efficient optimization techniques for robust learning, and 4) availability of benchmark datasets for training and validation (Agravat and Raval, 2021). Obtaining the tagged dataset is the most important step for DNN. The dataset is first made available, then split into training and validation sets using the necessary preprocessing methods for the task at hand. The DNN forces itself to learn the parameters when applied to the training data. The DNN evaluation over test data gauges the effectiveness of the model.

Predicting postoperative patients' survival days can significantly help medical practitioners with treatment planning and decision making. OS prediction deals with predicting survival days of brain tumor patients using handcrafted features or DNN features extracted from segmentation results and input images. Interpretation of OS predictions deals with finding these features' contribution to survival prediction.

Recent advances in tumor segmentation methods show the use of 2D, 3D, or hybrid U-Net DNNs. U-Net performance is further improved by assembling attention blocks (Marti Asenjo et al., 2020), residual connections between layers (Myronenko, 2018), and dense connections between layers of the network (Agravat and Raval, 2019a, 2019b; McKinley et al., 2018). In the Brain Tumor Segmentation Challenge (BraTS–2020) (Menze et al., 2014; Bakas et al., 2017; Bakas et al., 2018), an improvised version of the "no-new network" model with variation in preprocessing and input patches was proposed in (Isensee et al., 2020). Most end-to-end DNNs are capable of generating results matching human limits. However, they have a highly complex structure and many parameters. The DNN results on image segmentation or analysis are not human understandable. A similar nuance is found in OS prediction, where various complex machine learning (ML) models are used to predict patients' survival days. It works as a black box and creates massive friction between the reliability and high performance of DNNs.

The internal functioning cannot be known/identified and may be needed to accept the final output without justification. Consider a critical example of a brain tumor, where the abnormal tumor area does not appear clearly in the medical image in its initial stage. However, suppose the power of a DNN is used to identify such an area in its early stage. In that case, it could help the radiologist to locate the tumor. Such decision-making models are used by doctors only if they can understand and interpret the models' informative decisions. Interpretability of such black boxes is highly desirable for their wide acceptance in the medical field, where such random algorithm behavior is unacceptable. Therefore, increasing the interpretability of deep learning techniques is crucial for deploying these models in real-world domains.

The chapter focuses on the interpretability and explainability of ML models to visualize their internal workings and understand how these complex models make decisions to segment brain tumors accurately. This can help enhance the ML model's performance, which not only helps increase the patient's survivability and improves the efficiency of treatment but also helps in the continuous health monitoring process. It can also help the experts generate reproducible segmentation results and decide to what extent they can leverage it, which will not be subjective. Furthermore, interpretability enables us to understand the patterns learned by the model and authenticate if they are consistent with the domain knowledge of medical specialists. It increases end-user faith and reliability in the model's decisions. In summary, for a robust AI-based medical system, accountability of these powerful DNN models is a must, which led to the surge in interpretability domain research. Figure 6.1 depicts the significant growth of contributions in eXplainable AI (XAI) and the interpretability domain in the recent decade.

There is increasing research on XAI, with increasing usage in medicine. Some 2D and 3D models for brain tumor segmentation approaches are as follows. Saleem et al. (2021) used a saliency map for 3D visualization generated through the weighted sum of the product between the activation map and predicted weights of the segmentation. Natekar et al. (2020) used various methods for 2D visualization, such as a saliency map, Grad-CAM, and activation maximization, which validated measuring the model's uncertainty. The authors show the resemblance between human and network learning. Like humans, networks also learn global features first and then local features. Likewise, for interpreting the OS model, Charlton et al. (2021) used various model-agnostic methods such as Bayesian rule lists (BRLs), Shapley additive explanations (SHAPs), and local interpretable model-agnostic explanations (LIMEs). Rule lists are intuitively interpretable methods, including a series of if-else

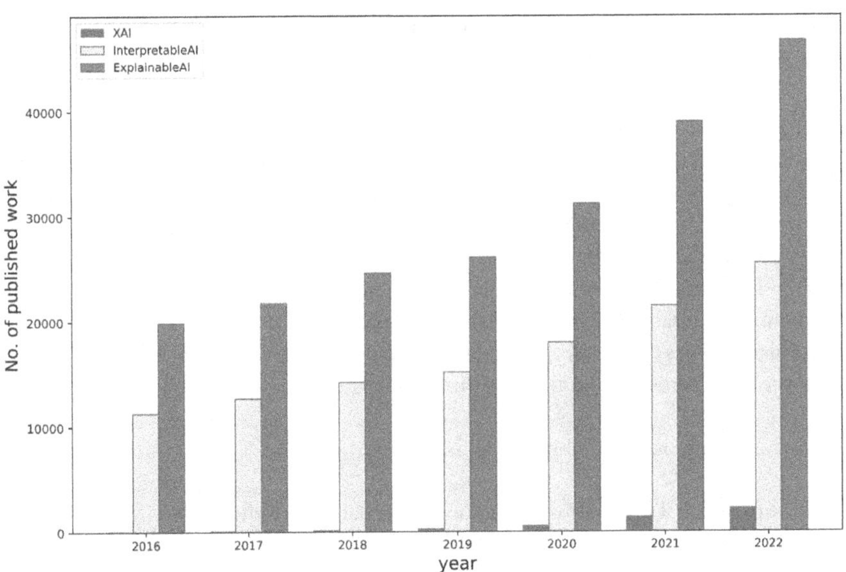

Figure 6.1 A trend in the total number of publications in the domain of XAI.

statements. In contrast, SHAP and LIME are called post-hoc methods applied to the trained model to understand features' local and global impact on survival prediction. The rest of the chapter is organized as follows: Section 6.2 introduces XAI, Section 6.3 focuses on XAI models for brain tumor segmentation and OS, and Section 6.4 concludes the chapter with future work.

6.2 Interpretability of ML Models

The lack of trust in black-box models can be a roadblock preventing their deployment in many real-world applications, particularly critical ones such as medical diagnosis. Responsible artificial intelligence systems play an essential role where moral principles and human values are involved (Platt, 2020; Molnar et al., 2019). Such systems not only give additional features to AI systems but also take responsibility as intelligent systems. Responsible AI systems are built on three crucial pillars. First and foremost, society as a whole needs to be ready to accept responsibility for the effects of AI. This implies that researchers and developers should receive training to help them understand their obligations when it comes to the creation of AI systems that have an immediate influence on society. Second, responsible AI emphasizes the requirement for methods that allow AI systems to consider and behave ethically and follow human values. This implies that algorithms and models should reflect, justify, and make decisions based on human values. They must defend their choices in light of how they will affect those ideals. Current (deep-learning) algorithms are unable to meaningfully connect choices to inputs. As a result, they are unable to provide adequate justification for their actions. The third is participation; to create ethical AI frameworks, it is important to comprehend how many individuals across cultures interact with and live with AI technologies. AI must be considered a component of socio-technical connections because it does not stand alone (Dignum, 2017). The second pillar of responsible AI is the focus on interpretability (Lipton, 2018). The motivation for interpretability includes:

1. Trust: This is simply the confidence that a model will perform well.
2. Causality: Any correlation that supervised models find might not always be causal. Unobserved causes may always be in charge of two related variables. However, supervised learning models' interpretations can produce hypotheses that researchers could evaluate through experimentation.
3. Transferability: the model is expected to generalize and transfer learning skills to unfamiliar situations where the environment is not stationary.
4. Informativeness: provide helpful evidence and assist human decision-makers without focusing on the model's inner workings.

Properties of any interpretable model include:

1. Transparency: This deals with the understandability of the entire model (simulatability), of all the components (decomposability), and training of the algorithm (algorithmic transparency).
2. Post-hoc interpretability: This consists of explanations that need not explain the exact process by which models work. It gives natural language explanations,

visualizations of learned models, and explanations by example (similarity with other examples). One advantage of this concept of interpretability is that we can interpret opaque models after the fact without sacrificing predictive performance.

The first step towards interpretable machine learning models for image processing is understanding the higher-level feature representation used by black-box models. To make it possible, we may need to encourage the models to learn feature representations that are intuitive and translatable to the human user. Uncovering and understanding the "hidden" feature representation of images learned by neural networks is a vital first step toward trustworthiness, interpretability, and subsequently explainability.

Interpretable models are explainable by default since the explanations can be immediately derived from the underlying model design. The explainability of DNNs must not be misleading, incomplete, or biased. True explainability – with foolproof and meticulous explanations – of black-box deep learning models is a non-trivial task (Platt, 2020). Researchers may argue that some insight is more desirable than none. However, we must be careful about how we interpret and use that insight. According to this distinction, interpretability is a subterm of the more general phrase of explainability and is equal to the word "transparency." Simple models with intrinsic transparency, such as rule-based learning, K-nearest neighbor, and decision trees, allow for direct observation of the decision boundaries by humans. Deep learning's weights and nonlinear activations are opaque, making it impossible to immediately interpret them as human knowledge.

The objectives of enhancing explainability are expressed by other often-used concepts in XAI, such as "trustworthiness," "reliability," and "transferability." Among these, explainability's primary goal is trustworthiness, with the latter being a required but not sufficient condition of trustworthiness. High performance and reproducibility are further prerequisites for acquiring total end-user trust.

The absence of innovative laws, understanding, and knowledge resulting from the application of deep learning algorithms in healthcare is one of the main complaints about this technology. Furthermore, if a deep learning model cannot be explained, it may be vulnerable to malevolent manipulation. To avoid any potential ethical problems, certain radiogenomic research chooses to focus only on manually created features and basic models like linear regression and decision trees because, despite possibly having superior performance, deeper models are thought to be more difficult to explain than their shallower equivalents. If deep learning is not used, the healthcare system will forfeit the potential high performance it can provide if the interpretability issue is solved (Liu and Hu, 2022).

6.2.1 Interpretability Characterization Criteria

Interpretability techniques can be characterized by criteria, as shown in Figure 6.2.

- Global or local: Global techniques describe the overall behavior of the model, whereas local techniques describe specific predictions. Local attention visualizations and global rule extraction (RE) techniques are two examples.

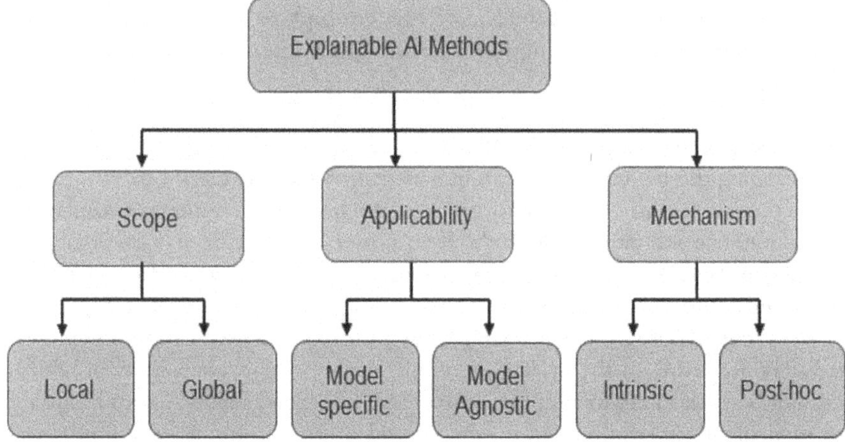

Figure 6.2 Ontology of explainable AI.

- Model-specific and model-agnostic methods: Any ML model can be utilized with model-specific or model-agnostic models after the model has been trained. The feature input and output pairs are often examined by these agnostic algorithms to function. Examining the core model parameters can help to clarify why model-specific approaches are restricted to particular model classes. Examples include model-specific methods like NeuroRule (Lu et al., 2017), which are exclusively effective for deciphering ANNs.
- Intrinsic (in-hoc) or post-hoc: Post-hoc explanation techniques and intrinsic explanation methods can both be classified as explanation methods depending on how the explainers are used. Once a prediction has been made, the AI system is then subjected to post-hoc procedures. In situations where the explanation is integrated within the AI system, such methods are typically opaque black boxes. Explanatory techniques could be intrinsic or in-hoc, for instance, computing attention weights through the intermediary layers of a neural network.
- Four main groups of interpretability techniques are:

6.2.1.1 Global and Model-Agnostic Methods

No matter how complicated, model-agnostic tools can be used on any machine learning model. These agnostic methods usually work by analyzing feature input and target output pairs. Furthermore, the interpretation method, which explains the entire model behavior, falls under global methods. It attempts to explain the crucial features and quantify their importance and how they interact and impact the target. Some of these methods are as follows:

1. Partial dependency plot (PDP) (Molnar et al., 2020) shows how changes in observable feature(s) affect the prediction of the target feature. If the observed

feature is essential, higher modulation of its value will affect the predicted value of the target variable more. If it is less important, its impact on the predicted target will be marginal. The supposition of feature independence is the most problematic aspect of PDPs. The assumption is that the feature(s) for which the partial dependence is computed is unrelated to other features.

2. Accumulated local effects (ALE) (Molnar et al., 2020) resolves the problem of PDP plots, where it uses the difference in predictions rather than the average value. It reduces the effect of correlated feature values.
3. Functional decomposition (Molnar et al., 2019) measures the complexity of the model through the decomposition of complex predictor functions into multiple simple functions. It measures any complex function through rubrics, like how complex a model is?, What is the interaction strength among the features? How many numbers of features are used?
4. Feature interaction, also called the H-statistic (Molnar et al., 2020), measures the joint effect of two features. The interaction between the two features is the variation in the prediction that occurs when the features are varied after the individual feature effects are taken into account.
5. Permutation feature importance (Scikit-Learn Developers (BSD License), 2007) is measured by the increase in the model's prediction error after we permute the feature's values. A feature is "essential" if changing its values tends to increase model error because the model depends on the feature for prediction in this case. A feature is "insignificant" if changing its values results in the same model error because the model overlooked the feature for the prediction. Mathematically, feature importance *(I)* for feature *j* of the input dataset *(D)* can be defined per Eq. 6.1:

$$I = S - \frac{1}{K}\sum_{k=1}^{K} s_{k,j} \tag{6.1}$$

   where ***S*** is a score of the model, ***K*** is the number of repetitions for shuffling data of the feature *j*, and $s_{k,j}$ is the score for the corrupt dataset for feature *j*.
6. Global surrogate model: Here, another surrogate model is trained and replaced with the black box model with the condition that it approximates the prediction function well and should be interpretable (like linear regression, decision tree). The main advantage is that it is easy to quantify how well it approximates the black-box model; at the same time, it is difficult to decide the threshold value to categorize the model as a well-generalized surrogate model (Elshawi et al., 2019).

6.2.1.2 *Global and Model-Specific Methods*

Model-specific methods are intrinsically interpretable by design. No post-processing of these models is needed to look into the working of these models. Global means it explains the holistic behavior of the model. Traditional ML models like decision tree (DT), linear regression (LR), KNN, naïve Bayes, rulefit, feature importance – XGBoost, random forest, and neural networks are such methods.

1. Feature weights using a neural network (NN) (Zeng and Martinez, 2004): This method weights a feature based on the strengths (weights) of links in the neural network, with a vital feature typically connected to strong links and having a more significant influence on the outputs. Feature weight *(F)* for an input node is calculated per Eq. 6.2:

$$F_i = \sum_{j=1}^{h} \sum_{l=1}^{k} Y_{i,j} \times Y_{j,k} \tag{6.2}$$

   where F_i is the feature weight for input node *(i)*, h, k is the hidden and output node, $Y_{i,j}$ is the weight of the link connecting input with hidden node, and $Y_{j,k}$ is the weight of the link connecting to the hidden output node.
2. NN layer visualization: Visualizing the filters in a trained deep neural network can help explain how the model works. We can visualize the filters from any layer of DNN. It may include a plot with multiple images, one for each channel, or compress all images down to a single image.

Similarly, visualizing a feature map (activation map) from different layer(s) can help us to understand where the model emphasizes an image. Figures 6.3(a) and (b) show the original image and feature map from the first layers, which shows the model learns general features initially. In contrast, later layers learn more refined or detailed features [shown in Figures 6.3(c–f)]. The initial layers feature contains brain images that can be easily visualized by looking at them. In contrast, deeper features extracted from the fifth block cannot be easily correlated with human understanding of fine features.

6.2.1.3 *Local and Model-Specific Methods*

1. Saliency maps (Simonyan et al., 2013) are defined as a method of visualizing the class learned by the DNN model. Specifically, given an image (*I*), desirable class (*C*), and trained DNN model, this method generates and image (*I*), which shows the presence of the given class. Mathematically, it can be defined as shown in Eq. 6.3:

$$S_c - \lambda \left\| I' \right\|_2^2 \tag{6.3}$$

where λ is the regularization parameter, and I is the locally optimized image found through back-propagating the gradient score of any class of interest (S_c) in a given image (*I*) obtained through the classification layer of the model. Here, the score is a highly nonlinear function, and hence the gradient is used to approximate the score after applying the Taylor expansion, as shown in Eq. 6.4.

$S_c(I) \approx w^T I + B$ where w is the derivative of score with regard to image I at point I_0 Moreover, it is defined as:

$$w = \frac{\partial S_c}{\partial I} \mid I_0 \tag{6.4}$$

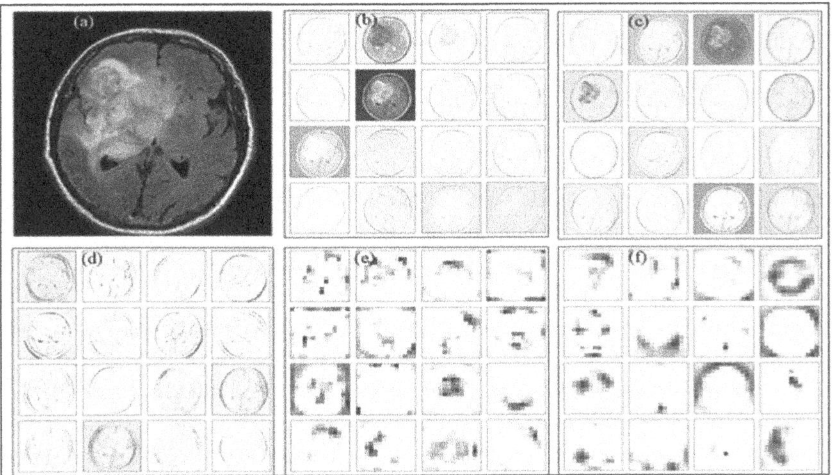

Figure 6.3 Visualization of the (a) original image and activation maps from the (b) first, (c) second, (d) fifth, (e) fifteenth, and (f) sixteenth block of the U-Net model.

2. DeconvNet (Zeiler and Fergus, 2014): The notion is to unravel the CNN propagating reversely to the image using DeconvNet, which is attached to each layer. To investigate a specific activation map, we turn off all other activations in the layer and feed the feature maps into the attached DeconvNet layer. Then we 1) unpool, 2) rectify (using Relu), and 3) filter to regenerate the activation map. This process is repeated until the input pixel space is attained. Here, gradient visualization is highly detailed but lacks class discriminative ability (Selvaraju et al., 2017).
3. Gradient-based methods: these include gradient-weighted class activation map (Grad-CAM) (Simonyan et al., 2013), guided Grad-CAM (G-CAM) (Selvaraju et al., 2017), guided attention inference network (GAIN) (Li et al., 2019), and high-resolution class activation mapping (HiResCAM) (Draelos and Carin, 2020). Grad-CAM is a method that tells where the model is looking while making the decision. It is a generalization of the class activation mapping (CAM) method, which requires particular CNN architecture. CAM necessitates a design that employs global average pooling (GAP) on the final feature maps, followed by a single fully connected layer that generates predictions. Unlike CAM, Grad-CAM does not need any specific layer architecture. When an image is fed into a trained network, G-CAM generates a heatmap for a specific class of interest using three steps: 1) calculating the output gradient for specific class with regard to N feature maps, 2) global average pooling (GAP) over the gradients to obtain class weights on the activation maps, and 3) generating a heatmap (H^{c}_{map}) averaging weighted activation maps. The procedure can be defined as shown in Eqs. 6.5 and 6.6:

$$\alpha_k^c = \left(\frac{1}{Z} \sum_i \sum_j \frac{\partial Y^c}{A_{ij}^k} \right) \tag{6.5}$$

$$H_{map}^c = ReLU\left(\sum_k \alpha_k^c A^k \right) \tag{6.6}$$

where Y^c is the score of c class, A is the activation map with width i and height j, and α_k^c is neuron importance weights. While Grad-CAM discriminates between classes well and identifies relevant image regions, it fails to highlight fine-grained details like guided backpropagation (Springenberg et al., 2014) and deconvolution (Zeiler and Fergus, 2014). At the same time, guided Grad-CAM incorporates the best aspects of Grad-CAM and guided backpropagation. Li et al. (2019) proposed an attention-based mechanism to explain the decision of the DNN model. This end-to-end method helps to learn target-specific tasks and attention maps which can help further improve performance. Further, Draelos and Carin (2020) proposed the HiResCAM method to highlight only those locations of the image the model used for prediction. The Grad-CAM method fails to ensure localization because of averaging effect of gradients.

4. Occlusion sensitivity maps (Zeiler and Fergus, 2014): This method helps to visualize what part of the input image affects the output classification result. The basic working of this method is to hide some portion of an image and see how it affects the decision of the DNN output result while backpropagating gradients. The confidence measure is used to quantify the performance of the model. Occurring of the crucial part of the image will downgrade the confidence measure, which testifies to its significance in classifying a particular class as output.

6.2.1.4 *Local and Model-Agnostic Methods*

Various local explanation methods which do not have access to the internal structure of the model use post-hoc explanation to approximate the behavior of a black box with the help of relationship between feature values and the predictions. Various such methods are as follows:

1. Individual conditional expectation (ICE) (Goldstein et al., 2015): ICE plots disintegrate the visual output of PDPs. This shows the dependence of the target feature on input features sample-wise. PDP shows the average behavior of features on the target feature, which shows global behavior, whereas ICE plots each instance. ICE can show the complex interaction between input and response features, whereas PDP averages out such complex behavior.
2. Local interpretable model-agnostic explanations (Ribeiro et al., 2016): This is a method to explain individual prediction from the black box by replacing it with an interpretable surrogate model. The surrogate model was trained to approximate the black box predictor function. The internal function is that it generates a new perturbed dataset and replaces the black-box model *(F)* with an explainable one *(G)*. Mathematically local interpretable model for a sample x can be defined per Eq. 6.7:

$$\varphi(x) = argarg\, L(F, G, \pi_x) + \omega_x \tag{6.7}$$

where $g \in G$ (interpretable model), ω_x is the complexity of model g (should be low), f is the black-box model, and $\neq_x$ is the proximity measure between the instance and x.

3. Anchors (Ribeiro et al., 2018): This method uses decision rules to explain individual predictions of the model. The decision rules consist of if-else statements called anchors that justify the decision taken for a particular prediction. In other words, for instances where the anchor holds, the prediction is (almost) always the same. The main advantage of this method is that it is easy to interpret and has high precision when compared to other model agnostic methods. Ribeiro et al. (2018) showed the applicability of anchor methods on diverse models and datasets.
4. Shapley additive explanations (Lundberg and Lee, 2017): This method assigns weight values that signify feature importance in individual predictions. It calculates the Shapley value for each feature, which signifies its contribution to the overall prediction of the target value. The Shapley value of a specific feature is calculated by looking at all the feature combinations with or without the feature of interest.

6.2.2 Interpretable and Explainable Models

In the medical domain, models are trained to address different tasks. In Gaur et al. (2022), the authors used a system composed of a restricted Boltzmann machine (RBM) for unsupervised feature learning and a random forest classifier (RFC) to jointly consider existing correlations between imaging data, features, and target variables. The system enhances the interpretability of automatically extracted features. Global interpretation helped to correctly understand the relevant relationships in data, and local interpretation focused on voxel- and patient-level predictions. The structure of ECG signals depends on the waveform features' relationship to arrive at a diagnosis. This 1D layer relationship interpretation was proposed in Maweu et al. (2021) with the help of understanding the evolution of learned features across the layers, comparative study of learned features and ECG waveform features, and misclassification of the target class.

The image is modulated by perturbation-based techniques to determine the significance of particular regions, such as an occlusion sensitivity analysis to identify the most important areas for categorization (Zeiler and Fergus, 2014). Using a variational autoencoder (VAE), the authors in Uzunova et al. (2019) replace problematic regions with corresponding healthy tissue (VAE). When optical coherence tomography pictures of the eye are used in different imaging studies, the VAE perturbations are used to identify diseased regions. The pathology included pigment epithelium detachments, intraretinal fluid, subretinal fluid, and an MRI of the brain (pathology consisted of stroke lesions). A VAE produced better pathological localization than straightforward blurring or constant-value perturbations, they also demonstrated.

To create saliency maps, the authors in Zintgraf et al. (2017) employed prediction difference analysis. By measuring the predicted changes for each pixel, a pertinent value was given to each pixel. Textual explanation is a part of XAI. It is generated as output with the help of image captioning (visual explanation) (van der Velden et al., 2022). Much more specific model agnostic methods are explained in the next section, which mainly focuses on semantic segmentation tasks like tumor segmentation.

6.3 Model-Agnostic Methods for Brain Tumor Segmentation

The taught DNN idea can be interpreted by neurons in the network's top layer. However, the upper layer is abstract and difficult for people to see. In contrast, network input is often interpreted. Therefore, something that is both interpretable and indicative of the abstract learned idea at the output layer is required for the input domain (Holzinger et al., 2017).

According to the authors in Jin et al. (2019), there are two ways to interpret glioma images: by analyzing feature properties and by providing examples. In the XAI literature, feature attribution is the most prevalent type of justification. Doctors acknowledged the necessity to comprehend the crucial elements that fit with recognized medical paradigms during a discussion with physicians about their requirements for XAI. Features are displayed along with information about the pathological change types, importance rankings, and image locations. Text descriptions, color maps (or saliency maps), or segmentation maps superimposed on input images can all be used to provide this information. The strategies for generalized feature attributes interpretability are:

1. Input perturbations: Multiple input image perturbations were used to generate a single explanation using LIME (Saleem et al., 2021). Several such repetitive forward passes result in time-consuming image analysis. Therefore, activation maximization can be used as an analysis framework that searches for an input pattern to produce a maximum model response for a specific quantity of interest. The authors in Kumar et al. (2021) used an explanation-driven CNN approach with LIME and SHAP to detect three types of brain tumors.
2. For applications requiring explainable predictions in medical image analysis, gradient-based techniques are most frequently used. Gradients are manipulated using guided backpropagation (Springenberg et al., 2014) and Grad-CAM (Selvaraju et al., 2017) to draw attention to the pixels that make the greatest contributions to the forecast. These approaches, however, are inaccurate when it comes to the whole class coverage and do not work well for locating numerous instances of a class in an image. Explainable learning has also been used to segment brain gliomas (Natekar et al., 2020; Zhou et al., 2016). To identify brain tumors, deep neural networks were used in conjunction with 2D Grad-CAM (Natekar et al., 2020). Due to it being a 2D-only approach, it shares the same drawbacks as earlier classification explanation techniques. By creating 3D heatmaps to illustrate the significance of segmentation output, another method that expands class activation mapping (CAM) (Saleem et al., 2021) was introduced in Zhou

et al. (2016). Despite being incredibly classist, it sacrificed performance for model complexity to make CNN transparent. Without any architecture alteration or performance reduction, NeuroXAI (Lu et al., 2017) was proposed to make the current DL models for brain imaging research interpretable. It contained seven cutting-edge backpropagating XAI techniques that could produce 2D and 3D visual interpretations. It demonstrated promising explanation results to showcase MRI classification and segmentation of brain tumors.

3. Activation-based methods: For a quicker and more understandable classification of a brain tumor into five different classes, the authors in Kumar et al. (2021) used a subtractive spatial lightweight convolutional neural network, which was composed of three processes: subtractive probable pixel normalization model, lightweight CNN, and CAM.
4. Example-based interpretability: This technique provides better contextual information about model learning and facilitates clinician reasoning. No such technique is identified in the literature for classification or segmentation problems of glioma images.

6.3.1 XAI Evaluating Metrics

Interpretability methods can be evaluated at three points (Pereira et al., 2018):

1. Functionality-grounded evaluation: They use a class of validated proxy models or regularizers to evaluate interpretable methods. The proxy models are chosen based on the class of problems (e.g., decision trees). The evaluation focuses only on improving the prediction/classification performance of the naïve model.
2. Human-grounded evaluation: Human-grounded evaluation is most appropriate when one wishes to test more general notions of the quality of an explanation of the model. The approach will depend on the explanation, regardless of its post-hoc interpretation or the correctness of the associated prediction, for example, binary choice – humans are asked to select the better-quality explanations out of two given forward simulations or predictions. Alternatively, humans are given input and explanation and asked to predict correct output, or they are given counterfactual simulation; that is, humans are given input, output, and an explanation and asked to correct the explanation for the desired output.
3. Application-grounded evaluation: This evaluation involves human experiments within an actual application, for example, working with the doctor for disease diagnosis. Here the system must deliver its intended task. In this type of application, high standards of experimental design are desired. It is not an easy evaluation metric, and it directly tests the objective the system is built for; thus, performance for that objective gives strong evidence of success.

The evaluation of current XAI glioma imaging techniques is scant to nonexistent. It's possibly because current XAI research is less concerned with the practical difficulties of implementing XAI in clinical settings and more concerned with exposing the model's predictions and assessing how well the learned model matches doctors'

Table 6.1 Medical Domain Problem and Appropriate Evaluation Metrics

Medical Domain Problem	*Evaluation Metric*
Classification	Accuracy
	Sensitivity or recall
	Specificity
	Precision
	F1-score
	Area under ROC curve (AUC)
Segmentation	Dice score
	Sensitivity
	Specificity
	Precision
	False-positive rate
	False-negative rate

prior knowledge. Investigation into the clinical use of XAI for glioma imaging is only getting started. It has a lot of unresolved problems that need to be investigated.

In addition, different medical imaging tasks use different evaluation metrics depending on the problem. A summary of some of the evaluation metrics is shown in Table 6.1.

6.3.2 OS Prediction Interpretation

The 3D U-Net model (Isensee et al., 2020) is utilized for OS prediction. This model is a robust segmentation model to obtain a segmentation map. Various shapes, locations, and radiomics features are extracted from segmentation and input (only FLAIR MRI scan). The feature selection step follows the feature extraction step, which allows selection from a wider range of available features. The local and global role of features can be explored and visualized with standard PDP and SHAP methods.

6.3.2.1 PDP ISOlate Plots

Various shape, location, and radiomics features from the segmentation map and input images are extracted for OS prediction. Features dimensions are reduced using PI feature importance (Scikit-Learn Developer, 2022) and the Spearman correlation coefficient method. PDP tools visualize the effect of age features across all the features. Figure 6.4 shows the PDP plot for the age feature vs. all the features for OS prediction.

6.3.2.2 SHAP Force Plot

The SHAP force plot helps visualize the features' impact on predicting a particular sample. The baseline value is the average of all predicted values of all the samples. In contrast, the output value is the actual value of the particular sample. As shown in Figure 6.5, the features in dark grey push the predicted value towards a positive value (increase), whereas the features in light grey push the predicted value towards

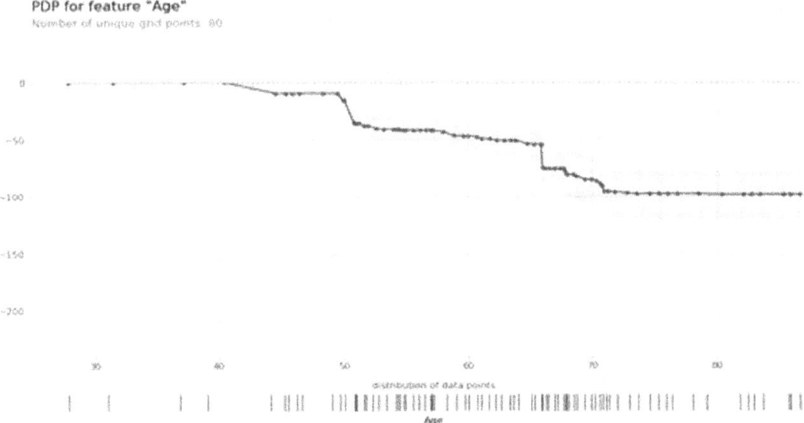

Figure 6.4 PDP plot where *X*-axis shows the distribution of age feature and *Y*-axis shows the average value of age feature with regard to all features.

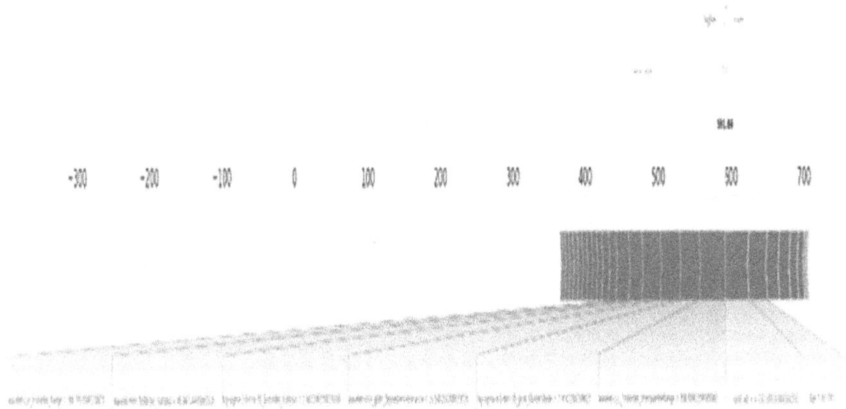

Figure 6.5 SHAP force plot of a single instance. The features in light grey push the predicted value towards a positive value (increase), whereas the features in light grey push the predicted value towards a negative value (decrease). The length of features indicates the magnitude of their impact on particular samples.

a negative value (decrease). The length of features indicates the magnitude of their impact on particular samples. In the SHAP force plot, only those features whose contribution is more significant than 5% of the total contribution are displayed.

6.3.2.3 *SHAP Feature Importance Plot*

The concept behind the importance of SHAP features is straightforward: It is important to have features with high absolute Shapley values. We average the absolute

Shapley values per feature across the data to get the global importance (G_i) (Molnar, 2018):

$$G_i = \frac{1}{n}\sum_{j=1}^{n}\left|\varphi_i^{(j)}\right| \tag{6.8}$$

As shown in Figure 6.6, the SHAP feature importance plot arranges all the features in decreasing order according to their SHAP value to show global impact, where the first feature has maximum contributions to the prediction of the target feature.

The research domain of XAI is in the nascent stage, and it is too early to declare any model a panacea for explainability. Similarly, some of these methods are in the developing stage and yet to confront many dynamic situations dealing with different problems. In the previous sections, we have discussed various methods which have shown significant improvement in seeking a rationale for decision-making while predicting the output. However, some of the methods fail in some cases(s). For example, methods based on perturbation (permutation importance, PDP, and ICE) fail if features are correlated to each other because they draw sample data that is not feasible in reality. Some of the methods take too much time (e.g., SHAP, feature visualization). At the same time, a few of them can be very fragile (Zeiler and Fergus, 2014), where Ghorbani et al. (2019) demonstrated that introducing slight fluctuation to an image yields the exact prediction. However, for the explanation,

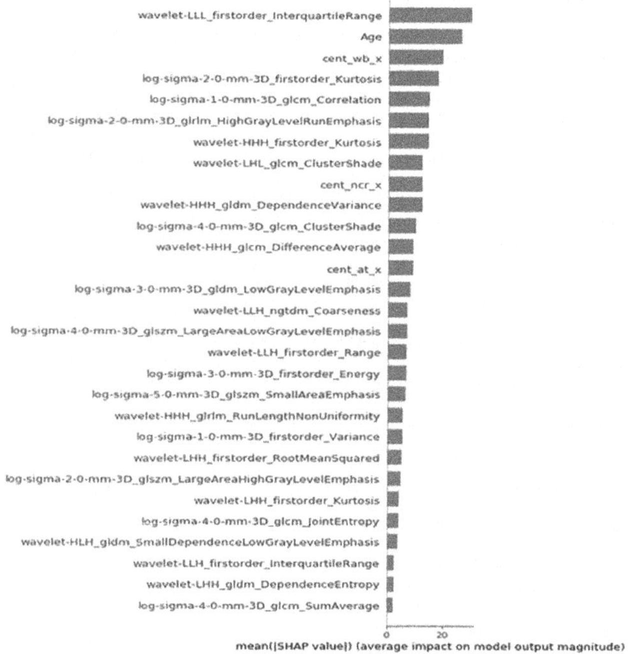

Figure 6.6 SHAP feature importance plot in decreasing order with the SHAP value.

very different pixels are highlighted. Some researchers found a lack of consistency when quantifying these methods' performance (Tomsett et al., 2020).

6.4 Conclusion

AI techniques are widely used to address various medical domain problems using medical images. Implementation of the entire life cycle of the AI model for this domain has various challenges, like 1) availability of training data; 2) model training; 3) evaluation and deployment of the AI model in clinics; 4) safety and privacy issues of data; 5) ethical, financial, and legal barriers in development and distribution of AI models; and 6) clinical acceptance. Clinical acceptance of such methods requires interpretable and explainable AI models to support a transparent decision-making process. The chapter includes various properties of explainability and interpretability along with the approaches of the models to achieve those properties. These approaches are categories in scope, applicability, and mechanism. Various model-agnostic approaches for brain tumor segmentation and OS prediction are summarized in the chapter. In the end, OS prediction of brain tumor patients is demonstrated with PDP and SHAP features analysis. In the future, these interpretable models can be used in many diagnostics and surgery-related tasks and use federated learning for medical data safety. The participation of medical practitioners in designing and developing AI models for better interpretability and explainability is very important.

References

Agravat, Rupal R., and Mehul S. Raval. "A survey and analysis on automated glioma brain tumor segmentation and overall patient survival prediction." *Archives of Computational Methods in Engineering 28*, no. 5 (2021): 4117–4152.

Agravat, Rupal R., and Mehul S. Raval. "Brain tumor segmentation and survival prediction." In *International MICCAI Brainlesion Workshop*, pp. 338–348. Cham: Springer, 2019a.

Agravat, Rupal R., and Mehul S. Raval. "Prediction of overall survival of brain tumor patients." In *TENCON 2019–2019 IEEE Region 10 Conference (TENCON)*, pp. 31–35. New York: IEEE, 2019b.

Bakas, Spyridon, Hamed Akbari, Aristeidis Sotiras, Michel Bilello, Martin Rozycki, Justin S. Kirby, John B. Freymann, Keyvan Farahani, and Christos Davatzikos. "Advancing the cancer genome atlas glioma MRI collections with expert segmentation labels and radiomic features." *Scientific Data 4*, no. 1 (2017): 1–13.

Bakas, Spyridon, Mauricio Reyes, Andras Jakab, Stefan Bauer, Markus Rempfler, Alessandro Crimi, Russell Takeshi Shinohara, et al. "Identifying the best machine learning algorithms for brain tumor segmentation, progression assessment, and overall survival prediction in the BRATS challenge." *arXiv Preprint arXiv:1811.02629* (2018), pp. 1–49.

Charlton, Colleen E., Michael Tin Chung Poon, Paul M. Brennan, and Jacques D. Fleuriot. "Interpretable machine learning classifiers for brain tumour survival prediction." *arXiv Preprint arXiv:2106.09424* (2021), pp. 1–62.

Dignum, Virginia. "Responsible artificial intelligence: Designing AI for human values." *ITU Journal: ICT Discoveries, 1* (2017): 1–8.

Draelos, Rachel Lea, and Lawrence Carin. "Use hirescam instead of grad-cam for faithful explanations of convolutional neural networks." *arXiv e-Prints* (2020): arXiv-2011.

Eleanor Platt, Interpretable and Explainable Deep Learning for Image Processing. *CDT Data Science Blog*, 2020. https://blogs.ed.ac.uk/datasciencecdt/2020/05/13/interpretable-and-explainable-deep-learning-for-image-processing/.

Elshawi, Radwa, Mouaz H. Al-Mallah, and Sherif Sakr. "On the interpretability of machine learning-based model for predicting hypertension." *BMC Medical Informatics and Decision Making 19*, no. 1 (2019): 1–32.

Fathi Kazerooni, Anahita, Sanjay Saxena, Erik Toorens, Danni Tu, Vishnu Bashyam, Hamed Akbari, Elizabeth Mamourian et al. "Clinical measures, radiomics, and genomics offer synergistic value in AI-based prediction of overall survival in patients with glioblastoma." *Scientific Reports 12*, no. 1 (2022): 1–13.

Gaur, Loveleen, Mohan Bhandari, Tanvi Razdan, Saurav Mallik, and Zhongming Zhao. "Explanation-driven deep learning model for prediction of brain tumour status using MRI image data." *Frontiers in Genetics* (2022): 448.

Ghorbani, Amirata, Abubakar Abid, and James Zou. "Interpretation of neural networks is fragile." *Proceedings of the AAAI Conference on Artificial Intelligence 33,* no. 1 (2019): 3681–3688.

Goldstein, Alex, Adam Kapelner, Justin Bleich, and Emil Pitkin. "Peeking inside the black box: Visualizing statistical learning with plots of individual conditional expectation." *Journal of Computational and Graphical Statistics 24*, no. 1 (2015): 44–65.

Hanif, Farina, Kanza Muzaffar, Kahkashan Perveen, Saima M. Malhi, and Shabana U. Simjee. "Glioblastoma multiforme: A review of its epidemiology and pathogenesis through clinical presentation and treatment." *Asian Pacific Journal of Cancer Prevention: APJCP 18*, no. 1 (2017): 3.

Holzinger, Andreas, Chris Biemann, Constantinos S. Pattichis, and Douglas B. Kell. "What do we need to build explainable AI systems for the medical domain?." *arxiv Preprint arXiv:1712.09923* (2017), pp. 1–28.

Isensee, Fabian, Paul F. Jäger, Peter M. Full, Philipp Vollmuth, and Klaus H. Maier-Hein. "nnU-Net for brain tumor segmentation." In *International MICCAI Brainlesion Workshop*, pp. 118–132. Cham: Springer, 2020.

Jin, Weina, Mostafa Fatehi, Kumar Abhishek, Mayur Mallya, Brian Toyota, and Ghassan Hamarneh. "Applying artificial intelligence to glioma imaging: Advances and challenges." *arXiv Preprint arXiv:1911.12886* (2019), pp. 1–31.

Kumar, Ambeshwar, Ramachandran Manikandan, Utku Kose, Deepak Gupta, and Suresh C. Satapathy. "Doctor's dilemma: Evaluating an explainable subtractive spatial lightweight convolutional neural network for brain tumor diagnosis." *ACM Transactions on Multimedia Computing, Communications, and Applications (TOMM) 17*, no. 3 (2021): 1–26.

Li, Kunpeng, Ziyan Wu, Kuan-Chuan Peng, Jan Ernst, and Yun Fu. "Guided attention inference network." *IEEE Transactions on Pattern Analysis and Machine Intelligence 42*, no. 12 (2019): 2996–3010.

Lipton, Zachary C. "The mythos of model interpretability: In machine learning, the concept of interpretability is both important and slippery." *Queue 16*, no. 3 (2018): 31–57.

Liu, Qian, and Pingzhao Hu. "Extendable and explainable deep learning for pan-cancer radiogenomics research." *Current Opinion in Chemical Biology* 66 (2022): 102111.

Lu, Hongjun, Rudy Setiono, and Huan Liu. "Neurorule: A connectionist approach to data mining." *arXiv Preprint arXiv:1701.01358* (2017).

Lundberg, Scott M., and Su-In Lee. "A unified approach to interpreting model predictions." *Advances in Neural Information Processing Systems* 30 (2017): 1–12.

Marti Asenjo, Jaime, and Alfonso Martinez-Larraz Solís. "MRI brain tumor segmentation using a 2D-3D U-net ensemble." In *International MICCAI Brainlesion Workshop*, pp. 354–366. Cham: Springer, 2020.

Maweu, Barbara Mukami, Sagnik Dakshit, Rittika Shamsuddin, and Balakrishnan Prabhakaran. "CEFEs: a CNN explainable framework for ECG signals." *Artificial Intelligence in Medicine* 115 (2021): 102059.

McKinley, Richard, Raphael Meier, and Roland Wiest. "Ensembles of densely-connected CNNs with label-uncertainty for brain tumor segmentation." In *International MICCAI Brainlesion Workshop*, pp. 456–465. Cham: Springer, 2018.

Menze, Bjoern H., Andras Jakab, Stefan Bauer, Jayashree Kalpathy-Cramer, Keyvan Farahani, Justin Kirby, Yuliya Burren, et al. "The multimodal brain tumor image segmentation benchmark (BRATS)." *IEEE Transactions on Medical Imaging 34*, no. 10 (2014): 1993–2024.

Molnar, C. *Interpretable Machine Learning: A Guide for Making Black Box Models Explainable*. Leanpub, 2018.

Molnar, Christoph. *Interpretable Machine Learning*. Lulu. com, 2020. https://leanpub.com/interpretable-machine-learning.

Molnar, Christoph, Giuseppe Casalicchio, and Bernd Bischl. "Quantifying model complexity via functional decomposition for better post-hoc interpretability." In *Joint European Conference on Machine Learning and Knowledge Discovery in Databases*, pp. 193–204. Cham: Springer, 2019.

Myronenko, Andriy. "3D MRI brain tumor segmentation using autoencoder regularization." In *International MICCAI Brainlesion Workshop*, pp. 311–320. Cham: Springer, 2018.

Natekar, Parth, Avinash Kori, and Ganapathy Krishnamurthi. "Demystifying brain tumor segmentation networks: interpretability and uncertainty analysis." *Frontiers in Computational Neuroscience* 14 (2020): 6.

Ostrom, Quinn T., Gino Cioffi, Kristin Waite, Carol Kruchko, and Jill S. Barnholtz-Sloan. "CBTRUS statistical report: primary brain and other central nervous system tumors diagnosed in the United States in 2014–2018." *Neuro-oncology 23*, no. Supl 3 (2021): iii1–iii105.

Pereira, Sérgio, Raphael Meier, Richard McKinley, Roland Wiest, Victor Alves, Carlos A. Silva, and Mauricio Reyes. "Enhancing interpretability of automatically extracted machine learning features: Application to a RBM-random forest system on brain lesion segmentation." *Medical Image Analysis* 44 (2018): 228–244.

Ribeiro, Marco Tulio, Sameer Singh, and Carlos Guestrin. "Anchors: High-precision model-agnostic explanations." *Proceedings of the AAAI Conference on Artificial Intelligence 32*, no. 1 (2018).

Ribeiro, Marco Tulio, Sameer Singh, and Carlos Guestrin. "Why should I trust you?" Explaining the predictions of any classifier." In *Proceedings of the 22nd ACM SIGKDD International Conference on Knowledge Discovery and Data Mining*, California, pp. 1135–1144, 2016.

Rindi, Guido, David S. Klimstra, Behnoush Abedi-Ardekani, Sylvia L. Asa, Frederik T. Bosman, Elisabeth Brambilla, Klaus J. Busam, et al. "A common classification framework for neuroendocrine neoplasms: An International Agency for Research on Cancer (IARC) and World Health Organization (WHO) expert consensus proposal." *Modern Pathology 31*, no. 12 (2018): 1770–1786.

Saleem, Hira, Ahmad Raza Shahid, and Basit Raza. "Visual interpretability in 3D brain tumor segmentation network." *Computers in Biology and Medicine* 133 (2021): 104410.

Scikit-Learn Developers (BSD License). (2007, July 12). 4.2. Permutation feature importance. *Scikit-Learn*. Retrieved July 12, 2022, from https://scikitlearn.org/stable/modules/permutation_importance.html

Selvaraju, Ramprasaath R., Michael Cogswell, Abhishek Das, Ramakrishna Vedantam, Devi Parikh, and Dhruv Batra. "Grad-cam: Visual explanations from deep networks via gradient-based localization." In *Proceedings of the IEEE International Conference on Computer Vision*, Venice, Italy, pp. 618–626, 2017.

Simonyan, Karen, Andrea Vedaldi, and Andrew Zisserman. "Deep inside convolutional networks: Visualising image classification models and saliency maps." *arXiv Preprint arXiv:1312.6034* (2013), pp. 1–8.

Springenberg, Jost Tobias, Alexey Dosovitskiy, Thomas Brox, and Martin Riedmiller. "Striving for simplicity: The all convolutional net." *arXiv Preprint arXiv:1412.6806* (2014), pp. 1–12.

Tomsett, Richard, Dan Harborne, Supriyo Chakraborty, Prudhvi Gurram, and Alun Preece. "Sanity checks for saliency metrics." *Proceedings of the AAAI Conference on Artificial Intelligence 34*, no. 4 (2020): 6021–6029.

Uzunova, Hristina, Jan Ehrhardt, Timo Kepp, and Heinz Handels. "Interpretable explanations of black box classifiers applied on medical images by meaningful perturbations using variational autoencoders." In *Medical Imaging 2019: Image Processing*, vol. 10949, pp. 264–271. Washington, DC: SPIE, 2019.

van der Velden, Bas HM, Hugo J. Kuijf, Kenneth GA Gilhuijs, and Max A. Viergever. "Explainable artificial intelligence (XAI) in deep learning-based medical image analysis." *Medical Image Analysis (*2022): 102470.

Zeiler, Matthew D., and Rob Fergus. "Visualizing and understanding convolutional networks." In *European Conference on Computer Vision*, pp. 818–833. Cham: Springer, 2014.

Zeng, Xinchuan, and Tony R. Martinez. "Feature weighting using neural networks." In *2004 IEEE International Joint Conference on Neural Networks (IEEE Cat. No. 04CH37541)*, vol. 2, pp. 1327–1330. New York: IEEE, 2004.

Zhou, Bolei, Aditya Khosla, Agata Lapedriza, Aude Oliva, and Antonio Torralba. "Learning deep features for discriminative localization." In *Proceedings of the IEEE Conference on Computer Vision and Pattern Recognition*, Las Vegas, NV, pp. 2921–2929. 2016.

Zintgraf, Luisa M., Taco S. Cohen, Tameem Adel, and Max Welling. "Visualizing deep neural network decisions: Prediction difference analysis." *arXiv Preprint arXiv:1702.04595* (2017).

7 Identification of MR Image Biomarkers in Brain Tumor Patients Using Machine Learning and Radiomics Features

Jayendra M. Bhalodiya

Contents

7.1 Introduction

Brain tumors can be benign or malignant. Particularly, gliomas, which originate from glial cells of the brain, may present as low grade (Forst et al., 2014) (stage I and II) or high grade (Nayak and Reardon, 2017) (stage III and IV). Determining the stage during patient diagnosis is of great clinical interest, as they require different surgical treatments. Moreover, tumor diagnosis involves non-invasive and invasive procedures. Non-invasive procedures like magnetic resonance imaging (MRI) and invasive techniques like tissue biopsies are common in practice. However, invasive biopsies are painful to patients and may not be sufficient to thoroughly assess tumor microstructure.

In the literature, as part of tumor diagnosis, researchers have developed various imaging sequences to assess tumor microstructure qualitatively and quantitatively (Nilsson et al., 2018). One such sequence is contrast-enhanced T1-weighted (ceT1) MRI, which shows tumor core structures with higher intensity separately from cystic/

DOI: 10.1201/9781003333425-7

necrotic structures (Padhani, 2002). Another imaging sequence is apparent diffusion coefficient, which has the potential to become a virtual biopsy tool due to its suitability in quantitative assessment (le Bihan, 2013). Such techniques can provide useful biomarkers but may increase patient scanning time to acquire images for each biomarker.

Over time, researchers have adopted data analysis of radiomics features to identify cancer biomarkers, as they provide a number of quantitative measures non-invasively (van Griethuysen et al., 2017; Aerts et al., 2014). Such radiomics features are well-determined image features. Their standardized definitions can be found in an initiative (Zwanenburg et al., 2020). Moreover, researchers developed open-source tools such as pyradiomics to extract radiomics features within tumor microstructure. This posed a new challenge of understanding the biological meaning of image features to validate them and assess their potential as biomarkers (Tomaszewski and Gillies, 2021; Smits, 2021). In literature, researchers addressed such challenges by showing correlation between radiomics and histology features (Bobholz et al., 2020), radiomics and digital pathology slice features (Geady et al., 2020), radiomics and physiologic features in gliomas (Hu et al., 2015), radiomics features and molecular characteristics in glioblastoma (Ellingson, 2015), and a review of radiogenomics studies (Bodalal et al., 2019).

In this chapter, we have systematically shown radiomics feature extraction and their clinical validation using gene expressions to identify MRI-based image biomarkers. We used brain tumor segmentation (BraTS) challenge data (Menze et al., 2015) to acquire MRI scans and associated ground truth. The corresponding gene expression data are collected out of the Cancer Genome Atlas (TCGA) (Tomczak et al., 2015) repository and processed using the TCGA Assembler2 (TA2) tool (Wei et al., 2018). All the data and extraction tools are open access. The identified radiomics features are tested using test-retest experiments, and their validation and biological meaning are elaborated on using Pearson correlation and earlier findings.

This chapter is organized into five sections: (1) "Introduction," (2) "Materials and Methods," (3) "Results," (4) "Discussion," and (5) "Conclusion." The introduction poses the problem statement, summarizes the literature review, and gives a brief about the chapter. The materials and methods section elaborates upon the dataset and methods to address the identified problem. Further, the results section presents image features and genes which are identified in a systematic way. Their significance is further discussed in the discussion section, followed by a conclusion.

7.2 Materials and Methods

7.2.1 Materials

We used 285 glioma patients' MRI data, comprising 210 high-grade glioma (HGG) and 75 low-grade glioma (LGG) patient images. MRI sequences include T1-weighted (T1) and ceT1 MRI. All the patients' data were anonymized. Moreover, we utilized the ground truth of tumor segmentation associated with each MRI. This ground truth is the segmented tumor area. The segmentation of the whole tumor, which consists of the peritumoral edema, tumor core including necrotic/cystic components, and contrast-enhanced tumor core, was used for analysis. Dataset and ground truth are publicly available in the multimodal BraTS data repository (Menze et al., 2015). Multiple institutions contributed anonymized MRI data, and various raters curated and assessed ground truth in the BraTS dataset. Specific data acquisition, curation, and patient characteristics are available in the respective articles (Menze et al., 2015; Bakas et al., 2017; Bakas et al., 2018).

7.2.2 *Methods*

We aim to identify magnetic resonance (MR) image biomarkers to distinguish glioma patients. For that, we performed our procedure in five steps: (1) preprocessing of MRI data, (2) radiomics feature extraction from MR images, (3) identification of top-performing radiomics features in classifying gliomas using random forest, (4) statistical analysis to identify significant radiomics features, and (5) validation of radiomics features using gene expressions to identify potential image biomarkers. These steps are elaborated upon in the methods sections.

7.2.2.1 *Data Preprocessing*

We selected T1 and ceT1 MRI sequences from the BraTS dataset. Images contained 3D brain volumes in neuroimaging informatics technology initiative (NIfTI) standard. MR images were ensured to contain skull-stripped brain images. Moreover, we preprocessed images to have standardized intensity values; that is, each image was normalized to zero-mean unit-variance of intensity values. MR images were registered with their respective ground truth tumor segmentation using NIfTI header information. The segmentation ground truth was available in the dataset. Alternatively, brain tumor segmentation techniques (Bhalodiya et al., 2022; Agravat and Raval, 2021; Agravat and Raval, 2020a, 2020b) can be employed to segment various tumor regions.

7.2.2.2 *Radiomics Feature Extraction from MR Images*

We extracted 214 features in each glioma patient. These included 107 features extracted from each ceT1 and T1 MR sequences. Among these 107 features, there were seven different types: (1) shape features, (2) first-order statistics features, (3) grey-level cooccurrence matrix (GLCM) features, (4) gray-level dependence matrix (GLDM) features, (5) gray-level run length matrix (GLRLM) features, (6) gray-level size zone matrix (GLSZM) features, and (7) neighboring grey tone difference matrix (NGTDM) features. Names of all the calculated features are available in Table 7.1. Extraction was accomplished utilizing an open-source Python library, pyradiomics. No image filters were used while extracting features. Tumor areas in each image were selected using their segmentation mask available in ground truth data files. Image intensities were normalized before extracting radiomics features. Moreover, intensities were interpolated using B-spline. Mathematical definitions and implementation of all features can be found on the GitHub page (PyRadiomics, 2023).

7.2.2.3 *Identification of Top-Performing Radiomics Features in Classifying Gliomas Using Random Forest*

We identified top-performing radiomics features in three steps: (1) feature reduction using correlation coefficient, (2) k-fold cross-validation utilizing random forest

Table 7.1 Names of Radiomics Features Derived and Calculated through MR Images

Shape Features	*First-Order Features*	*GLDM Features*	*GLCM Features*
Elongation	10th percentile	Dependence entropy	Autocorrelation
Flatness	90th percentile	Dependence non-uniformity	Cluster prominence
Least axis length	Energy	Dependence non-uniformity normalized	Cluster shade
Major axis length	Entropy	Dependence variance	Cluster tendency
Maximum 2D diameter column	Interquartile range	GLNU	Contrast
Maximum 2D diameter row	Kurtosis	Gray-level variance	Correlation
Maximum 2D diameter slice	Maximum	HGLE	Difference average
Maximum 3D diameter	Mean absolute deviation	LD emphasis	Difference entropy
Mesh volume	Mean	LD HGLE	Joint entropy
Minor axis length	Median	LGLE	Inverse difference (ID)
Sphericity	Minimum	LD LGLE	ID moment (IDM)
Surface area	Range	SD emphasis	IDM normalized
Surface volume ratio	Robust mean absolute deviation	SD HGLE	ID normalized
Voxel volume	Root mean squared	SD LGLE	Informational measure of correlation (IMC) 1
	Skewness		IMC 2
	Total energy		Inverse variance
	Uniformity		Joint energy
	Variance		Difference variance
			Sum of squares
			Maximal correlation coefficient
			Maximum probability
			Sum average
			Sum entropy
			Joint average

GLRLM features	**GLSZM features**	**NGTDM features**
GLNU	GLNU	Busyness
GLNU normalized	GLNU normalized	Coarseness
GLV	GLV	Complexity
HGL run emphasis	HGL zone emphasis	Contrast
Long run emphasis	Large area emphasis	Strength
Long run HGLE	Large area HGLE	
Long run LGLE	Large area LGLE	
LGL run emphasis	LGL zone emphasis	
Run entropy	Size zone non-uniformity	
Run length non-uniformity	Size zone non-uniformity normalized	
Run length non-uniformity normalized	Small area emphasis	
Run percentage	Small area HGLE	
Run variance	Small area LGLE	
Short run emphasis	Zone entropy	
Short run HGLE	Zone percentage	
Short run LGLE	Zone variance	

Note: LD is large dependence. SD is small dependence. HGLE is high gray-level emphasis. LGLE is low gray-level emphasis. GLNU is gray-level non-uniformity. GLV is gray-level variance. HGL and LGL refer to high and low gray level, respectively.

classifier in distinguishing glioma types, and (3) identifying top-performing radiomics features using MR images.

7.2.2.3.1 FEATURE REDUCTION USING CORRELATION COEFFICIENT

The radiomics feature extraction step provided us with 214 radiomics features per subject. To reduce the number of features, we performed two steps: (1) computed correlation coefficient among features and (2) reduced highly correlated features. We assessed the intraclass correlation coefficient (ICC) within each imaging sequence features set; that is, each T1 and ceT1 MR images features set was tested for ICC. We computed ICC values into four categories: (1) poor correlation, that is, ICC less than 0.5; (2) moderate correlation, that is, ICC between 0.5 (inclusive) and 0.75; (3) good correlation, that is, ICC between 0.75 (inclusive) and 0.9; and (4) excellent correlation, that is, ICC greater than or equal to 0.9. Moreover, we visualized hierarchical feature clusters based on the distance among correlated features. The cluster threshold was 0.7. After visualizing Pearson correlation coefficients and cluster dendrogram, we plotted the Pearson correlation coefficient matrix. Features with a Pearson correlation coefficient > 0.95 were considered highly correlated and were reduced. Visualization plots and the number of reduced features are noted in the "Results" section.

7.2.2.3.2 K-FOLD CROSS-VALIDATION UTILIZING RANDOM FOREST CLASSIFIER IN DISTINGUISHING GLIOMA TYPES

After reducing the number of features, we divided the data subjects into three groups named training data, validation data, and test data. We tested k = 5 and k = 10 for the split. We noted that k = 10 provided better classification accuracy with our data samples. Therefore, we continued our experiments with k = 10. Our dataset contains two types of glioma patients to classify, HGG and LGG. As the data split process was automated, we made sure that in each set, the count of high-grade glioma patients remained at least half of the set population, and the count of low-grade glioma patients was at least one-third of the set population. This condition allowed us to prepare sets with both types of glioma data samples.

After the k-fold split of data samples, we used the training dataset to train a random forest classifier. We assigned 100 to the random forest estimator (decision trees within the forest) count. The maximum depth of the decision trees happens until all leaves have fewer than two samples or the leaves are pure (i.e., same data labels in the data points). All samples had equal weight. Bootstrap samples were used while building the trees rather than all the samples. The class labels were assigned as high-grade glioma to class 1 and low-grade glioma to class 0. All tests were performed using an open-source Python package, scikitlearn, which provides the function RandomForestClassifier for experiments (Pedregosa et al., 2011).

7.2.2.3.3 IDENTIFY TOP-PERFORMING RADIOMICS FEATURES USING MR IMAGES

Using the trained classifier, we noted the feature importance score (Gini importance) (Pedregosa et al., 2011) while predicting class labels. The feature importance score was calculated as the (normalized) aggregate decrease of the measure that the feature contributed during predictions. We sorted features per these score values to identify top-performing 25 features. These scores were computed using the accuracy score metrics implementation in scikitlearn (Pedregosa et al., 2011).

7.2.2.4 *Statistical Analysis to Identify Significant Radiomics Features*

After identifying top-performing 25 features, we again trained the random forest classifier using only these 25 features values from the training dataset. The new classifier was then tested with a validation set and test set to find the prediction accuracy. We statistically assessed the top-performing features. For that, we repeated the k-fold split, classifier training, validation set predictions, and test set predictions 1000 times in an automatic manner. After each repeated test, we noted the top-performing 25 features in each test. At the end of 1000 tests, we short-listed features that were found in more than 95% of repeat tests. These short-listed features are significant features to be considered potential MR image biomarkers. Moreover, we noted the image feature values in each patient to observe the overall value range in this dataset.

7.2.2.5 *Validation of Radiomics Features Using Gene Expressions to Identify Potential Image Biomarkers*

We validated the identified radiomics features in each patient using gene expressions. For that, we used an open-access tool, TA2, to collect genomics data from the TCGA database for each patient. We downloaded genomic data including mRNA expressions for the respective patient IDs using cancer type "GBM" (glioblastoma) or "LGG" (low-grade glioma) and assay platform "gene.normalised_RNAseq", which provided normalized RNA sequence data. The downloaded raw data were processed to calculate gene expressions using TA2. We used the "processRNASeqData()" function of TA2 to calculate gene expressions. After that, gene expression scores were correlated with both tumor types, that is, low- and high-grade glioma. Genes that can distinguish between these two glioma types were noted separately. Moreover, radiomics features and gene expressions were correlated with each other using Python. The Pearson correlation coefficient was measured to estimate the correlation between radiomics features and genes. The correlated genes were further discussed to understand their biological characteristics. Moreover, we discussed genes reported by previous studies. Overall, gene expression correlation and discussion of gene biological characteristics were used to identify potential image biomarkers from the MRI-based radiomics features.

7.3 Results

First, we extracted 214 radiomics features from each patient using pyradiomics. After that, we prepared data frames of radiomics feature values, patient IDs and corresponding glioma types. These data frames were then computationally tested using Python. In particular, intraclass correlation among the radiomics features was calculated within the T1 and ceT1 MRI sequences data frames individually. While calculating the correlation coefficient, the subjects with missing feature values were dropped. We noted that T1 MRI features had moderate intraclass correlation for an average of 2*k* (*k* = number of features) random raters. The value range of ICC2k was 0.6676 (confidence interval: [0.61, 0.72]). Moreover, we show the correlation coefficient among individual features and cluster dendrogram in Figure 7.1.

We noted that the feature set included features with good (≥0.75 and <0.9) and excellent (≥0.9) correlation values. Similarly, we examined the radiomics features of contrast-enhanced T1-weighted MRI. During this assessment, we dropped 27 patients who did not have enhanced tumor cores to extract features. We depict correlation coefficient values and cluster dendrogram for contrast-enhanced T1-weighted MRI features in Figure 7.2.

We noted that ceT1 MRI features had a moderate intraclass correlation for an average of 2*k* (*k* = number of features) random raters. The ICC2k value range was 0.6789 (confidence interval: [0.62, 0.73]). In addition, Figure 7.2 also shows a hierarchical cluster dendrogram of feature correlation.

After the feature correlation shown in Figures 7.1 and 7.2, we reduced highly correlated features with a Pearson correlation value > 0.95 and dropped 49 highly correlated features of T1 MRI. Moreover, 53 highly correlated features of ceT1 MRI were dropped. After that, we combined the remaining features of T1 and ceT1 MRI and examined the combined data frame to reduce highly correlated features. However, no features were found to be dropped from this combined data frame. Overall, we preserved a total of 112 features from both MRI sequences for further analysis.

We assessed radiomics features for glioma classification. For that, we repeated classification tests 1000 times and assessed the results of each test. In each test, we randomly and automatically split the data samples into training, validation, and test datasets per 10-fold cross-validation. Twenty-seven patients were dropped due to contrast region unavailability in the ceT1 MRI. Accordingly, the test set contained 25 patients, the validation set contained 23 patients, and the training set contained 210 patients. The training set was utilized in training a random forest classifier with 100 tree estimators. Each test provided 25 top-performing features and forecast correctness on validation and test sets. Detailed steps are given in the "Methods" section. We analyzed the results of this evaluation and noted the features that were top performing in more than 95% of tests. We noted that the average classification accuracy using top-performing features in the randomly selected validation set was 0.82±0.06 (mean ± standard deviation), and the test set was 0.82±0.06 (mean ± standard deviation). In addition, we found three radiomics features of GLSZM called large area emphasis, large area high gray-level emphasis, and zone variance in T1 MRI were top-performing features in more than 95% of tests. Moreover, we found a first-order statistics feature called range in ceT1 MRI was a top-performing feature in more than 95% of tests.

Validation of radiomics features with gene expressions showed that the four genes postmeiotic segregation increased: (1) 1 homolog 2 pseudogene 2 (PMS2P2), (2) small ubiquitin-like modifier 1 pseudogene 3 (SUMO1P3), (3) TAR DNA binding protein pseudogene (LOC643387), and (4) heterogeneous nuclear ribonucleoprotein

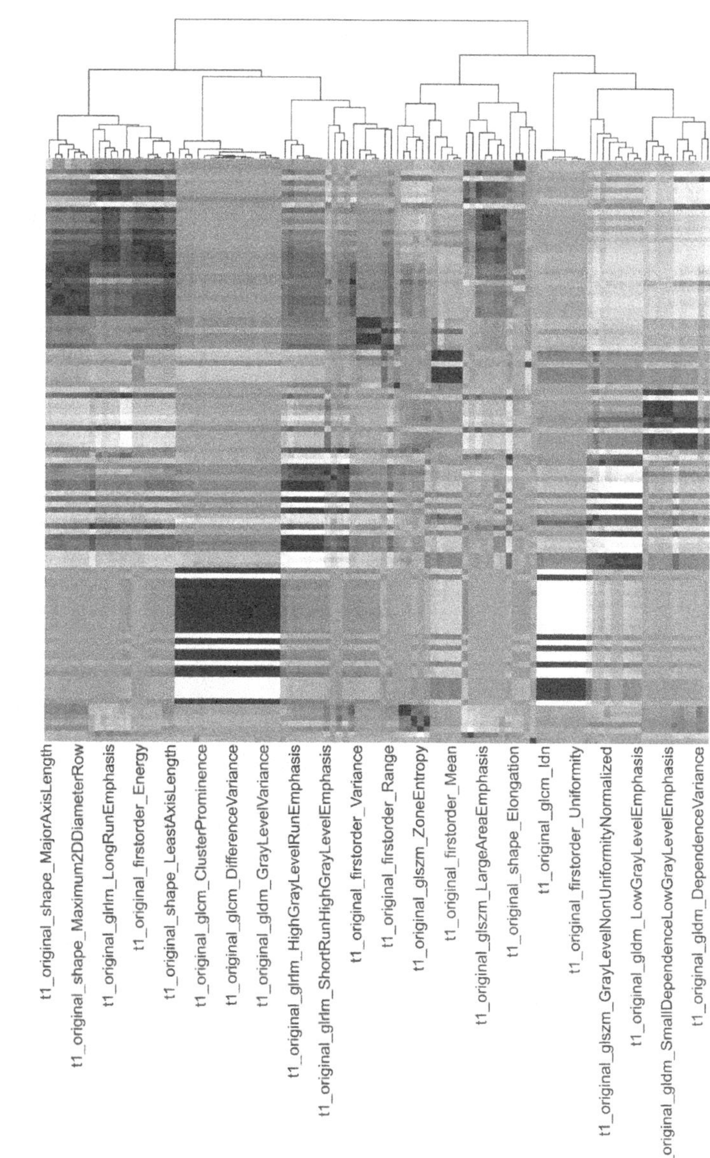

Figure 7.1 Image shows correlation and clusters among radiomics features in T1-weighted MRI. The darker shade shows positive values of the Pearson correlation coefficient, which indicates features with correlation in the same direction. The lighter shade shows negative values, which indicates features with correlation in opposite directions.

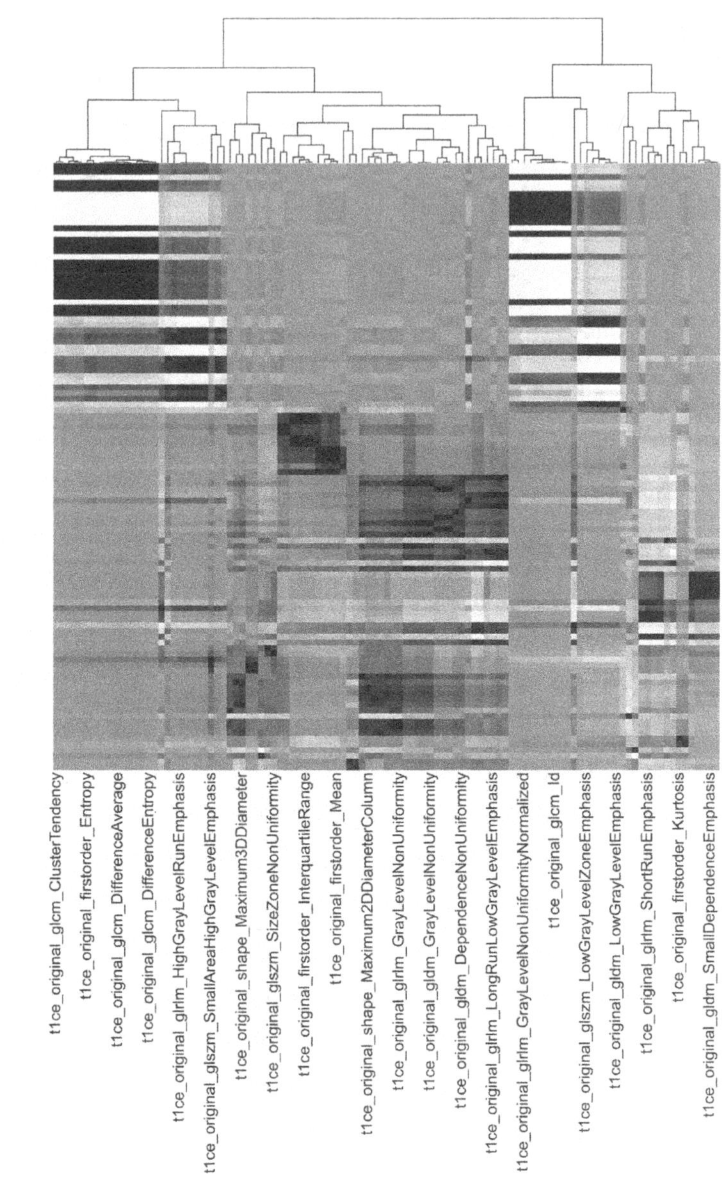

Figure 7.2 Image shows correlation and clusters among radiomics features in contrast-enhanced T1-weighted MRI. The darker and lighter shades show positive and negative values of the Pearson correlation coefficient, respectively. Positive and negative values indicate features with correlation in the same and opposite directions, respectively.

A3 pseudogene 1 (HNRNPA3P1). These genes were correlated the most with tumor types compared to other genes. We presented the *P* values of significant correlation between tumor type and genes and identified features and genes. Here, *P* value refers to the probability of finding greater than or equal to the absolute value of the calculated correlation coefficient using random data samples from the same dataset. In particular, high-grade gliomas were correlated the most with PMS2P2 (correlation coefficient: 0.91, $P < 0.001$) and SUMO1P3 (correlation coefficient: 0.91, $P < 0.001$), and low-grade gliomas were correlated the most with LOC643387 (correlation coefficient: 0.90, $P < 0.001$) and HNRNPA3P1 (correlation coefficient: 0.86, $P < 0.001$). Moreover, the identified significant radiomics features were correlated the most with four gene expressions. In specific, the large area emphasis feature of T1 MRI was correlated the most with ankyrin repeat and SOCS box containing 11 (ASB11) genes (correlation coefficient: 0.80, $P < 0.001$), the large area high gray-level emphasis feature of T1 MRI was correlated the most with the WAP four-disulfide core domain 10A (WFDC10A) gene (correlation coefficient: 0.80, $P < 0.001$), the zone variance feature of T1 MRI was correlated the most with the cocaine and amphetamine-regulated transcript prepropeptide (CARTPT) gene (correlation coefficient: 0.77, $P < 0.001$), and the range feature of contrast-enhanced T1-weighted MRI was correlated the most with the ectonucleoside triphosphate diphosphohydrolase 7 (ENTPD7) gene (correlation coefficient: 0.61, $P < 0.001$). A list of correlated genes corresponding to the radiomics features and tumor type is provided in Tables 7.2 and 7.3.

Moreover, we discuss the gene properties and biological characteristics of genes corresponding to the tumor type and radiomics features in the discussion section to further assess the relevance among image features and genes.

7.4 Discussion

In this chapter, we have shown a step-by-step procedure to identify radiomics features as potential image biomarkers. The aim is to use these biomarkers to distinguish between brain tumor patients with low-grade and high-grade gliomas.

We used T1 and ceT1 MRI sequences as they are routinely used in clinics to diagnose brain tumor patients. NIfTI header information of MRI was used to ensure registration between data files and ground truth segmentation files. All the data

Table 7.2 Tumor Type Correlation with Genes

Tumor Type	*Gene*	*Pearson Correlation Coefficient*	*P-Value*
HGG	PMS2P2	0.91	$P < 0.001$
HGG	SUMO1P3	0.91	$P < 0.001$
LGG	LOC643387	0.90	$P < 0.001$
LGG	HNRNPA3P1	0.86	$P < 0.001$

Note: HGG is high-grade gliomas and LGG is low-grade gliomas.

Table 7.3 Radiomics Features Correlation with Genes

Radiomics Feature	*Gene*	*Pearson Correlation Coefficient*	*P-Value*
LAE of T1wMRI	ASB11	0.80	$P < 0.001$
LAE of T1wMRI	KRTAP4–3	0.76	$P < 0.001$
LAE of T1wMRI	NF1P1	0.76	$P < 0.001$
LAE of T1wMRI	OR2B2	0.76	$P < 0.001$
LAE of T1wMRI	URAD	0.76	$P < 0.001$
LAE of T1wMRI	CRYGB	0.75	$P < 0.001$
LAE of T1wMRI	SLC22A25	0.75	$P < 0.001$
LAE of T1wMRI	UMOD	0.75	$P < 0.001$
Large area high gray-level emphasis of T1wMRI	WFDC10A	0.80	$P < 0.001$
Zone variance of T1wMRI	CARTPT	0.77	$P < 0.001$
Zone variance of T1wMRI	CDX4	0.76	$P < 0.001$
Zone variance of T1wMRI	FSCB	0.76	$P < 0.001$
Range of ceT1wMRI	ENTPD7	0.60	$P < 0.001$

Note: T1wMRI and ceT1wMRI are T1- weighted and contrast-enhanced T1-weighted magnetic resonance imaging, respectively. LAE refers to large area emphasis feature.

samples were anonymized. They were collected from a benchmark framework of brain tumor segmentation challenge to encourage reproducibility of the findings using open-access datasets.

We extracted radiomics features from MR images using Python pyradiomics to encourage open-science practices. Their implementation in Python script, mathematical formulas, feature definition, and relevance to literature for each feature is available as open-access data. Moreover, our extracted features, listed in Section 7.2.2.2 and Table 7.1, are similar to features listed in the standardization initiative of image biomarkers (Zwanenburg et al., 2020). Therefore, the use of these features helps to build on the efforts of non-invasive image biomarkers-based clinical diagnosis. All features were extracted using original intensity values without any filters.

Before beginning the model training and experiments, we evaluated dataset feature correlations using correlation coefficients and hierarchical cluster dendrograms, as elaborated on in Section 7.2.2.3.1 and the corresponding results in Figures 7.1 and 7.2. We categorized the features into four categories based on their correlation values. These results helped us to visualize and identify highly correlated features, which we reduced to have efficient computation and avoid overfitting of our classifier.

We chose a random forest classifier to train our model and predict glioma types because random forest collectively uses multiple decision trees, which provide better classification decisions than an individual decision tree. Particularly when trees of a random forest are built using uncorrelated or minorly correlated features and use features having predictive power, they predict better in a forest than individually. We ensured this by visualizing and reducing highly correlated features, as mentioned in

Section 7.2.2.3.1 and the corresponding results. Subsequently, we identified 25 top-performing features in each test to select features with predictive power, as described in Section 7.2.2.3.3 and the corresponding results. The classifiers built using these top-performing features were trained, validated, and tested using data samples, as described in Section 7.2.2.3.2.

Moreover, random forest allows bagging of features, that is, choosing *n* training samples with repetitions allowed, and allows selecting random features while building individual trees of the forest. Such training facilities help to build classifiers that provide similar performance on different datasets. Therefore, as mentioned in Section 7.2.2.4. and the corresponding results, the random forest helped us to classify glioma types with similar accuracy on the validation set (0.82 ± 0.06) and test set (0.82 ± 0.06) with a minor standard deviation during 1000 repetitive experiments.

After the 1000 repetitive experiments, we noted the top-performing features in more than 95% of tests. Definitions of these features are as follows.

T1 MRI features:

- Large area emphasis: This is a GLSZM feature. It calculates the distribution of larger size areas within the image. A higher value of large area emphasis means a higher number of larger size zones within the image.
- Large area high gray-level emphasis: This is a GLSZM feature. It calculates the joint distribution of bigger areas with greater gray levels.
- Zone variance: Zone variance is a GLSZM feature. It calculates the variance in zone size volumes.

ceT1 MRI features:

- Range: Range is a first-order statistics feature. It means the range of grey values, that is, a maximum minus minimum of grey values within the region of interest.

As shown in Table 7.2, genes correlated the most to the tumor types were PMS2P2 and LOC643387. In the literature, PMS2P2 involvement is reported in the DNA mismatch repair system, and it is noted as a promising gene to modulate the risk of cancer (Caja et al., 2020). Additionally, SUMO1P3, which is also notably correlated with tumor type, is a potential indicator of cell proliferation, migration, and invasion in glioma patients (Lou et al., 2020). Its expression relates to glioma growth, as reported in the literature (Lou et al., 2020). Moreover, SUMO1P3 is a potential biomarker in bladder cancer (Zhan et al., 2016), breast cancer (NA-ER et al., 2021), and gastric cancer (Mei et al., 2013) to identify cancer stage and prognosis. LOC643387 has several functional associations with clinical conditions, including low-grade gliomas, as noted by the Harmonizome (Rouillard et al., 2016). HNRNPA3P1 has a significant correlation with patient survival in cervical cancer, cervical squamous cell carcinoma, and endocervical adenocarcinoma (Ding et al., 2016). Moreover, it is noted as one of the top biomarkers that segregate activated from resting NK cells in bladder cancer patients (Sun et al., 2021). Thus, HNRNPA3P1 has the potential as a biomarker.

Moreover, as shown in Table 7.3, the genes correlated the most to the significant radiomics features are ASB11, WFDC10A, CARTPT, and ENTPD7. ASB11 is used in BIK ubiquitination that determines cell survival. Such blocking of BIK degradation can potentially be used in anti-cancer strategies (Chen et al., 2019). WFDC10A is a protein-coding gene. It belongs to the telomeric cluster in chromosome 20q12-q13. As described in a study (Adam et al., 2019), telomeres can be visualized as high-intensity image features after staining. That could be the probable reason for its high correlation with large area HGLE feature (Table 7.3), as this feature also refers to higher-intensity areas in the image. CART peptides are involved in processes such as body weight, food digestion, reward systems, and the endocrine system (Rogge et al., 2008). CARTPT is detected in many cancer patients (mostly breast cancer), and it is an FDA-approved drug target ("Expression of CARTPT in Cancer – Summary – The Human Protein Atlas" 2022). Moreover, CART immunoreactivity (CART-LI) is detected as a tumor biomarker in neuroendocrine tumor patients (Bech et al., 2008). ENTPD7 is detected in cancer tissues, as reported by the Human Protein Atlas. Moreover, circular RNA generated from ENTPD7 is found as a promoter of cell proliferation in glioblastoma patients (Zhu et al., 2020). In addition, ENTPD5 is identified as a potential target gene for cancer patient treatment (Vogiatzi et al., 2016). Therefore, the correlation of radiomics features with such genes validates their potential for biomarker consideration. However, genes such as caudal type homeobox 4 (CDX4) and fibrous sheath CABYR binding protein (FSCB) have a higher correlation coefficient with radiomics features, but they are not profoundly detected as cancer biomarkers in the literature. Therefore, such genes need further verification before consideration as potential biomarkers.

Image features are emerging biomarkers which can be validated, and their biological meaning can be explained through histology and genomics (Tomaszewski and Gillies, 2021). This chapter selected genomics to explain the features. First, the image features were identified using artificial intelligence and radiomics methods. These image features were used with a random forest classifier to distinguish between LGG and HGG. Further, the biological explanation of these features was established with gene correlation.

7.5 Conclusions

We identified MRI-based image biomarkers using radiomics features and machine learning to aid brain tumor diagnosis. The identified radiomics features were large area emphasis, large area high gray-level emphasis and zone variance in T1 MRI and range in ceT1 MRI. Moreover, these radiomics features were found to significantly correlate with gene expressions of ASB11, WFDC10A, CARTPT, and ENTPD7, and previous studies show that these genes are notable in cancer and tumor studies. Therefore, the identified radiomics features have the potential to be considered image biomarkers.

Acknowledgments

We have presented results using data generated by the TCGA Research Network, which can be accessed at www.cancer.gov/tcga.

References

Adam, Nancy, Erin Degelman, Sophie Briggs, Rima Marie Wazen, Pina Colarusso, Karl Riabowol, and Tara Beattie. 2019. "Telomere Analysis Using 3D Fluorescence Microscopy Suggests Mammalian Telomere Clustering in HTERT-Immortalized Hs68 Fibroblasts." *Communications Biology* (Nature Research) 2 (1). doi: 10.1038/s42003-019-0692-z.

Aerts, Hugo JWL., Emmanuel Rios Velazquez, Ralph TH. Leijenaar, Chintan Parmar, Patrick Grossmann, Sara Carvalho, Johan Bussink, et al., 2014. "Decoding Tumour Phenotype by Noninvasive Imaging Using a Quantitative Radiomics Approach." *Nature Communications* 5 (1): 4006. doi: 10.1038/ncomms5006.

Agravat, Rupal R., and Mehul S. Raval. 2020a. *Brain Tumor Segmentation and Survival Prediction. Lecture Notes in Computer Science (Including Subseries Lecture Notes in Artificial Intelligence and Lecture Notes in Bioinformatics)*, vol. 11992 LNCS. Cham: Springer International Publishing. doi: 10.1007/978-3-030-46640-4_32.

Agravat, Rupal R., and Mehul S. Raval. 2020b. "Brain Tumor Segmentation and Survival Prediction." *Lecture Notes in Computer Science (Including Subseries Lecture Notes in Artificial Intelligence and Lecture Notes in Bioinformatics)* 11992: 338–348. doi: 10.1007/978-3-030-46640-4_32.

Agravat, Rupal R., and Mehul S. Raval. 2021. "3D Semantic Segmentation of Brain Tumor for Overall Survival Prediction." *Lecture Notes in Computer Science (Including Subseries Lecture Notes in Artificial Intelligence and Lecture Notes in Bioinformatics)* 12659: 215–227. doi: 10.1007/978-3-030-72087-2_19.

Bakas, Spyridon, Hamed Akbari, Aristeidis Sotiras, Michel Bilello, Martin Rozycki, Justin S. Kirby, John B. Freymann, Keyvan Farahani, and Christos Davatzikos. 2017. "Advancing The Cancer Genome Atlas Glioma MRI Collections with Expert Segmentation Labels and Radiomic Features." *Scientific Data* (The Author(s)) 4: 1–13. doi:10.1038/sdata.2017.117.

Bakas, Spyridon, Mauricio Reyes, Andras Jakab, Stefan Bauer, Markus Rempfler, Alessandro Crimi, Russell Takeshi Shinohara, et al., 2018. "Identifying the Best Machine Learning Algorithms for Brain Tumor Segmentation, Progression Assessment, and Overall Survival Prediction in the BRATS Challenge." *ArXiv*. http://arxiv.org/abs/1811.02629.

Bech, Paul, Virginia Winstanley, Kevin G. Murphy, Amir H. Sam, Karim Meeran, Mohammad A. Ghatei, and Stephen R. Bloom. 2008. "Elevated Cocaine- and Amphetamine-Regulated Transcript Immunoreactivity in the Circulation of Patients with Neuroendocrine Malignancy." *The Journal of Clinical Endocrinology and Metabolism* (The Endocrine Society) 93 (4): 1246–1253. doi: 10.1210/jc.2007-1946.

Bhalodiya, Jayendra M., Sarah N. Lim Choi Keung, and Theodoros N. Arvanitis. 2022. "Magnetic Resonance Image-Based Brain Tumour Segmentation Methods: A Systematic Review." *Digital Health* (SAGE Publications Inc) 8: 1–19. doi: 10.1177/20552076221074122.

Bobholz, Samuel A., Allison K. Lowman, Alexander Barrington, Michael Brehler, Sean McGarry, Elizabeth J. Cochran, Jennifer Connelly, et al., 2020. "Radiomic Features of Multiparametric MRI Present Stable Associations with Analogous Histological Features in Patients with Brain Cancer." *Tomography* (Grapho Publications LLC) 6 (2): 160–169. doi: 10.18383/j.tom.2019.00029.

Bodalal, Zuhir, Stefano Trebeschi, Thi Dan Linh Nguyen-Kim, Winnie Schats, and Regina Beets-Tan. 2019. "Radiogenomics: Bridging Imaging and Genomics." *Abdominal Radiology* (Springer New York LLC) 44 (6): 1960–1984. doi: 10.1007/s00261-019-02028-w.

Caja, Fabian, Ludmila Vodickova, Jan Kral, Veronika Vymetalkova, Alessio Naccarati, and Pavel Vodicka. 2020. "Dna Mismatch Repair Gene Variants in Sporadic Solid Cancers." *International Journal of Molecular Sciences* (MDPI AG) 21: 1–29. doi: 10.3390/ijms21155561.

Chen, Fei Yun, Min Yu Huang, Yu Min Lin, Chi Huan Ho, Shu Yu Lin, Hsin Yi Chen, Mien Chie Hung, and Ruey Hwa Chen. 2019. "BIK Ubiquitination by the E3 Ligase

Cul5-ASB11 Determines Cell Fate during Cellular Stress." *Journal of Cell Biology* (Rockefeller University Press) 218 (9): 3002–3018. doi: 10.1083/JCB.201901156.

Ding, Zijian, Songpeng Zu, and Jin Gu. 2016. "Evaluating the Molecule-Based Prediction of Clinical Drug Responses in Cancer." *Bioinformatics* 32 (19): 2891–2895. doi: 10.1093/bioinformatics/btw344.

Ellingson, Benjamin M. 2015. "Radiogenomics and Imaging Phenotypes in Glioblastoma: Novel Observations and Correlation with Molecular Characteristics." *Current Neurology and Neuroscience Reports* (Current Medicine Group LLC) 1 (15): 506. doi: 10.1007/s11910-014-0506-0.

Expression of CARTPT in Cancer – Summary – The Human Protein Atlas. 2022. Accessed March 14. www.proteinatlas.org/ENSG00000164326-CARTPT/pathology.

Forst, Deborah A., Brian v. Nahed, Jay S. Loeffler, and Tracy T. Batchelor. 2014. "Low-Grade Gliomas." *The Oncologist* (Oxford University Press (OUP) 9 (4): 403–413. doi: 10.1634/theoncologist.2013-0345.

Geady, C., H. Keller, I. Siddiqui, J. Bilkey, NC. Dhani, and DA. Jaffray. 2020. "Bridging the Gap between Micro- and Macro-Scales in Medical Imaging with Textural Analysis – A Biological Basis for CT Radiomics Classifiers?" *Physica Medica* 72: 142–151. doi: 10.1016/j.ejmp.2020.03.018.

Hu, Leland S, Shuluo Ning, Jennifer M Eschbacher, Nathan Gaw, Amylou C Dueck, Kris A. Smith, Peter Nakaji, et al., 2015. "Multi-Parametric MRI and Texture Analysis to Visualize Spatial Histologic Heterogeneity and Tumor Extent in Glioblastoma." *PLoS ONE* 10 (11): 1–14. doi: 10.1371/journal.pone.0141506.

le Bihan, Denis. 2013. "Apparent Diffusion Coefficient and Beyond: What Diffusion MR Imaging Can Tell Us about Tissue Structure." *Radiology* (Radiological Society of North America) 268 (2): 318–322. doi: 10.1148/radiol.13130420.

Lou, J.-Y, J. Luo, S.-C. Yang, G.-F. Ding, W. Liao, R.-X. Zhou, C.-Z. Qiu, and J.-M. Chen. 2020. "Long Non-Coding RNA SUMO1P3 Promotes Glioma Progression via the Wnt/β-Catenin Pathway." *European Review for Medical and Pharmacological Sciences* 24: 9571–9580.

Mei, Danyi, Haojun Song, Kai Wang, Yichao Lou, Weiliang Sun, Zhong Liu, Xiaoyun Ding, and Junming Guo. 2013. "Up-Regulation of SUMO1 Pseudogene 3 (SUMO1P3) in Gastric Cancer and Its Clinical Association." *Medical Oncology* 30 (4): 709. doi: 10.1007/s12032-013-0709-2.

Menze, Bjoern H., Andras Jakab, Stefan Bauer, Jayashree Kalpathy-Cramer, Keyvan Farahani, Justin Kirby, Yuliya Burren, et al., 2015. "The Multimodal Brain Tumor Image Segmentation Benchmark (BRATS)." *IEEE Transactions on Medical Imaging* 34 (10): 1993–2024. doi: 10.1109/TMI.2014.2377694.

NA-ER, A., Y-Y. XU, Y-H. LIU, and Y-J. GAN. 2021. "Upregulation of Serum Exosomal SUMO1P3 Predicts Unfavorable Prognosis in Triple Negative Breast Cancer." *European Review for Medical and Pharmacological Sciences* 25: 154–160. http://gepia.can.

Nayak, Lakshmi, and David A. Reardon. 2017. "High-Grade Gliomas." *Continuum (Minneap Minn)* 23 (6): 1548–1563. doi: 10.1212/CON.0000000000000554.

Nilsson, Markus, Elisabet Englund, Filip Szczepankiewicz, Danielle van Westen, and Pia C. Sundgren. 2018. "Imaging Brain Tumour Microstructure." *NeuroImage* 182: 232–250. doi: 10.1016/j.neuroimage.2018.04.075.

Padhani, Anwar R. 2002. "Dynamic Contrast-Enhanced MRI in Clinical Oncology: Current Status and Future Directions." *Journal of Magnetic Resonance Imaging* (John Wiley & Sons, Ltd) 16 (4): 407–422. doi: 10.1002/jmri.10176.

Pedregosa, Fabian, Gaël Varoquaux, Alexandre Gramfort, Vincent Michel, Bertrand Thirion, Olivier Grisel, Mathieu Blondel, et al., 2011. "Scikit-Learn: Machine Learning in Python."

Journal of Machine Learning Research 12 (85): 2825–2830. http://jmlr.org/papers/v12/pedregosa11a.html.

PyRadiomics. 2023. *AIM-Harvard/Pyradiomics*. https://github.com/AIM-Harvard/pyradiomics.

Rogge, G., D. Jones, GW. Hubert, Y. Lin, and MJ. Kuhar. 2008. "CART Peptides: Regulators of Body Weight, Reward and Other Functions." *Nature Reviews Neuroscience* 9 (10): 747–758. doi: 10.1038/nrn2493.

Rouillard, Andrew D., Gregory W. Gundersen, Nicolas F. Fernandez, Zichen Wang, Caroline D. Monteiro, Michael G. McDermott, and Avi Ma'ayan. 2016. "The Harmonizome: A Collection of Processed Datasets Gathered to Serve and Mine Knowledge about Genes and Proteins." *Database* 2016: baw100. doi: 10.1093/database/baw100.

Smits, Marion. 2021. "MRI Biomarkers in Neuro-Oncology." *Nature Reviews Neurology* 17 (8): 486–500. doi: 10.1038/s41582-021-00510-y.

Sun, Yuhan, Alexander James Sedgwick, Md Abdullah-Al-Kamran Khan, Yaseelan Palarasah, Stefano Mangiola, and Alexander David Barrow. 2021. "A Transcriptional Signature of IL-2 Expanded Natural Killer Cells Predicts More Favorable Prognosis in Bladder Cancer." *Frontiers in Immunology* 12. www.frontiersin.org/article/10.3389/fimmu.2021.724107.

Tomaszewski, Michal R., and Robert J. Gillies. 2021. "The Biological Meaning of Radiomic Features." *Radiology* (Radiological Society of North America) 298 (3): 505–516. doi: 10.1148/radiol.2021202553.

Tomczak, Katarzyna, Patrycja Czerwińska, and Maciej Wiznerowicz. 2015. "The Cancer Genome Atlas (TCGA): An Immeasurable Source of Knowledge." *Wspolczesna Onkologia* (Termedia Publishing House Ltd) 19: A68–A77. doi: 10.5114/wo.2014.47136.

van Griethuysen, Joost J. M, Andriy Fedorov, Chintan Parmar, Ahmed Hosny, Nicole Aucoin, Vivek Narayan, Regina GH. Beets-Tan, Jean-Christophe Fillion-Robin, Steve Pieper, and Hugo JWL. Aerts. 2017. "Computational Radiomics System to Decode the Radiographic Phenotype." *Cancer Research* 77 (21): e104 LP-e107. doi: 10.1158/0008-5472.CAN-17-0339.

Vogiatzi, Fotini, Dominique T. Brandt, Jean Schneikert, Jeannette Fuchs, Katharina Grikscheit, Michael Wanzel, Evangelos Pavlakis, et al., 2016. "Mutant P53 Promotes Tumor Progression and Metastasis by the Endoplasmic Reticulum UDPase ENTPD5." *Proceedings of the National Academy of Sciences of the United States of America* (National Academy of Sciences) 113 (52): E8433–E8442. doi: 10.1073/pnas.1612711114.

Wei, Lin, Zhilin Jin, Shengjie Yang, Yanxun Xu, Yitan Zhu, and Yuan Ji. 2018. "TCGA-Assembler 2: Software Pipeline for Retrieval and Processing of TCGA/CPTAC Data." *Bioinformatics* 34 (9): 1615–1617. doi: 10.1093/bioinformatics/btx812.

Zhan, Yonghao, Yuchen Liu, Chaoliang Wang, Junhao Lin, Mingwei Chen, Xiaoying Chen, Chengle Zhuang, et al., 2016. "Increased Expression of SUMO1P3 Predicts Poor Prognosis and Promotes Tumor Growth and Metastasis in Bladder Cancer." *Oncotarget* 7 (13): 16038–16048. www.impactjournals.com/oncotarget.

Zhu, Fei, Cheng Cheng, Hong Qin, Hongsheng Wang, and Hailong Yu. 2020. "A Novel Circular RNA CircENTPD7 Contributes to Glioblastoma Progression by Targeting ROS1." *Cancer Cell International* (BioMed Central Ltd) 20 (1). doi: 10.1186/s12935-020-01208-9.

Zwanenburg, Alex, Martin Vallières, Mahmoud A. Abdalah, Hugo JWL. Aerts, Vincent Andrearczyk, Aditya Apte, Saeed Ashrafinia, et al., 2020. "The Image Biomarker Standardization Initiative: Standardized Quantitative Radiomics for High-Throughput Image-Based Phenotyping." *Radiology* 295 (20). doi: 10.1148/radiol.2020191145.

8 Explainable Artificial Intelligence in Breast Cancer Identification

Pooja Bidwai, Smita Khairnar, and Shilpa Gite

Contents

8.1 Introduction

Artificial intelligence (AI) has recently shown considerable potential in healthcare. However, challenges with explainability make AI applications in healthcare settings complex. Significant studies have been undertaken on explainable artificial intelligence (XAI) to address the constraint of AI methodologies' black-box nature. Compared to intelligent systems, including deep learning, XAI could give simultaneous decision-making model justifications. Competent healthcare is the application of technology like cloud-based solutions and the Internet of Things (IoT), with artificial intelligence to allow practical, accessible, yet personalized health service (Weng

DOI: 10.1201/9781003333425-8

et al., 2017a). Similar systems provide significant medical checking via healthcare software on cell phones or wearables, empowering individuals to take charge of their health. Healthcare data acquired at the user end could also be communicated to medical experts for further analysis (Kakadiaris et al., 2018a), earlier diagnosis of diseases, and treatment plan selection in conjunction with AI (Liu et al., 2019a).

XAI is critical in a wide range of real-world challenges (Mukund Deshpande et al., 2022). Researchers are developing various software-based approaches to address real-world societal concerns (Zhang et al., 2022). Computer vision and associated subjects address many problems, including social, technical, financial, commercial, pharmaceutical, and security challenges.

Those technologies encompass ML, artificial intelligence, and deep learing (DL). The most critical thing about newly developed AI algorithms is their better performance across various metrics (Weng et al., 2017b; Kakadiaris et al., 2018b; Liu et al., 2019b). Clinical diagnosis is now the most important of the several real-world concerns since it greatly influences human life (Adadi and Berrada, 2020; Kleinbaum and Kleinbaum, 1994). Any human disease diagnostics must be accurate to provide the best therapy advice to a patient. In medicine, there are various methods of diagnosing conditions. Many disease symptoms are used to make a diagnosis. However, in many illnesses, the broad symptoms are identical. As a result, it is essential to employ several diagnostic approaches. Conventional image processing, computer vision (CV), and complex AI algorithms are used to diagnose images (Mukund Deshpande et al., 2022) The value of XAI has been extensively recognized in academia and industry in recent times. The deep learning model's decision-making procedure is difficult to grasp due to its incredible complexity.

Explainability is the process of presenting AI decision-making in human-understandable words in a wider view. The various end users concentrate on distinct aspects of explainability. AI professionals or scientists are much more focused on the model or algorithm's explainability. Health practitioners or physicians, on the other hand, are primarily concerned with clinical inference/prediction. Figure 8.1 depicts the classification of XAI approaches.

XAI approaches are mainly categorized as in-hoc and post-hoc methods (Adadi and Berrada, 2020). The intrinsic category of applicability includes all models with an easy-to-interpret internal structure and is white box in nature (Zhang et al., 2022). Post-hoc XAI approaches estimate black-box behavior by identifying correlations among feature values with prediction. Further, they are subclassified as model agnostic and model specific. Among the most often utilized post-hoc XAI systems are perturbation-based and decision-set approaches. Various post-hoc methods are shown in Figure 8.1. Linear regression (LR) (Kleinbaum and Kleinbaum, 1994), logistic regression, k-nearest neighbor, rule-based learners, general additive models, Bayesian models, and decision trees are examples of in-hoc approaches.

In addition, the interpretability and explainability of the results of many machine learning algorithms may not be instantly available, which might be a challenge. Because of this, these methods should demand the application of XAI strategies to ensure the predictability of their models. The steps involved in the explainable AI approach are illustrated in Figure 8.2. In the first, second, and third stages of

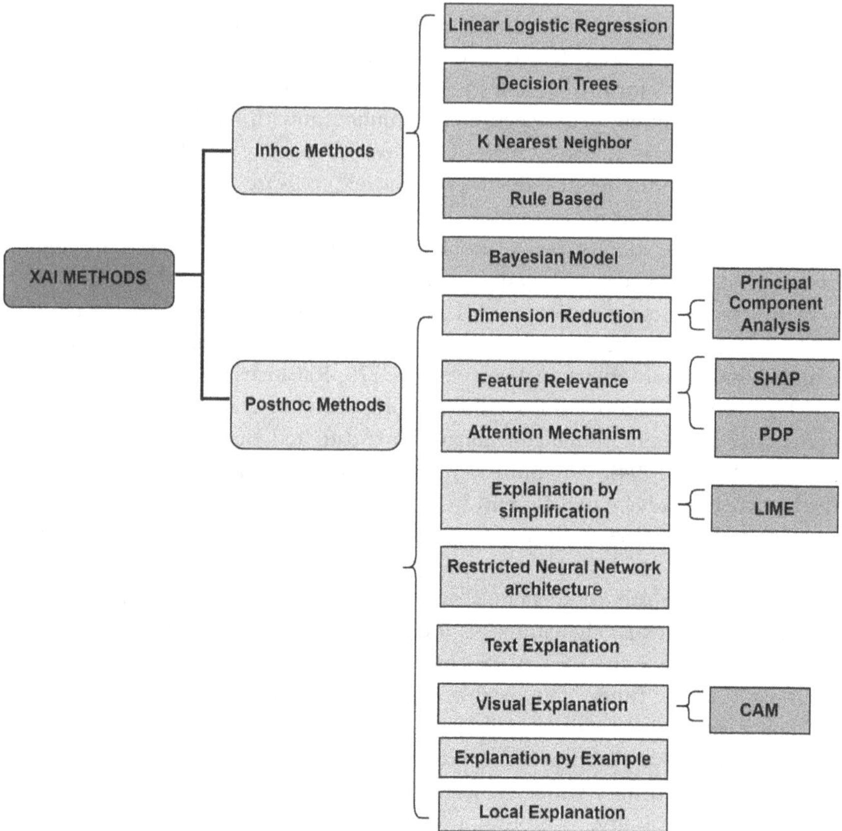

Figure 8.1 Taxonomy of XAI methods.

the building process, there is evidence of decision-making processes that can be explained. The steps involved in the framework are outlined in the following paragraphs. During the early explainability phase, one helps form a varied team of subject-matter experts who are familiar with the artificial intelligence they are building. The use of techniques that allow for offline explainability presents an opportunity to improve the system and is vital for the future acceptance of AI (Bahador, n.d.).

Trust is of the utmost significance in all aspects of life, including business dealings, day-to-day activities, and medical diagnostics. The fact that an automated system may be trusted over one that is "micro-controlled" by its users is what differentiates the two types of systems. Micro-controlling a system gives its users greater control over its every action. The value of a system declines as its management demands increase, which in turn necessitates an increase in staffing levels (Ilias Papastratis, 2021).

When a system conforms to our mental model, we develop confidence in it, since it will not surprise us. Users who are aware of a system's limitations are more likely to benefit from it than from those whose results are deemed unreliable. With

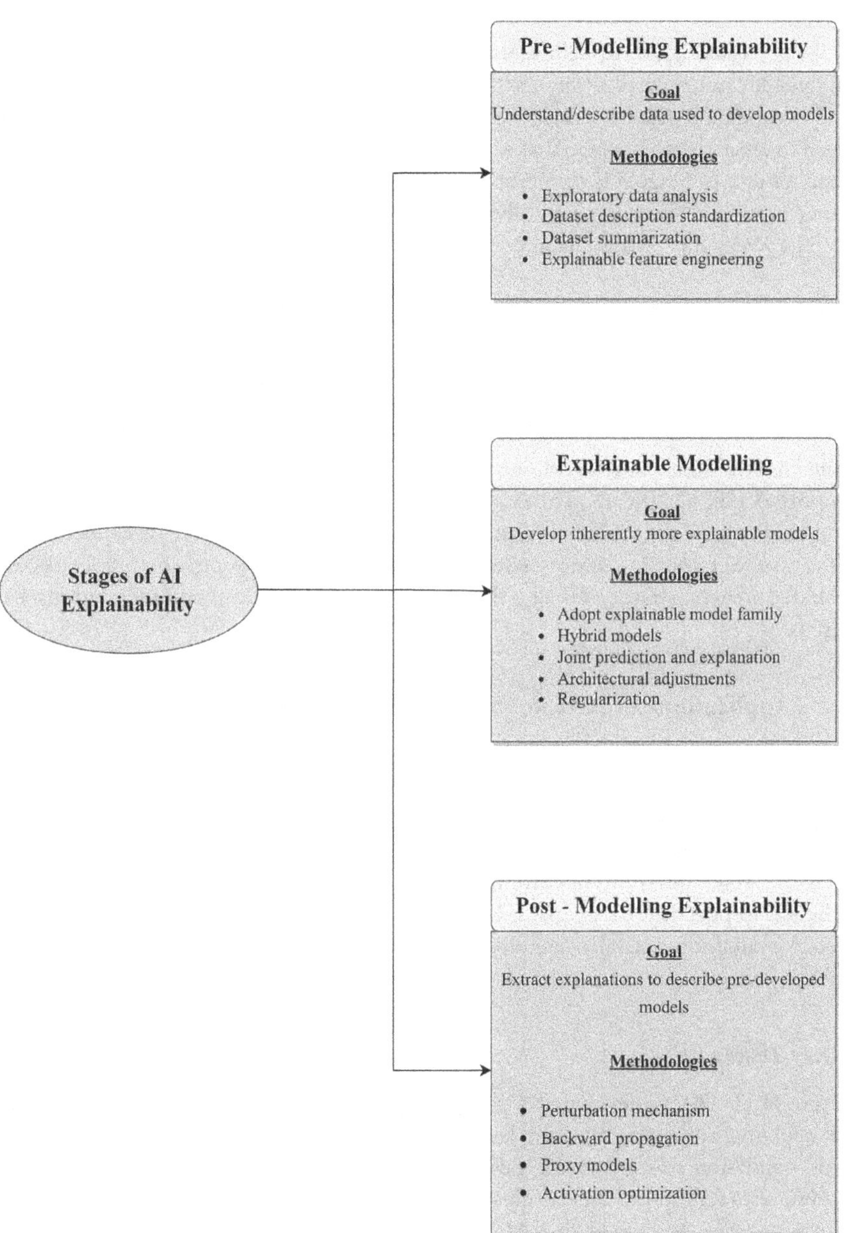

Figure 8.2 Stages involved in the explainable AI process.

explanations, it is faster to design any model. In this circumstance, the ability to explain AI judgments is beneficial. This clarifies the second step of the XAI model (Dağlarli, 2020).

Stages 1 and 2 aim to help users conceptually understand how AI systems work. Individuals can then critically analyze how AIs work and determine when to trust and accept their results, projections, or recommendations. To scale this up, you'll need to create business logic that will gradually apply the same "reasoning" to a large number of AIs. Stage 3 is concerned with creating interoperability between AIs and other types of software, specifically business logic software.

The highlights of this chapter are:

- The most recent survey in clinical diagnosis and surgical procedures utilizing XAI.
- The study of applications of XAI in breast cancer identification.
- Discussion on various XAI frameworks and future directions of XAI in healthcare.

The chapter's outline is as follows: The introduction discusses artificial AI and its importance in healthcare. The second section gives applications of XAI in surgery and diagnosis. Section 8.3 discusses recent work on XAI in breast cancer identification. Section 8.4 discusses several explainability concepts, including LIME, SHAP, and what-if-too. Finally, the conclusion and future recommendations are discussed.

8.2 Applications of XAI in Diagnosis and Surgery

Few studies have investigated XAI's potential in medical AI applications. This research focuses on the medical applications of XAI in diagnostics and surgery. Figure 8.3 depicts the general pipeline of an application. With the help of the intrinsic XAI method, it is easier for medical practitioners to study medical data and make decisions accordingly with the help of medical XAI applications, whereas in post-hoc XAI, black-box methods can be applied to medical data for decision making and also enable post-hoc XAI methods to explain black-box techniques.

8.2.1 Diagnosis

Kavya et al. (2021) developed a computer-aided system for allergy diagnosis. After applying numerous machine learning (ML) algorithms, the authors used k-fold cross-validation to choose the best-performing ML method. They built an random forest (RF) to produce a rule-based approach regarding the XAI methodology. Amoroso et al. developed an XAI framework for breast cancer therapy (2021). The clustered and dimensional methodology was utilized by the researchers, and the result indicated that the method can determine the most relevant medical characteristic for patients even while inventing oncological drugs. Dindorf et al. proposed a pathology-independent spine postural classification (2021). The researchers used a

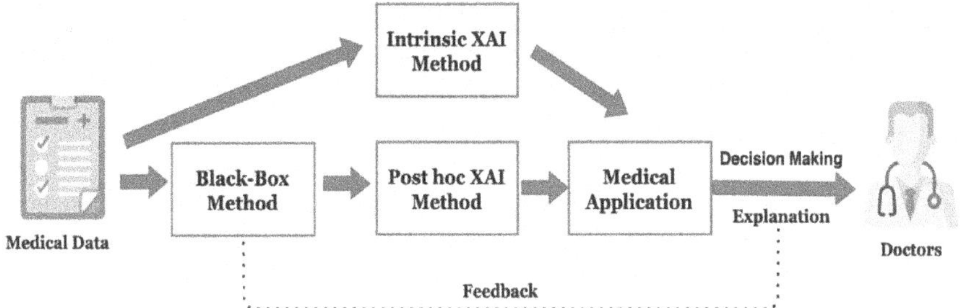

Figure 8.3 The overall process of a medical XAI application.

support vector machine and RF as ML classifiers and local interpretable model-agnostic explanations (LIME) to describe the classifier's predictions. El-Sappagh et al. suggested an RF framework for Alzheimer's disease (AD) diagnosis and progress detection (2021).

In addition, shapley additive explanations (SHAP) was utilized to select the key properties in the classifiers first. Following that, the researchers used a fuzzy rule-based technique. SHAP might be able to offer a local justification concerning features that influence patients' medical diagnosis/progression prediction interpretations. Furthermore, the fuzzy rule-based system might produce natural language forms to assist patients and doctors in comprehending the AI model. The study Peng et al. (2021) describes intrinsic XAI approaches such as logistic regression, decision tree (DT), and kNN to complicated models, including SVM, XGBoost, and RF, in this work. The researchers also used the post-hoc methods SHAP, LIME, and partial dependence plots (PDPs) (Friedman, 2001).

Rocco et al. (2020) introduced an XAI program to detect glioblastoma, combining topological and textural characteristics. Furthermore, the researchers measured the suggested AI model for glioblastoma multiforme (GBM) classification using fluid-attenuated inversion recovery (FLAIR) magnetic resonance imaging. Regarding explainability, the researchers computed the local feature relevance to the sample in the test set using LIME XAI approaches. Meldo et al. suggested a computer-aided lung cancer detection approach with explanatory sentences (2020). The suggested system is divided into two parts: the first is a local post-hoc XAI model constructed with LIME, and the other is a plain language translation of the main elements. Chang et al. demonstrated an explainable deep neural network (EDNN) (2020). The model was trained using data from the Taiwan Aging and Mental Illness (TAMI) cohort, which included 200 schizophrenia patients and healthy controls. The suggested approach attained an 84.0% accuracy in grey matter (GM) and a 90.22% accuracy in white case (WM) using the TAMI cohort (WM). In terms of explainability, the system provided a 3D visualization of the subject's brain imaging data, allowing the diagnostic process to be optimized. Magesh et al. suggested a CNN-based model for detecting early Parkinson's disease (PD) (2020). This publication's dataset included 642 single-photon emission computed tomography

(SPECT) images from the Parkinson's Progression Markers Initiative (PPMI) database. In addition, the authors used transfer learning on the CNN-based model. LIME, a post-hoc XAI approach, was used.

8.2.2 *Surgery*

Yoo et al. developed a multi-class classification XGBoost algorithm for enhanced laser therapy selection (2020). The researchers verified the suggested technique on participants who had already had refractive surgery at the B&VIIT Eye Centre and obtained an external validation dataset accuracy of 78.9%. This also gives a clinical grasp of the SHAP methodology's machine learning process. Kletz et al. (2019) and Chittajallu et al. suggested an explainable artificial intelligence system, XAI-CBIR, for medical training (International Society for Olfaction and Chemical Sensing, 2019, IEEE Sensors Council, and Institute of Electrical and Electronics Engineers). XAI-CBIR is an example-based explanation of the XAI approach. It gives answers by obtaining illustrative examples. It retrieves semantic characteristics from minimally invasive surgery (MIS) video sequences using a self-supervised deep learning technique. Additionally, a saliency map was employed to explain why the algorithm believes the retrieved image is comparable to the search query. The XAI-CBIR system can retrieve MIS movies depending on their contents. The suggested approach was tested on the Cholec80 dataset, and the proportion of relevant frames among the top 50 recovered structures was 64.42%, 99.54%, and 99.09% for three stages. They also used a saliency map to guide them. This survey suggests that various ML and DL methods can be used in XAI applications. However, it is difficult to predict which method will give better results since results may vary depending on the dataset size, datatype, and so on; also, there is no uniform machine learning or XAI software that can handle diagnosis and surgery task

8.3 Applications of XAI in Breast Cancer

Breast cancer has emerged as one of the most prevalent forms of cancer in women around the globe, and it poses a significant risk to the affected individual's physical and emotional health. Artificial intelligence (AI) has started to be fully integrated with mammography, magnetic resonance imaging, ultrasound, and other diagnostic tools in recent years due to the advancement of AI and the collection of medical data. This will help doctors diagnose diseases. On the other hand, the breast cancer diagnosis model based on natural language processing (NLP) cannot extract the semantic information of the mammography report successfully. The image quality significantly impacts the current breast cancer diagnosis model based on computer vision (CV). The trust in the current diagnostic models is similarly poor due to the lack of model interpretability. Hence, there is a need for explainable AI models for breast cancer identification.

Incorporating deep learning principles into AI technologies necessitated the incorporation of an explainable component, particularly when these models were being developed for patient screening in the identification of breast cancer, due to the high risk involved (Zhang et al., 2022). Many artificial intelligence techniques for data-driven categorization cannot be explained, particularly "black box" techniques such as deep learning, such as IBM Watson, which were recently utilized in breast cancer treatment. However, in medical systems, black boxes are often disliked by doctors since they prefer to understand why a machine makes a recommendation. Autonomous decision-making systems are commonly perceived as a threat and a loss of control ("Explainable Artificial Intelligence Approach in Combating Real-Time Surveillance of COVID19 Pandemic from CT Scan and X-Ray Images Using Ensemble Model – Enhanced Reader").

For early identification of breast cancer, machine learning algorithms like SVM, random tree, and J48 are explored (Khairnar et al., 2021). Identification is provided graphically through a user interface to give explanations in visual form (Lamy et al., 2019). A general overview of the case-based reasoning approach (CBR) approach is shown in Figure 8.4. Montebello et al. proposed deep learning techniques Resnet-50 and VGG-16 and highlighted pixels in mammograms to generate a map for the identification of breast cancer (la Ferla et al., 2021). The authors assessed the accuracy of the weakly-supervised DL algorithms used to locate breast tumors using the class activation map. The weakly supervised DL algorithms produced good diagnostic results for internal validation sets, with area under curve (AUC) values of 0.92–0.96, which were not significantly different from those of fully supervised DL algorithms with either human or automated region of interest (ROI) annotation (AUC, 0.92–0.96) (Kim et al., 2021). Scientific evaluation of explainable DL approaches will be crucial if DL is to be embraced in standard patient treatment.

Researchers have recently concentrated on explainable medical systems to help medical professionals and offer helpful interpretations so that any specialist may grasp a system's predictions (Lamy et al., 2019). Brunese et al. (2020) focused on coronavirus detection using X-ray pictures. They suggested using a deep convolutional network to extract information from photos and determine if a patient has pneumonia or coronavirus. The impacted areas of the X-ray are then marked, and visual explanations are provided using Grad-CAM (Xu et al., 2020). Using statistical equivalence, effective auto-labeling for chest X-ray imagery with an explainable model is explored in Kim et al. (2022). There is a definite demand for comprehensible AI techniques because reliable AI must enable biomedical experts to assume accountability for their decisions (Hu et al., 2022; Müller et al., 2022).

Since the description of the underlying medical condition is vague, explanations of conclusions about the malignancy of skin lesions from dermoscopic pictures need specific clarity. A multi-modal concept-based XAI framework for healthcare image analysis that offers clear text interpretations and visual representations of the explanations to support the predictions has been proposed as ExAID (Lucieri et al., 2022).

Compared to conventional image processing methods, these approaches have been shown to give considerable gains in accuracy and other measurement criteria. Despite their high precision, these methods are not employed commercially for many diagnostic applications. The inexplicability of these algorithms is the main contributing factor. Understanding what occurs behind the "black box" of these frameworks is quite challenging. Therefore, explainability and interpretability are

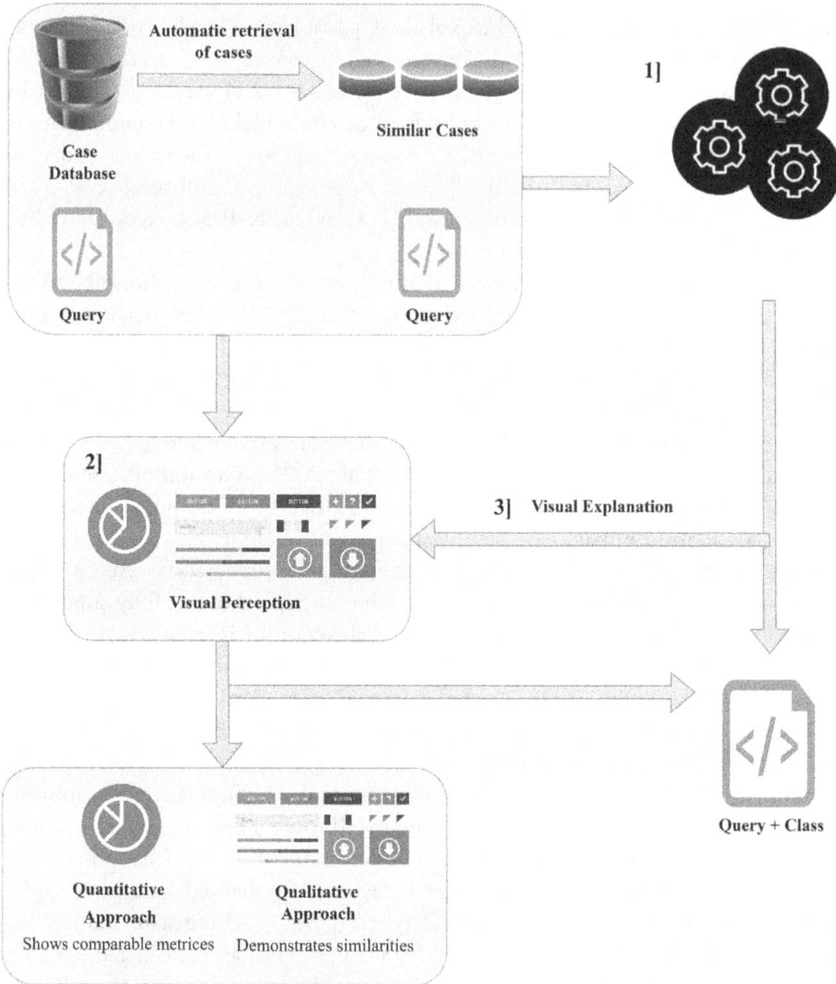

Figure 8.4 General overview of case-based approach with a visual interface.

required in these algorithms to support the diagnostic choice. Diagnostic decision-making expertise must build confidence in diagnosing abnormalities in the medical field (Tran et al., 2021).

8.4 Various XAI Frameworks

8.4.1 LRP

The layer-wise relevance propagation (LRP) (Montavon Grégoire et al., 2019) method grows potentially extremely complex deep neural networks while bringing such explainability. Using a set of propagation rules created explicitly for this purpose works by sending the prediction backward through the neural network. Medical image analysis has made use of LRP. From MR scans of the brain, researchers employed LRP to pinpoint the areas causing Alzheimer's. When they compared the saliency maps generated by LRP with guided backpropagation, they discovered that LRP was more accurate at detecting areas known to have Alzheimer's disease (Böhle et al., 2019).

8.4.2 *Local Interpretable Model-Agnostic Explanations*

LIME (Adadi and Berrada, 2018) is a method that focuses on understanding the model rather than trying to explain it fully. It does this by perturbing the input of data samples and seeing how the predictions change. The influence of changing a single data sample's feature values on the outcome is then seen. When the results of a model are observed, this is frequently related to the interests of humans (Ribeiro, n.d.).

The aim is to understand the black box model's decision-making process, or why and how the machine learning model generated a particular prediction. It makes sense how LIME works. Consider a situation where all you have is a black-box model that you may feed data points into to obtain model predictions. LIME examines what occurs to predictions when different versions of your data are fed into the machine learning model (Yang et al., 2022). To offer reliable reasons for glaucoma predictions from healthy and diseased pictures, ML employs LIME to explain outcomes coherently using local interpretable model-agonistic explanation (Kamal et al., 2022).

8.4.3 *SHAP*

Shapley additive explanations (Hussain et al., 2022) distribute credit for a model's outcome open outcome among its input features using cooperative game theory. It is required to match a model's input features with players in a game and its function with the game's rules to combine game theory with machine learning models (Yang et al., 2020). Figure 8.5 depicts the SHAP model for explanations.

8.4.4 *What-If-Tool*

What-if-tool (WIT) (Mukund Deshpande and Shailesh Gite, 2021) is an interactive visual tool created to explore machine learning models. It allows users to inspect, assess, and contrast machine learning models to better comprehend a classification or regression model. Everyone from a developer to a product manager to a researcher to a student can utilize it for their goal due to its user-friendly interface and minimal reliance on complicated coding. WIT is an open-source visualization tool published by Google as part of the PAIR (People + AI Research) initiative. PAIR gathers researchers throughout Google to examine and reimagine how humans engage with AI technologies (Thimoteo et al., 2022).

8.4.5 *AIX360*

AIX360 (Arya et al., 2020), also known as AI Explainability 360, is an extendable free software toolset created by IBM research that may assist in understanding ML identification of labels during the development lifecycle. The AIX360

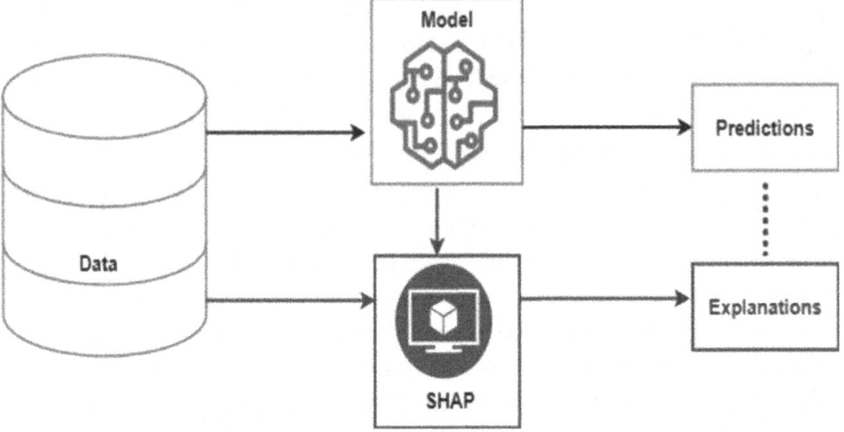

Figure 8.5 SHAP model.

toolkit attempts to provide a uniform, extensible, and user-friendly programming interface and accompanying software architecture to handle the various explainability methodologies hired by diverse stakeholders. The objective is to be accessible to algorithm engineers and data scientists, who may not be experts in explainability.

8.4.6 DeepLIFT

This technique uses the difference between each neuron's activity and its "reference activation" to give contribution scores. DeepLIFT (Linardatos et al., 2021) considers both positive and negative contributions independently and can reveal dependencies that other approaches do not. Scores may be swiftly computed in a single backward pass. DeepLIFT examines the distinction between an output and a "reference" output in the same way that it explores the difference between an input and a "reference" input. The reference input is the default or "neutral" input chosen based on the job at hand.

8.4.7 ELI5

ELI5 (Linardatos et al., 2021) is a Python library that aids in explaining and debugging machine learning classifier predictions. To view and troubleshoot various ML models, the ELI5 Python toolkit uses a standardized API. It supports every algorithm in the Scikit-Learn library, including the fit() and predicts() techniques. You can explain white-box models (such as linear regression and decision trees) and black-box models with it because it has built-in support for several ML frameworks (Keras, XGBoost, LightGBM), and models for classification and regression can both use it.

8.4.8 Activation Atlases

A robust explainable AI framework is Activation Atlases (Pawar et al., 2020). Google and Open AI created this cutting-edge method to show how neural networks interact. Additionally, it keeps track of how information and different layers help neural networks broaden their scope. The technique also offers a visual picture of the inner workings of convolutional vision networks. In addition to this, it gains a general understanding of the concepts included inside the hidden levels. This is done to make information obtained from the web easier for individuals to comprehend.

8.4.9 Rulex Explainable AI

Forecasting models for first-order conditional logic rules are developed by a start-up company called Rulex (Joshi et al., 2021). In addition to this, it assists in rapidly presenting findings that are comprehensive and can be utilized by anyone. The primary machine learning method, known as logic learning machine (LLM), approaches the problem differently than standard AI does. In addition to this, it provides comprehensive language conditional logic rules that can be used to forecast decisions. The instructions it offers also create forecasts that are easy to understand.

8.4.10 Skater

Skater (Oracle) is a model-neutral framework that provides model interpretation for any model. This makes it possible to aid in the development of interpretable machine learning systems, which are typically needed for application in the real world. It is a free software Python program that was developed to explain the uncovered elements of a black box framework on a global and local scale. Skater was initially a branch of LIME, but it eventually developed as a separate framework with a wide variety of features and capabilities that enable model-agnostic interpretation of any black-box models. Skater has a vast range of features and capabilities. The project started as a research venture to discover ways to improve the interpretability of prediction "black boxes" for practitioners as well as other researchers.

8.4.11 explAIner

A single framework called explAIner (Spinner et al., 2019) aids users in comprehending deep learning and machine learning models. The framework also includes tools for analyzing models using various explainable methods. The optimization process is then monitored and guided using these justifications, creating better designs. The explAIner may integrate high-level explainable ways to analyze a model's performance metrics with interactive graph display.

8.5 Discussion and Future Directions

It is crucial to look at the traits of a black box that could render a decision for the wrong reason. It is a significant issue that might seriously affect how well the system performs if used in the real world. Most of the techniques, especially the ones

Table 8.1 Summary of XAI Tools Used in Breast Cancer-Related Study

Reference	*Year*	*XAI Frameworks/Tools Used*	*Application*	*Methodology*	*Discussion*	*Limitations*
(Amoroso et al., 2021)	2021	Dimension reduction	Breast cancer therapy	The cluster of feature analysis	The adopted dimensional reduction method determines subspace where patient distances are employed by hierarchical clustering to select the best groupings.	XAI evaluation is not done.
(Hussain et al., 2022)	2022	LIME, Grad-CAM	Breast lesion classification	Multi-class feature clustering, deep learning models for training	LIME gives better explanations than Grad-CAM in few results.	The exact amount of contributions for the classification of breast lesions is not provided by the used tools.
(Lamy et al., 2019)	2019	Rainbow boxes using scatterplots	Breast cancer identification	Case-based reasoning approach for visual representations	Extensive user research in a controlled environment is conducted as part of the clinical validation of the visual case-based reasoning approach.	The method majorly relies on color for identifying classes.
(Binder et al., 2021)	2021	Explanations of the classifier decisions using heatmaps	Breast cancer profiling	Explainable ML technique for morphological, molecular, and clinical breast cancer histology profiling	XAI method that is easily explicable makes it possible to evaluate the connection between morphological and molecular cancer features.	The method can be evaluated using available XAI tools.

that use credit, are open-source implementations. Corporate interest is growing in explainability, notably the identification approaches that may be applied to various corporate applications.

Deep learning techniques, primarily used during diagnosing of diseases, have greatly improved in explaining their choices. Recognizing the factors that affect a choice can assist model developers in overcoming issues with dependability, enabling end users to gain confidence and make better judgments. The goal of almost all these methods is to ascertain local explainability. Saliency maps, which emphasize the effect of different captured images, are produced by most deep network interpretability algorithms using image categorization. The LIME and SHAP methods for showing feature associations and significance are the most complete and widely used approaches to describing any black-box model. Grad-CAM, visual explainability, has recently shown good growth in interpretability and explainability.

To increase the reliability of medical diagnoses, some crucial factors must be considered in addition to the reasonable explainability of already existing AI algorithms. The decision period and the clinical expert's assessment of the accuracy of the diagnosis come first in line with this. To increase confidence in the implementation and diagnosis, it must be done. The examination of explainability models that could warrant the need for adjustments and enhancements to the XAI algorithm, if any, must consider experts' advice.

Further study direction would involve combining various decision-making sources, like clinical information and imaging techniques, then assigning model decisions to each. This may mimic a clinician's diagnostic process, in which a judgment is made based on images and a person's physical features. Although explainable models increase confidence in diagnosing diseases, they still need to be extensively researched before being used economically.

8.6 Conclusion

Health assessment is always of the utmost importance since doctors' recommendations for therapy depend on an accurate diagnosis. Diagnostics based on symptoms can be complex in many respects since they are often similar across diseases. Therefore, it turns out that computerized tomography and medical tests are the superior choices for making the correct diagnosis. To establish trust, imaging tests usually require manual forecasts. Pathologists' or radiologists' skills and technical understanding are critical factors in manual diagnosis. Researchers created specific software frameworks to give helpful diagnostics for the medical industry. These frameworks used AI, computer vision, and image processing techniques, which were more accurate yet inexplicable. In this chapter, the top XAI frameworks are detailed. This included Rulex XAI, LIME, SHAP, What-If-Tool, AIX360, activation atlases, and many others. The researchers use these frameworks to describe how AI models are black boxes. In any scenario, it's possible to think that explainable AI still has a lot of undiscovered opportunities to research in the coming future. According to the survey results, medical XAI is a potential future research direction. The chapter seeks to guide medical specialists and AI scientists while creating medical XAI solutions.

References

Adadi, A., and M. Berrada. 2020. Explainable AI for healthcare: From black box to interpretable models. In *Embedded Systems and Artificial Intelligence: Proceedings of ESAI 2019, Fez, Morocco*, pp. 327–337. Singapore: Springer.

Adadi, Amina, and Mohammed Berrada. 2018. "Peeking Inside the Black-Box: A Survey on Explainable Artificial Intelligence (XAI)." *IEEE Access* (Institute of Electrical and Electronics Engineers Inc.) 6: 52138–52160. doi: 10.1109/ACCESS.2018.2870052.

Amoroso, Nicola, Domenico Pomarico, Annarita Fanizzi, Vittorio Didonna, Francesco Giotta, Daniele la Forgia, Agnese Latorre, et al., 2021. "A Roadmap towards Breast Cancer Therapies Supported by Explainable Artificial Intelligence." *Applied Sciences* 11 (11). doi: 10.3390/app11114881.

Arya, Vijay, Rachel KE. Bellamy, Pin-Yu Chen, Amit Dhurandhar, Michael Hind, Samuel C. Hoffman, Stephanie Houde, et al., 2020. "AI Explainability 360: An Extensible Toolkit for Understanding Data and Machine Learning Models." *Journal of Machine Learning Research* 21. http://aix360.mybluemix.net.

Bahador, Khaleghi. n.d. *The How of Explainable AI: Pre-Modelling Explainability*. https://Towardsdatascience.Com/the-How-of-Explainable-Ai-Pre-Modelling-Explainability-699150495fe4.

Binder, Alexander, Michael Bockmayr, Miriam Hägele, Stephan Wienert, Daniel Heim, Katharina Hellweg, Masaru Ishii, et al., 2021. "Morphological and Molecular Breast Cancer Profiling through Explainable Machine Learning." *Nature Machine Intelligence* 3 (4): 355–366. doi: 10.1038/s42256-021-00303-4.

Böhle, Moritz, Fabian Eitel, Martin Weygandt, and Kerstin Ritter. 2019. "Layer-Wise Relevance Propagation for Explaining Deep Neural Network Decisions in MRI-Based Alzheimer's Disease Classification." *Frontiers in Aging Neuroscience* (Frontiers Media S.A) 10 (JUL). doi: 10.3389/fnagi.2019.00194.

Brunese, Luca, Francesco Mercaldo, Alfonso Reginelli, and Antonella Santone. 2020. "Explainable Deep Learning for Pulmonary Disease and Coronavirus COVID-19 Detection from X-Rays." *Computer Methods and Programs in Biomedicine* (Elsevier) 196: 105608. doi: 10.1016/J.CMPB.2020.105608.

Chang, Yu Wei, Shih Jen Tsai, Yung Fu Wu, and Albert C. Yang. 2020. "Development of an Al-Based Web Diagnostic System for Phenotyping Psychiatric Disorders." *Frontiers in Psychiatry* (Frontiers Media S.A) 11. doi: 10.3389/fpsyt.2020.542394.

Dağlarli, Evren. 2020. "Explainable Artificial Intelligence (XAI) Approaches and Deep Meta-Learning Models." In *Advances and Applications in Deep Learning*, edited by Marco Antonio Aceves-Fernandez. Rijeka: IntechOpen. doi: 10.5772/intechopen.92172.

Dindorf, Carlo, Jürgen Konradi, Claudia Wolf, Bertram Taetz, Gabriele Bleser, Janine Huthwelker, Friederike Werthmann, et al., 2021. "Classification and Automated Interpretation of Spinal Posture Data Using a Pathology-Independent Classifier and Explainable Artificial Intelligence (Xai)." *Sensors (MDPI)* 21 (18). doi: 10.3390/s21186323.

El-Sappagh, Shaker, Jose M. Alonso, S. M. Riazul Islam, Ahmad M. Sultan, and Kyung Sup Kwak. 2021. "A Multilayer Multimodal Detection and Prediction Model Based on Explainable Artificial Intelligence for Alzheimer's Disease." *Scientific Reports* (Nature Research) 11 (1). doi: 10.1038/s41598-021-82098-3.

Friedman, Jerome H. 2001. "999 Reitz Lecture Greedy Function Approximation: A Gradient Boosting Machine 1." *The Annals of Statistics* 29.

Hu, Brian, Bhavan Vasu, and Anthony Hoogs. 2022. "X-MIR: EXplainable Medical Image Retrieval." *Proceedings – 2022 IEEE/CVF Winter Conference on Applications of Computer Vision, WACV 2022*: 1544–1554. doi: 10.1109/WACV51458.2022.00161.

Hussain, Sardar Mehboob, Domenico Buongiorno, Nicola Altini, Francesco Berloco, Berardino Prencipe, Marco Moschetta, Vitoantonio Bevilacqua, and Antonio Brunetti. 2022. "Shape-Based Breast Lesion Classification Using Digital Tomosynthesis Images: The Role of Explainable Artificial Intelligence." *Applied Sciences* (MDPI AG) 12 (12): 6230. doi: 10.3390/app12126230.

Ilias Papastratis. 2021. *Explainable AI (XAI): A Survey of Recents Methods, Applications and Frameworks*. https://Theaisummer.Com/Xai/.

International Society for Olfaction and Chemical Sensing, IEEE Sensors Council, and Institute of Electrical and Electronics Engineers. 2019. *ISOEN 2019 : 18th International Symposium on Olfaction and Electronic Nose : 2019 Symposium Proceedings : ACROS Fukuoka,* May 26–29.

Joshi, Gargi, Rahee Walambe, and Ketan Kotecha. 2021. "A Review on Explainability in Multimodal Deep Neural Nets." *IEEE Access* (Institute of Electrical and Electronics Engineers Inc) 9: 59800–59821. doi: 10.1109/ACCESS.2021.3070212.

Kakadiaris, Ioannis A., Michalis Vrigkas, Albert A. Yen, Tatiana Kuznetsova, Matthew Budoff, and Morteza Naghavi. 2018a. "Machine Learning Outperforms ACC/AHA CVD Risk Calculator in MESA." *Journal of the American Heart Association* (American Heart Association Inc) 7 (22). doi: 10.1161/JAHA.118.009476.

Kakadiaris, Ioannis A., Michalis Vrigkas, Albert A. Yen, Tatiana Kuznetsova, Matthew Budoff, and Morteza Naghavi. 2018b. "Machine Learning Outperforms ACC/AHA CVD Risk Calculator in MESA." *Journal of the American Heart Association* 7 (22). American Heart Association Inc. doi:10.1161/JAHA.118.009476.

Kamal, Md. Sarwar, Nilanjan Dey, Linkon Chowdhury, Syed Irtija Hasan, and KC. Santosh. 2022. "Explainable AI for Glaucoma Prediction Analysis to Understand Risk Factors in Treatment Planning." *IEEE Transactions on Instrumentation and Measurement* 71. doi: 10.1109/TIM.2022.3171613.

Kavya, R., J. Christopher, S. Panda, and YB. Lazarus. 2021. "Machine Learning and XAI Approaches for Allergy Diagnosis." *Biomed Signal Process Control* 69: 102681.

Khairnar, Smita, Sudeep D Thepade, and Shilpa Gite. 2021. "Effect of Image Binarization Thresholds on Breast Cancer Identification in Mammography Images Using OTSU, Niblack, Burnsen, Thepade's SBTC." *Intelligent Systems with Applications* 10 (11): 46. doi: 10.1016/j.iswa.2021.20.

Kim, Doyun, Joowon Chung, Jongmun Choi, Marc D Succi, John Conklin, Maria Gabriela Figueiro Longo, Jeanne B. Ackman, et al., 2022. "Accurate Auto-Labeling of Chest X-Ray Images Based on Quantitative Similarity to an Explainable AI Model." *Nature Communications* 13 (1). doi: 10.1038/s41467-022-29437-8.

Kim, Jaeil, Hye Jung Kim, Chanho Kim, Jin Hwa Lee, Keum Won Kim, Young Mi Park, Hye Won Kim, So Yeon Ki, You Me Kim, and Won Hwa Kim. 2021. "Weakly-Supervised Deep Learning for Ultrasound Diagnosis of Breast Cancer." *Scientific Reports* (Nature Research) 11 (1). doi: 10.1038/s41598-021-03806-7.

Kleinbaum, DG., and DG. Kleinbaum. 1994. "D.G.Logistic Regression." In *Springer*. Berlin/Heidelberg, Germany: Springer.

Kletz, Sabrina, Klaus Schoeffmann, and Heinrich Husslein. 2019. "Learning the Representation of Instrument Images in Laparoscopy Videos." *Healthcare Technology Letters* (Institution of Engineering and Technology) 6: 197–203. doi: 10.1049/htl.2019.0077.

la Ferla, Michele, Matthew Montebello, and Dylan Seychell. 2021. *An XAI Approach to Deep Learning Models in the Detection of Ductal Carcinoma in Situ*, June. http://arxiv.org/abs/2106.14186.

Lamy, Jean Baptiste, Boomadevi Sekar, Gilles Guezennec, Jacques Bouaud, and Brigitte Séroussi. 2019. "Explainable Artificial Intelligence for Breast Cancer: A Visual Case-Based

Reasoning Approach." *Artificial Intelligence in Medicine* (Elsevier B.V.) 94: 42–53. doi: 10.1016/j.artmed.2019.01.001.

Linardatos, Pantelis, Vasilis Papastefanopoulos, and Sotiris Kotsiantis. 2021a. "Explainable Ai: A Review of Machine Learning Interpretability Methods." *Entropy* (MDPI AG) 23 (1): 18. doi: 10.3390/e23010018.

Liu, Tianyu, Wenhui Fan, and Cheng Wu. 2019a. "A Hybrid Machine Learning Approach to Cerebral Stroke Prediction Based on Imbalanced Medical Dataset." *Artificial Intelligence in Medicine* (Elsevier B.V) 101. doi: 10.1016/j.artmed.2019.101723.

Liu, Tianyu, Wenhui Fan, and Cheng Wu. 2019b. "A Hybrid Machine Learning Approach to Cerebral Stroke Prediction Based on Imbalanced Medical Dataset." *Artificial Intelligence in Medicine* (Elsevier B.V) 101. doi: 10.1016/j.artmed.2019.101723.

Lucieri, Adriano, Muhammad Naseer Bajwa, Stephan Alexander Braun, Muhammad Imran Malik, Andreas Dengel, and Sheraz Ahmed. 2022. "ExAID: A Multimodal Explanation Framework for Computer-Aided Diagnosis of Skin Lesions." *Computer Methods and Programs in Biomedicine* (Elsevier Ireland Ltd) 215. doi: 10.1016/j.cmpb.2022.106620.

Magesh, Pavan Rajkumar, Richard Delwin Myloth, and Rijo Jackson Tom. 2020. "An Explainable Machine Learning Model for Early Detection of Parkinson's Disease Using LIME on DaTSCAN Imagery." *Computers in Biology and Medicine* (Elsevier Ltd) 126. doi: 10.1016/j.compbiomed.2020.104041.

Montavon, Grégoire, et al. 2019. "Layer-Wise Relevance Propagation: An Overview." *Explainable AI: Interpreting, Explaining and Visualizing Deep Learning* 2019: 193–209.

Marco Tulio Ribeiro. n.d. *LIME – Local Interpretable Model-Agnostic Explanations*. https://Homes.Cs.Washington.Edu/~marcotcr/Blog/Lime/.

Meldo, Anna, Lev Utkin, Maxim Kovalev, and Ernest Kasimov. 2020. "The Natural Language Explanation Algorithms for the Lung Cancer Computer-Aided Diagnosis System." *Artificial Intelligence in Medicine* (Elsevier B.V) 108. doi: 10.1016/j.artmed.2020.101952.

Mukund, Deshpande, Nilkanth, and Shilpa Shailesh Gite. 2021. *A Brief Bibliometric Survey of Explainable AI in Medical Field A Brief Bibliometric Survey of Explainable AI in Medical Field A Brief Bibliometric Survey of Explainable AI in Medical Field*. https://digitalcommons.unl.edu/libphilprac.

Mukund, Deshpande, Nilkanth, Shilpa Gite, Biswajeet Pradhan, and Mazen Ebraheem Assiri. 2022. "Explainable Artificial Intelligence–A New Step towards the Trust in Medical Diagnosis with AI Frameworks: A Review." *Computer Modeling in Engineering & Sciences* (Computers, Materials and Continua, Tech Science Press): 1–30. doi: 10.32604/cmes.2022.021225.

Müller, Heimo, Andreas Holzinger, Markus Plass, Luka Brcic, Cornelia Stumptner, and Kurt Zatloukal. 2022. "Explainability and Causability for Artificial Intelligence-Supported Medical Image Analysis in the Context of the European In Vitro Diagnostic Regulation." *New Biotechnology* 70: 67–72. doi: 10.1016/j.nbt.2022.05.002.

Oracle. *Skater*. https://Oracle.Github.Io/Skater/Overview.Html.

Pawar, Urja, Donna O'shea, Susan Rea, and Ruairi O'reilly. 2020. *Explainable AI in Healthcare. 2020 International Conference on Cyber Situational Awareness, Data Analytics and Assessment (CyberSA)*, pp. 1–2.

Peng, Junfeng, Kaiqiang Zou, Mi Zhou, Yi Teng, Xiongyong Zhu, Feifei Zhang, and Jun Xu. 2021. "An Explainable Artificial Intelligence Framework for the Deterioration Risk Prediction of Hepatitis Patients." *Journal of Medical Systems* (Springer) 45 (5). doi: 10.1007/s10916-021-01736-5.

Rucco, Matteo, Giovanna Viticchi, and Lorenzo Falsetti. 2020. "Towards Personalized Diagnosis of Glioblastoma in Fluid-Attenuated Inversion Recovery (FLAIR) by

Topological Interpretable Machine Learning." *Mathematics* (MDPI AG) 8 (5). doi: 10.3390/MATH8050770.

Spinner, Thilo, Udo Schlegel, Hanna Schäfer, and Mennatallah El-Assady. 2019. "ExplAIner: A Visual Analytics Framework for Interactive and Explainable Learning." *CoRR* abs/1908.00087. http://arxiv.org/abs/1908.00087.

Thimoteo, Lucas M., Marley M. Vellasco, Jorge Amaral, Karla Figueiredo, Cátia Lie Yokoyama, and Erito Marques. 2022. "Explainable Artificial Intelligence for COVID-19 Diagnosis Through Blood Test Variables." *Journal of Control, Automation and Electrical Systems* (Springer) 33 (2): 625–644. doi: 10.1007/s40313-021-00858-y.

Tran, Khoa A., Olga Kondrashova, Andrew Bradley, Elizabeth D. Williams, John V. Pearson, and Nicola Waddell. 2021. "Deep Learning in Cancer Diagnosis, Prognosis and Treatment Selection." *Genome Medicine* (BioMed Central Ltd) 13 (1): 1–17 doi: 10.1186/s13073-021-00968-x.

Weng, Stephen F., Jenna Reps, Joe Kai, Jonathan M. Garibaldi, and Nadeem Qureshi. 2017a. "Can Machine-Learning Improve Cardiovascular Risk Prediction Using Routine Clinical Data?" *PLoS ONE* (Public Library of Science) 12 (4). doi: 10.1371/journal.pone.0174944.

Weng, Stephen F., Jenna Reps, Joe Kai, Jonathan M. Garibaldi, and Nadeem Qureshi. 2017b. "Can Machine-Learning Improve Cardiovascular Risk Prediction Using Routine Clinical Data?" *PLoS ONE* (Public Library of Science) 12 (4). doi: 10.1371/journal.pone.0174944.

Xu, Y., X. Yang, L. Gong, H. C. Lin, T. Y. Wu, Y. Li, and N. Vasconcelos. 2020. Explainable object-induced action decision for autonomous vehicles. In *Proceedings of the IEEE/CVF Conference on Computer Vision and Pattern Recognition*, Virtual, pp. 9523–9532.

Yang, Guang, Qinghao Ye, and Jun Xia. 2022. "Unbox the Black-Box for the Medical Explainable AI via Multi-Modal and Multi-Centre Data Fusion: A Mini-Review, Two Showcases and Beyond." *Information Fusion* (Elsevier B.V) 77: 29–52. doi: 10.1016/j.inffus.2021.07.016.

Yang, Zebin, Aijun Zhang, and Agus Sudjianto. 2020. *GAMI-Net: An Explainable Neural Network Based on Generalized Additive Models with Structured Interactions*, March. http://arxiv.org/abs/2003.07132.

Yoo, Tae Keun, Ik Hee Ryu, Hannuy Choi, Jin Kuk Kim, In Sik Lee, Jung Sub Kim, Geunyoung Lee, and Tyler Hyungtaek Rim. 2020. "Explainable Machine Learning Approach as a Tool to Understand Factors Used to Select the Refractive Surgery Technique on the Expert Level." *Translational Vision Science and Technology* (Association for Research in Vision and Ophthalmology Inc) 9 (2). doi: 10.1167/tvst.9.2.8.

Zhang, Yiming, Ying Weng, and Jonathan Lund. 2022. "Applications of Explainable Artificial Intelligence in Diagnosis and Surgery." *Diagnostics* (MDPI) 12 (2): 237. doi: 10.3390/diagnostics12020237.

9 Interpretability of Self-Supervised Learning for Breast Cancer Image Analysis

Gitika Jha, Manashree Jhawar, Vedant Manelkar, Radhika Kotecha, Ashish Phophalia, and Komal Borisagar

Contents

9.1 Introduction

One of the top reasons for unnatural deaths in every country of the world is cancer, as stated in a report by the World Health Organization (WHO) ("The Top 10 Causes of Death" 2020). Breast cancer is the second most commonly diagnosed cancer (11.7% of total cases) worldwide among women (Sung et al., 2021). According to WHO, cancer can be cured in 30–50% of patients if detected early ("Cancer" 2022). The current strategy for combating this disease entails early detection and treatment. Patients with stage 0 and I cancer have a 98% chance of a 10-year survival rate, as opposed to patients with stage III cancer, who have a 65% chance of the same (ASCO, 2021). In order to enhance the survival rate of this disease, more patients must be diagnosed at

DOI: 10.1201/9781003333425-9

an early stage. Moreover, accurate categorization of benign lesions can save patients from having to take needless medication. On the other hand, breast cancer affects 8% of women at some point in their lives. According to statistics, one out of every eight women in the United States will be affected by this illness over their lifetime. It also accounts for 14% of cancers in Indian women. This cancer is characterized by abnormal cell proliferation in the breast ("Basic Information About Breast Cancer" 2021), and the type of cell determines what type of cancer it will be. The cells can begin to grow in many parts of the organ, like the lobules, connective tissue, and ducts. Also, it metastasizes from one part to the other via blood and lymph vessels.

Symptoms of breast cancer may or may not be present ("Bilateral or Double Mastectomy: What to Expect and Recovery" 2022). There are various unchangeable risk factors like genetic mutations, aging, and consumption of certain drugs like diethylstilbestrol (DES). There is a much higher risk of breast and ovarian cancer for people with inherited changes in breast cancer gene 1 (BRCA1) and breast cancer gene 2 (BRCA2) genes ("Breast Cancer Risk Factors You Can't Change" 2019). One way to confirm the presence of breast cancer is via screenings. Although screenings cannot prevent breast cancer, they can be helpful in its early detection. There are various treatments for breast cancers that are done with doctors' consultations. Though breast cancer is commonly detected in females, 1% of the total patients are males ("Breast Cancer" 2016).

Pathologists use breast cancer classification to develop a systematic and structured prognosis, the most common being binary classification (benign tumor/malignant tumor) as shown in Figures 9.1 and 9.2. Machine learning (ML) approaches are now widely used in this scenario. They exhibit excellent prediction performance and diagnostic capability. Examining the medical images is the most effective approach to diagnosing breast cancer. Medical imaging modalities used for diagnosis include infrared thermography (IRT), digital mammography (DM), and ultrasound (US). Mammograms are X-rays of the breast, and they are best for early detection, unlike MRIs and other screening techniques, which are recommended for high-risk patients. As a tool for aiding radiologists and physicians in identifying problems, these modalities produce images that have lowered fatality rates by 30 to 70% (Zhang and Sejdić, 2019). However, because image interpretation is operator dependent and involves ability, information technology is required to increase the diagnostic speed and accuracy while giving another opinion to experts and trained professionals. Furthermore, as these diagnoses depend on a doctor's personal assessment, the diagnostic efficiency varies, increasing the risk of misdiagnosis. Deep learning (DL) and ML approaches have proliferated in biomedical applications to help medical workers with jobs like these. Computer-aided diagnosis (CAD) employs classification algorithms and automated feature extraction and can be a valuable tool for clinicians and specialists in spotting anomalies (Doi, 2007).

Mammography-based computer-aided diagnosis has proven successful in terms of reliability (Ramadan, 2020). As a traditional DL approach, convolutional neural networks (CNNs), have demonstrated their efficacy in this field of CAD based on mammograms (Ramadan, 2020). However, collecting and annotating a large number of mammograms can be costly and time consuming. Moreover, improving the diagnostic accuracy of a mammography-based CAD with a small dataset remains a difficult task, as suggested by multiple papers. One, in particular, Mori et al. (2017), explains the

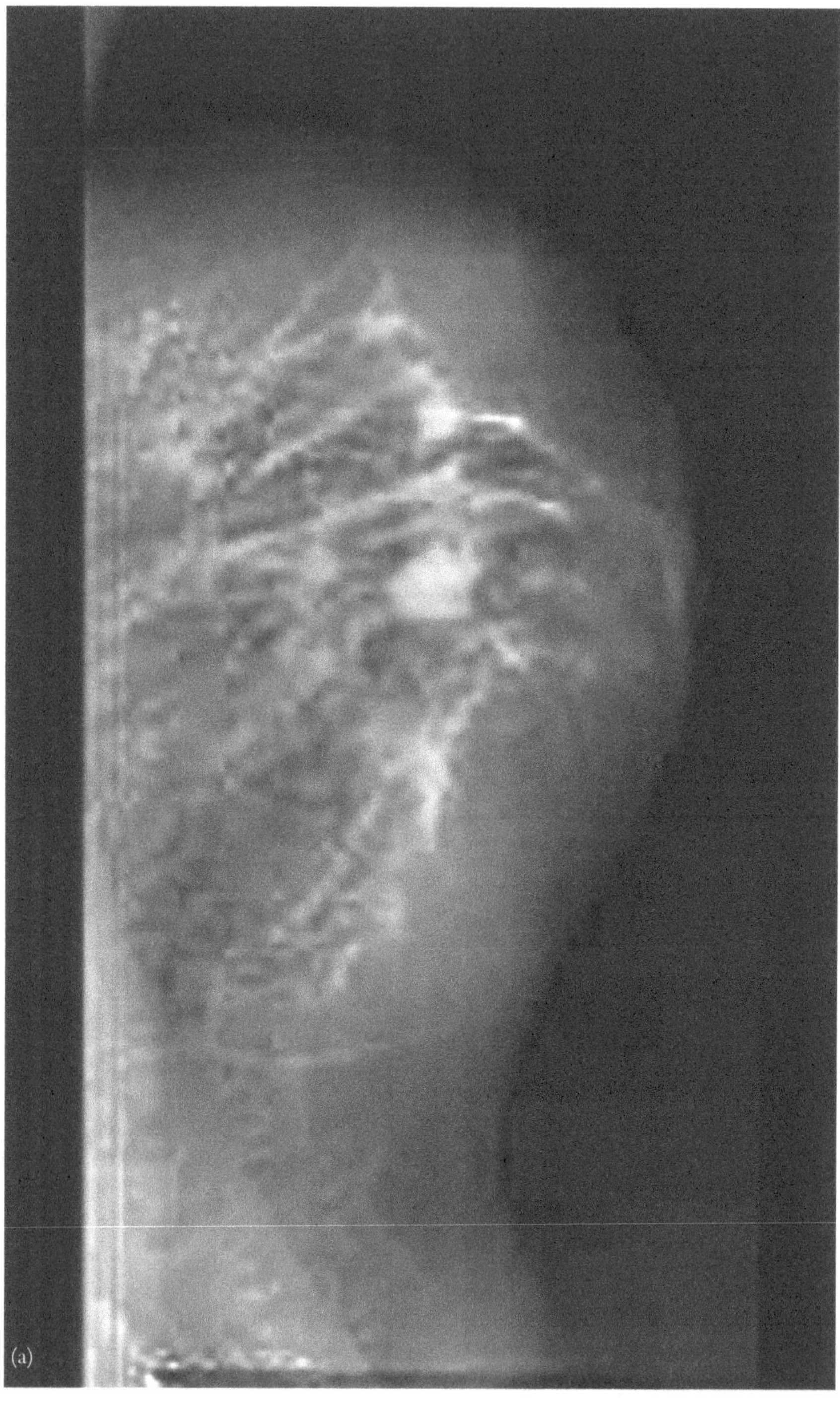

Figure 9.1 (a) Benign mammogram (left) and (b) malignant mammogram (right) from the dataset (Cui et al., 2021). (Continued)

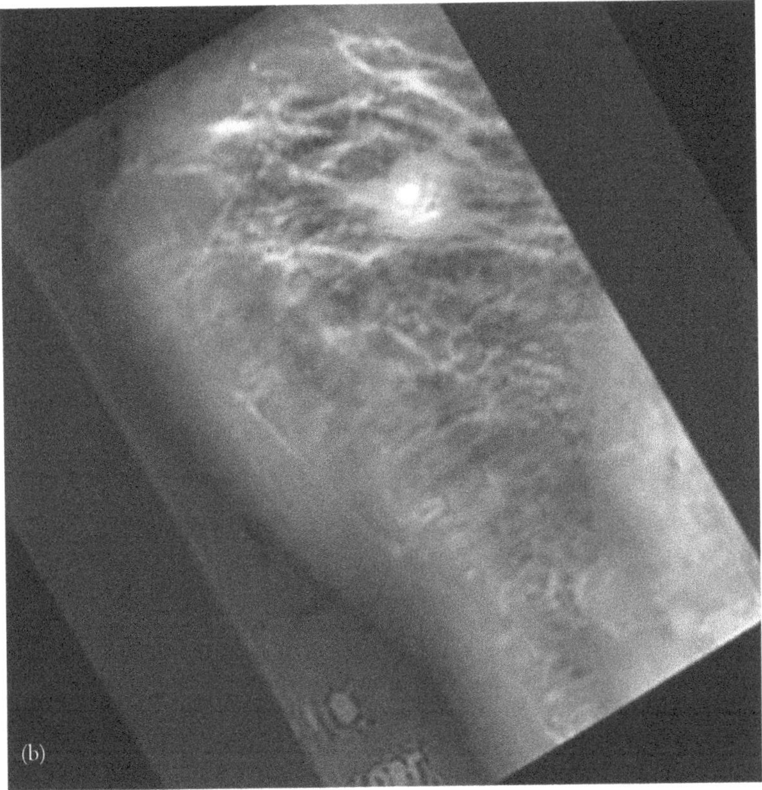

Figure 9.1 (b) (Continued)

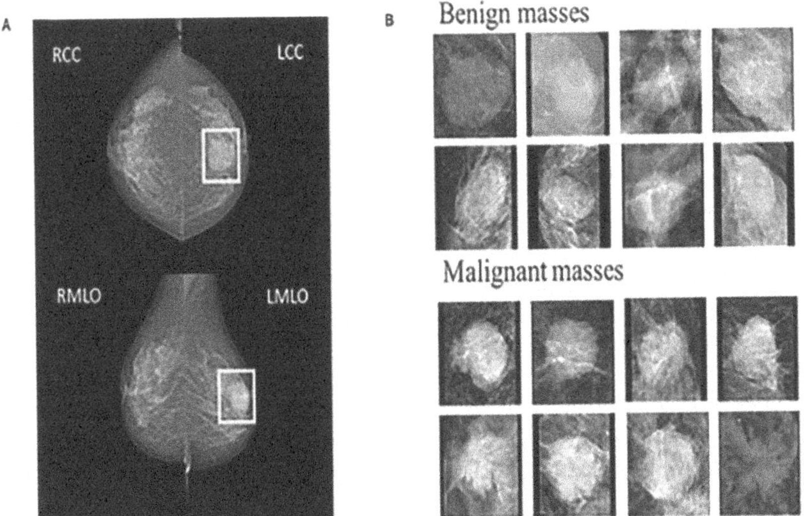

Figure 9.2 Benign masses vs malignant masses in mammograms (Cui et al., 2021).

model's performance concerning the available medical data for training and how much the availability of big data affects the results in traditional ML and DL methods.

In order to create a good model for detecting breast tumors accurately, a sufficient number of samples are required for training. High-quality annotated medical data are not readily available at times. Moreover, the datasets might be smaller, or unlabeled data might outnumber labeled data. Data labeling done manually is required for supervised learning, which is usually a tedious, time-consuming, and error-prone operation; this challenge is overcome through self-supervision. Recent developments in unsupervised learning in computer vision and natural language processing (NLP) have greatly influenced the viability of using vast amounts of unlabeled data. Self-supervised machine learning techniques that produce fictitious labeling as supervision have been crucial to these results. Contrastive learning, which uses the instance bias pretext task, has taken over in the field of computer vision. It performs competitively with traditional supervised learning, and in some downstream tasks like object detection, it even outperforms it. It is primarily instrumental when the datasets are large and thus becomes a faster approach (Daisuke et al., 2021).

The recent advances in algorithms like DL, random forest, and others have shed light on its applications in medical imaging. Such methods make it promising to apply advanced techniques in medical applications and surpass the current state-of-the-art schemes. Since strong augmentation based self-supervised learning (SSLs) is the most recent advancement in the computer vision field, it has not received much attention in the medical imaging field to date (Azizi et al., 2021). More specifically, in the breast cancer image analysis field using screening mammograms, SSL is a very new approach (Miller et al., 2022).

The work done by Miller et al. (2022) targets the same problem as our work. While they focused more on tiled-patch pretraining, our work performs whole image classification directly. Their work focuses on two datasets: the Curated Breast Imaging Subset of Digital Database for Screening Mammography (CBIS-DDSM) and the Chinese Mammography Database (CMMD). We have individually applied our proposed approach to three different datasets: Digital Database for Screening Mammography (DDSM) (Lee et al., 2017), MIAS ("Mammographic Image Analysis" 2021), and INBreast (Moreira et al., 2012). Moreover, to get the best results from a self-supervised learning approach, we combined the three datasets using random sampling and evaluated our approach on a much smaller dataset, confirming that self-supervised learning with a smaller, unannotated dataset can achieve accuracies as high as supervised learning approaches.

The proposed method, if incorporated into the process of diagnosing patients, will act as an assistant to medical personnel. Using a tool like this has the potential to save a substantial percentage of lives by making a proper diagnosis quicker than traditional methods.

In order to make the model interpretable and explainable, it is crucial to understand how the network works with objects and understand the importance of pixels that decide the output of the classifier. Therefore, to implement this, we use saliency maps. First, the model is trained with the datasets, then preprocessed, retrieving the gradient from the image. In this case, the image can be a testing sample from the datasets.

This chapter aims to create a novel approach to image analysis used in breast cancer detection from tumor segmentation and to apply self-supervised learning as a method of analysis in which smaller medical datasets can be leveraged to find better accuracy by manipulating data instances to populate the dataset further. Several attempts have been made to correctly evaluate the accuracy of data classification by various algorithms in terms of effectiveness and efficiency to analyze the results, creating a tool that will help radiologists, doctors, and other researchers study breast cancer further and save lives.

9.1.1 Contributions of This Chapter

The major contributions of this chapter are:

1. Proposition of a novel approach in analyzing scans that can help detect tumors and determine if they are malignant or benign.
2. Comprehensive analysis and comparison of the application of algorithms on different open-source mammogram and ultrasound datasets like DDSM, MIAS, and INbreast.
3. Interpretation and explanation of the model using saliency maps.

The following is an overview of the structure of the chapter: Section 9.2 gives a summary of the related works in the field in the form of a literature survey and the concept of self-supervised learning. Section 9.3 explains the proposed approach and datasets used. Section 9.4 explores the results and analyzes them. Finally, Section 9.5 discusses the limitations, future scope, benefits to society, and conclusions.

9.2 Related Works

This section presents the existing literature for traditional approaches followed by the core concepts of self-supervised learning, after which there are comparisons of algorithms used in the literature. Furthermore, the importance of model explainability and interpretability are also elaborated on.

9.2.1 Existing Literature

The existing state of the art in both traditional methods and self-supervised learning is described in this chapter. Moreover, the chapter presents the most recent developments in these fields in this section along with certain limitations faced by the current literature.

9.2.1.1 About Traditional Computer-Aided Diagnosis Systems

Wang et al. (2020) utilize a CNN-based CAD for breast cancer classification. The paper uses Inception-v3 for effective feature extraction, with satisfactory results. The preferred approach gets an area under curve (AUC) value of 0.9468 after assessing

316 breast lesions, basing their verification process on five human reviewers' diagnoses. Compared to the standard feature extraction approaches like principal component analysis (PCA) or histogram of oriented gradients (HOG), the model achieves a greater than 10% improved AUC value.

The CBIS-DDSM dataset was utilized by Shen et al. (2019) to optimize the breast cancer diagnosis process on mammography screening. Lesion markers are only necessary during the preliminary training iteration in this approach, and subsequent stages simply necessitate image-level annotations, eliminating the need for scarce lesion labels. The single best individual model obtained a per-image accuracy of 88% on an experimental testing dataset of digitized mammograms from the CBIS-DDSM dataset, while four-model averaging boosted the accuracy to 91%.

Algorithms were utilized by Ribli et al. (2018) to identify and categorize abnormalities in mammograms. Faster region-based convolutional neural network (R-CNN) is the approach method used in this paper. This R-CNN incorporates some of convolutional layers that are trained to recognize and localize items in the picture, independently of their class, on top of the initial network's final convolutional layer. The suggested approach achieves a classification accuracy with an AUC of 0.95 on the public INbreast database. The approach provided here took second place in the Digital Mammography DREAM Challenge (2022) with an accuracy of 85%. When employed as a detector on the INbreast dataset, the system obtains high sensitivity yet a very low false-positive score per data sample. This model's classification performance was only tested on the small INbreast dataset, and this is a limitation of the proposed method.

Harvey et al. (2019) discuss how deep learning facilitates the process of breast cancer mammogram screening. The approach shows how practitioners used CAD models in the beginning and then what challenges were faced and how better systems were eventually developed to train these datasets. It mainly discusses all the relevant material that is available on breast cancer screening and how it can be used for further research purposes. The paper also talks about a deep learning system made by the authors called mammography intelligent assessment (MIA), which understands the models and acts as a second opinion that gives case-wise callback results to patients. The paper also states that while the research on using 3D digital breast tomosynthesis (DBT) is going ahead quickly, it will require more time to interpret, which is a major reason it is not as commonly used.

Geras et al. (2017) discuss why the deep learning models that give high accuracy to natural images cannot be used for mammograms. In medical photos, precise details are required for detection, whereas in natural images, coarse structures are most important. Because of this discrepancy, existing network designs designed for natural images are insufficient because they function on significantly downscaled images to save memory, which conceals information needed to make good forecasts. Thus, the paper uses the BI-RADS dataset to achieve a probabilistic accuracy of 0.688, whereas radiologists achieved 0.704. One of the constraints was the fact that because of limited computing resources, any systematic survey for optimal hyperparameters could not be performed.

Muduli et al. (2022) propose using a CNN with a DL approach for both mammograms and ultrasound images. The proposed approach tests their unique model with only five learnable layers on INbreast, DDSM, and MIAS mammogram datasets as well as BUS-1 and BUS-2 ultrasound datasets (Al-Dhabyani et al., 2020). Using fewer layers, the suggested approach succeeded in achieving lower computational cost, maximized the speed of learning, and improved performance accuracy when put against the pre-defined CNN models. The suggested algorithm attains an AUC of 0.965 on the MIAS, 0.906 on the DDSM, 0.912 on the INbreast, 1 on the BUS-1, and 0.89.7 on the BUS-2 dataset. The model also eliminates the need for manual extraction of features and eliminates all feature reduction activities. Subsequently, the suggested approach is more time efficient.

Wu et al. (2020) propose a deep CNN model based on over 1 million scans and achieve an average AUC value of 0.895 in predicting whether a breast tumor is malignant. The proposed approach verified the results from a novel two-stage network design by presenting radiologists with a portion of the screening mammogram exams. The hybrid approach also demonstrates that the average likelihood of malignancy by the neural network and radiologists provides better accuracy than either of them independently.

Yassin et al. (2018) surveyed various ML techniques used in image modalities to detect BC. The approach discovered that digital mammograms had been used in the majority of the papers. The support vector machine (SVM) technique achieved an accuracy in the range 90%–99.5% for DMs, with two achieving 100% accuracy. Artificial neural networks (ANNs) used for DMs gave 90–98.14% accuracy. K-nearest neighbor (KNN) registered the highest accuracy of 98.69% for DMs. According to the data that was gathered, it was difficult to compare approaches extensively due to a number of issues. The datasets used for evaluation, the image samples shortlisted for evaluation, the amount of sample data used, and the assessment process employed are some of these considerations. The main limitation of the paper is that it is difficult to compare approaches fully due to a number of issues. Furthermore, the parameter tuning used in various approaches differs from one method to another, creating yet another barrier to a meaningful comparison of diverse methods.

While these methods have been extremely beneficial in furthering the research in the field of breast cancer, there came a need to address the limitations of medical data availability as well as employing the approach of self-supervised learning in this use case.

9.2.2 Self-Supervised Learning

Recently, machine learning has had several breakthroughs and continues to have an impact across a variety of disciplines. Data availability is a common thread that runs through all of these fields. Machine learning algorithms have reached or even outperformed human performance (Wiens and Shenoy, 2018). Due to the expansion in the available datasets that are relevant clinically, scholars have now started to apply ML approaches to a broad variety of healthcare practices, from diagnosing to prognosis tasks. Machine learning methodologies are widely divided into three categories: supervised learning, unsupervised learning, and reinforcement learning.

This chapter explores a specific ML approach called self-supervised learning. Previously, a large percentage of clinical data was discarded (or not even collected in the first place). This constraint stemmed from the data's bulk and complexity, as well as the lack of means for gathering and storing it. Medical sample collection is always a time-consuming procedure that necessitates a lot of overhead and time from skilled personnel for labeling purposes. Self-supervision allows to utilization of a fraction of the labeled samples required for deep learning classification tasks. Due to the expense of gathering medical data and labeling them, datasets for identifying cancer with mammography images are often tiny and potentially non-representative, unlike in conventional object identification, where big, diversified datasets can be leveraged. This makes training and evaluating such models difficult, raising concerns about their reliability and generalizability.

The SSL approach uses the annotated and unannotated data together to enhance the effectiveness of the training models. This approach does not use information already known or labeled beforehand but instead learns from scratch. This enables the model to uncover different aspects of medical scans that were not apparent to the classifier beforehand.

9.2.2.1 SimCLR

Traditionally, pretraining done using an unsupervised learning approach is followed by supervised fine-tuning to make the best out of a smaller batch of data that is unlabeled. In contrast to the more common and popular approaches, the SimCLR framework uses all the unlabeled samples in a task-independent manner. By employing this method using a task-specific method, the massive structure may be refined and condensed into a rather reduced network with no loss of prediction performance after fine-tuning (Chen et al., 2020).

9.2.2.2 Drawbacks of SimCLR

The choice of image augmentation has an impact on contrastive approaches. SimCLR struggles to remove color distortion from its image augmentations. It indicates why the color histograms of crops from the same image are almost always the same (Chen et al., 2020). Color histograms fluctuate among images. As a result, when a contrastive task uses randomized cropping as visual augmentations, it is typically best to concentrate simply on colored histograms. As a consequence, there is no benefit for the representation to keep information. Instead, approaches like bootstrap your own latent (BYOL) maintain any data acquired by the desired representation in its online network in an effort to boost estimations (Grill et al., 2020). It retains more characteristics in its representation regardless if the augmented viewpoints of the same data sample have the exact same color histogram. As a result, BYOL is more resistant to image augmentation selections than contrastive approaches. This model is also less susceptible to systematic biases in the training data. This usually suggests that it is more generalizable to unobserved examples. In most benchmarks, BYOL outperforms SimCLR (Grill et al., 2020). More specifically, in medical imaging,

Miller et al. evaluate the results of BYOL vs. SimCLR, suggesting that SimCLR might not be best suited for mammographic image evaluation tasks (2022). Sample types of image augmentations used in BYOL are depicted in Figure 9.3.

9.2.2.3 The Promise of Self-Supervised Learning

Yin et al. (2020) used the University of California, Irvine (UCI), dataset for finding pattern classification techniques for breast tumor detection using magnetic resonance imaging scans. The review paper also discussed self-supervised and semi-supervised DL approaches as well as generative adversial networks (GANs) for differentiating the tumor types. The approach proposed in the paper can help in the early identification of heterogeneous tumors. The suggested approach employs innovative loss

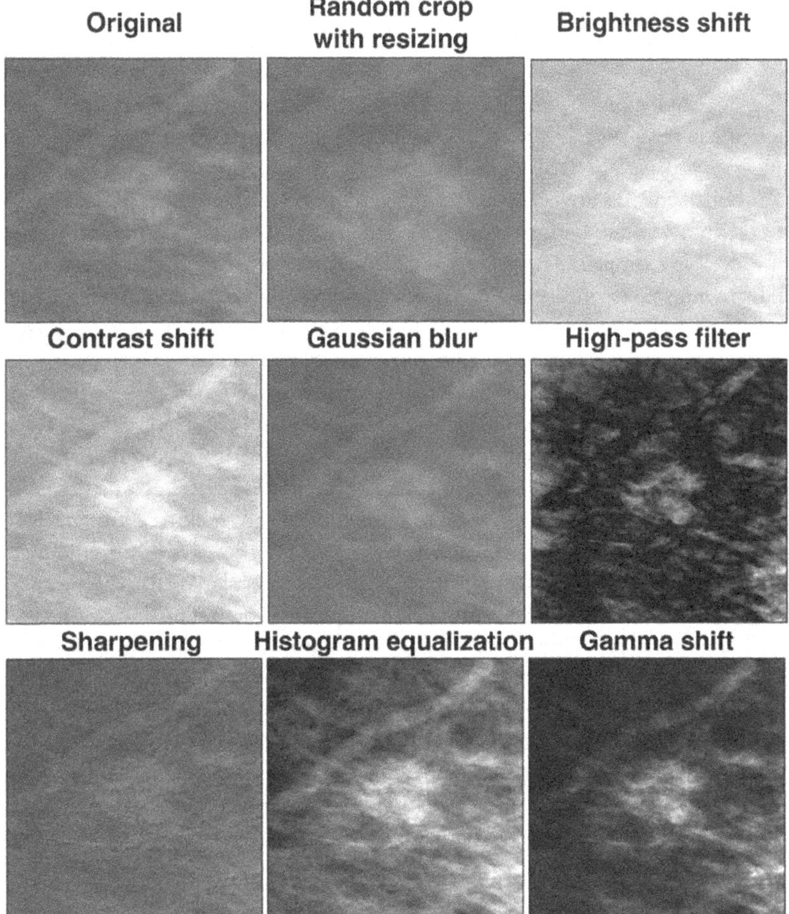

Figure 9.3 Sample types of image augmentations used in bootstrap your own latent (Miller et al., 2022).

functions that serve as the foundation for a produced confrontation learning methodology for tensorial Dynamic Contrast-Enhanced Magnetic Resonance Imaging (DCE-MRI). As a few of the methods mentioned are based on a type of imaging based on time-lapse, inferences about the disease's rate of progression are conceivable. This paper concludes DCE-MRI is among the most effective modalities for breast tumor imaging considering all the various approaches used to detect it but also states that the specificity of detection is low. Thus, it proposes that deep CNN should be used in order to make full use of these datasets.

Gong et al. (2021) propose a method of "task-driven self-supervised bi-channel networks" (TSBNs) in order to overcome the challenge of pretext tasks and fine-tuning mechanisms. The pretext task is a new gray-scale image mapping task that incorporates information about the mammogram's class label into the restoration effort in order to enhance the discriminative representation of features. After that, the suggested system merges several architectures, such as image retrieval and classifier, into a single framework which uses SSL in a novel way. It trains the bi-channel network models by training as well as increasing the transmission accuracy to exchange information from pretext to downstream task. The suggested approach surpasses traditional SSL algorithms based on fine-tuning on the open-source dataset, INbreast, based on the results. The pretext and downstream bi-channel networks are both given training, and the resulting trained representations of features in both networks are communicated to each other cooperatively. This approach improves downstream task performance while simultaneously addressing the issue of the usage of only a few samples. The suggested TSBN outperforms traditional fine-tuning–based SSL algorithms, according to experimental findings on the public INbreast dataset. The paper further plans to look into other alternatives to design different types of pretext tasks based on label information and medical data characteristics in the TSBN framework. The researchers also strive to increase the transfer performance across two separate networks in order to improve the downstream CAD model's classification accuracy.

Miller et al. (2022) investigate SSL strategies based on strong augmentation to solve the problem of the dearth of good-quality curated datasets for breast cancer. They propose a strategy for converting a pretrained model to making estimations on uniformly tiled patches to whole images, as well as an attention-based pooling technique that boosts the classification performance. They discovered that the best SSL model was BYOL as compared to SimCLR, swapping assignments between views (SWaV), and vision transformers masked auto encoding (ViT-MAE) based on annotated patch classification. BYOL was highly transferable from one dataset to another and also increased the sample labeling's data efficiency about fourfold. Considering annotated patch classification, BYOL outperformed other pretext task algorithms like SimCLR, SWaV, and ViT-MAE, achieving a test set accuracy of 76.3% on the dataset. This study shows that the fine-tuned models greatly enhance data efficiency, outperforming the supervised learning baseline in every subgroup.

9.2.2.4 Explainable AI and Applications in Healthcare

Oyama and Yamanaka (2018) examine the study of saliency map's architecture and also the impact of image classification using ImageNet on the saliency map estimation. First, it demonstrated that there is a significant association between saliency map estimation accuracy and image classification accuracy. Additionally, it was discovered that in order to estimate the saliency maps, both the architecture and the initialization technique using weights pre-trained with the ImageNet classification task are crucial. Second, DenseSal and DPNSal were used to examine the efficient architecture and training process for saliency map estimation. The network's ability to be resilient to the size of objects in images provided evidence that the multipath architecture is advantageous.

In order to explain black-box deep-learning systems, this work focuses on post-hoc explanation-by-example solutions to XAI. Three different post-hoc explanation techniques – factual, counterfactual, and semi factual techniques – are described in detail.

Mossman et al. (2006) demonstrate an effective method for object categorization. The research was also able to significantly enhance results as compared to simply uniformly sampling windows by defining saliency as the capacity of a classifier to identify features well by creating these saliency maps and biasing the random sampling of sub windows. As a result, a state-of-the-art categorization system that can process images in under 2 seconds is developed.

9.3 Methodology

The proposed approach is presented in Figure 9.4. A detailed breakdown of each aspect in the figure is elucidated as follows.

An input mammogram instance is fed to the system. The necessary image augmentations are made. A random patch of the images is selected and resized into a target size of 224 × 224 with a horizontal flip. Then, in a random order, the other image augmentation techniques are applied. Color dropping is performed where the image is converted into grayscale. Gaussian blurring is done where, for a 224 × 224 image, a 23 × 23 square Gaussian kernel is employed using a standard deviation uniformly sampled over [0.1, 2.0]. Color jittering is also performed, which includes shifting the saturation, contrast, brightness, and hue of the image by a random offset on all pixels. In order to implement these transformations, Kornia in PyTorch is used, which is a differentiable CV library.

The encoder is responsible for feature extraction from the base model and projecting them into a latent space with a lower dimension. Feature extraction will collect outputs from one of the last model layers. This is implemented using hooks,

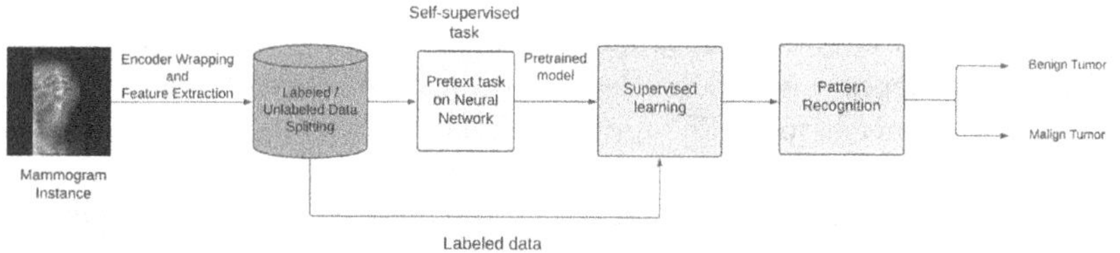

Figure 9.4 Proposed approach for breast cancer image analysis and prediction.

which are functions that execute automatically after a particular event. The projector is another module that is in charge of projecting the outputs down the lower dimensions. For BYOL's training code, PyTorch Lightning is used, which is a library for deep learning projects, which includes conveniences like multi-GPU training, experiment logging, model check pointing, and mixed-precision training.

Code for processing data samples can get messy and hard to maintain; ideally, the dataset code should be decoupled from the model training code for better readability and modularity. PyTorch provides two data primitives: torch.utils.data.DataLoader and torch.utils.data. The dataset allows you to use preloaded datasets as well as your own data. The dataset stores the samples and their corresponding labels, and DataLoader wraps an iterable around the dataset to enable easy access to the samples. This is used to create a custom dataset and data loader that can be easily iterable and can be used with ease with PyTorch lightning neural network modules. The dataset is divided into train, test (for supervised learning), and unlabeled data (for BYOL).

Following this, the BYOL architecture implements a target and an online network in which it minimizes the distance between representations of each sample and a transformation of that sample. These samples are usually alternative augmentations of the original image from the dataset. This is also referred to as a pretext task, and the model is trained on unlabeled data taken from the data loaders.

The learning rate and weight decay are similar to the ones used in the supervised learning task. The BYOL class will define the target, updated_target, optimizers, training_step, epochs, validation steps, learning rate, and other parameters.

The model is passed after the pretext class to do supervised learning and uses Resnet-18/34/50 for 25 epochs and a $1e^{-4}$ and $1e^{-6}$ learning rate, and weight decay is used. The results are then divided into benign and malignant samples as the results.

In order to make the model interpretable and explainable, we need to understand how the network works with objects and the importance of pixels that decide the output of the classifier; to implement this, we use saliency maps. The model is first trained with the datasets; then we preprocess and retrieve the gradient from the image. In this case, the image can be a testing sample from the datasets.

9.3.1 Bootstrap Your Own Latent

Bootstrap your own latent is a self-supervised learning approach that is akin to contrastive learning with the exception that it does not worry about whether dissimilar samples have differing representations (which is the contrastive part of contrastive learning) (Grill et al., 2020). Figure 9.5 shown the architecture of BYOL. The method merely ensures that similar samples have comparable representations. This difference may appear insignificant, but it has significant implications for training efficiency and generalization. Because BYOL does not require negative sampling, training is more effective. The negative equivalents can be ignored entirely because each training example is sampled just once in each epoch. Furthermore, the suggested method is less vulnerable to systematic biases in the training dataset, implying that it generalizes better to unobserved occurrences.

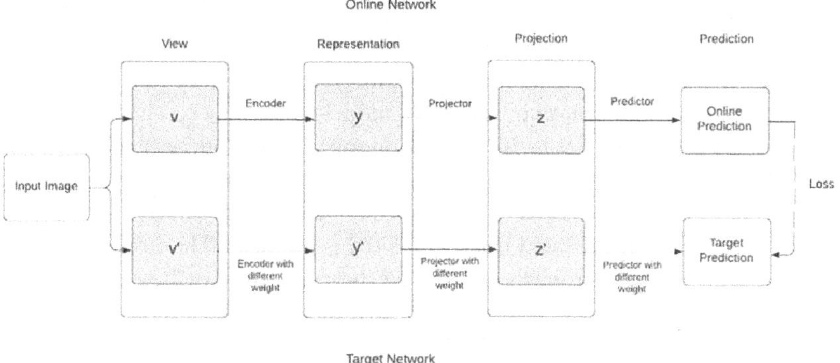

Figure 9.5 BYOL architecture (Grill et al., 2020).

BYOL additionally closes the gap between each sample's representations and transformations. Translation, rotation, blurring, color inversion, color jitter, Gaussian noise, and other transformations are examples. Though this chapter has used images as an example, BYOL can also be utilized with other forms of data. Models are often trained using a combination of transformations that can be used together or separately. If the model is expected to be invariant under a specific transformation, it should be incorporated into the training.

BYOL has two encoder networks that are identical. The first one is trained as normal, with every training batch updating its weights. A continuous mean of the first encoder's weights is used to update the second, also referred to as the "target" network. During training, a raw training batch is supplied to the target network, and a modified version of the very same batch is delivered to the other encoder. For its respective data, each network develops a low-dimensional, latent representation. Then, using a multi-layer perceptron, we try to anticipate the outcome of the target network. The correlation between this forecast and the output of the target network is maximized by BYOL.

The multilayer perceptron layer in a kind of feed-forward artificial neural network that learns to identify input modifications and estimates the target latent vector. As a result, weights no longer collapse to zero, allowing the model to learn self-consistent representations. This way, the overall performance of the model can be enhanced by this SSL method.

9.3.2 ResNet

The branch of computer vision (CV) has recently seen a number of developments. Since the introduction of deep CNNs, scientists are getting cutting-edge results on tasks like image identification and classification. As a result, over time, researchers have preferred to develop deeper neural networks (adding more layers) in order to accomplish these challenging tasks and improve classification accuracy. We often stack extra layers in Deep Neural Networks (DNNs), which increases accuracy and performance in order to tackle a challenging problem. The concept underlying adding further layers is that as time passes, the layers will learn complex traits (Great Learning Team, 2020). In the case of image recognition, for instance, the first layer may learn to recognize edges, the second may learn to recognize textures, the third may learn to recognize objects, and so on. The conventional CNN model does, however, have a threshold. This suggests that when more layers are built on top of a network, its performance declines. The neural network becomes more complex to train as more layers are added, and as a result, its accuracy starts to saturate and eventually degrades. Here, ResNet, or residual network, steps in and helps to solve this problem. The difficulty of training very deep networks has been reduced by the emergence of ResNet, which are composed of residual blocks. The first thing that occurs is that a direct link is made, skipping various stages in between. This is the "skip connection," which is at the core of residual blocks. The problem of disappearing gradient in deep neural networks is alleviated by ResNet's skip connections by allowing the gradient to pass through a supplementary bypass channel (Great Learning Team, 2020).

9.3.3 Data Sources and Sample Sizes

Three different open-source datasets were combined in order to get the best results: Digital Database for Screening Mammography, Mammographic Image Analysis Society, and INbreast. Randomly selected scans from these datasets were used to form a smaller, combined dataset to perform self-supervised learning efficiently. Samples from each of these datasets are shown in Figures 9.6 to 9.8.

DDSM is a resource used by the mammographic image analysis research community. There are about 2500 examples total in this database. Each case includes a photograph of each breast as well as details about the patient, including age, the American College of Radiology (ACR) breast density rating, any anomalies, and image details. Pixel-level data regarding the suspicious regions are paired with images

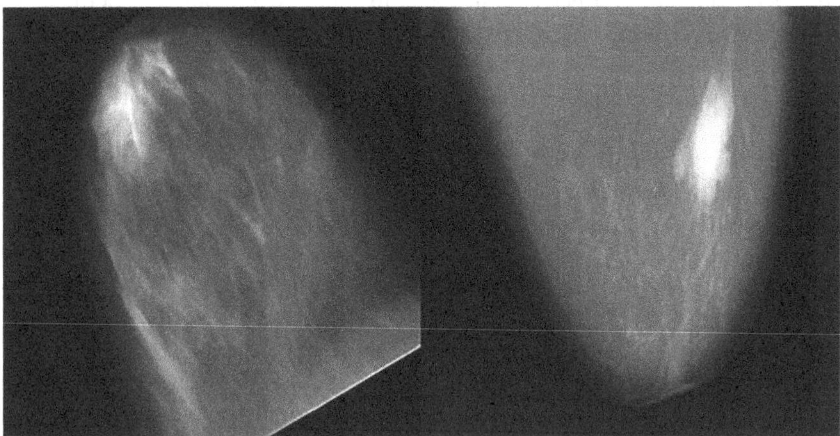

Figure 9.6 Benign sample (left) and malignant sample (right) from the DDSM dataset taken from Lee et al. (2017).

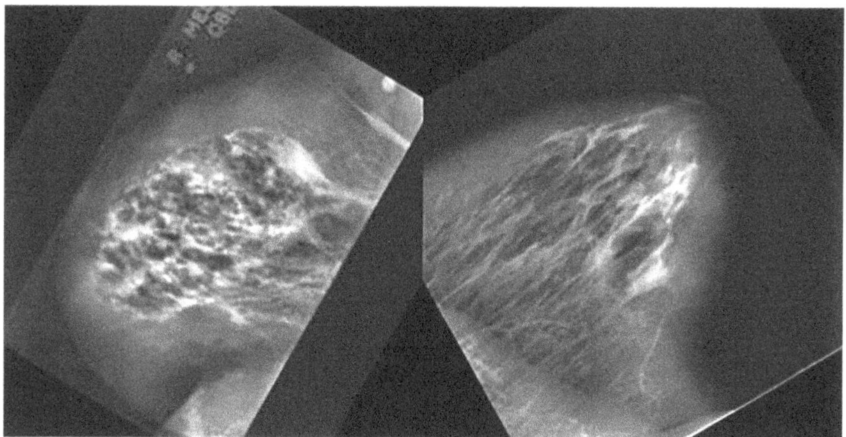

Figure 9.7 Benign sample (left) and malignant sample (right) from the MIAS dataset taken from "Mammographic Image Analysis" (2021).

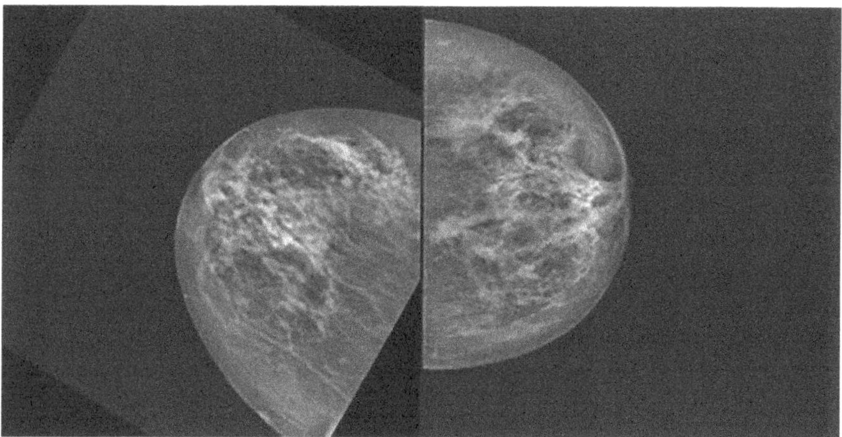

Figure 9.8 Benign sample (left) and malignant sample (right) from the INbreast dataset taken from Moreira et al. (2012).

that contain those regions. Performance metrics for automated image analysis systems can be computed using these mammograms and truth pictures.

MIAS ("Mammographic Image Analysis" 2021) has contributed to the collection of mammograms and the development of a digital database of the same. With the aid of a Joyce-Loebl microdensitometer, these mammograms have been digitally enhanced to 50-micron pixel edges. This database contains 322 digitized films and is available on 2.3-GB 8-mm tape. The radiologists have annotated the photographs that show anomalies. The database's photos are trimmed to 200-micron pixel boundaries and resized to 1024 × 1024 pixels overall. The University of Essex's Pilot European Image Processing Archive (PEIPA) provides access to mammographic pictures.

INbreast (Moreira et al., 2012) consists of 115 cases, which includes a total of 410 images. Out of this, women affected with both breasts make up around 90 cases; that is, four images in every case and about 21% of the cases are of mastectomy patients. This database was made for works related to breast cancer imaging and was made publicly available with a variety of cases. The INbreast database is built with full-field digital mammography (FFDM), in that it uses electrical signals to form images of the breast, which can then be viewed on screens. These mammograms are much better than digitized mammograms, as they can be maneuvered to improve their contrast and resolution. The clarified image then eliminates the need for advanced imaging and improves interpretations for medical practitioners.

9.3.4 Tools Used

For the implementation of proposed approach, the tools used were PyTorch, TensorFlow, and Keras. PyTorch libraries used were Kornia, Lightning module, and dataloaders.

9.3.5 Saliency Maps

Saliency maps are the derivatives of an AI's class probability *Pi* with respect to the input image *X*. Representation of a saliency map is shown is Equation 9.1 (Springenberg et al., 2014).

$$SaliencyMap = \frac{dX}{dPi} \tag{9.1}$$

As shown in Figure 9.9, the gradient does not stop at the initial layer of our network. Instead, we have to propagate it back to the input image *X* and the pixels *xi* (Springenberg et al., 2014).

Saliency maps give us a relevant quantification for every input pixel with respect to a certain class prediction *Pi*. The pixels important for a malignant sample should be highlighted near the cancerous areas. Otherwise, there is something very weird going

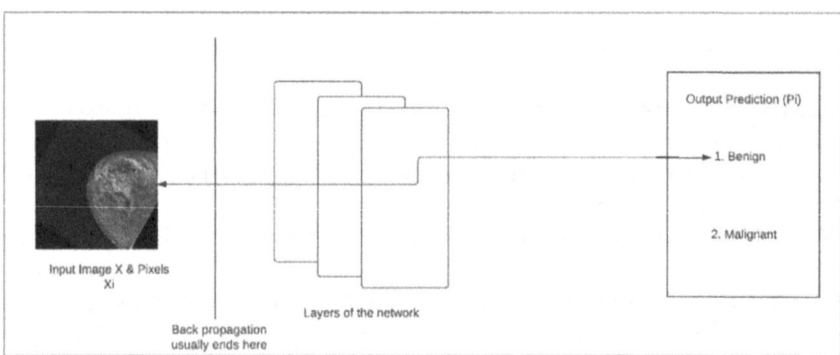

Figure 9.9 Working of the saliency map.

on. The good thing about saliency maps is that because they only rely on gradient calculations, all the commonly used AI frameworks are capable of giving us saliency maps almost for free. We do not have to modify the network architectures at all; we just have to modify the gradient calculations a little bit (Springenberg et al., 2014).

The locations of important information in an image are indicated on saliency maps. These regions relate to traits that, depending on how saliency is defined, are either uncommon or instructive. Low-saliency areas are related to background, while high-saliency areas correspond to objects or places where they are most likely to be found. In order to recognize and classify objects, a classification system can use this information as a prior. The majority of methods used thus far are independent of the task and are based on a bottom-up process. We contend that it is more advantageous for a classification system to be aware of the regions where the classifier can find factors to identify objects (Simonyan et al., 2013). The working of saliency maps with respect to the work presented in this paper is shown in Figure 9.9.

9.4 Results and Analysis

The basic architecture that has been used for the model is ResNet. Since it is designed for three input image channels, for the proposed approach, it had to be configured for one image channel size. With a batch size of 128, we trained this model for a period of 25 epochs. The time taken for the model to train was roughly 300 minutes. The learning rate was set to $1e^{-4}$, and the weight decay was set to $1e^{-6}$.

As shown in Figure 9.10, the highest accuracy achieved was on Resnet-18, which was 96.79% on the combined dataset. The model also gave an accuracy of 92.91% and 90.27% for the Resnet-34 and Resnet-50 architectures, respectively.

For the INbreast dataset, the Resnet-18 architecture gave an accuracy of 89.31%, whereas Resnet-34 and Resnet-50 achieved an accuracy of 87.64% and 88.47%, respectively. For the MIAS dataset, Resnet-18 gave the best accuracy of 98.73%, and

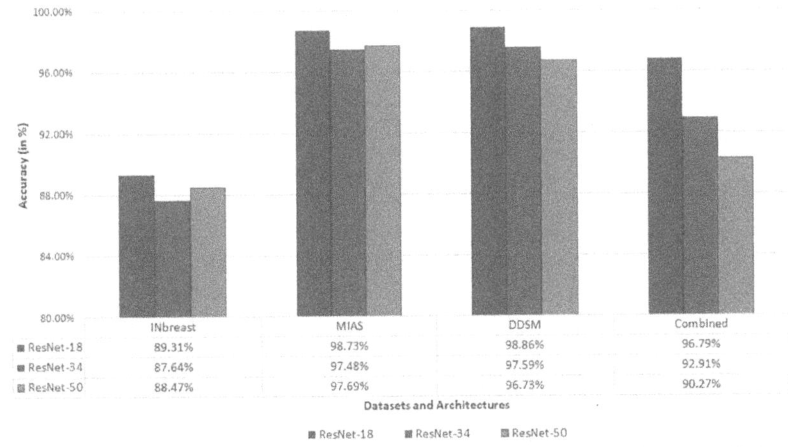

Figure 9.10 Performance comparison of the proposed approach using various architectures.

the worst accuracy was given by Resnet-34 at 97.48%. Resnet-50 gave an accuracy of 97.69%. For the DDSM dataset, Resnet-18 gave the best accuracy of 98.86%. Resnet-34 and Resnet-50 gave similar accuracies of 97.59% and 96.73%, respectively.

Different ResNet models showed varying accuracies on the same dataset. Our accuracies ranged from 87.64% to 98.86% on different datasets using different ResNet architectures. Average accuracy considering all of this was 94.85%. The results achieved by combining datasets with random sampling to get a smaller dataset were the best representation of self-supervised learning. The combined dataset included a total of 3906 samples, 1974 malignant ones and 1932 benign ones to get trained on, achieving the highest accuracy of 96.7% on the Resnet-18 architecture.

These results outperform the supervised learning baseline accuracy. Not only that, this also outperforms the results by Miller et al. (2022) using BYOL and fine-tuned ResNet-50–2x on the DDSM dataset, their evaluation achieving a maximum AUC of 0.803.

A loss curve is one of the most often used charts to debug a neural network during training. It gives a broad perspective of both the network's learning curve and the training process. Two periods can be used to log the loss:

- After each epoch
- After each iteration

The loss vs. epoch curve tells us whether the model is underfitted or overfitted. If the model has trained really fast, then it might be overfitted, and if training is extremely slow, then underfitting might be the issue. As shown in Figure 9.11, the curve for

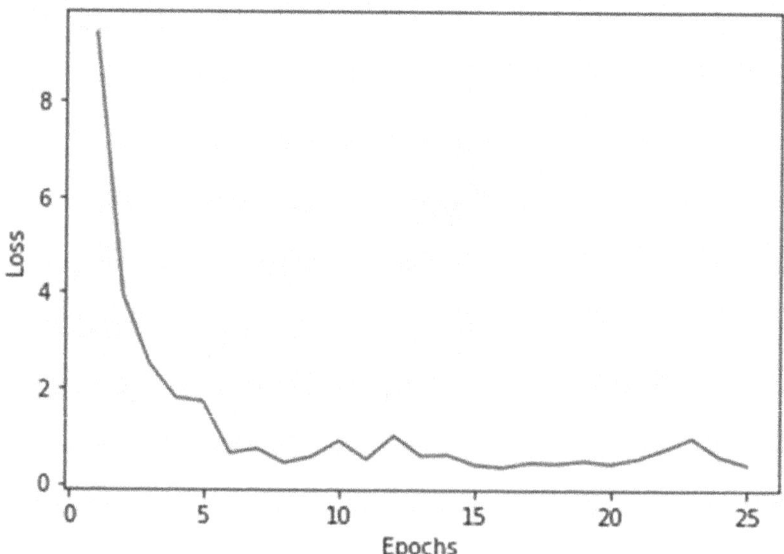

Figure 9.11 Analysis of loss vs. epochs Resnet-18 combined dataset.

the model proposed shows that after the tenth epoch, the curve has flattened, which means that the model has trained and all the other iterations are redundant.

Figure 9.12 represents the saliency maps for the given network. The brighter pixels are represented as pixels that have a greater effect on the output.

9.5 Conclusion and Future Scope

The results of the implementation demonstrate the efficacy of self-supervised learning for breast cancer prediction and analysis. The pretext task, powered by self-supervised learning, helps in populating the dataset to an extent that will help the model to learn sufficiently from the dataset. This novel approach will provide better accuracy on the dataset as compared to the original dataset, which is smaller and contains many unannotated data instances. This approach performed better than state-of-the-art methods on these datasets without compromising on accuracy.

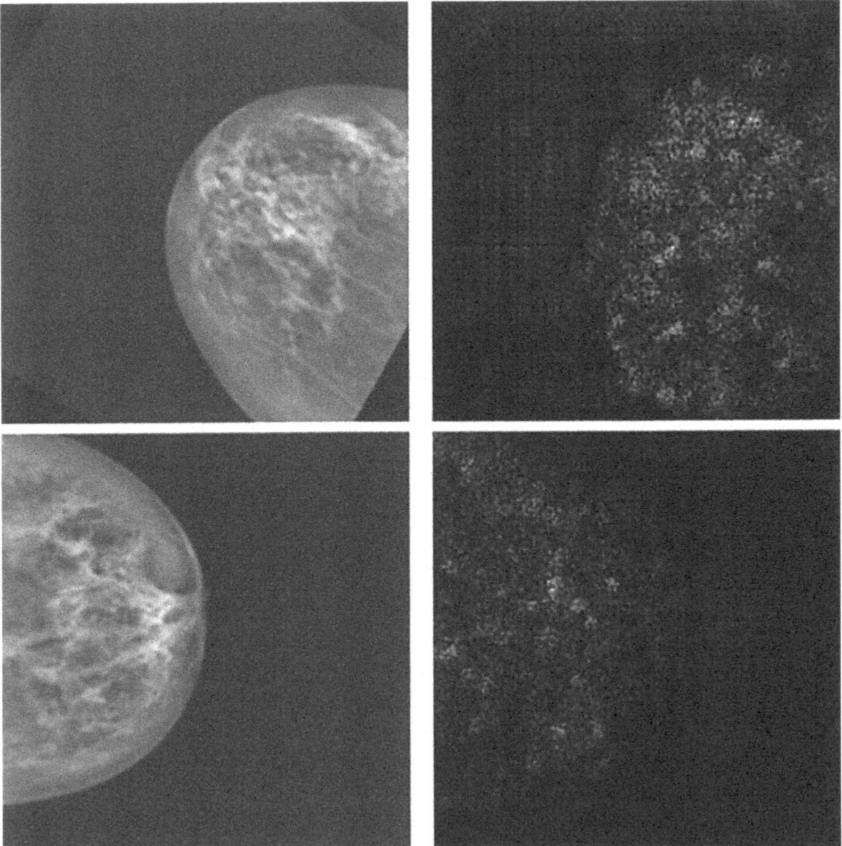

Figure 9.12 Saliency map for benign sample (upper), and malignant sample (lower) from the combined dataset.

Moreover, this model will be of extreme help to radiologists and other medical professionals as well as researchers, hopefully giving rise to more research in the field and aiding in saving many lives by predicting whether a tumor in a mammogram is malign or benign. As predictions become more accurate, better diagnosis of the patients can be done, and it will then help in decreasing the mortality rate. This strategy will assist in reducing the workload of medical personnel while also improving performance and transparency in the process.

Through the usage of these algorithms and machine learning models on a limited working dataset, the model can better help doctors or radiologists to analyze anomalies as compared to traditional machine learning approaches like supervised or unsupervised learning. This will help reduce medical misdiagnosis and will act as a tool to aid doctors in giving accurate predictions. The proposal is a novel method to analyze scans that can help detect tumors and determine if they are malignant or benign. The comprehensive analysis and comparison of the application of algorithms on different mammogram datasets like DDSM, MIAS, and INbreast make it more reliable and accurate. The increase in training datasets publicly accessible at large hospitals is critical for the development and advancement of medical imaging algorithms that might eventually enhance quality of patient care, making these study findings significant for future research.

In the future, validation of the model's utility should be done in real time by interpreting screening mammograms as they are produced. Moreover, among the various tasks of interest, the one investigated in this study, that is, predicting if the patient had a visible malignancy at the time of the screening mammography examination, is one of the simplest. A clear next step would be to anticipate the development of breast cancer before it is even detectable to a trained human eye.

This model can also be modified to make it suitable to be tested on other organs like the brain, and lungs as well. Further, various options would be analyzed to design different types of pretext tasks such as rotating images and zooming in or out based on label information and medical data characteristics. The final task would be to look for ways to maintain or improve accuracy on real-time, unseen data, because if the data encountered by the model have never been seen before, that could affect the learned anatomical features of the model.

The greatest breakthrough is that our model created for breast cancer image analysis is also interpretable and can be explained through saliency maps where a specific importance is given to each and every pixel in the mammogram scan. The brighter the pixel, the more importance the pixel has on the given feature. The saliency map represents the model's view of the mammogram instance.

The current limitation of this model does not take into account the unseen extreme cases, and specialized help from a medical practitioner is required. Also, medical projects can be very uncertain because of the implications involved. Hence, the final validations always lie with the subject matter expert.

References

Al-Dhabyani, Walid, Mohammed Gomaa, Hussien Khaled, and Aly Fahmy. 2020. "Dataset of Breast Ultrasound Images." *Data in Brief* 28: 104863. https://doi.org/10.1016/j.dib.2019.104863.

ASCO. 2021. *Understanding Statistics Used to Guide Prognosis and Evaluate Treatment.* www.cancer.net. Accessed: July, 2021.

Azizi, S., B. Mustafa, F. Ryan, Z. Beaver, J. Freyberg, J. Deaton, A. Loh, A. Karthikesalingam, S. Kornblith, T. Chen, and V. Natarajan. 2021. "Big Self-Supervised Models Advance Medical Image Classification. In *Proceedings of the IEEE/CVF International Conference on Computer Vision*, pp. 3478–3488. https://doi.org/10.1109/iccv48922.2021.00346.

Basic Information About Breast Cancer. 2021. *Centers for Disease Control and Prevention.* www.cdc.gov/cancer/breast/basic_info/. Accessed: September, 2021.

Bilateral or Double Mastectomy: What to Expect and Recovery. 2022. *Cancer Treatment Centers of America.* www.cancercenter.com/cancer-types/breast-cancer/treatments/surgery/double-mastectomy. Accessed: February 4, 2022.

Breast Cancer. 2016. *World Health Organization*, March 26. www.who.int/news-room/fact-sheets/detail/breast-cancer. Accessed: August, 2021.

Breast Cancer Risk Factors You Can't Change, September 2019. www.cancer.org, Accessed: July, 2021.

Cancer. 2022. *World Health Organization*, February 2. www.who.int/health-topics/cancer, Accessed: July, 2021.

Chen, Ting, Simon Kornblith, Mohammad Norouzi, and Geoffrey Hinton. 2020. "A Simple Framework for Contrastive Learning of Visual Representations | Proceedings of the 37th International Conference on Machine Learning." *2020 Guide Proceedings.* https://dl.acm.org/doi/abs/10.5555/3524938.3525087.

Cui, Yanhua, Yun Li, Dong Xing, Tong Bai, Jiwen Dong, and Jian Zhu. 2021. "Improving the Prediction of Benign or Malignant Breast Masses Using a Combination of Image Biomarkers and Clinical Parameters." *Frontiers in Oncology* 11. https://doi.org/10.3389/fonc.2021.629321.

Doi, Kunio. 2007. "Computer-Aided Diagnosis in Medical Imaging: Historical Review, Current Status and Future Potential." *Computerized Medical Imaging and Graphics* 31 (4–5): 198–211. https://doi.org/10.1016/j.compmedimag.2007.02.002.

Geras, Krzysztof J., Stacey Wolfson, Yiqiu Shen, Nan Wu, S. Gene Kim, Eric Kim, Laura Heacock, Ujas Parikh, Linda Moy, and Kyunghyun Cho. 2017. *High-Resolution Breast Cancer Screening with Multi-View Deep Convolutional Neural Networks*, March. http://arxiv.org/abs/1703.07047.

Gong, Ronglin, Jun Wang, and Jun Shi. 2021. *Task-Driven Self-Supervised Bi-Channel Networks for Diagnosis of Breast Cancers with Mammography*, January. https://doi.org/10.48550/arXiv.2101.06228

Great Learning Team. 2020. "Introduction to Resnet or Residual Network." *GreatLearning Blog*, September 28. www.mygreatlearning.com/blog/resnet/. Accessed: November, 2021.

Grill, Jean-Bastien, Florian Strub, Florent Altché, Corentin Tallec, Pierre H. Richemond, Elena Buchatskaya, Carl Doersch, et al., 2020. "Bootstrap Your Own Latent a New Approach to Self-Supervised Learning | Proceedings of the 34th International Conference on Neural Information Processing Systems." *2020 Guide Proceedings.* https://dl.acm.org/doi/abs/10.5555/*3495724.3497510.*

Harvey, Hugh, Edith Karpati, Galvin Khara, Dimitrios Korkinof, Annie Ng, Christopher Austin, Tobias Rijken, and Peter Kecskemethy. 2019. "The Role of Deep Learning in Breast Screening." *Current Breast Cancer Reports* (Current Medicine Group LLC) 1. https://doi.org/10.1007/s12609-019-0301-7.

Lee, Rebecca Sawyer, Francisco Gimenez, Assaf Hoogi, Kanae Kawai Miyake, Mia Gorovoy, and Daniel L. Rubin. 2017. "A Curated Mammography Data Set for Use in Computer-Aided Detection and Diagnosis Research." *Scientific Data* 4 (1): 170177. https://doi.org/10.1038/sdata.2017.177.

Mammographic Image Analysis. 2021. *Mammographic Image Analysis*. www.Mammoimage. Org. Accessed: September, 2021

Miller, John D., Vignesh Arasu, Albert Pu, and Margolies Laurie. 2022. *Self Supervised Deep Learning to Enhance Breast Cancer Detection on Screening Mammography*. https://arxiv.org/abs/2203.08812.

Moosmann, Franck, Diane Larlus, Frédéric Jurie, Frank Moosmann, and Frederic Jurie. 2006. *Learning Saliency Maps for Object Categorization*. http://lear.inrialpes.fr. Accessed: March, 2022.

Moreira, Inês C., Igor Amaral, Inês Domingues, António Cardoso, Maria João Cardoso, and Jaime S. Cardoso. 2012. "INbreast: Toward a Full-Field Digital Mammographic Database." *Academic Radiology*, 19 (2): 236–248. https://doi.org/10.1016/J.ACRA.2011.09.014.

Mori, Yuichi, Shin-ei Kudo, Tyler Berzin, Masashi Misawa, and Kenichi Takeda. 2017. "Computer-Aided Diagnosis for Colonoscopy." *Endoscopy* 49 (8): 813–819. https://doi.org/10.1055/s-0043-109430.

Muduli, Debendra, Ratnakar Dash, and Banshidhar Majhi. 2022. "Automated Diagnosis of Breast Cancer Using Multi-Modal Datasets: A Deep Convolution Neural Network Based Approach." *Biomedical Signal Processing and Control* 71. https://doi.org/10.1016/j.bspc.2021.102825.

Niizumi, Daisuke, Daiki Takeuchi, Yasunori Ohishi, Noboru Harada, and Kunio Kashino. 2021. "BYOL for Audio: Self-Supervised Learning for General-Purpose Audio Representation." *2021 International Joint Conference on Neural Networks (IJCNN)*, April. https://doi.org/10.1109/ijcnn52387.2021.9534474.

Oyama, Taiki, and Takao Yamanaka. 2018. "Influence of Image Classification Accuracy on Saliency Map Estimation." *CAAI Transactions on Intelligence Technology*, 3 (3): 140–52. https://doi.org/10.1049/trit.2018.1012.

Ramadan, Saleem Z. 2020. "Methods Used in Computer-Aided Diagnosis for Breast Cancer Detection Using Mammograms: A Review." *Journal of Healthcare Engineering* 2020: 1–21. https://doi.org/10.1155/2020/9162464.

Ribli, Dezso, Anna Horváth, Zsuzsa Unger, Péter Pollner, and István Csabai. 2018. "Detecting and Classifying Lesions in Mammograms with Deep Learning." *Scientific Reports* 8 (1). https://doi.org/10.1038/s41598-018-22437-z.

Shen, Li, Laurie R. Margolies, Joseph H. Rothstein, Eugene Fluder, Russell McBride, and Weiva Sieh. 2019. "Deep Learning to Improve Breast Cancer Detection on Screening Mammography." *Scientific Reports* 9 (1). https://doi.org/10.1038/s41598-019-48995-4.

Simonyan, K., A. Vedaldi, and A. Zisserman. 2013. "Deep Inside Convolutional Networks: Visualising Image Classification Models and Saliency Maps. *arXiv preprint arXiv:1312.6034*, pp. 1–15. http://code.google.com/p/cuda-convnet/. Accessed: March, 2022.

Springenberg, Jost Tobias, Alexey Dosovitskiy, Thomas Brox, and Martin Riedmiller. 2014. "Striving for Simplicity: The All Convolutional Net." *ArXiv.org*. https://doi.org/10.48550/arXiv.1412.6806.

Sung, Hyuna, Jacques Ferlay, Rebecca L. Siegel, Mathieu Laversanne, Isabelle Soerjomataram, Ahmedin Jemal, and Freddie Bray. 2021. "Global Cancer Statistics 2020: GLOBOCAN Estimates of Incidence and Mortality Worldwide for 36 Cancers in 185 Countries." *CA: A Cancer Journal for Clinicians* 71 (3): 209–249. https://doi.org/10.3322/caac.21660.

The Digital Mammography DREAM Challenge. 2022. *Synapse*. https://sagebionetworks.org/research-projects/digital-mammography-dream-challenge/ Accessed: September, 2021.

The Top 10 Causes of Death. 2020. *World Health Organization*, September 12. www.who.int/news-room/fact-sheets/detail/the-top-10-causes-of-death. Accessed: July, 2021.

Wang, Yi, Eun Jung Choi, Younhee Choi, Hao Zhang, Gong Yong Jin, and Seok Bum Ko. 2020. "Breast Cancer Classification in Automated Breast Ultrasound Using Multiview Convolutional Neural Network with Transfer Learning." *Ultrasound in Medicine and Biology* 46 (5): 1119–1132. https://doi.org/10.1016/j.ultrasmedbio.2020.01.001.

Wiens, Jenna, and Erica S. Shenoy. 2018. "Machine Learning for Healthcare: On the Verge of a Major Shift in Healthcare Epidemiology." *Clinical Infectious Diseases* 66 (1): 149–153. https://doi.org/10.1093/cid/cix731.

Wu, Nan, Jason Phang, Jungkyu Park, Yiqiu Shen, Zhe Huang, Masha Zorin, Stanislaw Jastrzebski, et al., 2020. "Deep Neural Networks Improve Radiologists' Performance in Breast Cancer Screening." *IEEE Transactions on Medical Imaging* 39 (4): 1184–1194. https://doi.org/10.1109/TMI.2019.2945514.

Yassin, Nisreen IR., Shaimaa Omran, Enas MF el Houby, and Hemat Allam. 2018. "Machine Learning Techniques for Breast Cancer Computer Aided Diagnosis Using Different Image Modalities: A Systematic Review." *Computer Methods and Programs in Biomedicine* (Elsevier Ireland Ltd) 156: 25–45. https://doi.org/10.1016/j.cmpb.2017.12.012.

Yin, Xiao Xia, Lihua Yin, and Sillas Hadjiloucas. 2020. "Pattern Classification Approaches for Breast Cancer Identification via MRI: State-of-the-Art and Vision for the Future." *Applied Sciences (Switzerland)* (MDPI AG) 10: 7201. https://doi.org/10.3390/app10207201.

Zhang, Zhenwei, and Ervin Sejdić. 2019. "Radiological Images and Machine Learning: Trends, Perspectives, and Prospects." *Computers in Biology and Medicine* 108: 354–370. https://doi.org/10.1016/j.compbiomed.2019.02.017.

10 Predictive Analytics in Hospital Readmission for Diabetes Risk Patients

Kaustubh V. Sakhare, Vibha Vyas, and Mousami Munot

Contents

10.1 Introduction

Surgical treatment is usually considered a cause of patients being readmitted to the hospital after being released. The CMS (Centers for Medicare and Medicaid Services) has established a threshold of 30 days for the typical readmission rate. The healthcare sector is constantly working to raise its score for the various metrics established by the CMS. These measurements help us determine which hospitals are safe or have lower fatality rates. Readmission rates are one of the measures hospitals attempt to keep low. The readmission rate benchmark takes into account readmissions to all hospitals, not simply the one where the patient was initially admitted.

DOI: 10.1201/9781003333425-10

Alarming data about public and commercial insurance systems in the United States and other countries are included in the majority of studies relating to readmission rates (Pfuntner et al., 2006). Medicare beneficiaries have a readmission rate of more than 17% after 30 days, and of those, 75% or so can be prevented (Pfuntner et al., 2006), costing the program $15 billion. Acute myocardial infarction, heart failure, and pneumonia were the first three conditions for which 30-day readmission statistics were reported. The likelihood of hospital readmission is significantly increased by a number of factors, including diabetes. The Hospital Readmission Reduction Program (HRRP), a value-based Medicare program, lowers hospital expenses in areas with a higher prevalence of readmissions (Jweinat, 2010) In an effort to reduce readmissions to hospitals, it was implemented in 2010 by Patient Care and the Affordable Care Act (ACA). The fine for hospitals with a greater readmission rate has increased during this time, or since the program was started, from 1% to 3%.

Patient readmission predictions can be better understood when we take patient data from the time of readmission to the date of discharge into consideration. These data must contain all of the crucial elements of the process depicted in Figure 10.1.

- Examine caregiver worries: This stage will assist us in comprehending readmissions from the perspective of the caregiver.
- Verify attendance at follow-up visits: Hospitals must ensure that patients show up for their follow-up appointments following procedures.
- Keep an eye out for medication problems: If a patient is given their prescriptions incorrectly or fails to take them as prescribed after surgery, it will result in readmissions.

The review of the most popular research in this area is aligned based on understanding the factors that increase or decrease hospital readmission rates, predictive analysis (PA) for hospital readmission consider the impact of diabetes risk level on hospital readmissions. The patient admission process to the hospital is shown in

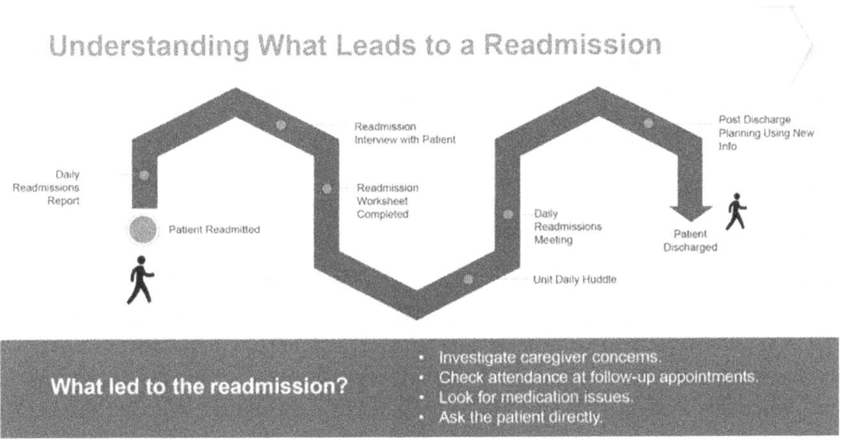

Figure 10.1 Readmission process.

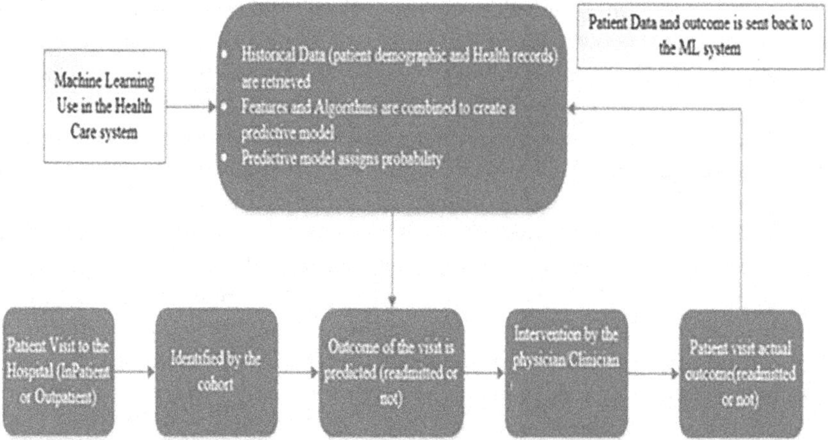

Figure 10.2 Hospital management data science approach.

Figure 10.2. Understanding the relationship between the healthcare system and machine learning will result from this.

The outline of the article is: Section 10.1 summarizes the introduction of the research work in prediction of health readmission. Section 10.2 details the various approaches in data analytics in healthcare and PA using machine learning. Interpretability in healthcare and ML in readmission prediction is detailed in Section 10.3. Section 10.4 introduces various ML-related research publications, along with the challenges in data preparation and model building. Section 10.5 presents the data preparation section and discussion. Conclusion of the study and future research directions are given in the conclusion.

Major contributions of this paper are:

- Investigating the factors impacting hospital readmission
- Understanding readmission rate issue for patients with diabetes
- Investigation of various practices of data analytics and predictive analytics in healthcare
- Investigation of interpretability and machine learning in readmission prediction

10.2 Data Analytics in Healthcare

Healthcare analytics uses a large amount of collected data and analyzes it to gain further insights, such as the impact of a location on patient recovery. Applications and systems that can manage large amounts of data are used in this procedure to retrieve or deduce hidden or relevant information from them. Health organizations can utilize this information to allocate resources to enhance patient care while also maximizing revenue and public health. Treatments for chronic diseases and readmission rates rank among the largest expenditures to the healthcare sector. Predictive analytics will reduce expenses of the people who are foreseen with high risk and can be treated by setting the early diagnosis to prevent readmission. Predictive analytics can be employed in the field of diabetes to diagnose the disease, forecast risk factors, anticipate readmissions, and prevent diabetes.

10.2.1 Predictive Analytics Using Machine Learning

In recent years, analytics in healthcare has become very well known. PA is a major factor. Compared to data mining, this is more advanced. There are a vast amount of medical data available for analysis as a result of hospitals adopting systems and applications that collect patient information like as symptoms, the cause of a disease, and its repercussions (Poon et al., 2014). Interpretable models in predictive analytics have no expectations for the dataset, they let the data lead the way. The predictive analytics algorithms get trained on the input data to give predicted output. While unsupervised learning discovers clusters or groupings, supervised learning uses techniques including classification, regression, and time-series analysis (Poon et al., 2014). Seven different kinds of regression models, each with its own significance and application, have been described by Xu et al. (2017). The list of predictive models also includes expert systems, support vector machines, neural networks, decision trees, and cluster models. The healthcare system is still cautious about integrating machine learning into its routine operations despite the availability of numerous models because of problems with interpretability. Clinical practitioners, radiologists, and other professionals who work in the hospital system will utilize these tools most frequently, and they like simple solutions.

10.3 Interpretability in Healthcare

These days, there are a lot more prospects and a demand for machine learning models that can be understood. These models enable users, such as doctors, to validate the model before taking any action. The information provided by these models allows users to approve or reject forecasts. Therefore, it is necessary to ensure that these technologies are accessible to users so that they may be employed in the hospital healthcare system. It's crucial to comprehend the fundamental concept of interpretability before studying how it's applied in ML. The degree to which a user can comprehend why a decision was reached is known as interpretability. The machine learning model with approachable solutions is widely recognized, as it is easier to comprehend why predictions are done.

There are several criteria used to categorize various ML interpretability strategies; some of those are in model, pre-model, and post-model groupings and a model outcome–based grouping. By the results of the prediction model, interpretability approaches are categorized (Molnar, 2019). Examples of these strategies include every feature's summary statistics, which relate to model prediction, and visualization summary, which describes many strategies that can only be seen and cannot be displayed using a table (Ahmad et al., 2018, Boehmke and Greenwell, 2019, Carvalho et al., 2019). In contrast to models used in other industries, ML predictive systems in healthcare will make an impact on patients' health. The users of such models must have faith in their forecasts. Users of interpretable machine learning can analyze, comprehend, and perform more analysis to support the development of ML systems.

10.3.1 Machine Learning in Readmission Prediction

Many studies have been conducted in the field of medicine to devise ML-based readmission forecasts. According to work (Hopkins et al., 2020) carried out at university in Wisconsin, machine learning can reduce unplanned readmissions. Understanding the predictive indicators for clinical spine surgery helps in estimating readmission, while the results indicate that sanctions for spine surgery under the hospital readmission reduction program need to be reassessed. As early readmissions following spinal fusion are one of the cost factors after surgeries or procedures (Bernatz and Anderson, 2015, Stopa et al., 2019), a different study by the National Surgical Registry (Goyal et al., 2019) examined whether ML-based predictive systems can accurately forecast discharge to home and non-home facilities at the same time to estimate unplanned early readmissions.

Machine learning is employed in one study (Awan et al., 2019) to investigate reasons behind readmission due to heart failure and the effect of using the right model and measurements. The finding shows that as compared to others, multilayer perceptron based feed forward network handles the class imbalance very well. Another study (Da et al., 2019) demonstrated that deep learning techniques are substantially more effective at predicting diabetes readmissions when structured data are present than naive Bayes and support vector classifier (SVC) models. It also demonstrated that textual data are a factor in predicting hospital readmissions. Random forest is said to outperform usage of the more common ML models, according to a study (Ramírez and Herrera, 2019). These conclusions will help in proper clinical decision making. One study (Strack et al., 2014) revealed that readmission and HbA1c depend only on primary diagnosis. Another (Bojja and EI-Gayar, 2019) focused on the use of ML models to predict readmissions; however, detailed analysis is required regarding the diabetic risk level of patients as well as the effectiveness of classifiers. The goal of this study is to create a model for readmission predictions that will consider the risk level of diabetic patients and different factors that must be taken into account.

10.4 Machine Learning–Based Research Publications in Readmission Prediction

Prior to selecting the optimum model, this study evaluates various classifiers. This section summarizes a few of the relevant research articles that were used in this study. Several trends in hospital readmissions have been studied. According to a study on disadvantaged populations, readmission rates for patients with acute myocardial infarction have decreased dramatically for these groups (Boccuti and Casillas, 2017). These diagnostics primarily served people with low incomes and high risk conditions. It also looked at how readmission rates as a result of different diseases affect hospital financial performance. Using the co-morbidity index, it studied that how risk stratification is done for various diseases. It is possible to predict health outcomes using this index and chronic medical conditions (Schneeweiss et al., 2003). The medical conditions from the aforementioned classes were identified using International Statistical Classification of Diseases (ICD) codes. This will assist healthcare professionals in educating patients about care management programs, which will raise hospital ratings and decrease readmissions. Numerous exploratory studies have been conducted in an effort to understand the clinical basis of the system (Caruana et al., 2015, Che et al., 2016).

Successful predictive models must have both accuracy and interpretability as essential characteristics. Many cutting-edge models are constructed using aggregated characteristics, such as the risk variables discovered using lasso regression (Caruana et al., 2015) and the results of applying the appropriate model and metrics (Awan et al., 2019). Some machine learning studies have contradictory findings, which is likely a result of the failure to recognize the issue of class imbalance. This study develops and evaluates a method for estimating 30-day heart failure readmission or fatality rates. The Virginia Hospital and Healthcare Association (VHHA) conducted research to determine the relationship between a diabetes diagnosis and hospital readmissions. According to the findings, people with primary and secondary clinical diagnoses of diabetes have a greater risk of readmission.

In a meeting held by the SAS Global Forum (Munnangi and Chakraborty, 2015), an SVM method was employed, and it was discovered that inpatient and outpatient visits, diagnoses, the kind of admission, and the patient's condition were important components in the analysis. Decision trees beat logistic regression in a study that compared the ability to predict readmissions based on diabetics (Duggal et al., 2016). The readmission section in the hospital, the patient's inclusive medical history, and the stay in the hospital are factors that helped or were significant, but the problem of class disparity has not been addressed. However, a paper (Hempstalk and Mordaunt, 2016) demonstrated better outcomes using logistic regression than with decision trees and naïve Bayes. Weight, type of diabetes, medication use, and having operations were all associated in another study using logistic regression models (Ruan et al., 2020). In terms of estimating the risk of hypoglycemia, the XGBoost model fared better than the logistic regression model. In another study, models created using naive Bayes, random forest, Ada boost, and neural networks are compared, and it is shown that utilizing random forest produces better prediction outcomes (Bhuvan et al, 2016). A number of characteristics, such as the source of the admission, the number of inpatient stays, and the number of diagnoses, are related aspects that serve as good predictors but neglect to take into account the issue of class imbalance. These findings show that despite the fact that there have been several studies on readmissions, there has been very little research on diabetes, and the studies that have been conducted on the condition have not addressed the issue of class imbalance.

A diabetic patient's care is also quite expensive; therefore this has been a very heavy load on inpatients and is expanding tremendously. If the rates of readmission for diabetic patients can be decreased, Medicare and hospital expenses may be decreased, and patient care may also be provided with higher quality. Finding out how diverse factors, like better discharge plans, affect diabetes patients' readmission rates is another important task. By creating interpretable models, it is possible to lower readmission rates and determine which features are crucial.

10.4.1 Discussion

The readmissions rate is a significant issue in the US hospital healthcare system. If hospitals don't maintain the CMS-set benchmark rate, they risk severe fines. The causes of readmissions are many, but diabetes plays a significant role in raising the likelihood of developing a number of other conditions, which in turn results in increased readmission rates. As previously indicated, a lot of studies are carried out utilizing machine learning to develop prediction models for everything from disease diagnosis to hospital readmissions. Most research has discovered a correlation between them. There are numerous models that can predict readmissions, but fewer studies have been conducted on diabetes and readmissions than on other diseases, and the majority of these studies have not addressed the issues with class imbalance. As a result, the predictive system to consider predicting readmission in a diabetic patient will benefit the hospital. However, hospital systems are quite specific, and healthcare ML models are closely examined since the outcomes have an impact on a patient's life. Furthermore, the model will not be accepted if it is not understood. The goal of this project is to present an interpretable model as a predictive system enabled to forecast readmission for diabetic and non-diabetic patients.

10.5 Data Preparation

This section describes the processes taken to analyze the dataset and how the model building steps were put into practice. This section describes the dataset, describes how the dataset was prepared using various techniques, handles missing values, and transforms categorical variables into numerical to aid with exploratory data analysis (EDA) and model construction. Bivariate and univariate analyses are used in the EDA section.

10.5.1 Dataset Description

This study makes use of a publicly accessible diabetes dataset from the UCI ML repository, which contains information from 130 US hospitals during a ten-year period. An abstract of this information was taken from the Health Facts Database (Strack et al., 2014).

Based on a study about readmissions for diabetic illness, this dataset was compiled (Strack et al., 2014). This information comprises various encounter types; provider specialties; and patient databases with attributes such as age, diagnosis at the clinical level, medication followed, results from the lab, and pharmacy and hospital characteristics. These data come from the same patients' inpatient (IP), outpatient (OP), and emergency department (ED) records. The information here represents both standalone hospitals and integrated hospital delivery networks (Strack et al., 2014). These data include information which is taken from the database with 50 attributes.

10.5.2 Data Preparation

The discussion provides a detailed explanation of the many procedures involved in getting the data ready for modeling. Find the dataset's missing and incorrect values:

Table 10.1 The Missing Values

Attribute Name	*Missing Values in the Attribute*	*% of Missing Values*
weight	98569	96.8
race	2273	2.23
diag_3	1423	1.4
diag_2	358	0.3
diag_1	21	2.0
medical_speciality	49949	49.0
payer_code	40256	39.5

Since ML algorithms do not handle datasets with missing values, locating and handling missing data is a crucial step. Missing values in datasets are a common occurrence, particularly in the healthcare industry where information is lost for a variety of causes, such as faulty or missing data entry. The missing values are handled by removing columns with significant missing data. Sometimes replacing the missing values by some other central tendency or even removing those columns would impact the healthcare data. The data can be kept unchanged rather than imputing them anyway. The invalid values, once replaced, exhibit the behavior of missing values, as given in Table 10.1.

10.5.2.1 Elimination of Variables

Features that won't have an impact on the analysis are removed in this step. Two columns in the dataset have unique values, and features with unique values are also excluded from the dataset. Null values are handled with the observation that there are very few values are missing and so those null values are discarded. In the data, Gender has only three values, which are dropped.

10.5.2.2 Feature Engineering

Feature engineering explains all the derived features in detail. This step explains the selection of all derived and new features used in the model building. When observing the dataset with regard to the different patient classes and the purpose of their visits, a parameter is proposed called Service Utilization, the feature is devised considering emergency, outpatient, and inpatient visits.

Diabetic patients after admission to the hospital are particularly prescribed with changes in medication. The dataset which is considered for the study has 23 drugs information which is observed with similar changes and hence correlated with readmission rates. The factor treated in one of the scenarios is the number of medications used by the patient; the higher the number of medications, the more care needed for the patient during the readmission. The dataset also represents the basic three types of diagnosis as primary, secondary, and additional. Primary has 848 distinct values, secondary has 923 values, and additional has 954 values. Certain disease categories are identified in the clinical diagnosis: respiratory, diabetes, genitourinary and musculoskeletal injury, neoplasm, respiratory, digestive, circulatory, and others. The research, however, is focused on diabetes and circulatory disease.

The Comorbidity column is devised to verify circulatory disease and diabetes. Also, the two columns Diabetes and Circulatory Disease are maintained when a patient has these values, as given in Figure 10.3.

10.5.2.3 Transformation to Numerical Variables

The features are transformed to numerical form using the data dictionary's metadata. Attributes like admission type ID, admission source ID, and discharge disposition ID are all listed as numerical values, and when cross-referenced with the data dictionary, it revealed that they are categorical instead. The dataset also undergoes a duplicate check. No records are redundant.

10.5.2.4 Outlier Check

The research uses box plots to do an outlier check on the numerical columns. Few columns have outliers, as illustrated in Figure 10.4, yet these values are left in the dataset, as they would be relevant to future research.

10.5.2.5 Exploratory Data Analysis

The dataset is analyzed using Tableau Python visualization tools to compile the various attributes. Utilizing visualizations, the entire dataset's features are examined. Univariate and bivariate analysis is carried out.

Comorbidity	Diabetes (250.xx)	Circulatory disease (390-459)
0	✗	✗
1	✓	✗
2	✗	✓
3	✓	✓

Figure 10.3 Comorbidity.

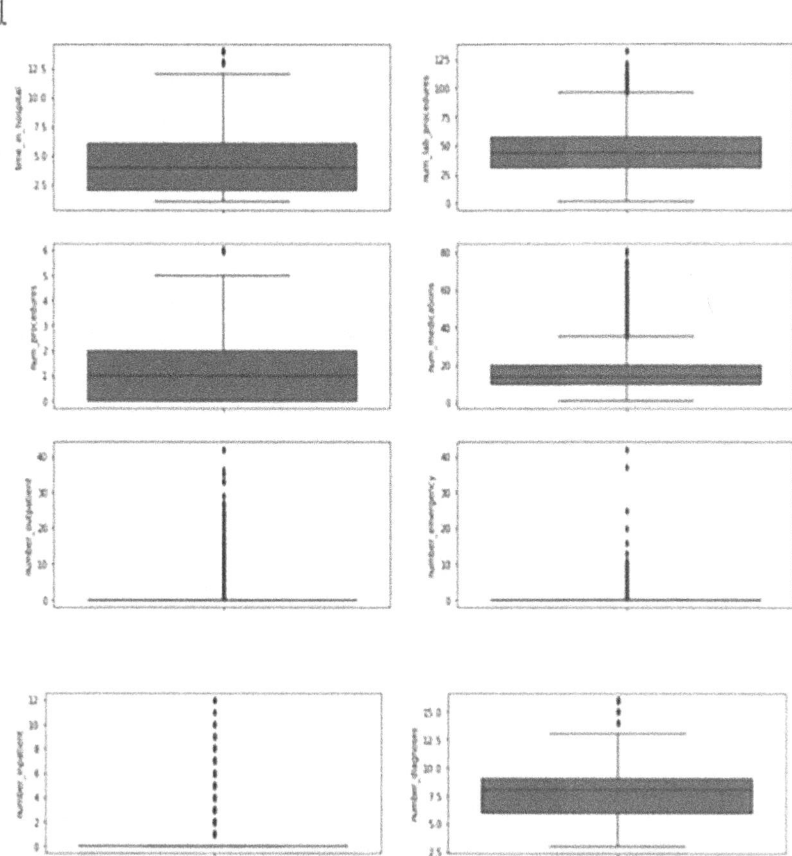

Figure 10.4 Outlier detection in the dataset.

10.5.2.6 Univariate Analysis

Visualizations are carried out in this step to demonstrate the influence of various features on the number of patients in the cleaned dataset. According to Figure 10.5, Caucasians make up the majority of patients, followed by African Americans. As the data are from US hospitals, where the population of Caucasians and African Americans will be higher than that of other races, it is unlikely that this information will offer any new insights. Figure 10.6 illustrates that the majority of patients are above 60 years old. The number of patients between the ages of 80 and 90 is lower than that between 60 and 80. This gives the potential age group for the analysis.

According to Figure 10.7, the majority of admissions are emergency and elective, yet it need to be noted, as depicted in Figure 10.8, that most patients stay two to five days.

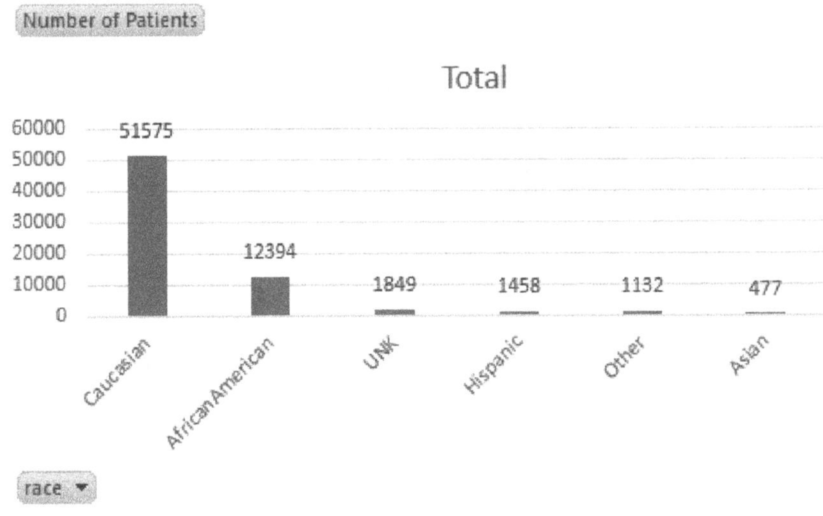

Figure 10.5 Patient count based on race.

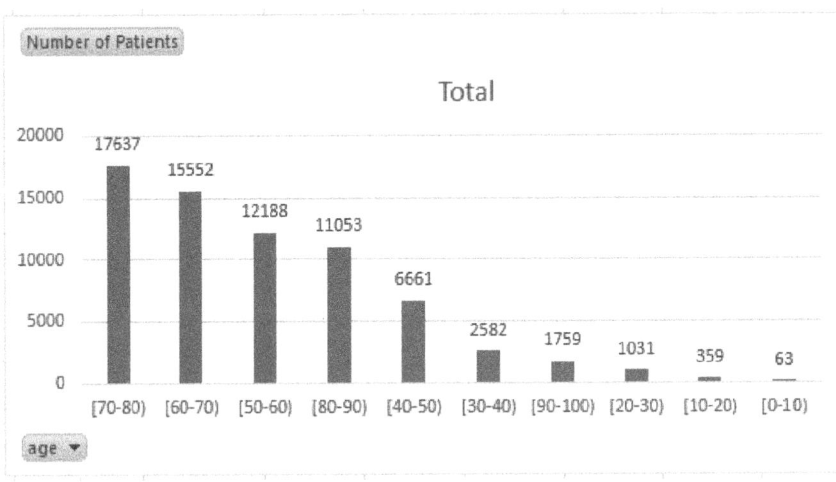

Figure 10.6 Age-wise patient count.

The majority of patients, as depicted in Figure 10.9, have not undergone any surgeries. More information will be revealed by additional investigation using other parameters such as number of medications. As depicted in Figure 10.10, the majority of patients are taking between 10 and 25 different medications.

Figure 10.11 from this dataset depicts the number of outpatients, while Figure 10.12 gives the inpatient count. The inpatient and outpatient count is one of the measuring factors to be considered for hospital readmission.

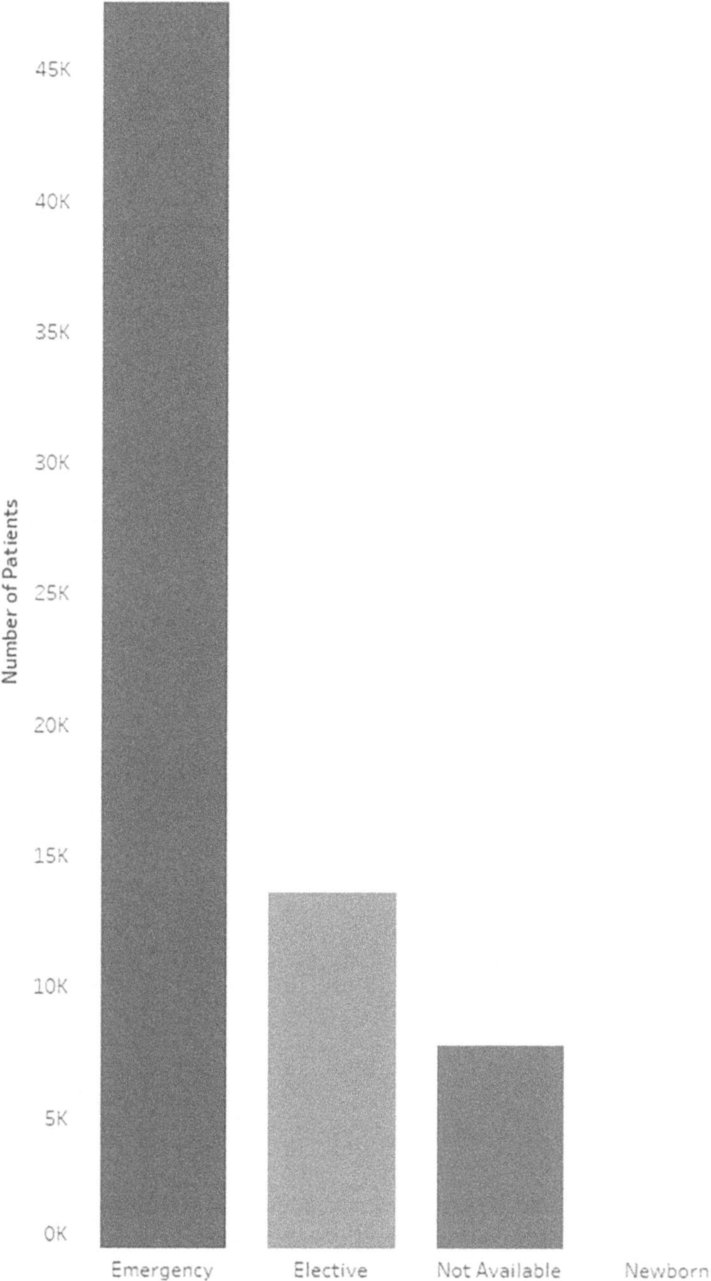

Figure 10.7 Patient counts for different admission types.

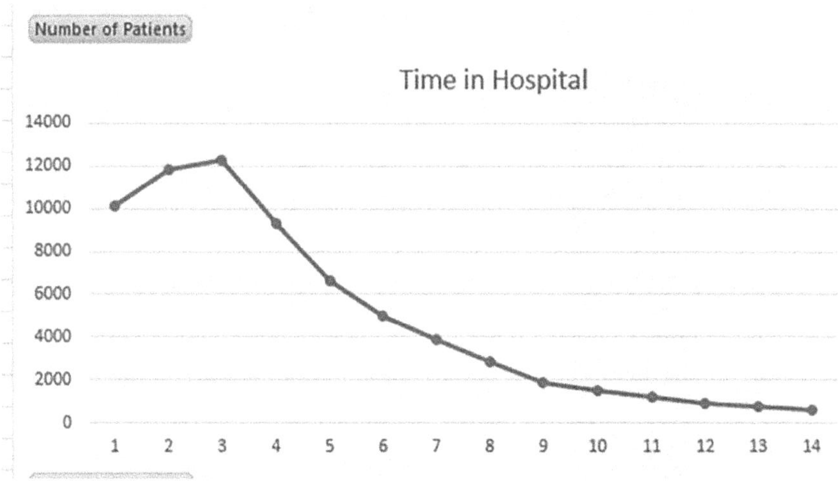

Figure 10.8 Patient count based on time spent in hospital.

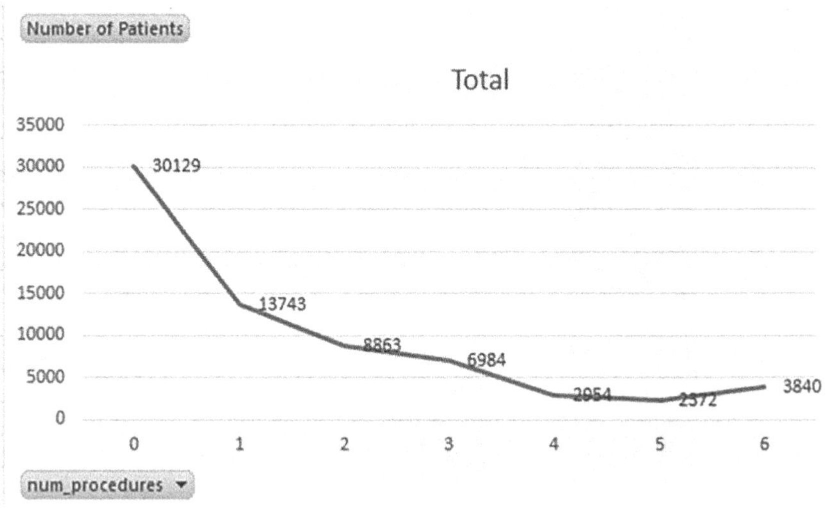

Figure 10.9 Patient counts per procedures.

Emergency count is given in Figure 10.13, while diagnosis count is given in Figure 10.14.

A1C Result: This statistic shows the patient's body's blood sugar level. A patient is diagnosed with diabetes if their value is greater than 6.5. As demonstrated in Figure 10.15, the majority of the patients in the dataset are represented as none. Understanding this result may be made easier with additional analysis using the readmission flag.

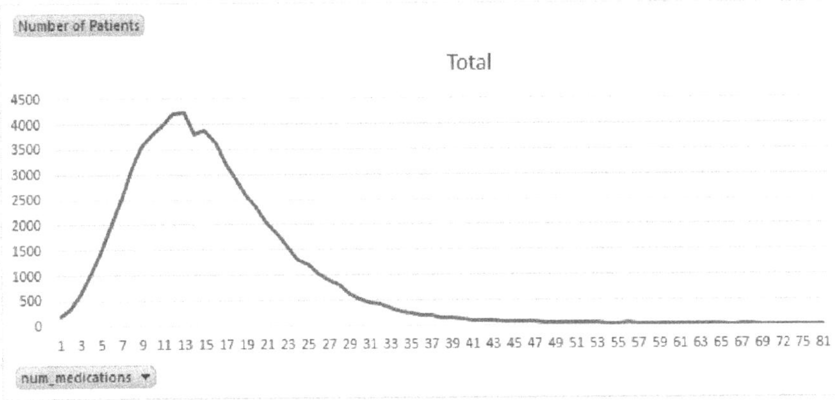

Figure 10.10 Patient count per medications used.

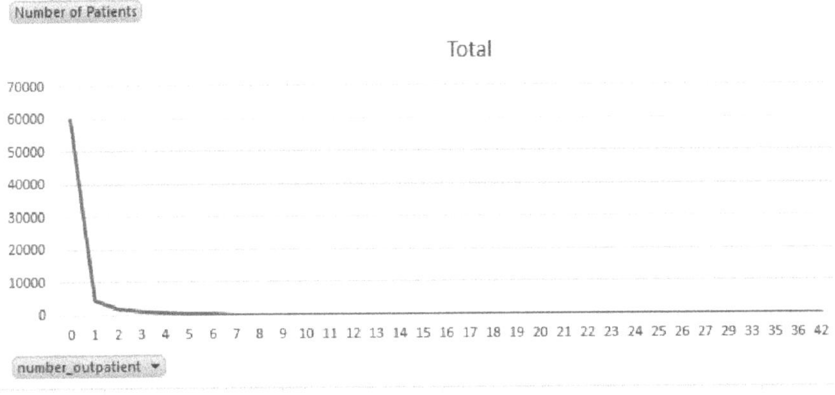

Figure 10.11 Outpatient count.

The patient's blood glucose and insulin levels are illustrated in Figure 10.16; a value greater than 200 denotes diabetes in the patient. The majority of the data are zero, which is identical to the A1C result. Understanding this result may be made easier with additional analysis using the readmission flag. According to the max glu serum and A1C results plots, which are shown in Figure 10.17, the majority of patients have the value none, and it appears that about 75% of patients were taking medications.

Figure 10.18 shows that 41% of patients did not require readmission. Figure 10.19 depicts that the outpatient and inpatient data are skewed towards the left, while the others are normally distributed.

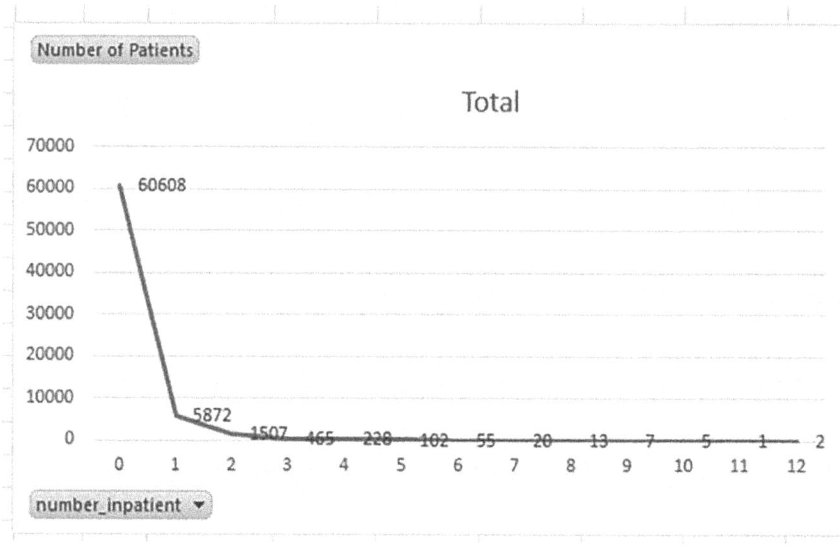

Figure 10.12 Inpatient count.

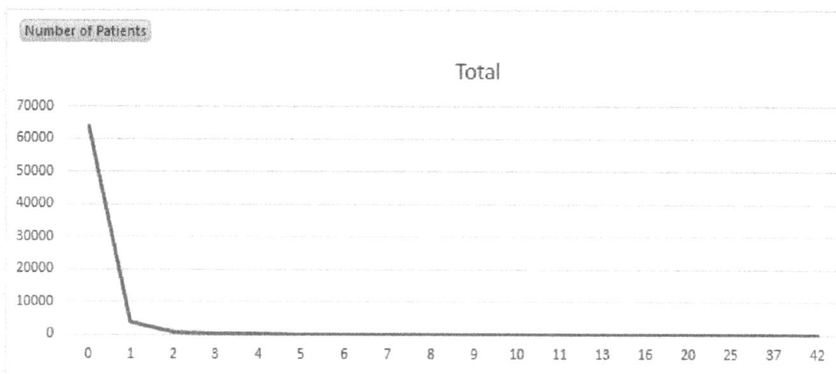

Figure 10.13 Patient count per emergency.

10.5.2.7 *Bivariate and Multivariate Analysis*

Bivariate analysis takes into account the readmission probability to discover high-risk patients. The likelihood that an event will occur divided by the total number of events is the probability of that event. In this instance, the likelihood of a patient being readmitted is calculated using the rationale

Readmission probability of the patient = Patient readmitted/(Patient readmitted + Patient not readmitted)

No readmission probability of the patient = Patient not readmitted/(Patient not readmitted + Patient readmitted)

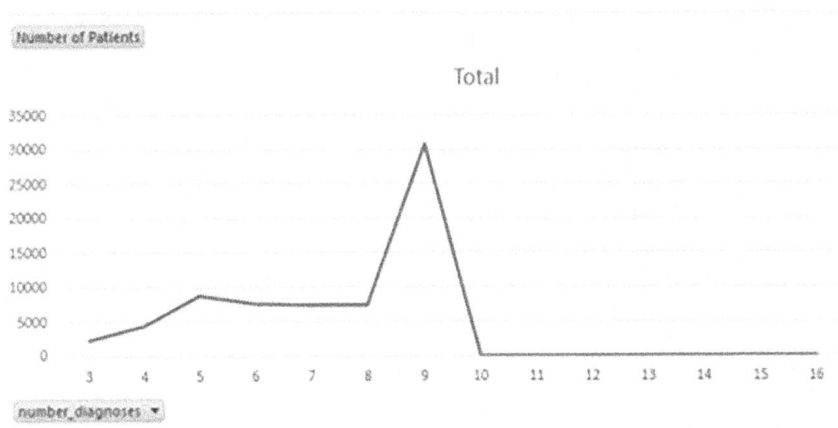

Figure 10.14 Patient count per diagnosis.

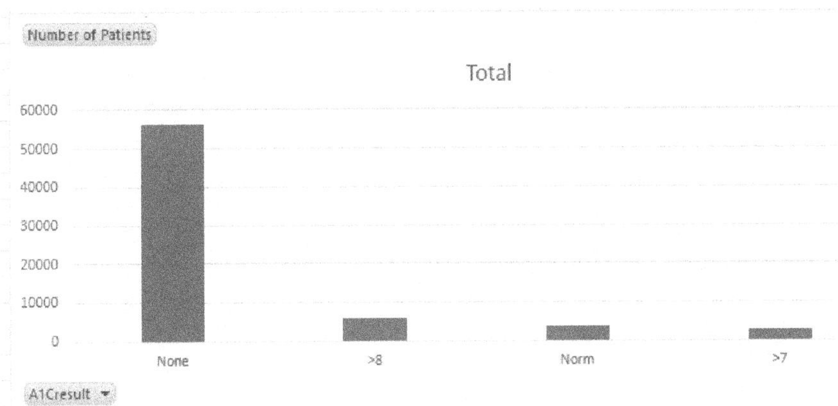

Figure 10.15 Patient count per A1C result.

The study focuses on different dataset attributes to compare the likelihood of readmission vs. likelihood of non-readmission.

Figure 10.20 shows that female patients are more prone to readmission.

The readmission increases particularly for the patients with age higher than 40; also, it is lower for the age group 90 to 100 because there are fewer records for them. As seen in Figure 10.21, the readmission rate is also noticeably higher for patients in the 10 to 20 age range.

As shown in Figure 10.22, the readmission rate is significant when a patient has both diabetes and a circulatory condition or solely a circulatory condition.

According to Figure 10.23, a patient's readmission rate is higher if they are hospitalized for a longer duration. This may be the result of the patient having to stay for a prolonged period of time after being admitted for a procedure.

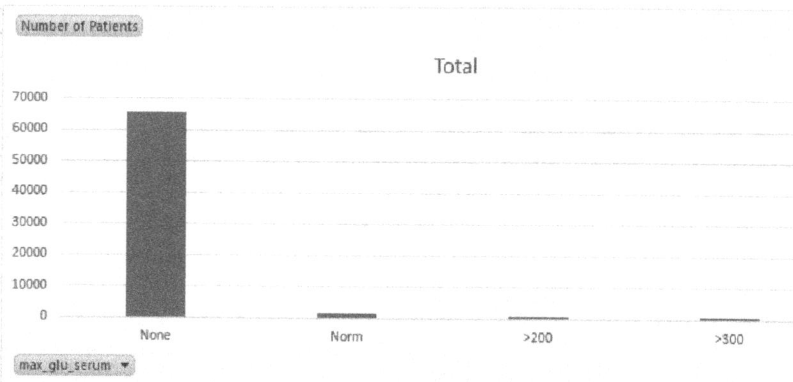

Figure 10.16 Patient count per glucose and insulin level

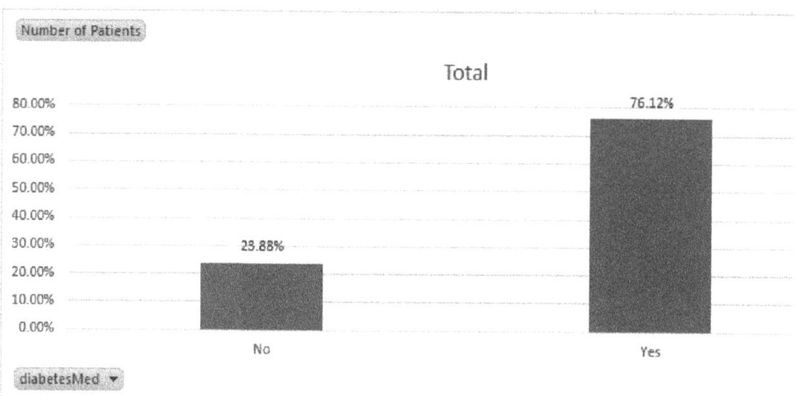

Figure 10.17 Patient count per diabetes medication.

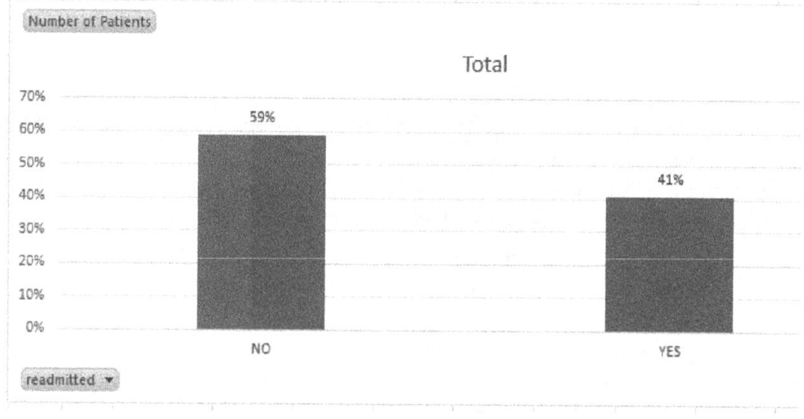

Figure 10.18 Patient count per readmission flag.

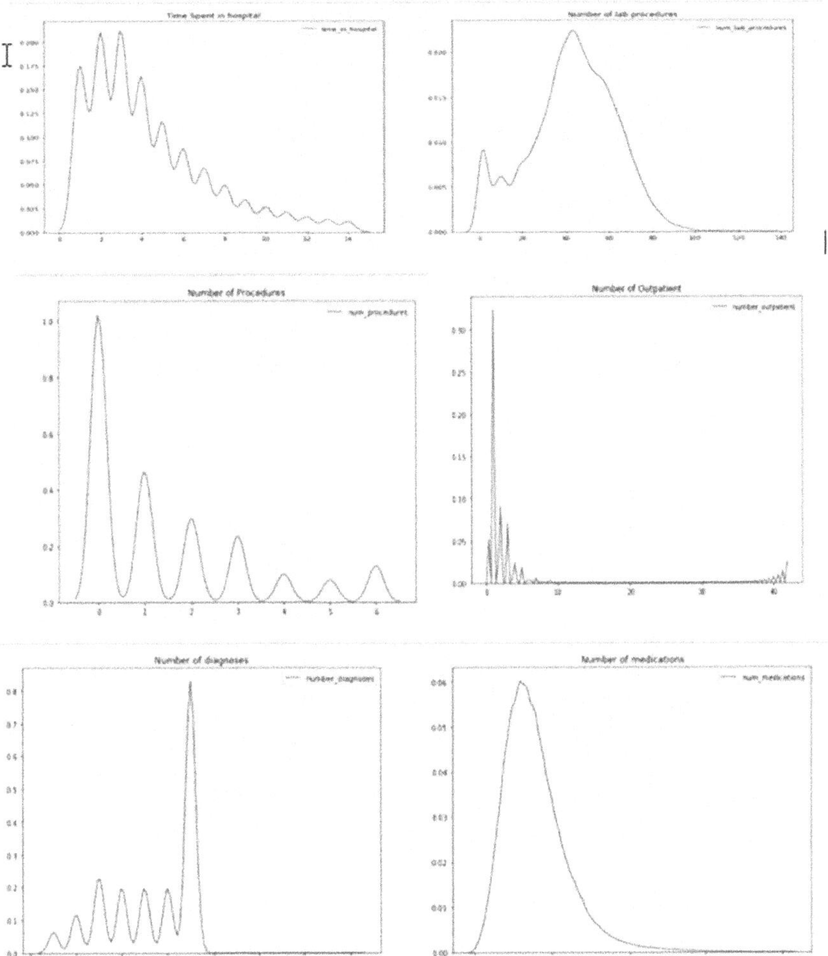

Figure 10.19 Distribution of numerical features.

If the number of medications is higher, the readmission rate is high, as shown in Figure 10.24.

Figure 10.25 shows that the more diagnoses, the higher the readmission rate.

If age is >40, there will be more medications, ultimately resulting in an increased readmission rate, as shown in Figure 10.26.

Miglitol, acarbose, and nateglinide are evaluated against insulin per the comparison: The delivery of insulin was the only medicine that significantly varied among individuals; all other medications were taken by all patients in the same amounts. Taking off all but the insulin column from Figure 10.2 gives list of medications

Several significant conclusions can be drawn from the outcomes of exploratory data analysis, including:

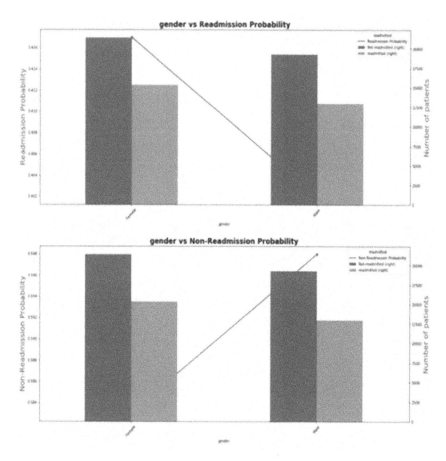

Figure 10.20 Plot of gender per readmission and probability of non-readmission.

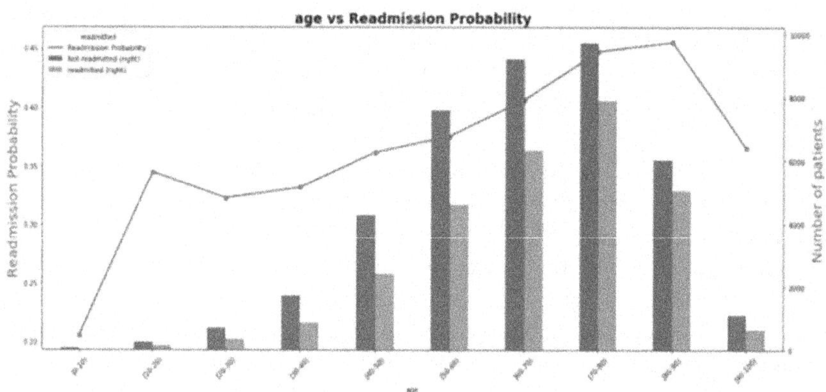

Figure 10.21 Age vs readmission/non-readmission probability.

(Continued)

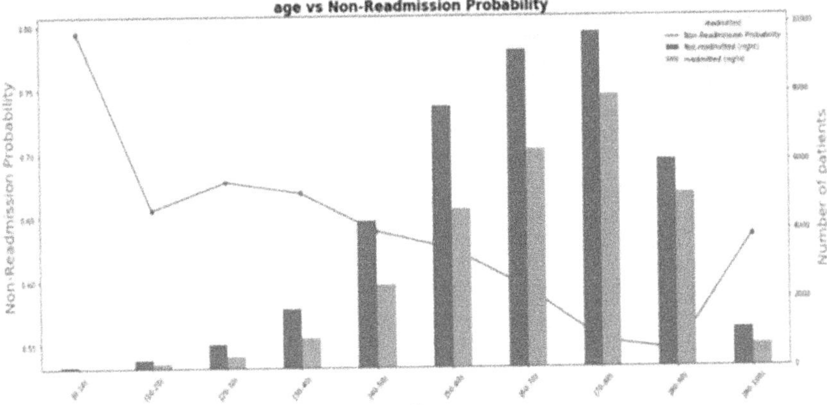

Figure 10.21 (Continued)

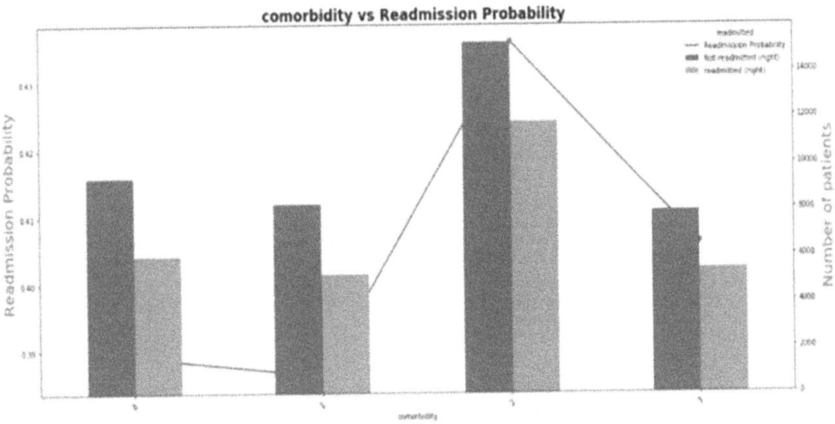

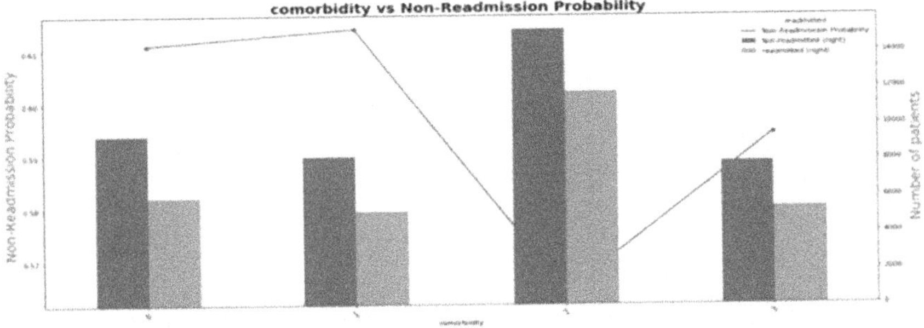

Figure 10.22 Comorbidity vs readmission/non-readmission probability.

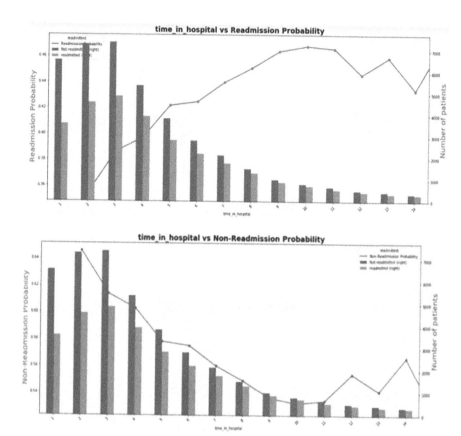

Figure 10.23 Plot of time in hospital with readmission and non-readmission rate.

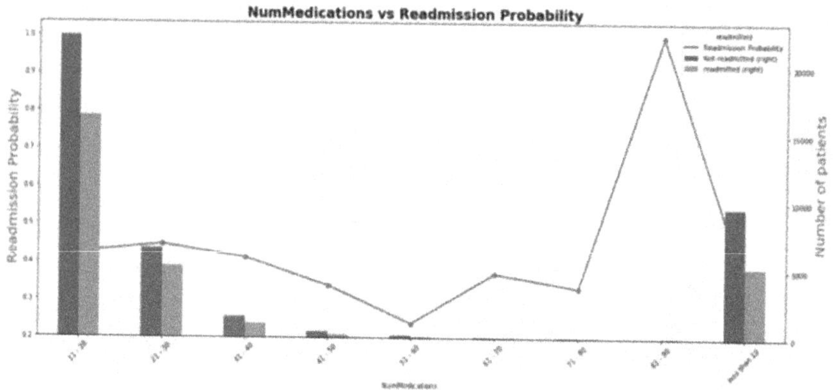

Figure 10.24 Plot of medications vs. readmission probability. (Continued)

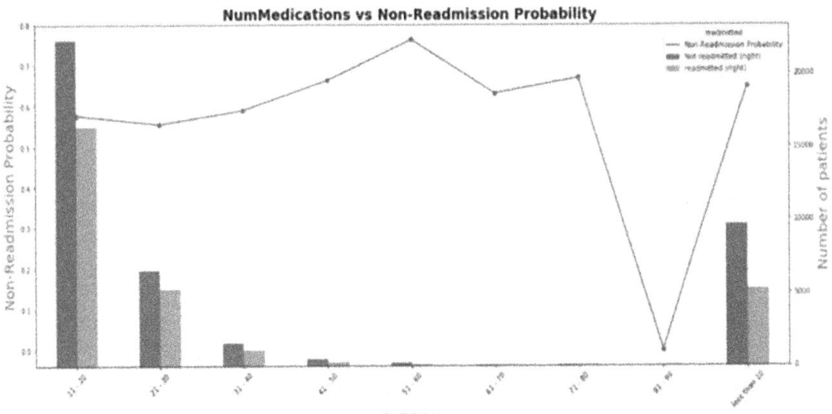

Figure 10.24 (Continued)

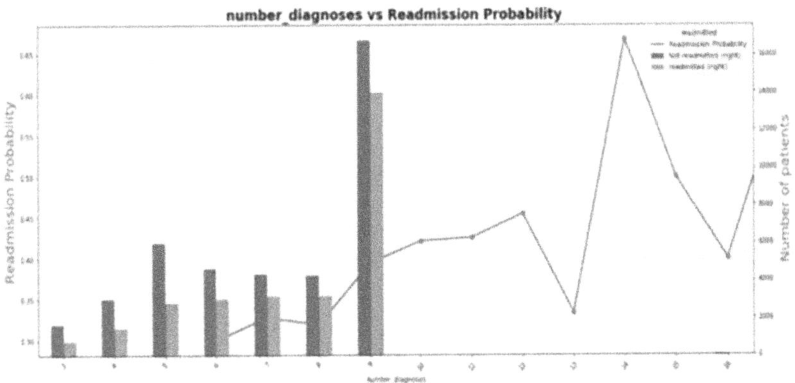

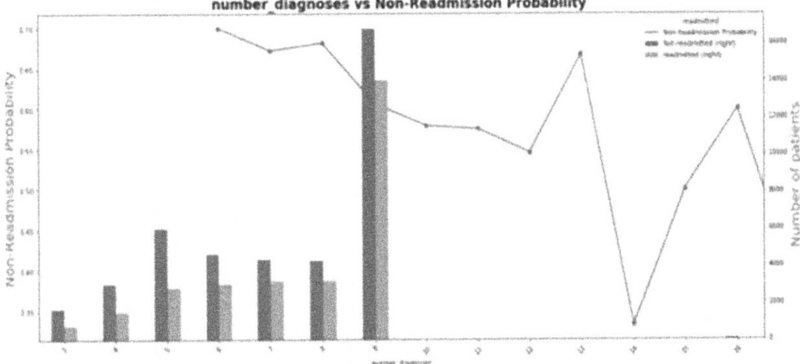

Figure 10.25 Plot of diagnoses vs. readmission rate.

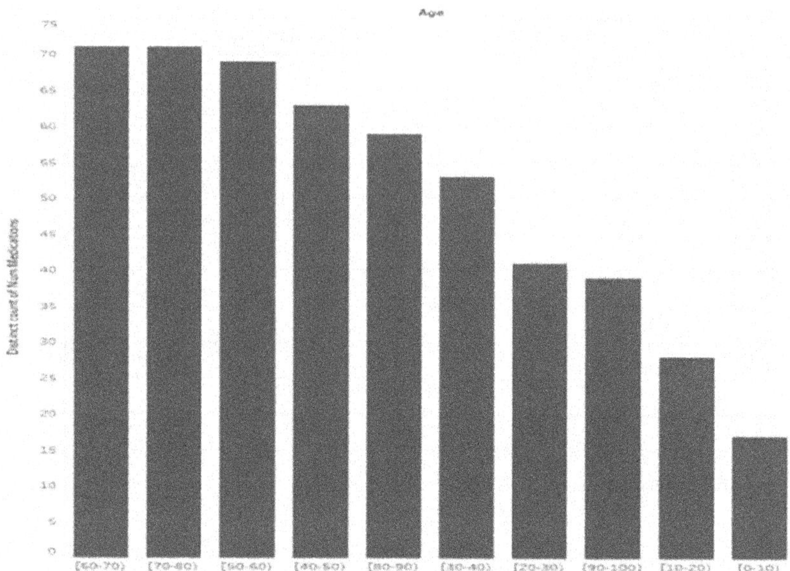

Figure 10.26 Relationships between medications and age.

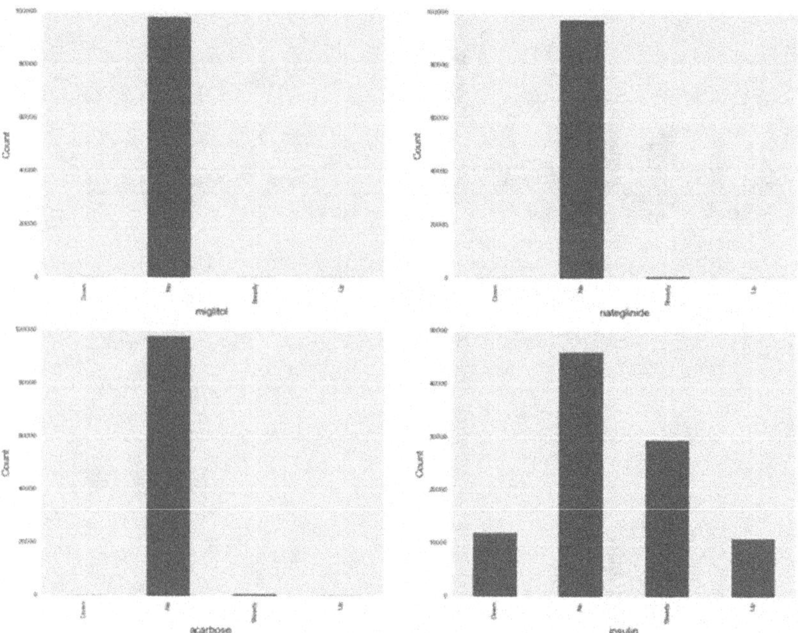

Figure 10.27 Comparing different diabetic medications.

- It may not come as a surprise that people with primary diagnoses of diabetes received better care for their diabetes than those with admitting diagnoses of circulatory or respiratory disorders.
- The ICD9 codes identify the primary, secondary, and tertiary medical diagnoses.
- Diabetes ICD9 code: 250.xx.

10.6 Conclusion

In the healthcare sector, readmission is an issue, and many hospitals still struggle to achieve the CMS Hospital Rating System's standards. Studies on readmission for various diagnoses are reviewed in this chapter; only a small number of studies cover diabetes. The data skewness is even limitedly addressed. In contrast to models in other sectors, ML prediction models for diabetes are unusual, as those forecasts might have an effect on a patient's health. As a result, users of such models must have faith in the models' predictions. In order to create decision support systems that can anticipate readmissions for usage in hospitals, interpretable models are therefore required. The research potential is seen in understanding and handling the readmission data and adopting suitable preprocessing techniques on the readmission data. The exploratory data analysis to analyze factors affecting hospital readmissions, identify the key features, build a predictive system, and perform comparative analysis are explored in great depth in the chapter. Various techniques are adopted to try out visualizations on different features to find the relationship between readmission and risk level. This is the major contribution of this research. Model building to take into account those primary and derived features shall be considered in the next phase of research work.

References

Ahmad, M.A., Teredesai, A. and Eckert, C., (2018) Interpretable machine learning in healthcare. In: *Proceedings–2018. IEEE International Conference on Healthcare Informatics* (ICHI), pp. 559–560.

Awan, S.E., Bennamoun, M., Sohel, F., Sanfilippo, F.M. and Dwivedi, G., (2019) Machine learning-based prediction of heart failure readmission or death: implications of choosing the right model and the right metrics. *ESC Heart Failure 6*(2): 428–435.

Bernatz, J.T. and Anderson, P.A., (2015) Thirty-day readmission rates in spine surgery: Systematic review and meta-analysis. *Neurosurgical Focus 39*(4), p.E7.

Bhuvan, M.S., Kumar, A., Zafar, A. and Kishore, V., (2016) Identifying diabetic patients with high risk of readmission. *arXivLabs: 2016arXiv160204257B*, 10.

Boccuti, C. and Casillas, G., (2017) Aiming for fewer hospital U-turns : The Medicare hospital readmission reduction program. policy brief. *Kaiser Family Foundation Issue Brief*, pp. 1 –12. https://www.kff.org/medicare/issue-brief/aiming-for-fewer-hospital-u-turns-the-medicare-hospital-readmission-reduction-program/

Boehmke, B. and Greenwell, B.M., (2019). *Hands-on Machine Learning with R*. CRC Press.

Bojja, G.R. and El-Gayar, O., (2019) *Predicting Hospital Readmissions of Diabetic patients, s.l.: Annual Research Symposium*, Dakota State University.

Caruana, R., Lou, Y., Gehrke, J., Koch, P., Sturm, M. and Elhadad, N., (2015) Intelligible models for healthcare: Predicting pneumonia risk and hospital 30-day readmission. In: *Proceedings of the ACM SIGKDD International Conference on Knowledge Discovery and Data Mining*, pp. 1721–1730. New York: Association of Computing Machinary.

Carvalho, D.V., Pereira, E.M. and Cardoso, J.S., (2019) Machine learning interpretability: A survey on methods and metrics. *Electronics* (Switzerland) *8*(8), 832.

Charlie, X., Stephone, C. and Christina, P., (2017) *Beating Diabetes: Predicting Early Diabetes Patient Hospital Readmittance to Help Optimize Patient*, pp. 1–12. http://cs229.stanford.edu/proj2017/final-reports/5244347.pdf

Che, Z., Purushotham, S., Khemani, R. and Liu, Y., (2016) Interpretable Deep Models for ICU Outcome Prediction. AMIA – Annual Symposium proceedings. *AMIA Symposium*, 2016, 371.

DaP, J., et al., 2019. Prediction of Hospital Readmission for Heart Disease: A Deep Learning Approach. s.l., *Smart Health: International Conference, ICSH 2019, Shenzhen, China, July 1–2, 2019, Proceedings* 7. Springer International Publishing.

Duggal, R., Shukla, S., Chandra, S., Shukla, B. and Khatri, S.K., (2016) Impact of selected pre-processing techniques on prediction of risk of early readmission for diabetic patients in India. *International Journal of Diabetes in Developing Countries 36*, 469–476.

Goyal, A., Ngufor, C., Kerezoudis, P., McCutcheon, B., Storlie, C. and Bydon, M., (2019) Can machine learning algorithms accurately predict discharge to nonhome facility and early unplanned readmissions following spinal fusion? Analysis of a national surgical registry. *Journal of Neurosurgery: Spine 31*(4), 568–578.

Hempstalk, K. and Mordaunt, D.A., (2016) *Improving 30-Day Readmission Risk Predictions Using Machine Learning* (s.l.). Berlin: Research Gate.

Hopkins, B.S., Yamaguchi, J.T., Garcia, R., Kesavabhotla, K., Weiss, H., Hsu, W.K., Smith, Z.A. and Dahdaleh, N.S., (2020) Using machine learning to predict 30-day readmissions after posterior lumbar fusion: An NSQIP study involving 23,264 patients. *Journal of Neurosurgery: Spine.*

Jweinat, J.J., (2010) Hospital readmissions under the spotlight. *Journal of Healthcare Management 55*(4), 252–264.

Molnar, C., (2019) *Interpretable Machine Learning. A Guide for Making Black Box Models Explainable.* Book, Lean Publishing Process.

Munnangi, H. and Chakraborty, G., (2015) *Predicting Readmission of Diabetic Patients using the high performance Support Vector Machine algorithm of SAS® Enterprise Miner.* Berlin: Research Gate.

Pfuntner, A., Wier, L.M. and Steiner, C., (2006) Costs for hospital stays in the United States, 2011: Statistical Brief #168. *Healthcare Cost and Utilization Project (HCUP) Statistical Briefs.* Agency for Healthcare Research and Quality (US). https://europepmc.org/article/nbk/nbk121966

Poon, A.K., Juraschek, S.P., Ballantyne, C.M., Steffes, M.W. and Selvin, E., (2014) Comparative associations of diabetes risk factors with five measures of hyperglycemia. *BMJ Open Diabetes Research & Care 2*(1), e000002.

Ramírez, J.C. and Herrera, D., (2019) Prediction of diabetic patient readmission using machine learning. In: *Communications in Computer and Information Science,* pp. 78–88. Springer International Publishing.

Ruan, Y., Bellot, A., Moysova, Z., Tan, G.D., Lumb, A., Davies, J., van der Schaar, M. and Rea, R., (2020) Predicting the risk of inpatient hypoglycemia with machine learning using electronic health records. *Diabetes Care 43*(7), 1504–1511.

Schneeweiss, S., Wang, P.S., Avorn, J. and Glynn, R.J., (2003) Improved comorbidity adjustment for predicting mortality in Medicare populations. *Health Services Research 38*(4), 1103–1120.

Stopa, B.M., Robertson, F.C., Karhade, A.V., Chua, M., Broekman, M.L.D., Schwab, J.H., Awan, et al., (2019). Predicting non-routine discharge after elective spine surgery: External validation of machine learning algorithms using institutional data. *Neurosurgery 84*(5), E270.

Strack, B., Deshazo, J.P., Gennings, C., Olmo, J.L., Ventura, S., Cios, K.J. and Clore, J.N., (2014) Impact of HbA1c measurement on hospital readmission rates: Analysis of 70,000 clinical database patient records. *BioMed Research International 2014*, 1–11. https://doi.org/10.1155/2014/781670

11 Continuous Blood Glucose Monitoring Using Explainable AI Techniques

Ketan K. Lad and Maulin Joshi

Contents

11.1 Introduction

Diabetes mellitus occurs when the levels of glucose in a person's blood are imbalanced and can be considered a serious and long-term condition that may hamper the cure of various diseases. It is caused when patient's body is unable to produce enough insulin

DOI: 10.1201/9781003333425-11

or appropriately use generated insulin (Holt et al., 2010). Currently, the disease affects 537 million people worldwide, and this number is likely to increase up to 643 million by 2030 The figure may reach 783 million by 2045 (IDF Diabetes Atlas, 2021). Diabetes can be categorized into different types, Type 1 diabetes (T1D), Type 2 diabetes (T2D), and gestational diabetes (Holt et al., 2010). When insulin-creating cells of the pancreas are adversely affected by the immune system of a body, it causes T1D (Oviedo et al., 2017). As a result, the body produces either negligible insulin or no insulin at all. Living with T1D is a challenge for patients, as it requires taking a daily number of insulin injections or a pump, routine glucose monitoring, and periodic expert medical advice.

Continuous glucose monitoring (CGM) technology (Facchinetti, 2016) helps T1D patients have better glycemic control whenever conditions of hypo- or hyperglycemia arise. The condition in which the blood glucose (BG) level is low compared to the standard level is called hypoglycemia, and if the BG level is high compared to the standard level, it is called hyperglycemia (IDF Diabetes Atlas, 2021). Timely prediction of BG level may help to control patient health conditions. There are two types of measurement of blood glucose, invasive or non-invasive. In the invasive method, the person's fingertip is punctured for blood, and blood glucose is measured from that blood. This method is painful, and it is not convenient for CGM because several measurements of BG are done in a day. For non-invasive measurement, CGM sensors are used that measure BG without taking the person's blood (Facchinetti, 2016; Vashist, 2013). The non-invasive method is convenient for CGM and BG data collection. Some BG datasets are also available for researchers to help them in their research on diabetes (Marling and Bunescu, 2020; Journal of Community Health Research, 2018). CGM sensors are also associated with smart phones or the cloud to store the data. There are smartphone-based devices that provide alerts to patients about their BG level (Reddy et al., 2016). Recent studies (Dalla Man et al., 2014; Vettoretti et al., 2018) use simulators to generate synthetic data, which is useful for analysis.

Different artificial intelligence (AI) algorithms are available for CGM. BG data along with other features are used for training the model. In Gadaleta et al. (2019), a comparison among AI algorithms for BG monitoring is discussed. Some novel features are also extracted from the CGM data which represent the data more meaningfully and help the model improve performance (Islam et al., 2020). CGM data are not stationary because they are influenced by daily short-term activities such as amount of glucose generated due to intake of food items, insulin generation by the body, insulin injections, and routine exercise. The autoregressive integrated moving average (ARIMA) model (Yang et al., 2019) was introduced to deal with such data, and it could provide information about early hypoglycemic events.

Recently, deep learning (DL) has been used in the medical field for medical image data analysis (Zhang et al., 2021). A near-infrared spectroscopy (NIR)–based intelligent glucometer (iGLU) was developed to collect BG data non-invasively, and these data were applied to a deep neural network (DNN) for training (Jain et al., 2020; Joshi et al., 2020). The performance accuracy was good with less measurement error. Researchers have also used convolutional neural networks (CNNs) (Ghosh et al., 2020) to predict BG levels at an early stage using time series data and classify the patient according to glucose levels (Mhaskar, Pereverzyev and van der Walt, 2017). CNNs with a Gaussian kernel filter are also used in classification of BG, which improves model performance (Lekha and Suchetha, 2018). Researchers also worked on T2D diabetes patient data (Alhassan et al., 2018). A smart phone–based blood glucose inference application was developed which collected data from subjects and used a multi-division deep dynamic recurrent neural network–based algorithm for classification of blood glucose (Gu et al., 2017). DL-based GluNet, which was a multilayer dilated CNN, was developed for glucose forecasting after a 30- and 60-minute prediction horizon (Liu et al., 2020), and it was trained using time series data.

CGM provides a time series BG data which has a time dependency. A long short-term memory (LSTM) network is basically a type of recurrent neural network (RNN) that gives good performance on data representing time series (Alessandro et al., 2019). Gated fusion of two models, that is, CNN for feature extraction and LSTM for BG forecasting (Li et al., 2020), seems promising to show improvement in the prediction accuracy of a model. Parameter optimization of LSTM is an important and challenging task. In Wang et al. (2020), an LSTM-based blood glucose prediction model improved the parameter optimization of LSTM. The input parameters we consider to train a network have a causal relation. One input parameter may affect the others less or more. This causal relation–based causal recurrent neural network (CausalBG) was investigated, which is a combination of CNN and a gated recurrent unit (GRU), as an RNN improves prediction (He et al., 2020). Measurement of three- to four-month-long average blood glucose level is called glycosylated hemoglobin (HbA1c). In Zaitcev et al. (2020), a DNN model for prediction of HbA1c was developed.

DNN is called a black-box method because it predicts output but fails to explain the reason behind the decision. It means there is no explanation about the predicted output by the DNN. Explainable artificial intelligence (XAI) is also playing an important role to make a model explainable. XAI can explain how features contribute to a predicted output (Dave et al., 2020; Peng et al., 2021). Methods like local interpretable model-agnostic explanations (LIME) (Ribeiro et al., 2016), Shapley additive explanations (SHAP) (Lundberg and Lee, 2017), and partial dependence plots (PDPs) are used to explain complex models.

In this chapter, an XAI model is proposed for prediction of blood glucose level from given input parameters. It provides reasons for predictions and suggests contributions of each input parameter in the decision. It aims to achieve accuracy on a par with state-of-the-art techniques.

The rest of the chapter is ordered as follows: Section 11.2 discusses the state of the art on AI models for CGM with modules like data acquisition techniques, preprocessing, feature extraction, and machine learning algorithms. Section 11.3 contains the proposed framework of BG measurement and XAI. Section 11.4 contains the evaluation protocols used by researchers and discussion on the state of the art. Section 11.5 contains a summary of the chapter.

11.2 AI Models for Continuous Glucose Monitoring

Continuous glucose monitoring has several steps for measuring and predicting BG, as shown in Figure 11.1. It includes general steps: dataset generation, preprocessing, feature extraction, AI algorithm, BG prediction, and performance evaluation. First, data are collected from various subjects. This dataset is passed through preprocessing

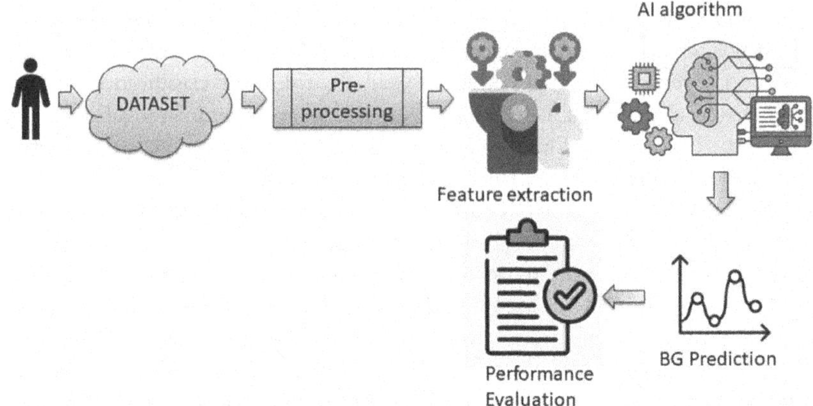

Figure 11.1 General diagram of continuous glucose monitoring using AI.

to reduce the effect of missing data or outliers. Subsequently, features are extracted and applied as an input to an AI algorithm. The AI algorithm trains the model using data, and then the model makes a prediction of the BG value when test data are applied. The evaluation protocol evaluates the model performance using the actual and predicted BG values.

11.2.1 Data Acquisition and Public Datasets

CGM requires proper data from diabetes patients for prediction. Non-invasive method–based sensors or devices are used to collect blood glucose data (Vashist, 2013; Yang et al., 2019; Jain et al., 2020; Joshi et al., 2020), which is then stored for further processing. Publicly available datasets like ohioT1DM data (Marling and Bunescu, 2020), RT_CGM (Journal of Community Health Research, 2018), and ABC4D project data (Reddy et al., 2016) collected under clinical trials are used for research work. In the ABC4D project, data were collected by participants using Dexcom CGM devices for six consecutive weeks. The OhioT1DM dataset contains 12 T1D diabetes clinical datasets which were taken during eight weeks of clinical trial. In Zaitcev et al. (2020), data of 759 people with T1D are used. This data collection was made during people's visits to Sheffield Teaching Hospitals between 2013 and 2015. In Gu et al. (2017), 112 participants wore a CGM device for six days, and the UI app took a CGM reading every three minutes. In Li et al. (2020a), ten adult T1D subjects' clinical data are used. The dataset is composed of glucose, meal, insulin, and associated timestamps. In some research, virtual datasets are also used. UVA/Padova T1D simulator (Chiara et al., 2014) (Vettoretti et al., 2018; Li et al., 2020a, 2020b; He et al., 2020), approved by the US Food and Drug Administration (FDA), generates virtual data for adults as well as adolescent subjects. In addition, researchers can generate time-series data for specific time periods.

11.2.2 Preprocessing

Real datasets which are collected using CGM devices may contain some short or long missing periods during measuring blood glucose values that can affect prediction of future glucose values. Preprocessing is done for data cleaning. Data preprocessing has several purposes, like exclusion of outliers, interpolation or extrapolation of data already acquired, computing useful features, and data alignment (Li et al., 2020a). According to errors in the dataset, specific preprocessing techniques will be applied for performance improvement of the algorithm. Outlier removal can be applied for correction of errors that have occurred in glucose measurements, data transmission, or incorrect behaviors by people at the time of recording. Sometimes, some readings are too small or too large and can be corrected by APPLYING appropriate thresholds for CGM data. a Gaussian kernel filter (Li et al., 2020a) is also used when data fluctuate with high frequency. Normalization as a preprocessing step removes undue bias among various inputs.

11.2.3 Feature Engineering

From the CGM data, relevant features are extracted to represent data more effectively to improve model learning performance. Time series data must be aligned to one another to generate multichannel data. DL-based models extract features by applying filters with different sizes. For better learning performance, relevant features are extracted from time series BG data and applied to models. In Li et al. (2020a), glucose, food, and insulin were utilized as inputs. In Li et al. (2020b), glucose, carbohydrate, insulin, amount of exercise, alcohol level, and stress were used as model inputs. In He et al. (2020), ten physiological and four external features were extracted from CGM data. In those studies, extracted physiological features were carbohydrate consumption, carbohydrate digestion, absorption, secretion and mass of insulin level, long-term effects of exercises and sleep quality on insulin, glucose mass, and glucose concentration.

11.2.4 State-of-the-Art Models for CGM

AI models are widely used in various applications due to their ability to solve complex problems. AI models generally are capable of recognizing a pattern from the set of data, training themselves, and then making certain decisions without the need of human intervention. Several DL algorithms are available for prediction once useful features are extracted from the dataset. Some models have the ability to extract features automatically and then make suitable predictions. Some of the advanced models which are used for prediction BG are described in the next sub-sections.

11.2.4.1 Auto-Regression Integrated Moving Average Model

ARIMA (Yang et al., 2019) has been used to analyze non-stationary behavior of time series data, and based on that prediction, models are built. Auto-regression refers to the use of lag values of changing variables. Integrated refers to the differencing of lag values to make time series data stationary. The moving average represents the residual error during prediction and uses the lag values of error in prediction.

The output of the ARIMA model can be expressed as follows (Yang et al., 2019):

$$y_i = \sum_{j=1}^{p} a_j y_{i-j} + \varepsilon_i + \sum_{j=1}^{q} b_j \varepsilon_{i-j}, i = m+1, m+2, \ldots, k \tag{11.1}$$

where p and q represent the number of lag values to be considered, y_{i-j} represents differenced data of blood glucose values, a_j and b_j are the model parameters, ε_i takes into account Gaussian white noise, and ε_{i-j} are lag values of the residual error. In this model, a differencing step is applied to eliminate the non-stationary nature of the data.

11.2.4.2 *Convolutional Neural Networks*

A CNN (Ghosh et al., 2020) has feed-forward architecture and the ability to learn highly complex features of input data. It consists of several processing layers, and each layer learns different features of the input data. High-level features are learned by the initial layers, and low-level features are learned by the deeper layers. A CNN has weight sharing features. The CNN architecture is shown in Figure 11.2.

A CNN has several pairs of convolutional and pooling layers. A fully connected (FC) layer is used at the end. Each convolutional layer contains a number of kernels called filters. Convolution operation is performed between filters and input metrics, which generates a feature map. Every kernel is assigned a random weight at the start of the training. After each training epoch, the weights are adjusted and meaningful features are extracted by the kernel. The pooling layer shrinks the feature maps to smaller maps, preserving the important information during shrinking. The last part of the CNN architecture is the FC that serves as the output layer. The output of the last convolutional or pooling layer is flattened and given as input to the FC layer. In a CNN, an activation function is used after every layer, which introduces non-linearity into the model.

11.2.4.3 *Dilated CNN Model*

A CNN comprises several convolution layers, a pooling layer, and a FC layer as output. Different-sized filters are applied in the convolution layer to extract the features. Convolution operation is performed between filter weights and convolution layer

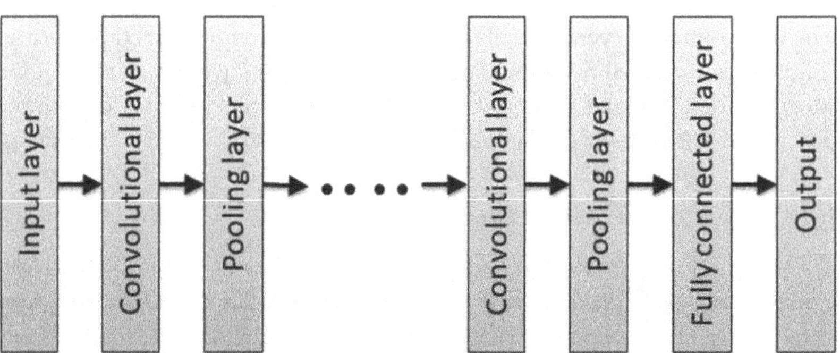

Figure 11.2 General architecture of CNN.

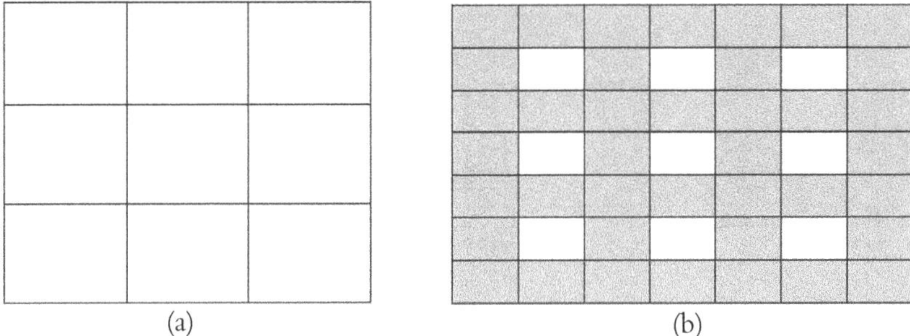

Figure 11.3 (a) 3 × 3 filter for convolution. 3 × 3 filters with random weights are used to perform convolution operation; (b) filter used for dilated convolution, which has a 7 × 7 receptive field.

data. Dilated convolution (Li et al., 2020b) means it expands the filter by inserting holes in it.

The difference between convolution and dilated convolution operation is explained using the filters used in them. For example, Figure 11.3(a) shows a 3 × 3 filter, which is used to perform convolution operation. Different kinds of filters with different sizes and weights are used for feature extraction. For dilated convolution, the same filter will be used with holes, as shown in Figure 11.3(b). This means that the same filter has a 7 × 7 receptive field in dilated convolution. Dilated CNN by skipping some of input values in each layer with certain steps betters data reception without adversely affecting computational cost.

11.2.4.4 Convolutional Recurrent Neural Network Model

CNNs as well as RNNs are part of a convolutional recurrent neural network (CRNN) (Li et al., 2020b). A CNN extracts the important features and serves as input to the RNN. An LSTM network is used, which learns time series data (Alessandro et al., 2019). The LSTM solves the gradient descent problem appearing in the RNN. The LSTM predicts BG levels for a 30- or 60-minute prediction horizon. Figure 11.4 shows the typical architecture of an LSTM.

LSTM comprises an input gate, forget gate, and output gate. The input gate controls information to be stored in long-term memory cells. The forget gate controls which data will be discarded from the LSTM cell. The output gate uses information received from current input, the output of the forget gate, and the output of the input gate and produces an output which is used in the next time step. The output of the LSTM cell is calculated by following equations:

$$C_t = i_t \star \overline{C_t} + f_t \star C_{t-1} \tag{11.2}$$

$$i_t = \sigma(W_h \left[h_{t-1} + x_t\right] + b_h \tag{11.3}$$

$$f_t = \sigma\left(W_f \left[h_{t-1} + x_t\right] + b_f\right) \tag{11.4}$$

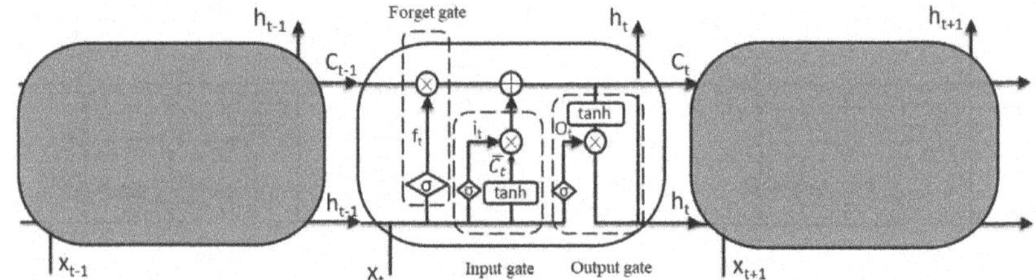

Figure 11.4 Architecture of LSTM. LSTM network comprising input, forget, and output gates. x_t, x_{t-1}, and x_{t+1} are current input, previous input, and next input, respectively. In the forget gate, x_t and h_{t-1} are added and passed through a sigmoid (σ) function and generate f_t. The forget gate controls which data will be discarded from the LSTM cell. In input gates, i_t and c_t , are used to generate new information, which will be stored in LSTM cells. C_{i-1} is an old cell state. The product of and f_t is added to the product *of* i_t and $\overline{C_t}$ to generate a new cell state. C_i C_t is passed through the hyperbolic tangential (tanh) function. h_t is a product of tanh (C_t) and O_t.

$$\overline{C_t} = tanh\left(W_c\left[h_{t-1} + x_t\right] + b_c\right) \tag{11.5}$$

$$h_t = O_t \star \left(tanh C_t\right) \tag{11.6}$$

$$O_t = \sigma\left(W_o\left[h_{t-1} + x_t\right] + b_o\right) \tag{11.7}$$

W_h, W_f, W_c, W_o = weights, b_h, b_f, b_c, b_o = bias, ⋆ operator is Hadamard product

11.2.4.5 Causal RNN Model

An RNN is used when temporal dependency is present in data. But sometimes features have a causal relation between them. A causal relation means a change in one feature value may affect the other feature value less or more. Features extracted from BG data have this kind of causal relation. The performance of conventional RNNs is not satisfactory on causal data, so the causal RNN was developed to overcome this problem. Causal RNN (He et al., 2020) first adopted the gated recurrent unit (GRU), which understands the non-linear time dependency of time series data. GRUs are used for BG prediction because they are computationally efficient at solving the vanishing gradient problem in conventional RNN. A sparse group lasso penalty is introduced with GRUs which automatically selects causal features and leaves other non-causal features. The sparse-group lasso adds l_1 and l_2 penalties across the weights of GRUs with the empirical loss function. l_1 and l_2 regularize the model and increase the robustness against outliers. The architecture of GRU is shown in Figure 11.5.

GRU comprises a reset gate and update gate. The reset gate finds the relevancy between the previous and current cell states and uses this information to update the current cell state. It decides the amount of information that will be neglected from the past cell. The update gate decides the amount of information that will be passed

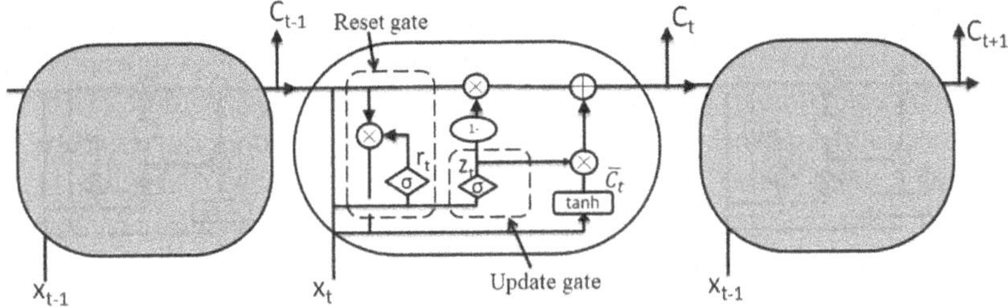

Figure 11.5 Architecture of GRU. GRU comprises reset and update gates. x_t, $x_{t-1,}$ and x_{t+1} are current input, previous input, and next input, respectively. The reset gate adds x_t and the previous cell state passing it through the sigmoid function to get r_t. The product of r_t and is added to x_t, and passed through the hyperbolic tangential (tanh) function, and gets. z_t is calculated by passing x_t and the previous cell state through the sigmoid function in the update gate. $1 - z_t$ is multiplied by and added to the product of z_t and to get .

to next cell. The output of each gate and the current state of the GRU cell are calculated by the following equations:

$$C_t = Z_t \star \overline{C_t} + (1 - Z_t) \star C_{t-1} \tag{11.8}$$

$$Z_t = \sigma\left(W_z\left[C_{t-1} + x_t\right] + b_z\right) \tag{11.9}$$

$$r_t = \sigma\left(W_r\left[C_{t-1} + x_t\right] + b_r\right) \tag{11.10}$$

$$\overline{C_t} = tanh\left(W_c\left[(r_t \star h_{t-1}) + x_t\right] + b_c\right) \tag{11.11}$$

W_z, W_r, W_c = weights, b_z, b_r, b_c = bias, $\star$ operator is Hadamard product

11.2.4.6 VMD-PSO-LSTM Model

A various mode decomposition–based particle swarm optimization (PSO) LSTM network, as described in Wang et al. (2020), was developed to solve the parameter optimization problem of LSTM. This model first decomposed CGM data using VMD and different frequency band components that were obtained in terms of the intrinsic mode function (IMF) of BG concentration. This process eliminated the non-stationary nature changes of BG values. An improved PSO algorithm was used to optimize LSTM model parameters.

11.3 Explainable AI

Today, AI is used widely in the healthcare industry for diagnosis of diseases. DL models are found in many fields because of their feature extraction ability and complex structure. Hundreds of parameters are used in DL model to provide the desired results. However, the general structure does not contain any explanation of the result. Explanation means how the deep learning network arrived at the decision. Medical experts generally distrust black-box AI models because of poor or no explanation; hence their use in actual clinical practice may be limited. Because of a lack of transparency and explainability, users also may get confused about the result and can have doubts about the reliability of the model. These facts direct AI models to be transparent with a view to increasing the level of trust among medical practitioners.

Figure 11.6 shows a conceptual diagram of an XAI (Dave et al., 2020)–based model that is able to interpret how the model has predicted a specific result. First, the model is trained using training data. Once reasonably good training and validation results are obtained, the model is ready to predict blood glucose values from the new test data. New test data are then applied to the XAI-based trained model. Using the data, the model predicts the blood glucose level, and XAI interprets the predicted result and explains the resulting outcome. Medical practitioners can validate their findings with the AI model's predicted results.

XAI methods can be used to get local and global explanations. Local explanations help to understand the reason behind decision-making for a single prediction, while global explanations provide an explanation about the overall behavior of the model. Local interpretable model-agnostic explanations (Ribeiro et al., 2016) are a commonly used local explanation method, while Shapley additive explanations (Lundberg and Lee, 2017) are broadly used as global interpretable method.

11.3.1 Local Interpretable Model-Agnostic Explanations

LIME is a local explanation method which helps the network provide interpretability for complex models. First, LIME performs data perturbation and creates an augmented dataset. Next, an interpretable model is trained by LIME on the new dataset. Finally, a LIME interpretable model is compared with the black-box model for the test dataset.

Let the original prediction function be y and g the explanation model. g belongs to G, which represents a set of explainable models. Here we need an explanation of

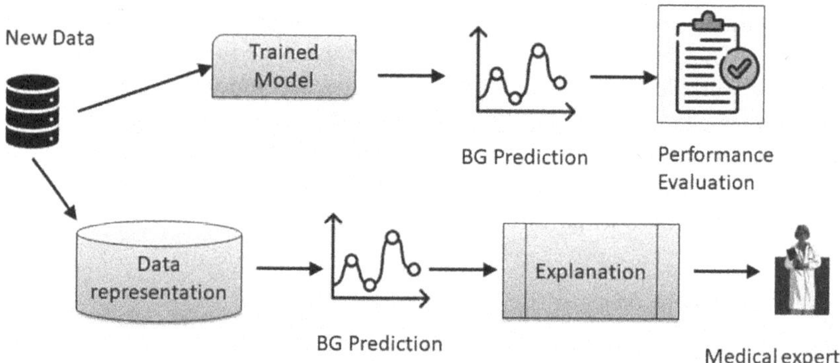

Figure 11.6 Conceptual diagram of XAI model in BG prediction (Dave et al., 2020).

the prediction $y(x)$ at input x. First x is converted to interpretable using the mapping function $h_x\left(x = h_x\left(x'\right)\right)$. After that, perturbation is done on and instances are created around. Every instance is assigned a weight . The instances which were close to get higher weight values, and lower weight values are assigned to instances which are far from . is added to measure the model complexity. The explanation produced by LIME is given in Eq. 11.12 that is defined in Ribeiro et al. (2016):

$$\xi\left(x\right) = \underset{g\epsilon G}{argmin}\ \mathcal{L}\left(y, g, \pi_x\right) + \Omega\left(g\right) \tag{11.12}$$

Using the perturbed dataset, optimization of $\mathcal{L}$ was carried out, and we get explanation $\xi\left(x\right)$.

11.3.2 *Shapley Additive Explanations*

SHAP calculates the Shapley values for each feature of a complex model to find the contribution of the features in predicting output (Lundberg and Lee, 2017). It is possible to interpret which feature contributed the most to predicting output from the Shapley value. In order to calculate the Shapley value, first a different subset of features is created. Then the prediction output is found using this subset, and the weighted sum of the prediction output is taken. The Shapley value is defined in Eq. 11.13 per Lundberg and Lee (2017):

$$\phi_j\left(x\right) = \sum_{s\subseteq\{x_1, x_2, \ldots, x_m\}\setminus\{x_j\}} \frac{|s|!\left(m - |s| - 1\right)!}{m!}\left(val\left(s \cup \left\{x_j\right\} - val\left(s\right)\right)\right) \tag{11.13}$$

where $\phi_j\left(x\right)$ is the Shapley value of x_j, x_j is a value of a feature, s is a subgroup of the model for a given feature, m represents the number of features available, and val is the corresponding predicted feature values.

11.4 Proposed XAI Based Fully Connected Network Model

In this section, the proposed XAI-based fully connected network (FCN) model is described. The dataset is obtained as mentioned in Jain et al., (2020). For our studies, we selected 96 participants' data. Table 11.1 summarizes the gender information of participants. Table 11.2 shows the dataset with features and targeted output used to train the FCN. The Sex column represents female as 0 and male as 1. Age represents subject age in years, and Weight represents weight in kg. ch1, ch2, and ch3 represent three sensors' output; 1300 nm absorption, 940 nm absorption, and 940 reflectance-infrared detectors were used to measure the glucose molecules present in blood, and these sensors' output were noted as ch1, ch2, and ch3, respectively, in the dataset. The sensors' outputs measure glucose molecules present in the blood and provide the equivalent voltage from 0 to 5 volts. These voltage values are converted to decimal using an analog to digital converter (ADC).

Figure 11.7 gives details of the proposed FCN. The proposed FCN contains a total of ten hidden layers, with ten neurons in each hidden layer. Multiple hidden

Table 11.1 Participants' General Age and Diabetic Related Information Used for Current Work (Jain et al., 2020)

Sample Basic Characteristics	*Testing*
Age in years **Male: 23–68** **Female: 26–73**	Gender-wise samples Male: 53 Female: 43
Age in years **Male: 24–68** **Female: 26–65**	Prediabetic Male: 16 Female: 16
Age in years **Male: 30–68** **Female: 30–73**	Diabetic Male: 28 Female: 22
Age in years **Male: 23–67** **Female: 35–62**	Healthy Male: 9 Female: 5

Table 11.2 Six Inputs and Targeted Output of Sample Dataset Used to Train Proposed FCN

Inputs						*Output*
Sex (M/F) **(0 = F, 1 = M)**	*Age (years)*	*Weight (kgs)*	*ch1*	*ch2*	*ch3*	*BG Level (mg/dl)*
0	60	51.0	3982.25	5920.19	208.44	105
0	60	77.0	4065.28	3925.95	275.30	140
1	24	98.0	4051.29	5580.95	226.53	213
1	42	70.0	3864.41	3771.65	207.04	98
0	60	62.0	3869.66	7093.48	233.64	158

layers help the FCN learn the complexity of features. The dataset contains one-dimensional tabular data, and the FCN is trained with this dataset. to are six input parameters: gender; age; weight; and three sensors' data, ch1, ch2, and ch3.

In order to train the FCN, we used inputs with two alternates with/without scaling inputs. In the first approach, we used data without scaled raw inputs whereby the same dataset was used to train the FCN with Min-Max scalar, which converts input data between 0 and 1. Eq. 11.14 is used to apply Min-Max scalar to each column's data.

$$Min - Max\ X' = \frac{X - X_{min}}{X_{max} - X_{min}} \tag{11.14}$$

where X is the input value on which scaling is applied, X' is the new value after applying scaling, and Xmin and Xmax are minimum and maximum value of each input parameter. The commonly used rectified linear (ReLU) activation function is

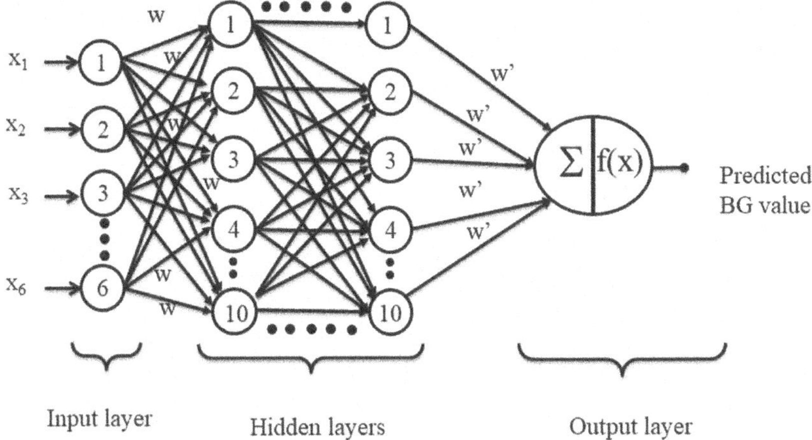

Figure 11.7 Architecture of proposed FCN.

used in each hidden layer neuron, whereas, in order to give linearity for predicting BG values in a wider range, we used a linear activation function f (x) at the output layer. We used adam as an optimizer, the mean squared error (MSE) function as a loss function, and root mean squared error (RMSE) as an evaluation protocol. In this work, XAI models using LIME and SHAP are implemented. LIME gives a local explanation, and SHAP gives a global explanation of the overall model.

11.5 Results and Discussion

11.5.1 Simulation Results

In order to validate the performance of the proposed FCN, the proposed work is compared with the FCN model proposed in Jain et al. (2020) on BG prediction, as both use the same dataset. The difference lies in the fact that in the proposed work, we have modified the architecture and used six input parameters – gender (sex), age, weight, and three sensors' data – of 96 people, whereas in Jain et al. (2020), three sensors' data of 93 people were used. We trained our model with non-scaled and scaled data. In one experiment, the FCN model is first trained with data that were not scaled by the Min-Max scaler. In the second set of experiments, the FCN model was trained with the data scaled by the Min-Max scaler. In this way, we can check the effect of scaling on model performance. The following performance evaluation parameters are used to evaluate the efficiency and performance of proposed methods.

11.5.1.1 Root Mean Square Error

RMSE is used to measure the performance of the regression model during training. RMSE is calculated per Eq. 11.15:

$$RMSE = \sqrt{\frac{1}{N}\sum_{k=1}^{N}\left(y_{k} - y_{k}\right)^{2}} \tag{11.15}$$

where y_k = *Actual output*, y_k = *Prediction output*, N = *number of predictions*

11.5.1.2 Mean Absolute Relative Difference

Mean absolute relative difference (mARD) is the average of the absolute difference between actual and predicted output. A lower value of mARD indicates that the prediction result is closer to the actual value. Typically, if a model or device has a mARD < 10%, it indicates good performance (Jain et al., 2020) (Joshi et al., 2020) (Li et al., 2020a, 2020b). mARD is calculated per Eq. 11.16):

$$mARD = \frac{1}{N}\sum_{k=1}^{N}\frac{\left|y_{k} - y_{k}\right|}{y_{k}} \tag{11.16}$$

where y_k = Actual output, y_k = Prediction output, N = number of predictions

11.5.1.3 Mean Absolute Deviation

Mean absolute deviation (MAD) is an important parameter that shows the average distance between each predicted value and the average of all predicted values. It shows how the predicted values are spread out (Jain et al., 2020; Joshi et al., 2020; Alessandro et al., 2019). MAD is calculated per Eq. 11.17:

$$MAD = \frac{1}{n}\sum\left(\hat{y}_{i} - \bar{y}\right) \tag{11.17}$$

where $\hat{y}_i$ = Prediction output , $\bar{y}$ = mean of $\hat{y}_i$, n = number of predictions

Table 11.3 summarizes the result comparison of the FCN models. Both proposed models outperform that of the work reported in Jain et al. (2020). The FCN model trained with scaled data provided mARD = 1.7%, MAD = 3.45 mg/dl, and RMSE = 6.27 mg/dl and performed better compared to other results.

Figures 11.8(a) and (b) show comparisons of the reference and predicted BG values for the proposed FCN model without and with scaling, respectively. It can easily be observed that the predicted BG values are very close to the reference values. Along

Table 11.3 Comparison of Proposed FCN Models

Sr no.	*Model*	*mARD (%)*	*MAD (mg/dl)*	*RMSE (mg/dl)*
1	FCN (Jain et al., 2020)	7.32	9.89	11.56
2	Proposed model (without scaling)	2.6	5.07	8.76
3	Proposed model (with scaling)	1.7	3.45	6.27

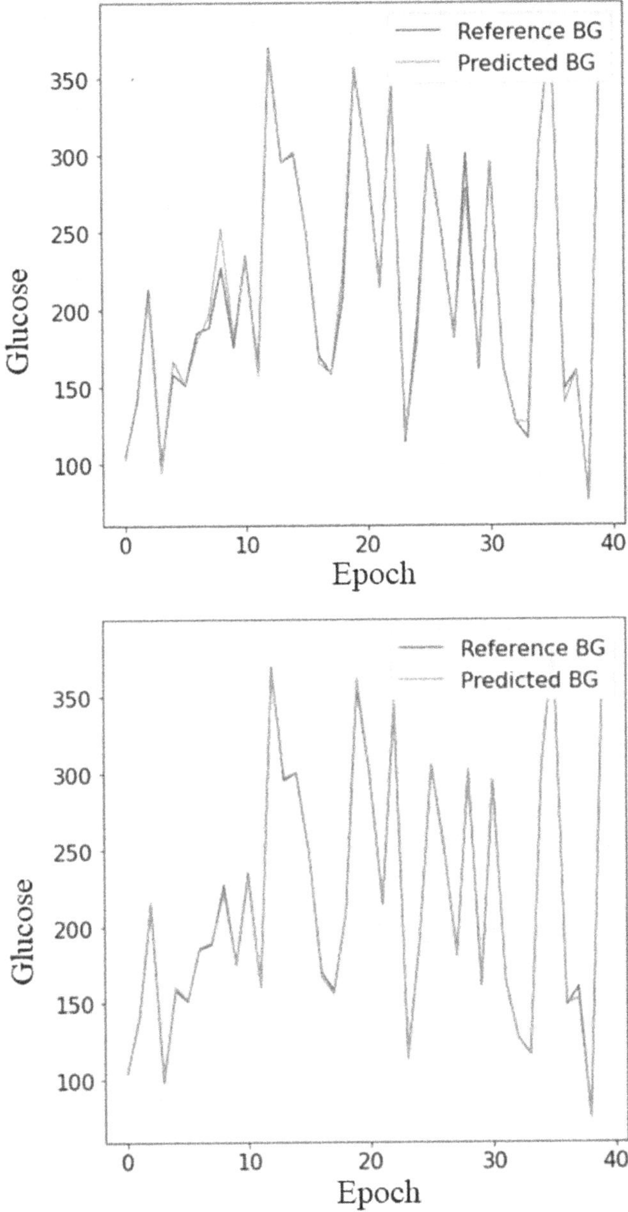

Figure 11.8 (a) Reference and predicted BG concentration for FCN model without scaling. (b) Reference and predicted BG concentration for FCN model with scaling.

with Table 11.3, it can be inferred that the FCN model with scaling has a lower RMSE after training because the predicted BG value is identically following the reference BG value. The model with scaling performed better because scaling scales all the feature data between 0 and 1. This helps the model train better and faster.

Clarke error grid analysis (CEGA) (Clarke et al., 1987) is used to analyze model accuracy. In CEGA, shown in Figures 11.9(a) and (b), the x- and y-axis represent the reference and predicted BG levels, respectively. The grid is divided into five zones, A–E. Zone A characterizes that predicted BG values do not diverge more than 20% from the reference value. Zone B characterizes that predicted BG values diverge more than 20% from the reference value but do not lead to much erroneous value. Zone C represents reference values inside the BG range (70 mg/dl to 180 mg/dl) but predicted values outside the range. Zone D characterizes reference values outside the BG range but predicted values inside the range. It represents failure detection of the model. Zone E represents reference values above 180 mg/dl or below 70 mg/dl but predicted values below 70 mg/dl or above 180 mg/dl, respectively. If the predicted output lies in Zone A and B, it is believed that the model gives the desired and clinically acceptable performance, whereas values in zones C, D, and E indicate erroneous and clinically unacceptable performance. Result values in Figure 11.9(a) and (b) show that in our proposed models, all the predicted outputs are in zone A. These facts show the efficacy of our models. The figures also highlight that both our proposed models, without scaling and with scaling, perform well, and both falling into Zone A. There is not much difference in the analysis of both proposed models.

11.5.2 Global Explanation of BG Prediction Using SHAP

In order to identify the impact of each feature on the prediction result, we calculate the mean SHAP value of the proposed deep neural network. Figure 11.10 represents a summary bar plot of the feature impact of the FCN using the mean SHAP value. The presented results show the contribution of each feature in predicting output. The left side shows the feature names arranged in such a way that the first feature impacts the prediction BG more and the last feature impacts it much less. It is observed that ch2 has more impact in prediction than other input parameters. The incorporation of new parameters, weight and age, has a greater contribution for the prediction of BG values, and that is the reason the proposed work outperforms the results in Jain et al. (2020).

Figure 11.11 represents the feature importance plot of the FCN using the SHAP value. The x-axis depicts the SHAP value of features calculates using different subsets of features. Zero, negative, and positive Shapley value represents no effect, negative effect, and positive effect of features, respectively. The y-axis on the left side represents the features by their names in descending order of their importance; that is, the most important is first and least important last. Light grey dots show low values, and dark grey dots show high values of features. This also indicates that the ch2 value contributes the most in predicting the BG value.

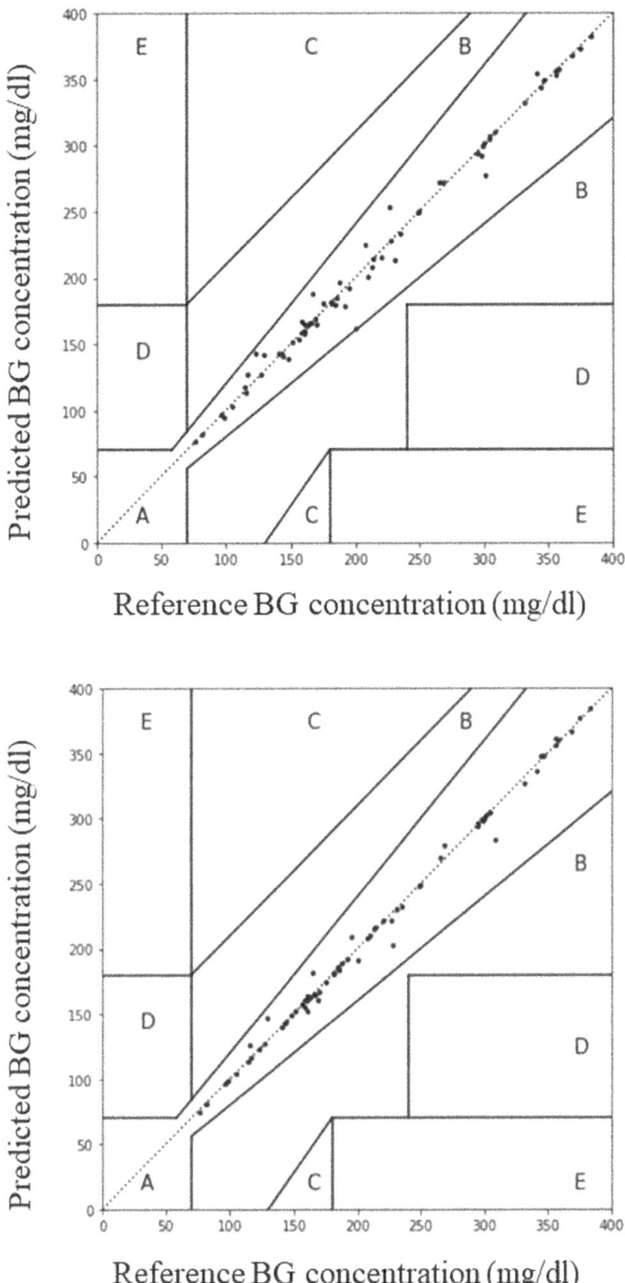

Figure 11.9 (a) Clarke error grid analysis of FCN trained without scaling. (b) Clarke error grid analysis of FCN trained with scaling.

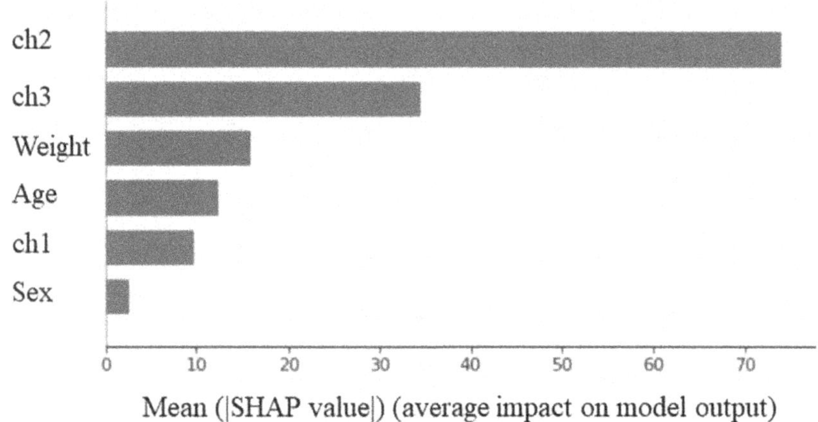

Figure 11.10 Summary bar plot of feature impact of the FCN.

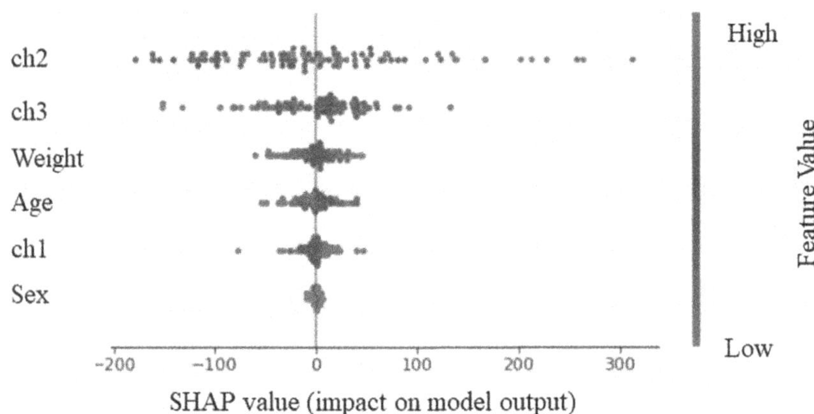

Figure 11.11 Feature importance plot of FCN using SHAP values.

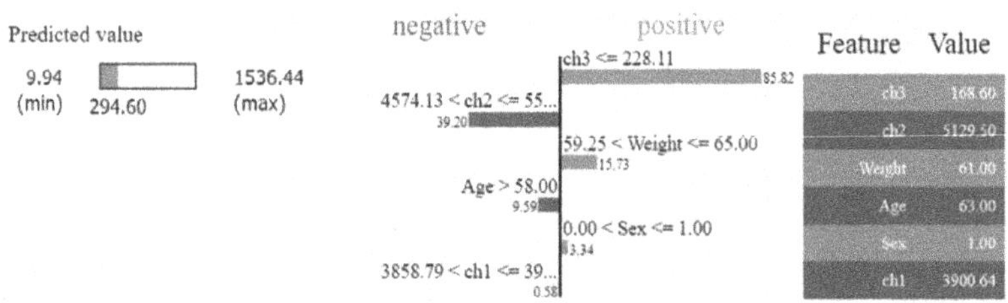

Figure 11.12 LIME explanation for a single BG prediction outcome.

11.5.3 Local Explanation of BG Prediction Using LIME

After discussing the global explanation of the FCN for prediction of BG concentration, it is also important to explain the individual prediction outcome. We used LIME for local explanation and randomly chose a single instance for local explanation of prediction outcome. Figure 11.12 shows a LIME explanation for a single BG prediction outcome. The left part indicates the prediction output of our proposed model. The center part gives features along with their weights. The color bar increases with higher weight values. Blue and orange in the figure indicate negative and positive feature contribution towards BG. In this particular instance, ch3 has a positive influence, while ch2 and ch1 have a negative influence on the BG value. Weight also contributes to high values of BG.

11.6 Conclusion

In this chapter, different algorithms used for blood glucose prediction are discussed. Explainable AI models are proposed for a BG prediction model. Simulation results show that the proposed FCN model trained with scaled data achieves good performance compared to similar work and also without a scaled model. Clarke error grid analysis demonstrates that the proposed model in this chapter gives the desired output for BG prediction. In this chapter, interpretability techniques like LIME and SHAP as explainable models were investigated for blood glucose prediction. The XAI technique SHAP provided a global explanation, while LIME provided a local explanation for the model's successful application. The Shapley value shows which features are more important for the FCN model and contributes more in BG prediction. LIME gives a prediction explanation of a single BG concentration. Further research can focus on implementation of the model with more physiological features and explain their relevancy with more model interpretability techniques.

References

Alessandro Aliberti, Pupillo Irene, Terna Stefano, Patti Enrico, and Acquaviva Andrea. 2019. "A Multi-Patient Data-Driven Approach to Blood Glucose Prediction." *IEEE Access* 7: 69311–69325. doi: 10.1109/ACCESS.2019.2919184.

Alhassan Zakhriya, A. Stephen McGough, Riyad Alshammari, Tahani Daghstani, David Budgen, and Noura Al Moubayed. 2018. "Type-2 Diabetes Mellitus Diagnosis from Time Series Clinical Data Using Deep Learning Models." In *International Conference on Artificial Neural Networks*, pp. 468–478. New York: Springer International Publishing. doi: 10.1007/978-3-030-01424-7_46.

Chiara Dalla Man, Francesco Micheletto, Dayu Lv, Marc Breton, Boris Kovatchev, and Claudio Cobelli. 2014. "The UVA/PADOVA Type 1 Diabetes Simulator: New Features." *Journal of Diabetes Science and Technology* 8 (1): 26–34. doi: 10.1177/1932296813514502.

Clarke WL., D. Cox, LA. Gonder-Frederick, W. Carter, and SL. Pohl. 1987. "Evaluating Clinical Accuracy of Systems for Self-Monitoring of Blood Glucose." *Diabetes Care* 10 (5): 622–628. doi: 10.2337/diacare.10.5.622.

Dave Devam, Het Naik, Smiti Singhal, and Pankesh Patel. 2020. *Explainable AI Meets Healthcare: A Study on Heart Disease Dataset*, pp. 1–23. http://arxiv.org/abs/2011.03195.

Facchinetti Andrea. 2016. "Continuous Glucose Monitoring Sensors: Past, Present and Future Algorithmic Challenges." *Sensors (Switzerland)* 16 (12): 1–12. doi: 10.3390/s16122093.

Gadaleta Matteo, Andrea Facchinetti, Enrico Grisan, and Michele Rossi. 2019. "Prediction of Adverse Glycemic Events From Continuous Glucose Monitoring Signal." *IEEE Journal of Biomedical and Health Informatics* 23 (2): 650–659. doi: 10.1109/JBHI.2018.2823763.

Ghosh Anirudha, Abu Sufian, Farhana Sultana, Amlan Chakrabarti, and Debashis De. 2020. "Fundamental Concepts of Convolutional Neural Network." *Recent Trends and Advances in Artificial Intelligence and Internet of Things. Intelligent Systems Reference Library* (Cham: Springer) 172: 519–567. doi: 10.1007/978-3-030-32644-9_36.

Gu Weixi, Yuxun Zhou, Zimu Zhou, Xi Liu, Han Zou, Pei Zhang, Costas J. Spanos, and Lin Zhang. 2017. "SugarMate: Non-Intrusive Blood Glucose Monitoring with Smartphones." *Proceedings of the ACM on Interactive, Mobile, Wearable and Ubiquitous Technologies* 1 (3): 1–27. doi: 10.1145/3130919.

He Miao, Weixi Gu, Ying Kong, Lin Zhang, Costas J. Spanos, and Khalid M. Mosalam. 2020. "CausalBG: Causal Recurrent Neural Network for the Blood Glucose Inference with IoT Platform." *IEEE Internet of Things Journal* 7 (1): 598–610. doi: 10.1109/JIOT.2019.2946693.

Holt Richard, Clive Cockram, Allan Flyvbjerg, and Barry Goldstein. 2010. *Text Book of Diadetes*, 4th edition. Hoboken: Willey-Blackwell. doi: 10.1002/9781444324808.ch2.

IDF Diabetes Atlas. 2021. *International Diabetes Federation*, 10th edition. Belgium: International Diabetes Federation. doi: 10.1016/j.diabres.2013.10.013.

Islam MS., MK. Qaraqe, SB. Belhaouari, and MA. Abdul-Ghani. 2020. "Advanced Techniques for Predicting the Future Progression of Type 2 Diabetes." *IEEE Access* 8: 120537–120547. doi: 10.1109/ACCESS.2020.3005540.

Jain Prateek, Amit M. Joshi, and Saraju P. Mohanty. 2020. "IGLU: An Intelligent Device for Accurate Noninvasive Blood Glucose-Level Monitoring in Smart Healthcare." *IEEE Consumer Electronics Magazine* 9 (1): 35–42. doi: 10.1109/MCE.2019.2940855.

Joshi Amit M., Prateek Jain, Saraju P. Mohanty, and Navneet Agrawal. 2020. "IGLU 2.0: A New Wearable for Accurate Non-Invasive Continuous Serum Glucose Measurement in IoMT Framework." *IEEE Transactions on Consumer Electronics* 66 (4): 327–335. doi: 10.1109/TCE.2020.3011966.

Journal of Community Health Research. 2018. *Diabetes Research Studies*. http://diabetes.jaeb.org/.

Lekha S., and MS. Suchetha. 2018. "Real-Time Non-Invasive Detection and Classification of Diabetes Using Modified Convolution Neural Network." *IEEE Journal of Biomedical and Health Informatics* 22 (5): 1630–1636. doi: 10.1109/JBHI.2017.2757510.

Li Kezhi, C. Liu, T. Zhu, Pau Herrero, and Pantelis Georgiou. 2020a. "GluNet: A Deep Learning Framework for Accurate Glucose Forecasting." *IEEE Journal of Biomedical and Health Informatics* (Institute of Electrical and Electronics Engineers Inc.) 24 (2): 414–423. doi: 10.1109/JBHI.2019.2931842.

Li Kezhi, John Daniels, Chengyuan Liu, Pau Herrero, and Pantelis Georgiou. 2020b. "Convolutional Recurrent Neural Networks for Glucose Prediction." *IEEE Journal of Biomedical and Health Informatics* 24 (2): 603–613. doi: 10.1109/JBHI.2019.2908488.

Lundberg Scott M., and Su In Lee. 2017. "A Unified Approach to Interpreting Model Predictions." *Advances in Neural Information Processing Systems* 30: 1–10.

Marling Cindy, and Razvan Bunescu. 2020. "The OhioT1DM Dataset for Blood Glucose Level Prediction: Update 2020." *CEUR Workshop Proceedings* 2675: 71–74.

Mhaskar Hrushikesh N., Sergei V. Pereverzyev, and Maria D. van der Walt. 2017. "A Deep Learning Approach to Diabetic Blood Glucose Prediction." *Frontiers in Applied Mathematics and Statistics* 3: 1–20. doi: 10.3389/fams.2017.00014.

Oviedo Silvia, Josep Vehí, Remei Calm, and Joaquim Armengol. 2017. "A Review of Personalized Blood Glucose Prediction Strategies for T1DM Patients." *International Journal for Numerical Methods in Biomedical Engineering* 33 (6). doi: 10.1002/cnm.2833.

Peng Junfeng, Kaiqiang Zou, Mi Zhou, Yi Teng, Xiongyong Zhu, Feifei Zhang, and Jun Xu. 2021. "An Explainable Artificial Intelligence Framework for the Deterioration Risk Prediction of Hepatitis Patients." *Journal of Medical Systems* 45 (5). doi: 10.1007/s10916-021-01736-5.

Reddy Monika, Peter Pesi, Maria Xenou, Chistofer Toumazou, Desmond Jonston, Patelis Georgiou, Pau Herrero, and Nick Oliver. 2016. "Clinical Safety and Feasibility of the Advanced Bolus Calculator for Type 1 Diabetes Based on Case-Based Reasoning: A 6-Week Nonrandomized Single-Arm Pilot Study." *Diabetes Technology and Therapeutics* 18 (8): 487–493. doi: 10.1089/dia.2015.0413.

Ribeiro Marco Tulio, Sameer Singh, and Carlos Guestrin. 2016. "'Why Should I Trust You?' Explaining the Predictions of Any Classifier." *NAACL-HLT 2016–2016 Conference of the North American Chapter of the Association for Computational Linguistics: Human Language Technologies, Proceedings of the Demonstrations Session*: 97–101. doi: 10.18653/v1/n16-3020.

Vashist Sandeep. 2013. "Continuous Glucose Monitoring Systems: A Review." *Diagnostics* 3 (4): 385–412. doi: 10.3390/diagnostics3040385.

Vettoretti Martina, Andrea Facchinetti, Giovanni Sparacino, and Claudio Cobelli. 2018. "Type-1 Diabetes Patient Decision Simulator for in Silico Testing Safety and Effectiveness of Insulin Treatments." *IEEE Transactions on Biomedical Engineering* 65 (6): 1281–1290. doi: 10.1109/TBME.2017.2746340.

Wang Wenbo, Meng Tong, and Min Yu. 2020. "Blood Glucose Prediction with VMD and LSTM Optimized by Improved Particle Swarm Optimization." *IEEE Access* 8: 217908–217916. doi: 10.1109/ACCESS.2020.3041355.

Yang Jun, Lei Li, Yimeng Shi, and Xiaolei Xie. 2019. "An ARIMA Model with Adaptive Orders for Predicting Blood Glucose Concentrations and Hypoglycemia." *IEEE Journal of Biomedical and Health Informatics* 23 (3): 1251–1260. doi: 10.1109/JBHI.2018.2840690.

Zaitcev Aleksandr, Mohammad R. Eissa, Zheng Hui, Tim Good, Jackie Elliott, and Mohammed Benaissa. 2020. "A Deep Neural Network Application for Improved Prediction of HbA 1c in Type 1 Diabetes." *IEEE Journal of Biomedical and Health Informatics* 24 (10): 2932–2941. doi: 10.1109/JBHI.2020.2967546.

Zhang Yudong, Juan Manuel Gorriz, and Zhengchao Dong. 2021. "Deep Learning in Medical Image Analysis." *Journal of Imaging* 7 (4). doi: 10.3390/jimaging7040074.

12 Decision Support System for Facial Emotion-Based Progression Detection of Parkinson's Patients

Bhakti Sonawane and Priyanka Sharma

Contents

12.1 Introduction

The goal of computer vision and machine learning (CVML) is to incorporate the human skill of data sensing, analysis, and action based on past and current data into machines. ML algorithm output and outcomes may now be understood and trusted by human users due to a collection of procedures and techniques known as explainable artificial intelligence (XAI). An XAI model should be able to explain the cause of a decision and any bias to the end user. It contributes to defining model correctness, fairness, and transparency and results in decision making supported by AI.

DOI: 10.1201/9781003333425-12

The emergence of CVML solutions has benefited the healthcare industry in numerous ways. By extracting useful knowledge from large-scale data using CVML algorithms and increasing access to clinical facilities, computer-based automated and objective evaluation solutions assist physicians in improving diagnosis.

One of the most fascinating applications of CVML is emotion detection using facial expressions. Emotion is a basic part of human interaction that may be expressed in a variety of ways, including facial expressions, gestures, voice, and physiological signs. In reaction to external social events, facial expression is the most visible and controlled nonverbal form. It is vital to understand facial expressions in order to communicate properly. Facial expression analysis is very important in medical diagnosis (Alvino et al., 2007). Physiological or behavioral responses might influence the posture or look of the face as a result of a medical condition. It delivers information about the patient's condition to the medical specialist. The way a patient's face is expressing himself or herself might give diagnostic information about the disease, the nature of the ailment, and certain key traits.

After Alzheimer's disease, Parkinson's disease (PD), which is focused on dopamine receptors, is the second most prevalent neurological illness (Li et al., 2018; Nilashi et al., 2016; Tsanas et al., 2009; Zhang et al., 2017; Zhao et al., 2014). It is a degenerative and chronic disease that results in a decrease in dopamine levels in the brain. The most prevalent symptoms of PD include tremors, stiffness, bradykinesia, and postural instability (Bologna et al., 2013; Postuma and Montplaisir, 2009). These symptoms are long-term, degenerative, and worsen over time. For various people, these indicators appear in variable degrees and combinations. The quality of life of PD patients is impacted by motor and non-motor symptoms, which may have an indirect impact on family and caregivers. Early detection of PD can help people improve and sustain their quality of life.

Facial bradykinesia is one of the most common symptoms in patients with PD. The loss and slowing of facial expression in both the upper and lower parts of the face are symptoms of this condition. Facial bradykinesia causes hypomimia or a lack of involuntary facial expression and expressive facial characteristics. A PD patient's face might have a "masked" or "poker" appearance, as though they are unconcerned with what is going on around them. Other observers are unable to discern the mental state of PD patients suffering from facial hypomimia when communicating with them, resulting in major social connection challenges (Bologna et al., 2013; Bandini et al., 2017).

Neurological impairment to the motor component of speech production, which affects the movement and coordination of the articulatory organs, is another common motor symptom (i.e., tongue, lips, and jaw). Dysarthria is the term used to describe these symptoms. Dysarthria affects a large percentage of PD patients, as is now well known. Dysarthria can occur at any stage of PD and worsen as the disease advances, according to a study (Bandini et al., 2016; Mutch et al., 1986). There is currently no cure for PD, although there are therapies available to help control the condition, such as dopaminergic medicines (Nilashi et al., 2016; Tsanas et al., 2009). Facial expressivity and dysarthria are measured manually in traditional PD assessments to objectively quantify the patient's expressive behavior and speech impairment. The gestalt evaluation ratings of observers are used in this traditional clinical PD assessment.

12.1.1 Scales for Measuring PD

The most commonly used scales are

- MDS-Unified Parkinson's Disease Rating Scale (UPDRS) (Goetz et al., 2008) is used for PD presence and severity tracking and assessed in terms of score (199 – severe, 0 – no disability).
- The Schwab and England Activities of Daily Living (ADL) Scale (Schwab, 1969) measures a person's ability to perform daily activities in terms of percentage.
- Hoehn and Yahr (H & Y) (Hoehn and Yahr, 1998) is used to assess PD symptom progress and the level of disability in terms of stages (1 through 5).
- Frenchay Dysarthria Assessment (FDA) (Enderby et al., 1980) measures articulatory and intelligibility evaluation of the speech in terms of percentage.

The MDS-UPDRS scale became one of the foundations of treatment and research in PD assessment. Interrogation on segments like mentation, behavior, and mood, motor portions, Schwab and England Activity of Daily Life, and the Modified H & Y Scale are all part of the scale. This is a common clinical test score used to determine the severity of PD. The first section of MDS-UPDRS scale covers mentation, behavior, and mood. The second section evaluates everyday activities. The third section is a clinician's assessment of the motor indications of PD. The fourth section discusses therapy-related problems. Sections 1, 2, and 4 of the report are based on interviews with patients and caregivers, whereas section 3 is based on an investigation. Each of the four sections of the MDS-UPDRS scale contains multiple points that a clinical expert scores independently. These scores range from 0 to 4, with 0 indicating no difficulties, 1 indicating minor issues, 2 indicating mild issues, 3 indicating moderate issues, and 4 indicating severe issues. During patient interviews, an expert clinician determines each scale response. Facial expression and hypomimia levels are discussed in the third section of the MDS-UPDRS scale. The score of the second point of the third section (item 3.2), which ranges from 0 to 4, determines the severity of the sickness.

Traditional medical procedures rely on the patient's clinical history and physical examination because no established biomarkers for PD diagnostic tests exist at this time. If re-evaluation is necessary on a regular basis, such time-consuming evaluations by experienced medical experts may become inconvenient. The creation of tools and approaches for both verbal and nonverbal communication channels become an alternate automated evaluation method. This work intends to aid clinicians in decision-making PD management. The use of ML approaches in an automated decision support system (DSS) to handle various issues associated with PD management is discussed in this paper. The rest of this chapter is organized as follows.

Major publications on facial expression-based PD evaluation are covered in Section 12.2, together with key publications on speech-based PD assessment. Section 12.3 discusses the proposed methodology for PD management. The real-life data procurement process is covered in this section. Results and discussion are presented in Section 12.4, followed by a conclusion in the last section.

12.2 Literature Review

Assessments based on facial expression made by clinicians are subjective and may differ from one another, as well as being impacted by a patient and ethnic background (Lumaka et al., 2017). Some studies in medical diagnostics have used CVML-based techniques to identify facial irregularities or abnormal features in order to give more information to medical doctors. Additionally, it can aid in the time-consuming process of managing data on human emotional behavior (Muhammad et al., 2017).

The structure for using the CVML approach to aid in diagnosis is often similar. In a generic model, various facial characteristics are derived from (preprocessed) input images or videos, which are then used to train classifiers that can gauge the severity of a symptom or categorize of a new sample in one of the predefined categories. Studies on face anomalies focus on areas believed to be affected in patients and compare morphological measurements to those anticipated in healthy controls. Thevenot et al. (2017) addressed automated assessment using CVML techniques to provide additional support for clinicians. Major challenges for such research are tracing the association between facial patterns and medical conditions by utilizing data from healthcare and in capturing the minute changes that the face produces when an expression changes. The majority of earlier research concentrates on characteristics that only perform well in peak intensity expressions. Consequently, they are inappropriate for quantifying expression changes (Alvino et al., 2007; Dagar et al., 2016; Pantic et al., 1999).

Facial bradykinesia is one of the most prevalent motor symptoms of PD. Facial expression and levels of hypomimia are covered in the third component of the MDS-UPDRS scale (item 3.2 of UPDRS). Facial masking is therefore an important biomarker for PD that needs to be taken into consideration (Bologna et al., 2013; Bowers et al., 2006; Gunnery et al., 2017; Tickle-Degnen et al., 2011). Some of the key of the literature on emotion-related automated facial expression quantification of patients is presented further in this section.

The authors in (Katsikitis and Pilowsky, 1988) developed a mathematical model based on 12 measures of the lips, brows, and eyes to evaluate the smile facial expression. In a study (Bowers et al., 2006), the researchers used an entropy metric to assess the timings and changes in facial movements in order to determine whether PD affected the voluntary expression of facial emotions. In another study (Wu et al., 2014), after displaying a movie clip to the individuals to elicit emotion, physiological signals were captured. Videos of the frontal face were gathered for research. Bandini et al. (2017) suggested a fully automated video-based method that obtained color video using the Microsoft Kinect Windows sensor. Additionally with facial bradykinesia, typical in PD patients is dysarthria. Speech intelligibility suffers with dysarthria as a result of imprecise articulation, fluctuating speech rate, and irregular speech prosody (Mutch et al., 1986). The second and third sections of the UPDRS deal with speech impairment in PD, with scores ranging from 0 (normal speech) to 4 (unintelligible speech).

There has been sporadic interest in classifying the speech impairment brought on by PD for many years. Some speech-based clinical DSS collect parameters from voice recordings to distinguish PD patients from healthy controls. Some clinical DSS techniques have taken into consideration the statistical mapping of speech characteristics to UPDRS or any other related scale score. On certain speech recordings, signal processing techniques may be applied, and machine learning techniques can be utilized to estimate an MDS-UPDRS or other scale rating. The important research is covered in more detail in this section.

Numerous studies concentrated on recordings of Oxford University research (Little et al., 2008). There have been 31 recordings of sustained vowel "a" phonation (23 were diagnosed with PD). A kernel support vector machine (SVM) classifier was used by the authors to extract different audio characteristics. In PD diagnosis, noted accuracy was 91.4%. Datasets from various open data repositories (like the University of California at Irvine [UCI] machine learning repository, Kaggle, or datasets containing their own speech recordings of PD patients) used these recordings and applied variety of classification techniques and feature selection methods (Nilashi et al., 2016; Berus et al., 2018; Chen et al., 2013; Orozco-Arroyave et al., 2016; Shahbakhi et al., 2014; Vásquez-Correa et al., 2018).

The majority of traditional speech-based PD management systems used a pipeline strategy. Getting low-dimensional handmade prosodic or spectral properties like noise to the harmonic ratio (NHR), jitter, shimmer, or Mel Frequency Cepstral Coefficients (MFCC) is the first step. Although these characteristics are straightforward to understand, they need the manual creation of predictive features by professionals. Even when customized acoustic features are frequently expertly developed, the human knowledge gap makes it hard to get all essential information. In order to get over these limitations, researchers are currently focusing on using deep learning to automate feature extraction and classification. This technique automatically collects auditory patterns without any prior expert knowledge (Nilashi et al., 2016; Zhang et al., 2017; Vásquez-Correa et al., 2018; Grover et al., 2018; Tripathi et al., 2020).

Research shows that many diagnostic systems based on CVML approaches for PD management are evaluating physiological signals, voice signals, handwriting patterns, and wearable sensors for gait analysis. These techniques use data from a variety of sources, including UCI, Kaggle, and others. Some of the popular datasets used are

- Daphnet Freezing of Gait Data Set (Bachlin et al., 2009), HuGaDB Database (Chereshnev et al., 2017), or HuMoD (Wojtusch et al., 2015) for gait-based analysis
- Parkinson's Disease Spiral Drawings Using Digitized Graphics Tablet dataset (Isenkul et al., 2014), PaHaW (Drotár et al., 2013), and NewHandPD (Pereira et al., 2016) for handwriting-based analysis
- Parkinson Speech dataset with Multiple Types of Sound Recordings dataset (Sakar et al., 2013), Parkinsons dataset (Bache and Lichman, 2013), Parkinsons Telemonitoring dataset (Tsanas et al., 2009), Parkinson dataset (Little et al., 2008), and Oxford Parkinson's Disease Telemonitoring Dataset (Rossi and Ahmed, 2015) for speech-based analysis
- Other signal analysis: Parkinson's Vision-Based Pose Estimation Dataset (Li et al., 2018) and Parkinsons Progression Markers Initiative PPMI (Marek et al., 2011)

12.3 Proposed Methodology

Based on emotional facial expression analysis and speech analysis, a clinical DSS architecture for PD treatment has been proposed, as shown in Figure 12.1

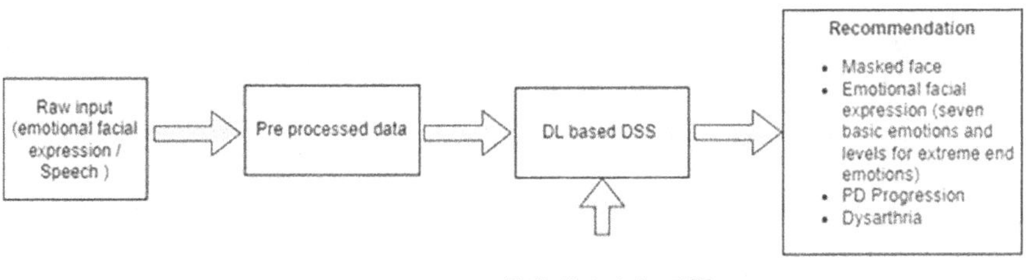

Figure 12.1 Proposed clinical DSS.

The objectives of this study are to propose DSS for various issues in PD management and are given as follows,

- Patients with PD who have a masked or expressionless face may have serious social issues with an outside observer. As a result, employing a deep learning (DL)–based technique, this study offers a binary classifier for masked face identification.
- Further, this work proposes a DSS that recognizes emotional face expression in seven basic categories and a DSS to grade extreme end emotions (happy and sad) into three levels of intensity to offer real-time feedback regarding facial expressive capabilities (low, medium, and high).
- Next, a DSS, a prediction model, is proposed as a way to potentially aid in the preparation of more customized care for PD patients. The video of all the patients is classified into three new classes depending on their Hoehn and Yahr stages. The DSS predicts the class that corresponds to the H & Y stages (a frequently used approach for summarizing how PD progress) based on emotional facial expression.
- Vocal impairment is widespread in PD, along with other movement disorders, and speaking function deteriorates as the disease progresses. As a result of the aforesaid facial expression-based analysis, this study recommends clinical DSS based on speech analysis to diagnose dysarthria (speech impairment) based on the DL approach.
- Finally, the next suggested DSS is a predictive model based on labial sound phrases that predict the matching class for the H & Y stage based on the transfer learning approach of DL.

12.3.1 Dataset

Due to ethical limitations, the data (facial expressions photos and raw speech data) of patients with PD is not available (free and online) for research work. As a result, the suggested DSS modules were trained and tested using data from openly accessible standard datasets during the early phase of implementation of this work.

12.3.1.1 Online Dataset

Four standard image datasets were used for this research work. Well-known image datasets included in this study are the Karolinska Directed Emotional Faces (KDEF) (Lundqvist et al., 1998), FACES (Ebner et al., 2010), Montreal Set of Facial Displays of Emotion (MSFDE) (Beaupré and Hess, 2005), and the Amsterdam Dynamic Facial Expression Set-Bath intensity variation (ADFES-BIV) (Wingenbach et al., 2016). For speech, the well-known TORGO (Rudzicz et al., 2012) dataset is used. During this phase, the study team collaborated with Lokmanya Tilak Municipal Medical College and Government Hospital (LTMMC & GH), Sion, Mumbai, and the real-life data collection procedure began. The obtained data from LTMMC & GH, Sion, Mumbai, are examined in the next stages of this research project.

12.3.1.2 Data Gathered from Lokmanya Tilak Municipal Medical College and General Hospital

Dr Sushant Sarang, a former assistant professor at the occupational therapy training school and center at LTMMC & GH, Sion, was the lead investigator in gathering the data necessary for the study (Sarang et al. under processing). Before beginning data collection, the ethical committee approval procedure (Ref. No. IEC/101/18 dated 24/01/2019) was followed, and the participants' permission was sought. The patients' age varied from 32 to 77 years old (mean: 58.71 years; SD: 12.35 years). Three patients were female, and 11 patients were male. During the period of the research, the disease lasted between 2 and 11 years (mean: 5.25 years, SD: 2.73 years). Before the experiment, each patient had a neurological evaluation. The UPDRS motor score (UPDRS part III) varied from 7 to 47 (21.5 to 13.55), whereas the Hoehn & Yahr illness stage ranged from 1 to 4 (2.07 to 0.8). All of the PD patients were on levodopa medication and were evaluated during their "on" state.

12.3.2 Data Gathering

This section presents the method for collection of facial expression videos of participants and then explains the method to collect speech data.

12.3.2.1 Methodology for Emotional Facial Expression Data Collection

Participants were requested to imitate facial expressions in two forms. First, participants were requested to imitate facial expressions for six basic emotions and then requested to imitate high-, medium-, and low-level facial expression variations for happy and sad emotions. Patients were shown small video clips (three to four secs) one by one consisting of different facial expressions. These video clips were generated using Abrosoft FantaMorph (Abrosoft Co, 2002) (powerful and easy-to-use morphing software). For this research work, its free license was received on request. Images of the well-known KDEF dataset were taken as input for the generation of videos for basis facial expressions (fear, happy, angry, disgust, surprise, and sad, along with neutral expression) and low-, medium-, and high-intensity level videos (for happy and sad facial expressions). Later, patients were asked to repeat the same, and then their expressions were recorded by web camera.

12.3.2.2 Methodology for Speech Data Collection

For this work investigation, audio recordings (labial sound phrases) of PD patients were gathered. To do this, the participants were asked to repeat three phrases, including "Baby hippopotamus," "British constitution," and "Rashtrapati" (a Hindi word). This work did not preserve any fixed content in these audio samples to enable testing on real-time unseen samples. The participants could say these words just once or several times. Thus, the lowest size of the audio that was gathered is 4 seconds long, and the largest size is 22 seconds. All of these mp4 extension samples were recorded on either a laptop or a smartphone with a sampling rate of 48 kHz (two stereo channels).

12.3.2.3 Ground Truth Labeling of Collected Data

The data were assessed by an expert rating team of behavioral therapists led by Dr Sushant Sarang from LTMMC & GH, Sion, Mumbai. On a projected screen, three different types of videos were played for the expert, who was then asked to assess them using a forced choice format as

- Seven-choice format (basic expression)
- Three-choice format (low-/medium-/high-intensity level videos [happy and sad emotion])
- Two-choice format (dysarthria/non-dysarthric for audios)

Although experts had limitless response time for the displayed videos, they were urged to answer as rapidly as they could. In order to guarantee confidentiality and eliminate mistakes and prejudice while recording participant responses, all of the recorded films were coded. Ultimately, based on DNN architecture, this study work proposes a DSS to handle various issues associated with PD management. Each solution is a sort of DSS in its own right, which is explained further in this section.

12.3.3 Masked Face Detection

A binary classifier based on a deep learning algorithm was used to detect the masked face. This work used a 14-layer convolutional neural network (CNN) architecture, which performs automatic feature extraction and classification as shown in Figure 12.2.

The input layer, which is the first layer, can handle inputs up to 128 × 128 pixels. The next layers consist of a convolutional layer, a batch layer, a ReLU layer, and a dropout layer. Five feature maps are produced by the first series of convolutional layers utilizing filter sizes of 12 × 12 and a stride of 2. Seven feature maps are produced using a second series convolutional layer with a filter size of 9 × 9 and a stride of 2.

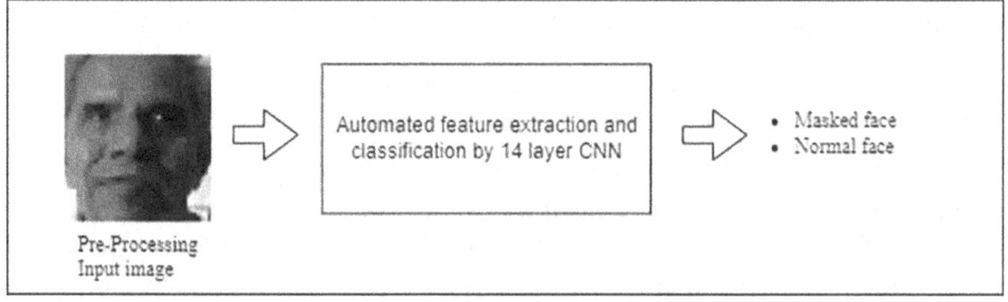

Figure 12.2 Masked face detection (Sonawane and Sharma, 2021a).

A dropout layer with a 50% dropout probability is used in networks to prevent overfitting. A maximum pooling layer, with filter size 2 × 2 and stride 2, is placed after each series. CNN acts as a binary classifier to recognize masked faces.

In order to represent images for the masked face category, this work used PD-related keywords (such as "Parkinson face," "masked face," and "hypomimia face") to search images in a search engine and finalized images for the masked face category. Preprocessing techniques such as the conversion of color images to grayscale to simplify further processing are used. The face region from the complete input images must be recognized and cropped in order to clearly capture facial characteristics. The images are then all similarly scaled to 128 × 128 size. The range of intensity values is finally brought to a normal distribution by performing image normalizing using min-max normalization. Flipping and sharpening data augmentation operations were done to the acquired images in order to prevent the model from being overfitted and to enhance its generalization.

On the test set, the proposed system had an overall classification accuracy of 85%. The confusion matrix is provided in Table 12.1, and its performance is given in Table 12.2.

It is observed that the resulting F1-score values were close to 1 for both classes, demonstrating the system's successful prediction of masked faces.

12.3.4 Automated Facial Expression Recognition

A system for automatically classifying emotional facial expressions into one of the seven fundamental categories is explained in this section. The automated approach that analyses facial expressions to identify emotion needs facial expression images from people of different ages, genders, and ethnicities (such as Americans, Indians, and Japanese). Consequently, this work employed images from three well-known datasets (KDEF, MSFDE, and FACES). Initially, faces are automatically cropped from every image in the training dataset to create facial images. The facial images are then subjected to a variety of preprocessing processes, such as grayscale conversion, image normalization, and scaling to 128 × 128 size. Data augmentation methods are also used to expand the number of images available. By applying flipping and sharpening, the suggested model can find patterns in huge amounts of data. From this, 30% image set

Table 12.1 Confusion Matrix for Masked Detection (Sonawane and Sharma, 2021a)

Predicted/Actual	*Normal Face*	*Masked Face*
Normal face	30	0
Masked face	9	23

Table 12.2 Performance of Masked Face Detection (Sonawane and Sharma, 2021a)

Performance Measure	*Normal Face*	*Masked Face*
Precision	0.76	1
Recall	1	0.71
F1-score	0.86	0.83

is utilized for testing, while the remaining 70% set is used as a training set. This work utilized a CNN for feature extraction and classification inspired by its success. Based on the performance, the committee of three different CNN variations (with different numbers of feature maps and filter sizes) was finalized.

The first convolutional layer of all CNN variations has 10 feature maps with filter size = 15 and stride = 2. A second convolutional layer of CNN1 has 20 feature maps with filter size = 15, and stride = 2 and a fully connected layer with 14 nodes. In CNN2, the second convolutional layer has 10 feature maps with filter size = 15, and stride = 2, and the fully connected layer has 50 nodes. In CNN3, the second convolutional layer has 15 feature maps with filter size = 15 and stride = 2, and the fully connected layer has 50 nodes. With a batch size of 128 and an initial learning rate of 0.001, each of these CNN variants was trained from scratch. Utilizing stochastic gradient descent, a loss function is optimized.

The proposed automated facial expression recognition (FER) method to classify facial expressions into seven fundamental emotion categories, as depicted in Figure 12.3.

The performance of the proposed approach on the test images is shown in Table 12.3 using various metrics.

According to the obtained F1-score value, it is observed that the CNN committee performs better when expressing good emotions like happiness than when expressing negative emotions like fear. A happy facial expression has the highest recognition accuracy because it is easier to distinguish from other emotional states visually. This finding is consistent with studies that demonstrate that in healthy persons, positive emotion (such as happiness) facial expressions are more likely to be detected than negative emotion facial expressions (Leppänen and Hietanen, 2004).

12.3.5 Expression Grader

This section discusses the emotional facial expression grader module, which categorizes emotional facial expression intensity into three categories (low, medium, and high). The extreme end emotions chosen for this experiment are happy and sad.

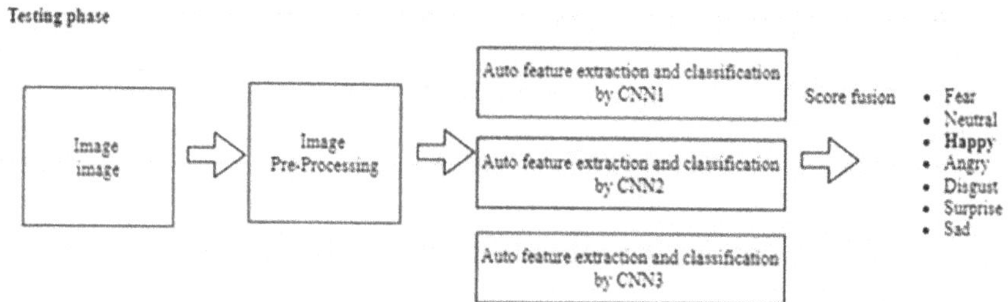

Figure 12.3 Automated facial expression recognition (Sonawane and Sharma, 2020).

Table 12.3 Performance of Automated Facial Expression Recognition (Sonawane and Sharma, 2020)

Performance Metrics	*Fear Emotion*	*Neutral Emotion*	*Happy Emotion*	*Angry Emotion*	*Disgust Emotion*	*Surprise Emotion*	*Sad Emotion*
Precision	00.95	00.87	00.95	00.86	00.90	00.88	00.85
Specificity	00.99	00.97	00.99	00.97	00.98	00.99	00.97
Accuracy	81.25	95.8	98.76	87.42	89.94	86.95	85.71
F1-score	00.88	00.91	00.97	00.87	00.90	00.88	00.85

The well-known MSFDE dataset, which contains morphed facial expression images of varied intensities, is used to train the expression grader. In this dataset, each emotion image is characterized in five levels (20%, 40%, 60%, 80%, and 100%). Since this work requires representative training images of the three classes (low, medium, and high), 20% of morphed images are grouped under the low-intensity group, 40% and 60% of morphed images are grouped under the medium-intensity group, and 80% and 100% morphed images are grouped under the high-intensity group. Grayscale facial images are extracted, normalized, and resized to 128 × 128 size as part of the preprocessing.

In this work, as shown in Figure 12.4, features of images with various intensities are recovered as activation of fully connected layer 1 of CNN variants (used for emotion detection module). Neutral images, as well as expected peak expression images features, are computed. Then, the SVM classifier that categorizes the input facial expression as having low, medium, or high intensities is trained using the extracted features difference. The implementation of the emotion grader is done independently for emotions of happiness and sadness.

An expression grader's performance is evaluated using videos of happy and sad human facial emotional expressions from the ADFES-BIV dataset utilizing a cross-dataset testing methodology. As the cross dataset includes videos, the peak expression frame is used from the input video to assess the expression grader's performance. The performance of the grader for three levels of happy and sad emotion videos from the ADFES-BIV dataset is shown in Table 12.4. It demonstrates that the performance of total intensity recognition on happy expressions seems to be higher than on sad emotions.

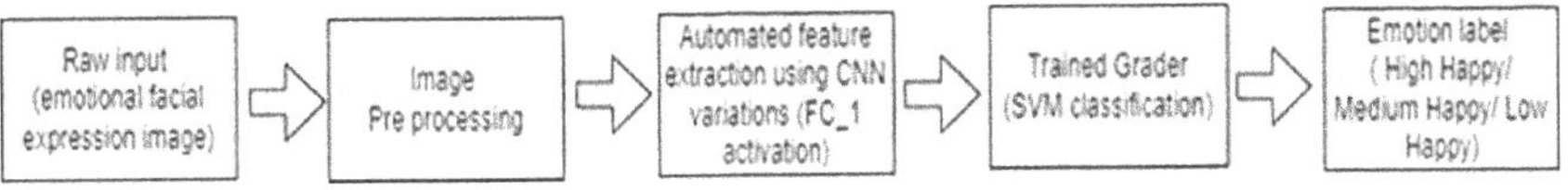

Figure 12.4 Emotional expression grader (Sonawane and Sharma, 2020).

Table 12.4 Performance of Emotional Intensity Level Detection (Sonawane and Sharma, 2020)

Emotion	*Level*	*Accuracy*
Happy	Low	75
	Med	68
	High	68
Sad	Low	83
	Med	33
	High	58

12.3.6 Dysarthria Detection

A pilot experiment using a deep learning approach to automatically detect dysarthric patterns in input speech is discussed in this section. The overall framework is given in Figure 12.5. Major steps involved in the overall framework are signal preprocessing, spectrogram generation, automated feature extraction and classification using a 12-layer CNN as shown in Figure 12.6.

The UA-Speech TORGO dataset from the University of Illinois is used in this study, and it contains dysarthric as well as non-dysarthric articulation. The TORGO dataset is chosen as it has a more diverse set of speakers and a larger set of speech samples. The proposed approach implementation shows 76.89% accuracy on a test sample of well-known TORGO dataset with fivefold validation.

12.4 Results and Discussion on Gathered Real-Life Data

In this section, data analysis on real-time data gathered from LTMMC & GH, Sion, Mumbai, is discussed. Peak expression frames were selected from all the videos of emotional facial expressions that had been gathered. The frame that is considered to have the greatest Euclidean distance from the video's neutral frame is the peak expression frame.

A brief summary of the analysis done on the peak frames of emotional facial expression videos and speech (real-life data) follows.

- In order to evaluate the effectiveness of the mask face identification module, this work has correlated its output considering participants' UPDRS (3.2) item scores and found it to be correlated with 86.84% accuracy using the peak expression frame of a patient with PD.

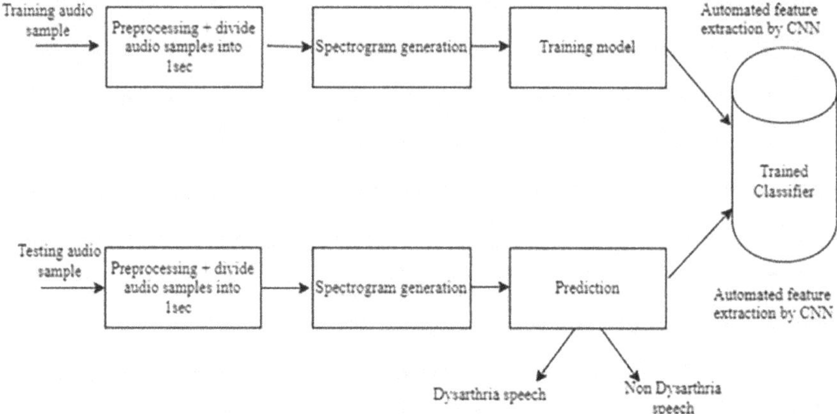

Figure 12.5 Framework for dysarthria detection (Sonawane and Sharma, 2021b).

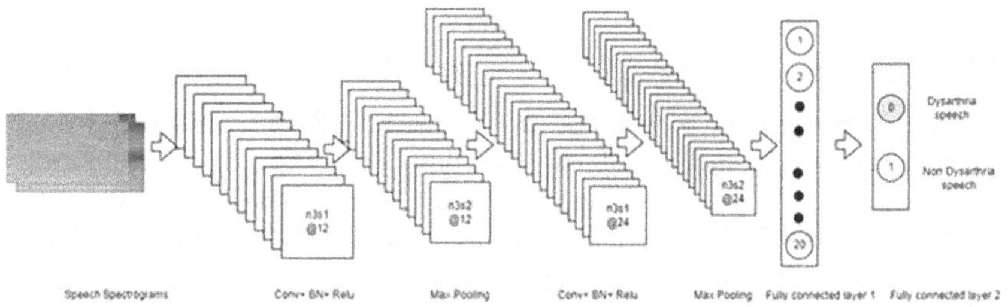

Figure 12.6 CNN used for dysarthria detection (Sonawane and Sharma, 2021b).

- In order to demonstrate the effectiveness of the system in giving real-time feedback for rehabilitation, this work also linked the output of the emotion detection module and the emotion grading module with the rating scores of experts. It has been noted that the emotion detection system's recognition accuracy is higher for the emotions of disgust, anger, and happiness than for the others. Further, the correlation of emotion grader with ratings from experts shows the performance of the system for high-intensity level happy and sad emotional expression videos is more than that of other level intensities. Additionally, happy emotional videos perform better on the system than sad emotional videos. This outcome is consistent with the findings of the authors in (Bandini et al., 2017) who noted that sad emotions are among the hardest to convey for both the normal and PD patient groups.
- Deep learning-based features are used to represent the frames of the emotional expression videos of PD patients in order to predict the class of PD severity based on facial expression quantification. Activation of fully connected layers of CNN variations used for the automated emotion detection module represents the features of frames of the videos. This work computed the Euclidean distance

between the features of peak expression frame from those of the neutral frame for facial expression videos of PD patients in order to measure the expressiveness of facial expression. In the beginning, this work mapped all the facial expression data of a patient with PD per their H & Y stages, into three new classes (mild, moderate, and severe). Then, a distinct combination of videos of each participant per group is formed. Five different statistics (max, min, mean, median, and standard deviation) are computed using Euclidean distances (for peak expression frame from the neutral frame) for each combination which helped this work to predict severity based on facial expression. KNN classifier was trained with 70% of the training data for three output classes while taking calculated statistics values into consideration as a dataset and using stratified sampling. KNN classifiers with $k = 5$ produce the best mean accuracy (94%) (Sarang et al. under processing). A confusion matrix is shown in Table 12.5, and it is observed that the model prediction was good for mild as well moderate classes.

- In addition, this research work divided all of the collected corpus data (labial sound phrases) of a patient with PD into three classes in order to indicate the severity of PD. Wavelet denoising is first used to preprocess the audio samples, and then each frame is separated into one second. Then, spectrograms with dimensions of 8193 × 8 × 1 are created for these samples. Here, this study tuned a 12-layer CNN to predict the severity of PD (which was used for dysarthria detection). Weights from layer 2 to layer 9 are transmitted through transfer learning. With the use of the fivefold cross-validation approach, CNN's mean accuracy was found to be 80.85%.
- Research opportunity: XAI in PD analysis.

Although DL models have been successful in PD analysis, one of the most significant challenges that still remains is the lack of transparency in terms of understanding the internals of it, which leaves users with not so clear knowledge of how it makes decisions. This becomes a matter of concern, especially when deep learning is used for decision making in medical-related applications. The outcome of DL models for medical applications should also be trusted by doctors, with proper validations on the accuracy of the outcomes. In order to trust them, doctors must comprehend the reasoning behind these decisions and contrast it with their prior domain expertise. Thus, it is undeniable that the use of DL models in the medical fields should offer a reasonable trade-off between accuracy and interpretability.

As a result, the use of a new branch of AI called XAI has recently emerged for explainable emotion detection (XED) and explainable face recognition (XFR) that

Table 12.5 Confusion Matrix Using KNN Classifier (Sarang et al. under processing)

	Class 1: Mild	*Class 2: Moderate*	*Class 3: Severe*
Class 1: Mild	100%		
Class 1: Moderate		100%	
Class 1: Severe	17.9%		82.1%

relates to providing quantitatively interpretable reasoning for the outputs of a facial or speech-based emotion detection system.

The model incorporates a facial matcher to associate the changes in a face geometry in reference to a particular emotion. The XAI model here will further generate a network attention map which best explains the regions in a probe image matched with a mated image. This provides ground truth for quantifying what image regions contribute to emotion matching.

Explainable face recognition has emerged in PD analysis (Sarica et al., 2022; Cavaliere et al., 2020; Das et al., 2022; Kim et al., 2022) (based on gait as well as speech analysis). There is a need for more study in this area due to the paucity of studies employing XAI to analyze facial expressions for PD management and refine the approach for XED.

12.5 Conclusion

In order to bridge the gap between ideal practice and actual clinical therapy, this study provides a collection of DSSs in PD management that has the potential to improve healthcare. The motor examination section of the UPDRS is commonly used to diagnose PD, a neurodegenerative condition characterized by increasing motor deficits, the severity of which is subjectively assessed by doctors during the execution of routine motor tasks. If regular re-assessments are required, this type of clinical evaluation is time consuming and difficult. Consequently, a targeted, automated, and contactless examination would enhance the diagnostic process. The efficacy of the assessment, which is typically hampered by inter-rater disagreements, would be enhanced with an objective, automated, contactless evaluation. This would also enable frequent treatment adaptation and the eradication of fluctuations.

Patients with PD have inflexible facial muscles, making it difficult for them to make facial emotions (masked face). For the management of PD, automatic facial expression analysis needs more research. This limited study may be the result of online data being unavailable owing to ethical restrictions. The current study suggested using clinical DSS to address various PD treatment concerns, with facial expression serving as a key biomarker. Since facial rigidity is a crucial indicator in the management of PD, detecting emotions in PD patients' facial expressions can be a crucial step in determining their stage of development.

Due to the lack of real-world data for PD connected to emotional facial expressions and speech, this project partnered with LTMMC & GH to get real-world data. The current research also suggested a multi-module architecture with the ability to recognize emotions and evaluate them for use in providing real-time feedback during rehabilitation. Patients with PD have stiffening of the face muscles with time. In this study, participants with PD were instructed to mimic facial expressions ranging from their least expressive to their most expressive. According to the study, facial expressions can help determine the H &Y stage class that best describes disease progress. Nowadays, dysarthria affects a significant portion of PD patients. It demonstrated how the illness had affected patients' ability to speak. This study demonstrates a favorable outcome when labial sound is used to predict the corresponding class of the H & Y stage.

In the future, the suggested methodology may be utilized to investigate numerous physiological signs in the non-invasive diagnosis of PD. Aside from that, the suggested model may be further adapted to another application area using the data augmentation and transfer learning technique. It can be utilized as a therapeutic decision support system in various neuropsychiatric illnesses, including schizophrenia, PSP, and amyotrophic lateral sclerosis (ALS), which cause changes in facial expression. It can also be used in rehabilitation therapy for mental illnesses like autism.

Acknowledgments

The authors are grateful to all the providers of the online dataset for providing free access to their data for this research work. The authors acknowledge Dean, Lokmanya Tilak Municipal Medical College and General Hospital (LTMMC & GH), Sion, Mumbai, for allowing real-life data collection in this study. The authors would like to thank Dr. Sushant Sarang, Dr. Rashmi Yeradkar, and their team for providing support during the data collection at LTMMC & GH for this study.

References

Abrosoft Co. (2002). *FantaMorph [software]* (Beijing). Available from www.fantamorph.com.

Alvino, Christopher, Christian Kohler, Frederick Barrett, Raquel E. Gur, Ruben C. Gur, and Ragini Verma. "Computerized measurement of facial expression of emotions in schizophrenia." *Journal of Neuroscience Methods 163*, no. 2 (2007): 350–361.

Bache, Kevin, and Moshe Lichman. "UCI machine learning repository." (2013): 2013.

Bachlin, Marc, Meir Plotnik, Daniel Roggen, Inbal Maidan, Jeffrey M. Hausdorff, Nir Giladi, and Gerhard Troster. "Wearable assistant for Parkinson's disease patients with the freezing of gait symptom." *IEEE Transactions on Information Technology in Biomedicine 14*, no. 2 (2009): 436–446.

Bandini, Andrea, Silvia Orlandi, Fabio Giovannelli, Andrea Felici, Massimo Cincotta, Daniela Clemente, Paola Vanni, Gaetano Zaccara, and Claudia Manfredi. "Markerless analysis of articulatory movements in patients with Parkinson's disease." *Journal of Voice 30*, no. 6 (2016): 766–e1.

Bandini, Andrea, Silvia Orlandi, Hugo Jair Escalante, Fabio Giovannelli, Massimo Cincotta, Carlos A. Reyes-Garcia, Paola Vanni, Gaetano Zaccara, and Claudia Manfredi. "Analysis of facial expressions in Parkinson's disease through video-based automatic methods." *Journal of Neuroscience Methods 281* (2017): 7–20.

Beaupré, Martin G., and Ursula Hess. "Cross-cultural emotion recognition among Canadian ethnic groups." *Journal of Cross-Cultural Psychology 36*, no. 3 (2005): 355–370.

Berus, Lucijano, Simon Klancnik, Miran Brezocnik, and Mirko Ficko. "Classifying Parkinson's disease based on acoustic measures using artificial neural networks." *Sensors 19*, no. 1 (2018): 16.

Bologna, Matteo, Giovanni Fabbrini, Luca Marsili, Giovanni Defazio, Philip D. Thompson, and Alfredo Berardelli. "Facial bradykinesia." *Journal of Neurology, Neurosurgery & Psychiatry 84*, no. 6 (2013): 681–685.

Bowers, Dawn, Kimberly Miller, Wendelyn Bosch, Didem Gokcay, Otto Pedraza, Utaka Springer, and Michael Okun. "Faces of emotion in Parkinsons disease: micro-expressivity and bradykinesia during voluntary facial expressions." *Journal of the International Neuropsychological Society 12*, no. 6 (2006): 765–773.

Cavaliere, Federica, Antonio Della Cioppa, Angelo Marcelli, Antonio Parziale, and Rosa Senatore. "Parkinson's disease diagnosis: towards grammar-based explainable artificial intelligence." In *2020 IEEE Symposium on Computers and Communications (ISCC)*, pp. 1–6. New York: IEEE, 2020.

Chen, Hui-Ling, Chang-Cheng Huang, Xin-Gang Yu, Xin Xu, Xin Sun, Gang Wang, and Su-Jing Wang. "An efficient diagnosis system for detection of Parkinson's disease using fuzzy k-nearest neighbor approach." Expert Systems with Applications 40, no. 1 (2013): 263–271.

Chereshnev, Roman, and Attila Kertész-Farkas. "Hugadb: Human gait database for activity recognition from wearable inertial sensor networks." In *International Conference on Analysis of Images, Social Networks and Texts*, pp. 131–141. Cham: Springer, 2017.

Dagar, Debishree, Abir Hudait, HK. Tripathy, and MN. Das. "Automatic emotion detection model from facial expression." In *2016 International Conference on Advanced Communication Control and Computing Technologies (ICACCCT)*, pp. 77–85. New York: IEEE, 2016.

Das, Arun, Jeffrey Mock, Farzan Irani, Yufei Huang, Peyman Najafirad, and Edward Golob. "Multimodal explainable AI predicts upcoming speech behavior in adults who stutter." *Frontiers in Neuroscience 16* (2022).

Drotár, Peter, Jiří Mekyska, Irena Rektorová, Lucia Masarová, Zdeněk Smékal, and Marcos Faundez-Zanuy. "A new modality for quantitative evaluation of Parkinson's disease: In-air movement." In *13th IEEE International Conference on Bioinformatics and Bioengineering*, pp. 1–4. New York: IEEE, 2013.

Ebner, Natalie C., Michaela Riediger, and Ulman Lindenberger. "FACES – A database of facial expressions in young, middle-aged, and older women and men: Development and validation." *Behavior Research Methods 42*, no. 1 (2010): 351–362.

Enderby, Pamela. "Frenchay dysarthria assessment." *British Journal of Disorders of Communication 15*, no. 3 (1980): 165–173.

Goetz, Christopher G., Barbara C. Tilley, Stephanie R. Shaftman, Glenn T. Stebbins, Stanley Fahn, Pablo Martinez-Martin, Werner Poewe, et al. "Movement disorder society-sponsored revision of the Unified Parkinson's Disease Rating Scale (MDS-UPDRS): scale presentation and clinimetric testing results." *Movement Disorders: Official Journal of the Movement Disorder Society 23*, no. 15 (2008): 2129–2170.

Grover, Srishti, Saloni Bhartia, Abhilasha Yadav, and K. R. Seeja. "Predicting severity of Parkinson's disease using deep learning." *Procedia Computer Science 132* (2018): 1788–1794.

Gunnery, Sarah D., Elena N. Naumova, Marie Saint-Hilaire, and Linda Tickle-Degnen. "Mapping spontaneous facial expression in people with Parkinson's disease: A multiple case study design." *Cogent Psychology 4*, no. 1 (2017): 1376425.

Hoehn, M. M., and M. D. Yahr. "Parkinsonism: onset, progression, and mortality." *Neurology 50,* no. 2 (1998): 318–318.

Isenkul, Muhammed, Betul Sakar, and Olcay Kursun. "Improved spiral test using digitized graphics tablet for monitoring Parkinson's disease." In *Proceedings of the International Conference on e-Health and Telemedicine*, Vol. 5, pp. 171–175, 2014.

Katsikitis, Mary, and I. Pilowsky. "A study of facial expression in Parkinson's disease using a novel microcomputer-based method." *Journal of Neurology, Neurosurgery & Psychiatry 51*, no. 3 (1988): 362–366.

Kim, Jeong-Kyun, Myung-Nam Bae, Kangbok Lee, Jae-Chul Kim, and Sang Gi Hong. "Explainable artificial intelligence and wearable sensor-based gait analysis to identify patients with osteopenia and sarcopenia in daily life." *Biosensors 12*, no. 3 (2022): 167.

Leppänen, Jukka M., and Jari K. Hietanen. "Positive facial expressions are recognized faster than negative facial expressions, but why?." *Psychological Research 69*, no. 1 (2004): 22–29.

Li, Michael H., Tiago A. Mestre, Susan H. Fox, and Babak Taati. "Vision-based assessment of parkinsonism and levodopa-induced dyskinesia with pose estimation." *Journal of Neuroengineering and Rehabilitation 15*, no. 1 (2018): 1–13.

Little, Max, Patrick McSharry, Eric Hunter, Jennifer Spielman, and Lorraine Ramig. "Suitability of dysphonia measurements for telemonitoring of Parkinson's disease." *Nature Precedings (*2008): 1–1.

Lumaka, Aimé, Nele Cosemans, Aimée Lulebo Mampasi, Gerrye Mubungu, Nono Mvuama, Toni Lubala, Sebastien Mbuyi-Musanzayi et al. "Facial dysmorphism is influenced by ethnic background of the patient and of the evaluator." *Clinical Genetics 92*, no. 2 (2017): 166–171.

Lundqvist, Daniel, Anders Flykt, and Arne Öhman. "Karolinska directed emotional faces." *Cognition and Emotion* (1998). https://doi.org/10.1037/t27732-000.

Marek, Kenneth, Danna Jennings, Shirley Lasch, Andrew Siderowf, Caroline Tanner, Tanya Simuni, Chris Coffey et al. "The Parkinson progression marker initiative (PPMI)." *Progress in Neurobiology* 95, no. 4 (2011): 629–635.

Muhammad, Ghulam, Mansour Alsulaiman, Syed Umar Amin, Ahmed Ghoneim, and Mohammed F. Alhamid. "A facial-expression monitoring system for improved healthcare in smart cities." *IEEE Access 5* (2017): 10871–10881.

Mutch, William J., Alison Strudwick, Sisar K. Roy, and Allan W. Downie. "Parkinson's disease: disability, review, and management." *The BMJ (Clin Res Ed) 293*, no. 6548 (1986): 675–677.

Nilashi, Mehrbakhsh, Othman Ibrahim, and Ali Ahani. "Accuracy improvement for predicting Parkinson's disease progression." *Scientific Reports 6*, no. 1 (2016): 1–18.

Orozco-Arroyave, Juan Rafael, F. Hönig, JD. Arias-Londoño, JF. Vargas-Bonilla, K. Daqrouq, S. Skodda, J. Rusz, and E. Nöth. "Automatic detection of Parkinson's disease in running speech spoken in three different languages." *The Journal of the Acoustical Society of America 139*, no. 1 (2016): 481–500.

Pantic, Maja, and Léon JM. Rothkrantz. "An expert system for multiple emotional classification of facial expressions." In *Proceedings 11th International Conference on Tools with Artificial Intelligence*, pp. 113–120. New York: IEEE, 1999.

Pereira, Clayton R., Silke AT. Weber, Christian Hook, Gustavo H. Rosa, and Joao P. Papa. "Deep learning-aided Parkinson's disease diagnosis from handwritten dynamics." In *2016 29th SIBGRAPI Conference on Graphics, Patterns and Images (SIBGRAPI)*, pp. 340–346. New York: IEEE, 2016.

Postuma, RB., and J. Montplaisir. "Predicting Parkinson's disease – Why, when, and how?." *Parkinsonism & Related Disorders 15* (2009): S105–S109.

Rossi, Ryan, and Nesreen Ahmed. "The network data repository with interactive graph analytics and visualization." In *Twenty-ninth AAAI Conference on Artificial Intelligence*. Palo Alto, CA: AAAI Press, 2015.

Rudzicz, Frank, Aravind Kumar Namasivayam, and Talya Wolff. "The TORGO database of acoustic and articulatory speech from speakers with dysarthria." *Language Resources and Evaluation 46*, no. 4 (2012): 523–541.

Sakar, Betul Erdogdu, M. Erdem Isenkul, C. Okan Sakar, Ahmet Sertbas, Fikret Gurgen, Sakir Delil, Hulya Apaydin, and Olcay Kursun. "Collection and analysis of a Parkinson speech dataset with multiple types of sound recordings." *IEEE Journal of Biomedical and Health Informatics 17*, no. 4 (2013): 828–834.

Sarica, Alessia, Andrea Quattrone, and Aldo Quattrone. "Explainable machine learning with pairwise interactions for the classification of Parkinson's disease and SWEDD from clinical and Imaging features." *Brain Imaging and Behavior* (2022): 1–11.

Schwab, Robert S. "Projection technique for evaluating surgery in Parkinson's disease." In *Third Symposium on Parkinson's Disease*, pp. 152–157. London: E & S Livingstone, 1969.

Shahbakhi, Mohammad, Danial Taheri Far, and Ehsan Tahami. "Speech analysis for diagnosis of Parkinson's disease using genetic algorithm and support vector machine." *Journal of Biomedical Science and Engineering 2014* (2014).

Sonawane, Bhakti, and Priyanka Sharma. "Deep learning based approach of emotion detection and grading system." *Pattern Recognition and Image Analysis 30*, no. 4 (2020): 726–740.

Sonawane, Bhakti, and Priyanka Sharma. "Review of automated emotion-based quantification of facial expression in Parkinson's patients." *The Visual Computer 37*, no. 5 (2021a): 1151–1167.

Sonawane, Bhakti, and Priyanka Sharma. "Speech-based solution to Parkinson's disease management." *Multimedia Tools and Applications 80*, no. 19 (2021b): 29437–29451.

Thevenot, Jérôme, Miguel Bordallo López, and Abdenour Hadid. "A survey on computer vision for assistive medical diagnosis from faces." *IEEE Journal of Biomedical and Health I nformatics 22*, no. 5 (2017): 1497–1511.

Tickle-Degnen, Linda, Leslie A. Zebrowitz, and Hui-ing Ma. "Culture, gender and health care stigma: Practitioners' response to facial masking experienced by people with Parkinson's disease." *Social Science & Medicine 73*, no. 1 (2011): 95–102.

Tripathi, Ayush, Swapnil Bhosale, and Sunil Kumar Kopparapu. "A novel approach for intelligibility assessment in dysarthric subjects." In ICASSP *2020–2020 IEEE International Conference on Acoustics, Speech and Signal Processing (ICASSP)*, pp. 6779–6783. New York: IEEE, 2020.

Tsanas, Athanasios, Max Little, Patrick McSharry, and Lorraine Ramig. "Accurate telemonitoring of Parkinson's disease progression by non-invasive speech tests." *Nature Preceding*s *(*2009): 1–1.

Vásquez-Correa, Juan Camilo, JR. Orozco-Arroyave, T. Bocklet, and E. Nöth. "Towards an automatic evaluation of the dysarthria level of patients with Parkinson's disease." *Journal of Communication Disorders* 76 (2018): 21–36.

Wingenbach, Tanja SH., Chris Ashwin, and Mark Brosnan. "Validation of the Amsterdam Dynamic Facial Expression Set–Bath Intensity Variations (ADFES-BIV): A set of videos expressing low, intermediate, and high intensity emotions." *PloS one 11*, no. 1 (2016): e0147112.

Wojtusch, Janis, and Oskar von Stryk. "Humod – A versatile and open database for the investigation, modeling and simulation of human motion dynamics on actuation level." In *2015 IEEE-RAS 15th International Conference on Humanoid Robots (Humanoids)*, pp. 74–79. New York: IEEE, 2015.

Wu, Peng, Isabel Gonzalez, Georgios Patsis, Dongmei Jiang, Hichem Sahli, Eric Kerckhofs, and Marie Vandekerckhove. "Objectifying facial expressivity assessment of Parkinson's patients: preliminary study." *Computational and Mathematical Methods in Medicine 2014* (2014).

Zhang, Jianxin, Weifeng Xu, Qiang Zhang, Bo Jin, and Xiaopeng Wei. "Exploring risk factors and predicting UPDRS score based on Parkinson's speech signals." In *2017 IEEE 19th International Conference on e-Health Networking, Applications and Services (Healthcom)*, pp. 1–6. New York: IEEE, 2017.

Zhao, Shunan, Frank Rudzicz, Leonardo G. Carvalho, César Márquez-Chin, and Steven Livingstone. "Automatic detection of expressed emotion in Parkinson's disease." In *2014 IEEE International Conference on Acoustics, Speech and Signal Processing (ICASSP)*, pp. 4813–4817. New York: IEEE, 2014.

13 Interpretable Machine Learning in Athletics for Injury Risk Prediction

Srishti Sharma, Mehul S Raval, Tolga Kaya, and Srikrishnan Divakaran

Contents

DOI: 10.1201/9781003333425-13

13.1 Introduction

The sports industry produces countless raw data which do not provide clear insight until processed and analyzed. Sports data analytics (SDA) is a rapidly growing area of research that makes use of easily accessible wearable devices, available computing power, and powerful AI/ML techniques for analyzing data to help develop products/services that facilitate the analysis of exponentially growing raw data about athletes by coaches/administrators to design/analyze strategies to maximize game performance and also address injury risk. The raw data can include opponent team game statistics or individual athlete data like physiological, training, and cognitive parameters. SDA augments the coaches'/administrators' ability to analyze athletes' data to get better insights into factors affecting a player's performance and risk factors contributing to injury. These insights can help them design better training and game strategies (Li and Xu, 2021; Sarlis and Tjortjis, 2020). Sports data analytics has been boosted due to the availability of wearable sensors. The availability of computing power, networking, and sophisticated machine learning (ML) techniques has made it possible to analyze data in real time (Li and Xu, 2021). It allows coaches to make informed decisions about training plans, team composition, profiling of an athlete, skill assessment and acquisition, on-field and off-field strategies, and change of players during games and to identify changes in rhythm and style of playing (Li and Xu, 2021; Sarlis and Tjortjis, 2020).

The technologies used in collecting on-field sports data include gyroscopes, triaxial accelerometers, goniometers, and sensors to measure physiological parameters such as heart rate and eye movement tracking (Gowda et al., 2017). The wearables have a small form factor, are lightweight, and are worn on the body (Düking et al., 2018). They monitor, transmit, and receive data from clouds and sometimes analyze locally and provide real-time biofeedback to the wearer. They usually monitor the individual's physiological parameters like blood oxygen, skin temperature, and heart rate and help develop customized programs for performance enhancement or health. Wearables allow recording and reporting of the player's movement during live matches. They allow coaches to track and plan match strategy. SDA will help analyze real-time large and complex data to analyze them from the perspective of game performance and injury risk. This can help coaches get better insights for developing good training and game strategies. Therefore, wearable technology applications have great potential provided the data are analyzed correctly. Sports data analysis also uses many other technologies for on-field measurements, like voice recognition within match analysis (Düking et al., 2018), which allows training and

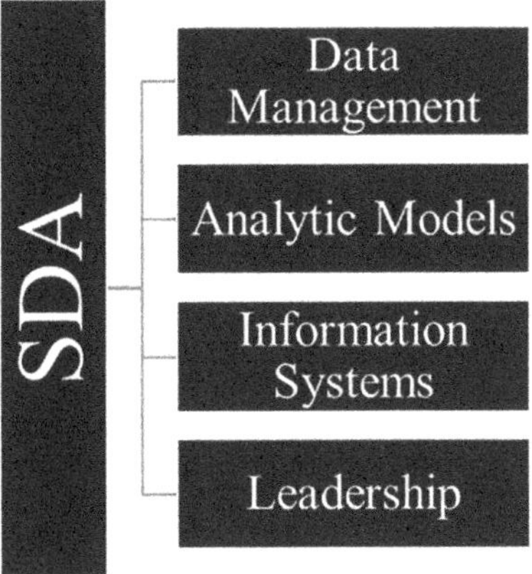

Figure 13.1 Components of SDA (Alamar, 2013).

recognition of verbally coded events recorded during a match by the human operator. Automated player tracking can be done using global positioning system (GPS) devices (Mangan et al., 2017) or infrared systems (Leser et al., 2014).

13.2 Framework for SDA

Successful SDA needs a robust framework for efficient usage (Alamar, 2013). There are four crucial components of the SDA framework (Alamar, 2013), as shown in Figure 13.1. The first part of data management deals with the protocols and processes of capturing and storing data. It has to ensure that storage allows the data to be easily accessed, manipulated, and used. The analytic model is the framework's foundation and uses algorithms to process the data. This module generates responses to queries from the coach and managers. The information system provides a mechanism for efficiently representing the processed data. The inference generated by analytic models must be presented to decision makers so that overall system efficiency increases. The fourth important part of the model is leadership, which is responsible for bringing organizational changes and introducing SDA. Developing an SDA system requires a change of mindset, and it must be able to justify the tangible benefits of analytics in decision-making.

The SDA approaches are sophisticated, as they utilize data from multiple sources such as images, videos, audio, survey forms, qualitative comments, and quotes (Alamar, 2013). The sources in sports give rise to Big Data, which is driven by 4 Vs: volume, variety, velocity, and veracity. The first dimension is *volume*, which is about the amount of generated and processed data. The second V, *variety*, can be in structured, semi-structured, or unstructured forms. The structured data are quantitative, such as numbers and values, while unstructured data are more qualitative, with data from sensors, text files, audio files, or videos. In general, it can have numerical data or categorical data in unstructured or various structured forms. For example, structured data could be numerical from a game score or number of minutes played or categorical, like responses to the cognitive state through a survey. Unstructured data could be a note from the coach or an interview. The data may be stored in a uniform format. However, very often, there are legacy systems that may need protocols for transforming data from one to another format.

The system must be ready to incorporate newer data types and analyses. So the third big V – *velocity* – addresses the speed at which new data are generated and moved around. The data can be stored at multiple levels at different sites and accessed via a distributed database. There are challenges associated with using data stored at different sources like centralized vs decentralized systems, large datasets vs small datasets, and preprocessed or unprocessed datasets. These challenges bring in the fourth dimension of big data – *veracity*. It is about the trustworthiness of the data, and its higher value means the importance of data and its analysis.

The data in the processing must be reliable and valid for generating reasonable inferences by the analytic model (Alamar, 2013). Wearable measurements will have variability, which is quantified using uncertainty. The measurements will be in a range of expected values instead of a single point. Measurements exhibit natural variability independent of human or instrument limitations. The uncertainty leads to the spread of measured values on repetitive observations. It could arise due to variations in the underlying physical process of the wearable or the judgment of the coach. Uncertainty gives rise to statistical or random errors which cannot be eliminated but reduced by conducting repeated observations of the athlete. Systematic bias or error is consistent and repeatable and usually creeps in due to device malfunction, human factors, duplication, ambiguity, and differences in data formats. The increase in ML can introduce algorithmic bias; as a result, its outcome may provide special privileges to one class (systematic and repeatable error). Bias can creep in due to limited computing power; the design of the algorithm; and the way data are selected, collected, preprocessed, and coded while training ML algorithms. Several human decisions during dataset assembling, programming hierarchy, design, and reinforcement of associations cause algorithmic bias.

Summarizing data often suffers from variability due to the following factors:

1. Algorithmic bias is due to social and institutional bias, technical bias, and emergent context bias.
2. Data uncertainty is due to errors in incorrect association. For example, the incorrect tagging of the player by the analyst or incorrect tagging of the ball possession in the team games.
3. Factors beyond the control may impact analysis, such as coach's selection bias.

The data quality is usually dealt with in the preprocessing of the analytic model. Errors and outliers can be addressed by data filtering, for example, removing outliers, interpolation or extrapolation, or smoothening. Errors due to randomness or variability can be addressed by statistical means (larger and repeated sampling or measurements. Tools can observe and detect bias within the algorithms. Explainable AI (XAI) can analyze the program outcome and detect existing bias. Open statistical tools and ML libraries help in developing a robust analytical framework for SDA. Analytics helps to establish the relationship between input and output by using regression analysis or classification. It can also help mine the hidden patterns in the data via clustering analysis. The emergence of deep learning (DL) and the integration of tools and applications has further accelerated the amalgamation of computer vision (CV), natural language processing (NLP), and speech processing (Alamar, 2013).

The development of SDA requires a key role from coaches. They must provide the features or functions that the framework must have to ease their tasks. Usually, coaches would demand a set of output variables, a summary of the statistics, a recording of the match, and different types of inferences using a dashboard. Data visualization plays an essential role in the dashboard development for the coach, for example, representing a person who is more prone to injury risk with red. Data visualization combines analysis and a graphical user interface (GUI) and helps to make sense of the big data and present inherent patterns. It also helps to reorganize complex data in presentable charts and modern visualization styles on the dashboard for the coach.

The coaches are domain experts and can help in developing and defining models both for data capture, identifying key characteristics/features, characterizing the relationship between them, defining measures for evaluating performance, and also validating the predictions or relationships determined by the AI/ML models for making predictions and/or inferences. They must have a fair idea of data analysis; otherwise, they will not be able to understand data limitations. They will be able to deeply understand the analytics and overcome some dataset-specific errors (Naik et al., 2022); for example, they may pinpoint errors made by data analysts and ensure robustness in analysis. It is vital to have close interactions between coaches and analysts; it will generate better real-time decisions. For example, a coach can view the inference and request analysis of a specific temporal sequence from a play. The analysis framework would have a similar flow, such as match-by-match performance analysis to target similar variables, or variables may evolve depending on the needs of the subject matter expert; for example, it is prevalent to perform what-if analysis for predictors. They may generate different probabilities for outcomes based on the scenarios, which helps in value assessment.

Recent developments in video analysis have greatly augmented SDA. The development of computer vision along with ML has enabled many critical SDA applications. The following section is devoted to getting a bird's-eye view of the use of CV-ML in SDA.

13.3 Vision-Based Analytics in Sports

Computer vision can facilitate the automatic processing of visual information. This is useful in applications like detection, tracking, classification, trajectory prediction, gameplay analysis and evaluations, and identifying actions and decisions. Figure 13.2 shows the broad application of CV in sports analytics. The CV module plays a primary role in data management of the SDA and deals with processes of capturing and storing visual data. It also interacts with analytic module of the SDA framework. The interactions lead to robust inference support in the SDA.

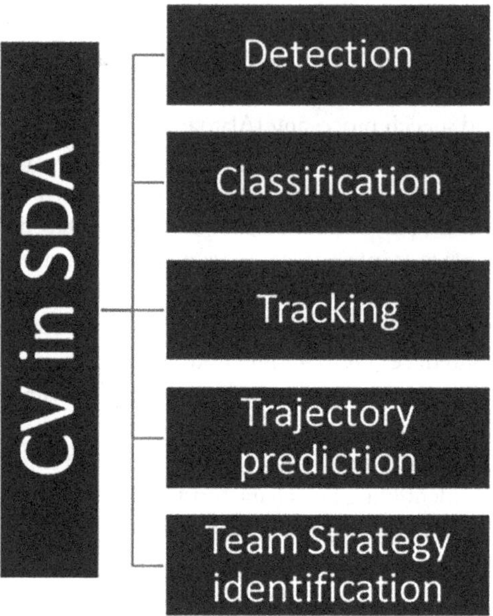

Figure 13.2 Some applications of CV in SDA.

The challenges faced by CV in developing the automated algorithms are as follows (Naik et al., 2022):

- The objects are heavily occluded.
- The scene is densely populated with subjects with similar appearances, such as the same team jersey color.
- The unconstrained environments on the field with unpredictable movements make detection difficult.
- The impact of perspective projection resulting in far-field players appearing smaller in the frame, the difference in viewing angle, and multiple cameras in the network.
- In team sports, there are sudden moves; balls change from player to player, and the game is fast paced.

We review the CV application in basketball, keeping our interest and past work with the Division I women's basketball team at Sacred Heart University, USA. It is a team sport, played by five players per side, and includes ball movements like passing, throwing, dribbling, shots, posting up, and shooting. The player's performance can be automatically analyzed by event classification and by identifying the player's action (Liu et al., 2021). Player detection and tracking (Ramanathan et al., 2016) are also essential in determining in-game performance. One of the exciting challenges that occur here is the movement of the ball across players. The occlusion among players will cause the tracker to lose the history and generate a new track and label. The performance of the tracking can be improved by studying the player's position on the court and estimating the ball's trajectory (Victor et al., 2021). By correlating the player's position and location of the ball, it is also possible to predict the player's movement (Victor et al., 2021). Extracting the shooting motion trajectory is also vital in basketball SDA (Li and Xu, 2021). Combined with image feature analysis of the basketball shooting, it allows for the development of complete quantitative tracking.

Technically, many issues have been observed in the previously mentioned CV methods that can be summarized as the following (Naik et al., 2022):

1. The game is usually played at a fast pace, and the algorithm cannot capture complex actions performed by the players. It can lower the accuracy of the CV algorithm.
2. Trajectory prediction in complex scenarios and uncertain situations fails. The game, player, and team dynamics do not allow a robust generation of predictions.
3. Tracking under severe occlusion is very challenging.
4. The cause of CV system failure includes the noisy nature of the data, difficult viewing angle, and foreground-background merging

13.3.1 Analytics Models for Computer Vision

The CV processes vision-based information with the help of machine learning. The application of CV and specific ML algorithms for basketball is shown in Table 13.1 (Naik et al., 2022). Basketball is a team sport with two teams comprising five players each competing against each other. The winning team will score more points than the losing team. The player can pass, throw, bounce, bat, and roll the ball, and restricting the desired movement of the player may result in a foul. Table 13.1 lists methods that can automate the task of analytics.

The game performance can be studied by recognizing the player's action from a recorded video (Liu et al., 2021). It helps to identify and analyze a sequence of steps taken by the player to complete an action. This in turn can improve training and game performance. The CNN performs motion recognition from frames of the video, then LSTM detects the key point and models the movement, and finally object detection reconstructs each movement (Liu et al., 2021). The approach failed to predict difficult actions, limiting its use. In basketball, scoring depends on the accuracy of the shooting. The establishment of an automated method for planning

Table 13.1 Suitable DL Techniques for CV Tasks in Basketball (Naik et al., 2022)

CV Task	*ML Algorithm*
Player's action recognition (Liu et al., 2021)	RNN or Bi-LSTM
Ball trajectory prediction (Li and Xu, 2021)	RNN and its variants
Multiplayer tracking in video (Fu et al., 2020)	YOLO family, region CNN family
Event recognition and classification (Wu et al., 2020)	CNN + RNN

Note: Convolutional neural network (CNN), recurrent neural network (RNN), long short term memory (LSTM), you look only once (YOLO).

of a shooting trajectory requires extraction and prediction of the ball trajectory (Li and Xu, 2021). The method uses shooting motion frames, features, and conditional variational RNNs to predict the trajectory of the ball. The method fails to predict trajectory in noisy and complicated scenarios. Belief maps (features extracted from deep neural network) are unable to accurately reflect the future positions of the ball, as players' positions are highly dynamic.

Tracking multiple players on a basketball court is a special case of multi-object tracking (Fu et al., 2020). This work uses several DL-based trackers and also provides a new dataset for basketball. Faster regional CNNs seem to be a better mechanism than you only look once (YOLO-v3) baseline approaches for multiplayer tracking. The faster R-CNN is an object detection architecture which uses a region proposal network for improved performance. YOLO-v3 is a real-time object detection algorithm, and it detects a specific object in videos or images. The joint detection and embedding method improves the efficiency of the algorithm. The tracker generates a new track and labels it under extreme occlusion scenarios. Motion patterns in team sports can accurately predict the activities (Wu et al., 2020) leading to an outcome. The method fuses local and global motion patterns for event recognition and classification in basketball. The first stage estimates the global motion from camera parameter adjustments, and a set of 3D CNNs recognize the events using local and global motions separately. The mean average precision (mAP) for activity recognition is 72.1%.

Data-driven ML approaches must be tested on various datasets to prove their generalization and robustness. With the availability of many off-the-shelf ML tools for a single task, it is important to understand performance metrics for informed selection. The preprocessing of video data and its mapping to various human-related activities is difficult, especially with the likelihood of fusing other data from different sensors. The mapping of low-level sensor data to high-level concept features needs significant computing resources. Data representation is vital in reducing the computing overhead without losing accuracy.

Apart from DL, some other ML techniques used in sports are summarized in Table 13.2. Clustering techniques are useful in extracting patterns from the data. This is an unsupervised form of learning, and it can identify hidden relationships or trends in the data. For example, it can help to place players with similar roles together. Dimensionality reduction techniques preserve maximal information in the data while reducing redundancy. Typical computer vision applications, as shown in Table 13.3, can implicitly use it for improvement. Prediction and classification are core problems in ML. It is important to predict the performance of a player or injury risk based on past records. Rule-based approaches are useful as both classifier and regressor. Rule-based analysis plays an important role during various data mining tasks. Text- and NLP-based approaches in conjunction with CV are opening many new dimensions in SDA.

13.3.2 General Challenges with Sports Analytics

There are several factors in human behavior that sports data analytics may find difficult to capture. For example, a player may deliberately mislead the opponent using

Table 13.2 ML Techniques for Team Sports (Naik et al., 2022)

ML Technique	*Purpose*
Clustering	Finding hotspots, extracting dimensions, clusters, and kernels from the data
Dimensionality reduction	Basis selection, visualization, variance preservation, class separability
Prediction	Injury – risk analysis, survival analysis in injury
Rule-based approaches	Analysis of positional data, human motion analysis (fuzzy rule base), event detection, and markup in soccer video
Association rules	Discovering rules for video analysis, video summarization, indexing, classification, semantic event detection
Decision tree	Classification, regression, accelerometer-based activity recognition – sitting, walking, jogging
Graph-based approaches	Tactic analysis, player and ball interaction analysis, analyzing team strategies
Text and NLP	Video analytics using audio features, model text into video analytics, characterizing video clips

gestures or coded signs (Alamar, 2013). Such nuances of human behavior are complicated to quantify. It results in unstructured data, which has to be handled in a specific way, for example, collecting such spoken words or gestures over periods and performing a time series analysis. It is also evident that the quality of data-driven approaches depends on the accuracy of the annotations, loss functions, and evaluation metrics. The only difficulty in implementing ML algorithms in sports is the model's accuracy, speed, and size. Deep representations can improve the accuracy, but with time and space complexity. The conventional DL architectures (RCNN family, YOLO family, VGG 16) used for detection, classification, trajectory prediction, and performance analysis are replaced by better paradigms like extreme learning machines (ELMs) and online learning algorithms, incremental learning, and reinforcement learning.

The developers of SDA use ML approaches as a black box, which can cause a missing link in the coach and analyst communication. As indicated in Section 13.2.1, continuous interactions between analyst and coach are necessary to improve the analysis's effectiveness. Therefore, analysts need to explain the decisions given by ML to the coach. It is facilitated by the use of explainable AI. In the following few sections, we discuss the case study to showcase the use of XAI in injury risk prediction.

13.4 Case Study – XAI in Injury-Risk Prediction

The case study aims to cover algorithms and processes in data gathering, data integration, model building, and decision-making to develop a fair and transparent system for injury prediction that quantifies and minimizes bias. We propose to develop a system for injury-risk prediction of anterior cruciate ligament (ACL) for the Division I college women's basketball team. Landing error scoring system (LESS) scores are computed for profiling players by performing video analytics using computer vision and machine learning techniques. The proposal characterizes fairness in terms of (i) biases and inconsistencies introduced during the data gathering and model building, (ii) the objectives in evaluating the algorithmic performance, and (iii) the transparency of decision making (i.e., explainable algorithms) by the AI/ML algorithms. We employ global-model and local-model agnostic explainable AI methods to explain the decisions of our AI/ML algorithms to the users. This helps to make data analytics–based reasoning accountable by addressing coaches' confirmation bias and motivated reasoning. It incorporates the coach's intuition and reasoning without introducing algorithmic bias. The system deployed on a trial basis uses the *fairness-accuracy* axis for the study.

13.4.1 ACL Injury in Sports

The anterior cruciate ligament connects the femur to the tibia. Sudden stopping, change in direction, jumping and landing uncomfortably, pivoting, or collision in basketball players cause an ACL injury (Li and Xu, 2021), more to lower extremities (Sarlis and Tjortjis, 2020) and for the aggressive player (Düking et al., 2018). Females are more likely to suffer it (Mangan et al., 2017), and the injury has a long recovery time with an increased risk of subsequent injury (Leser et al., 2014). ACL reconstruction (ACLR) is expensive (Gowda et al., 2017), and it can lead to osteoarthritis (Leser et al., 2014). However, the player returning to the same level of play after ACLR (Düking et al., 2018) is possible. Therefore, it is better to identify and prevent risk factors that can cause ACL.

Research suggests that jumping is critical for higher anterior cruciate ligaments (ACLs) in females (Alamar, 2013), especially landing techniques. Women's knees have less muscle mass, causing instability (Naik et al., 2022). For the ACL, risk can be sensed using a simple drop jump and countermovement jump (Liu et al., 2021). Hence, studying jump-landing biomechanics in females is crucial for identifying ACL risk. Biomechanical analysis using two-dimensional (2D) or three-dimensional (3D) motion can be used to quantify future ACL injury (Ramanathan et al., 2016). 3D motion analysis is a gold standard (Ramanathan et al., 2016) and needs multiple cameras with reflective markers (Victor et al., 2021). However, it has been shown that 3D biomechanical analyses can be approximated well by 2D captures (Li and Xu, 2021).

13.4.2 Computer Vision and ML for Landing Error Scoring System Score Computation

The landing error scoring system (LESS) is an inexpensive method that uses videos to estimate the risk of ACL injury (ACL Injury, 2022). It can identify at-risk athletes and be used during rehabilitation after ACLR (ACL Injury, 2022). It uses nine landing concepts and records videos (frontal and lateral) to assess foot, ankle, knee, hip, trunk, shoulder, neck, and head posture during a drop jump. Human judges then compute the LESS score, which matches performance validity against 3D motion analysis (Agel et al., 2007). LESS suffers from a subjective nature, requiring expert rater and video reviews post-recording (Thomas et al., 2021). Therefore, it is essential to automatically extract the LESS score from the videos (Gianotti et al., 2009).

The method uses the deep learning (DL)–based open-pose (Myklebust and Bahr, 2005) library to automatically extract features from the video frames to compute the LESS score. A dataset is also available to evaluate the ACL injury risk using computer vision (Liu et al., 2021). It has videos for drop jumps and countermovement jumps recorded by female university and club sports athletes. The automated process results match a qualified physiotherapist's LESS score. An ML approach using inertial and optoelectronic sensors predicts ACL risk and measures leg stability, mobility, and capability (Nagda et al., 2010). It compares nine classifiers and performs feature importance. DL, combined with CV, is a good choice for automated computation of the LESS score. It is possible without markers, expensive 3D motion analysis, and depth sensor cameras (Liu et al., 2021).

Compared to biomechanical assessment, LESS score computation is easy and fast, it can be performed without expensive laboratory equipment (ACL Injury, 2022), and it requires just few hours of administration training. LESS score measurements must be performed in a protected environment for consistency. It captures the fact that movement quality is a biomechanical risk factor and can capture a non-contact ACL injury very well. It has also been shown that ACL injury prevention programs pose no threat to the athlete. Automated LESS score computation has the potential to be used by the individual athlete as a screening tool. This will allow the LESS score to bring explainability and transparency into the screening process. Efforts are also being made to compute LESS scores in real time (LESS-RT) (Padua et al., 2009), which measures ten parameters. A study suggests that LESS-RT is a reliable tool for scoring landing mechanics.

13.4.3 Bias in the Player Selection, Data Modeling, and Algorithmic Decision Making

Coaches can design effective recruitment and training strategies if they factor in a player's role. Also, a proper nurturing environment can help develop good trust between the player and coach and reduce unfairness caused by perception (Hanzlíková et al., 2021; ACL Tears, 2022). In turn, it improves athletes' team identification and team cohesion tasks (Hanzlíková et al., 2021; ACL Tears, 2022). ML can be leveraged to develop such strategies. Algorithmic decision-making can compute the LESS score; however, it can result in unfairness. ML models can introduce biases in their decision-making due to the nature of the processes involved in collecting and sampling data and the lack of transparency in providing explanations. The interpolation techniques used to handle incompleteness in data can also result in inconsistencies due to variability in the predictions of the ML/DL models. In addition, some of the systemic sources of bias are due to chance behavior (due to inherent variability in entities, their environment, and interactions) and errors (model accuracy, unfairness in objective functions, nature of regularization, and statistical bias of estimators) (Blanchard et al., 2019). Moreover, in situations where algorithmic decisions lack transparency, managers and coaches tend to rely on their intuition and experience rather than on decisions based on data analytics (Bates and Hewett, 2016; 3D Biomechanics, 2022).

13.4.4 Mitigating Bias – Quantifying Fairness in ML

Data bias can impact algorithmic outcomes and includes measurement bias, omitted variable bias, representation bias, sampling bias, and longitudinal data fallacy (Blanchard et al., 2019). *Algorithmic bias* is purely due to the algorithm and influences user behavior. Bias can make algorithmic decisions unfair (Blanchard et al., 2019) and must be mitigated. For the present proposal, we define *fairness* as an *absence of prejudice or favoritism toward an individual or group based on their inherent or acquired characteristics* (Blanchard et al., 2019). The notion of fairness can be categorized into individuals, groups, and subgroups (Myer et al., 2010). *Group fairness* treats different groups equally, and one of the most popular fairness definitions is equalized odds (Padua et al., 2009). It states that protected and unprotected groups should have equal true positive rates (TPR) and false positive rates (FPR) (Padua et al., 2009). It is recommended to place bias mitigation in preprocessing, in-processing, and post-processing (Hanzlíková et al., 2020). Most classification methods for fair ML exclude protected attributes from decision-making, include users from sensitive groups, and use fairness notions like treatment disparity and impact disparity (Blanchard et al., 2019). Some methods treat protected attributes as noise and do not consider their impact on decision-making (Blanchard et al., 2019). Similarly, some methods use causal graphs and avoid paths that remove protected attributes from decision-making (Blanchard et al., 2019).

The approximation method LESS-RT (Padua et al., 2009) allows computation of real-time scores and also helps to understand the intuitive way coaches evaluate it. This will help to inject domain knowledge into automated LESS score computation and reduce algorithmic bias.

13.4.5 Explaining Decisions

Though the ML model may perform well, it may not help build trust as it cannot explain its own decisions. It has motivated the need for explainable AI (Dar et al., 2018), and it means developing systems as humans understand (Hebert-Losier et al., 2020) and facilitating fairness. XAI (Cao et al., 2017) incorporates pyramidal levels of fairness (top level, most challenging to achieve), accountability (mid-level, mid-tier difficulty to achieve), and transparency (bottom level, easy to achieve). Fairness ensures that ML algorithms are bias free. Accountability traces decisions back to the source or designer. Transparency explains how and why decisions are made.

Separating explanations and ML models allows for model, explanation, and representation flexibility (Taborri et al., 2021; De Backer et al., 2021). Global-model agnostic methods help to understand the general mechanism in data by studying the expected value from data distribution (De Backer et al., 2021). Examples are partial dependence plots (PDPs), permutation feature importance, or global surrogate models. On the other hand, methods like individual conditional expectation (ICE) and local interpretable model-agnostic explanations (LIME) can explain individual predictions (local-model agnostic methods) (De Backer et al., 2021). It makes sense to develop interpretable methods for deep neural networks (DNNs), as concepts and features are hidden in layers, allowing the use of computationally efficient gradients. There are techniques to find features that the DNN has learned (feature visualization or network dissection) or the contribution of each pixel to the prediction (saliency maps) to detecting concepts learned by DNN (testing with concept activation vectors; TCAV) (De Backer et al., 2021).

13.4.6 Research Gap and the Proposal

ACL injury is the most difficult an athlete may sustain, and it is very difficult to recover from it. Young women athletes are especially prone to ACL injury. It is very difficult for athletes to return to pre-ACL injury performance levels. Considering gravity of the injury risk and our association with a Division I women's' basketball team, the chapter aims to focus on ACL risk prediction. Identifying ACL injury is first step towards deployment of an ACL injury prevention program.

CV-ML methods (ACL Injury, 2022; Gianotti et al., 2009; Nagda et al., 2010; Liu et al., 2021) showed usefulness in predicting ACL injury. However, these methods must involve coaches during system development to gain wider acceptance. They merely show the possibility with no real correlation reported between the ACL risk predictions and decisions on the ground by the coach. None of the approaches (ACL Injury, 2022; Gianotti et al., 2009, Nagda et al., 2010; Liu et al., 2021) show the use of XAI, which leaves a semantic gap between the coach and the algorithm. The previous approaches do not discuss data or system uncertainty and biases. Therefore, the proposal aims at the following: (i) using XAI provides information suitable for auditable and provable ways for algorithmic decisions and building trust (De Backer et al., 2021), (ii) using transparent algorithmic decision-making brings coaches on board for informed decision-making, and (iii) the on-boarding of coaches infuses information based on their intuition and experience into the algorithms. It helps to overcome algorithmic bias. It is further tackled with better characterization of systems, the multiplicity of objective functions or consensus methods, and better sampling and statistical analysis. Thus, we envisage using XAI to promote humans in the loop, improving fairness at the coach level, which impacts algorithmic fairness. This establishes positive feedback in the interactions.

13.5 Material and Methods

13.5.1 Problem Statement

Ensuring fairness in profiling Women's Division I basketball athletes for ACL injury-risk assessment.

13.5.2 Participants

Division I female basketball athletes participated in the experimental protocol (Institutional Review Board approval number 170720A on 9/14/2020). The team members, strength coach, head coach, sports biomechanics, and graduate program director of exercise science are a part of the team.

13.5.3 Codifying Fairness and Indicator Metrics

The participants work together to agree on the project's fairness objectives and indicator metrics. Using the definition of fairness and evaluation metrics like equalized odds (Padua et al., 2009), classifying labels equally well for all values of features, or disparate impact (Blanchard et al., 2019), which compares the proportion of athletes who receive positive output for a protected and unprotected group.

13.5.4 Experimental Setup, Data Collection Protocol, and Data Annotations

The participants perform (i) drop jump and (ii) countermovement jump using standard protocols and over multiple trials. Three tripod cameras cover the fronto-parallel plane, the right-side lateral plane, and the left side to record the jumps. The reading from two force plates aligned with recorded video measurements ensures a sufficient sample size is available for the data. The public dataset (Liu et al., 2021) can be explored using principles of data-centric AI (Blanchard et al., 2019) or principle-centric AI (Blanchard et al., 2019). An expert in sports biomechanics identifies key frames in each video and evaluates them using a LESS protocol.

13.5.5 Automated Computation of the LESS Score and Validation Using Force Plates Measurement

The videos are processed to detect the key frames with initial contact and maximum knee flexion angle in all three views. Following the extraction of measurement, the LESS score is computed for test videos using ML algorithms. We also link the force plate measurements with the LESS scores to improve the validity of the results.

13.5.6 Fair Machine Learning Algorithms

We compute the LESS scores from the training sequence and then train a regression model to predict the LESS score for the testing sequences. Athletes with a higher LESS score re prone to injury risk and can be recommended for injury prevention programs (ACL Injury, 2022). A binary classifier based on the LESS score is trained for the player's profiling. Fairness is evaluated at all stages of the data pipeline.

Data preprocessing: Modify the training data based on the fairness metric and detect the bias after running tests on raw data. Use a reweighting algorithm (Blanchard et al., 2019) to change the weights of training data to mitigate bias at the data level.

In processing: adversarial debiasing (Blanchard et al., 2019) can be used to tackle bias. Post-hoc processing: AI bias mitigation (Blanchard et al., 2019) is applied to the predicted samples by tuning the labels to mitigate bias. Finally, we run the unit test for accuracy and bias and deploy the profiling model.

13.5.7 Explaining the Profiling Decision and Deploying the System

The recommendations for player profiling based on the LESS score (from the previous week's data) are provided to the coach on Monday morning to plan the exercise and training routine. Global and local model-agnostic techniques (De Backer et al., 2021) are used to explain the decisions to the coach. We anticipate deploying a multi-level flag system quantified after discussions with the coach. A neutral observer will be placed to keep tabs on whether algorithmic recommendations are followed by the coach. This helps us tune the algorithms and reduce bias due to error. This step links the algorithm output and coach perspective and brings fairness into the system.

The previous discussion proposes a framework to debias data and algorithms, then apply XAI techniques at the local and global level to understand decision-making. The framework will bring fairness to XAI. To further consolidate the idea, the following section shows the use of XAI for injury risk prediction on the actual data collected from the field.

13.6 Injury Risk Prediction Case Study

13.6.1 Dataset

Sixteen Division I women's basketball team athletes at Sacred Heart University, USA, were the subjects of this study. The daily sleep patterns of the athletes, combined with their training and survey data, were collected to predict their injuries using ML algorithms. A total of 2800 records, each with 38 features (37 input features and injuries), were collected from these athletes for 25 weeks.

A. Sleep monitoring: The daily sleep patterns and physiological measures such as heart rate, respiratory rate, and recovery patterns were collected via WHOOP strap (Fagan, 2021). A total of 22 features were measured daily (7/week). These features were awake hours, deep sleep hours, hours in bed, hours of sleep, heart rate variability (HRV), latency, light sleep hours, number of cycles, rapid eye movement (REM) sleep hours, recovery, respiratory rate (RR), restorative sleep hours, RHR, total cycle nap hours, total cycle sleep hours, wake periods, sleep consistency, sleep debt hours, sleep disturbances, sleep efficiency, sleep need, and sleep score.
B. Quantification of training load: Total work undertaken by the athlete in their metabolic conditioning, resistance training, and sports training was quantified in terms of a composite score. A total of six features were measured three times

a week. These features were daily average, monotony, repetitive training (RT) volume load, strain, week standard deviation, and week trimp total.

C. Survey: Athletes completed a short recovery and stress questionnaire using an online dashboard twice a week. It collected personal information on their emotional, mental, and overall recovery. The features were emotional balance (EB), lack of activation (LA), mental performance capability (MPC), muscular stress (MS), negative emotional state (NES), overall recovery (OR), overall stress (OS), and physical performance capability (PPC).
D. Game performance: Game performance measures an athlete's productivity during the game. Based on statistics collected during games, we measured performance using John Hollinger's game score equation (Hollinger and Hollinger, 2005).
E. Injuries: Injury records were taken from the medical reports generated during the season. They included information such as the date of injury, type of injury (contact or non-contact), and days of unavailability of the athlete.

13.6.2 Preprocessing

13.6.2.1 Data Imputation

The sleep monitoring and questionnaire data were incomplete due to the negligence of athletes in wearing WHOOP straps, improper attachment of the device to the wrist, and athletes not completing the surveys. This missing data could constitute a source of bias and impact injury prediction negatively. Hence, we utilized the multivariate imputation by chained equation (MICE) (Madley-Dowd et al., 2019) approach for imputing the missing values. In this approach, the feature values are input sequentially. The model uses prior imputed values to predict subsequent feature values. A MICE imputer is beneficial for all proportions of missing data and proves effective with the correctly specified imputation model (Madley-Dowd et al., 2019). Statistical measures of raw bias and percentage bias were calculated for all the imputed features and indicated effective imputation. The percentage bias (PB, ideal is <5%) of physical game performance capability (PPC) is 0.0004%, resting heart rate is 1.2%, and wake periods is 0.6%, indicating effective imputation.

13.6.2.2 Interaction Modeling

The interaction effect is when multiple features jointly contribute to the prediction of a target feature. Interaction modeling was performed over the dataset to analyze how a third feature influences the relationship between an independent and a target feature (Jaccard et al., 2003). For each pair of features, the two-way interaction effect was checked. Keeping a check on the significance level of the polynomial interaction terms on the target feature, forward selection and backward elimination of features was done to compute the optimal set of features for prediction. A random forest (RF) classifier was fit over datasets containing different combinations of significantly contributing features and two-way interaction terms. The achieved F2 score was kept as a check. The highest F2 score was obtained for the dataset with 14 features: 4 features from quantification of training load, 4 from sleep monitoring, 1 from survey data, 1 from game performance, 1 interaction feature from sleep monitoring, and 2 interaction features – a combination of sleep monitoring and game performance and one interaction feature – a combination of sleep monitoring and training load. The features were REM sleep, RR, monotony, strain, points, points, REM sleep, points and RR, week trimp total, sleep disturbances, EB, RT volume load, RT volume load, RR, REM sleep, and deep sleep.

13.6.2.3 Factor Analysis

There were several linear dependencies observed among the features in the dataset. For example, features such as awake hours, sleep disturbances, and wake periods are highly correlated. Sleep score was computed based on hours in bed, hours of sleep, and total cycle sleep hours. A high PPC implied a low MS, a high EB implied a low NES, and a high OS implied a low OR. Recovery was computed based on hours of sleep, HRV, RHR, and RR. The features daily average, weekly standard deviation, and week trimp total had a high correlation. These introduced redundancy and constituted a source of bias in the dataset. Hence, factor analysis was performed over the dataset to discover latent factors that were a linear combination of features sharing common variance (Srishti et al., 2022). It would provide a compact representation of the dataset, preserving each feature's impact on injury prediction.

Injuries were modeled as a weighted function of the seven latent factors that were discovered from the 36 input features of the dataset. Each latent factor is a weighted sum of a set of features sharing a common variance. The weights assigned to each feature are the correlation value (highest) between the feature and its allotted factor. Table 13.3 shows the categorization of features into factors.

Table 13.3 Categorization of Features into Factors

Factor	*Name*	*Features*
F0	Amount of sleep	Total cycle sleep hours, hours of sleep, sleep cycles, sleep score, hours in bed
F1	Perception	PPC, MPC, NES, EB, OS, OR, LA, MS
F2	Training	Week trimp total, daily average, RT volume load, weekly SD, strain, monotony
F3	Sleep interruptions	Sleep efficiency, wake periods, sleep disturbances, awake hours
F4	Sleep state	REM sleep hours, deep sleep hours, light sleep hours, restorative sleep hours
F5	Sleep required	Sleep need, sleep debt hours, sleep consistency, total cycle nap hours
F6	Physiological	HRV, RHR, recovery, respiratory rate, latency

Factor analysis results in reduced data dimensionality (helping interpretability). It also reduced the injury prediction model's computational complexity (quadratic speed-up).

13.6.2.4 Data Balancing

Due to only a few injuries during the season, the injury data were scarce compared to the entire dataset, leading to biased predictions. This dataset is called an imbalanced dataset, wherein minimal samples from the minority class make it difficult for the model to learn the decision boundary effectively. A straightforward preprocessing approach would be the duplication of records belonging to the minority class, which would introduce redundancy and bias, resulting in poor outcomes. Several sampling approaches are used to synthesize new records from minority classes to balance the dataset. We tried several oversampling, and undersampling techniques, such as synthetic minority oversampling technique (SMOTE) (Chawla et al., 2002) and its variants like ADASYN, TOMEK Links, ENN, and Borderline SMOTE. While SMOTE generates synthetic minority class samples that are in the direction of the existing minority class samples towards their nearest neighbors, borderline SMOTE (Han et al., 2005) generates synthetic samples along the borderline of the majority and the minority classes in the dataset, which is more suitable to injury risk prediction.

13.6.3 Injury Risk Prediction

The balanced dataset (352 records) was divided into training (289 records) and testing (63 records) datasets following the traditional 70:30 ratio. There were in all 11 injuries present, 9 in the training dataset and 2 in the testing dataset. Stratified tenfold cross-validation was made use of during training to ensure model estimates with a lower bias. We used the XGBoost Classifier for prediction due to its generalization capabilities and gradient boosting framework. As

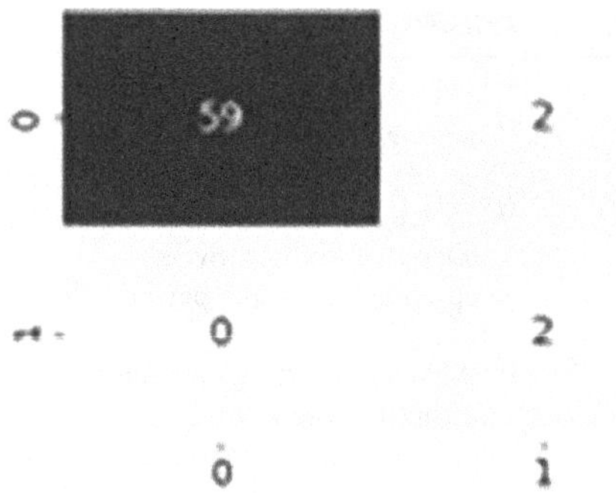

Figure 13.3 Confusion matrix on test set for injury prediction.

the data in our case were severely imbalanced, accuracy could not be used as a measure of evaluating model performance. Recall is more important than precision here. It is more critical to predict as many injuries as possible to help the coach in team assignment, as an injury to a player can strongly affect the results of a game. Therefore, we decided to use the F2 measure. The XGB classifier resulted in an F2 score of 0.83. Following is the confusion matrix that depicts four injuries predicted: two true negatives and two false negatives. There were 59 no injuries predicted.

In our case, false negatives are more acceptable than false positives.

13.6.4 Interpretability

13.6.4.1 Feature Importance (Sensitivity Analysis)

Sensitivity analysis (feature importance) explains the contribution of each independent feature to the target feature prediction. This technique facilitates dimensionality reduction and helps gain insights from a prediction model (Kowshalya et al., 2019). It helps understand the contribution of the dataset's unique feature to the target feature, thereby explaining decisions made by the prediction model. We applied Pearson's correlation (Kowshalya et al., 2019), XGBoost classifier-based feature importance (Hastie et al., 2009), and random forest–based feature importance (Hastie et al., 2009) over the dataset, setting injury as the target feature. A consensus-based approach was used to calculate the feature rank through a weighted rank-sum (hard voting). The following graph shows the features in order of their rank based on their aggregate feature importance score. REM sleep, respiratory rate, and monotony are the top three most significant features contributing to injury prediction.

Nevertheless, another popular tool used for sensitivity analysis is the SHAP values of features. Using a random forest, SHAP interpretations can compute the feature

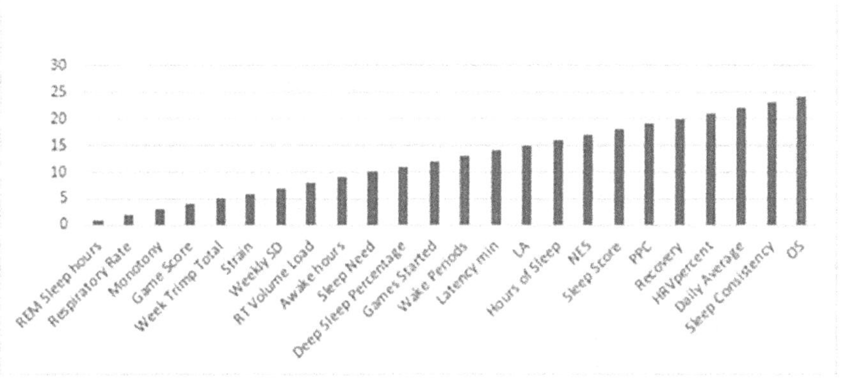

Figure 13.4 Features ranked based on importance scores (hard voting approach).

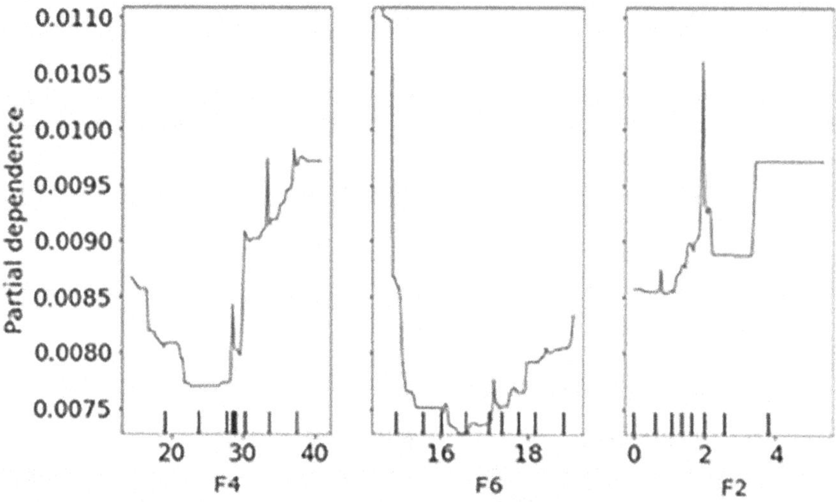

Figure 13.5 PDP for the F4 (left), F6 (middle), and F2 (right) with respect to injury.

importance score for independent features (Marcílio et al., 2020). We calculated the SHAP values for all dataset features for the target feature – injury. Per the SHAP values obtained, the top three most significant features are REM sleep (0.016), respiratory rate (0.011), and monotony (0.010).

13.6.4.2 *Partial Dependence Plots*

Partial dependence plots depict the impact of one or multiple independent features on the target feature. This shows the relationship (complex/linear/monotonic) between the independent and target features. We analyzed the impact of the top three most significant features on injury prediction.

The most significant feature is REM sleep, a constituent feature of factor 4 (F4). REM sleep is a state of restorative sleep. Around 20% to 25% of sleep time in the REM sleep state is suggested as an ideal (Miller et al., 2020). The PDP for REM sleep (F4) depicts that if the sleep time of athletes in the REM sleep state is <15% or >30%, it increases their chances of getting injured. The second most significant feature is a respiratory rate (RR), a constituent feature of factor 6 (F6). Twelve to 18 respirations per minute are considered normal (Miller et al., 2020). Any deviation from this range suggests an unusual pattern indicative of sleep disturbances, leading to an increase in the chances of injury. The third most significant feature is monotony, a constituent feature of factor 2 (F2). Monotony is indicative of the fluctuations in athletic training load. It shows a positive correlation with the risk of injury; that is, increased fluctuations would increase the chances of an injury.

13.7 Conclusion

The chapter presents the case of interpretable machine learning in injury risk prediction of the athlete. The field of sports data analytics is rapidly growing with the availability of sensors, wearable devices, computing power, and ML techniques. It is rapidly developing in both on-field and off-field analytics. The framework for SDA includes data, models, and information systems, and leadership plays an essential role in deployment decisions. The acceptance of analytics by the coach is key to the successful use of data in sports. A coach must be involved in piloting the system and then using it within the sports ecosystem. This chapter shows computer vision's vital role in capturing and augmenting the data collected from wearables. The simultaneous development of DNN has dramatically enhanced the robustness and accuracy of inferences. Data-driven approaches are increasingly becoming a norm but lack transparency in decision-making. The chapter explores XAI as a mechanism to study decisions by ML techniques.

The chapter proposes a framework to study injury risk prediction using automated LESS score computation from the video. The Division I basketball team at Sacred Heart University is under study. It has been observed that data collection and choice of algorithm can introduce a bias. Therefore, it is vital to debias data and algorithms, as indicated in the proposed framework. XAI can be significantly benefited from this debiasing. The ideas presented in the framework have been quantified with a case study on injury risk prediction. It discusses various features and performs sensitivity analysis. The partial dependence plots showcase the relationship between dependent and independent variables. This helps interpret the impact of variables on the target.

Acknowledgments

The authors wants to thank the players and coaching staff for cooperating. They are also grateful for the support from Welch College of Business & Technology, Sacred Heart University, CT, USA for obtaining the WHOOP straps and the research platform The authors acknowledge the help from Dr. Christopher Taber, Sacred Heart University, for helping us to understand the LESS parameters. The authors are also indebted to the Sacred Heart University research team for data collection, cleaning, processing, and making inferences. Part of this work is developed on a Workstation under the grant number GUJCOST/STI/2021-22/3858 by the Gujarat Council on Science and Technology, Government of Gujarat, India.

References

3D Biomechanics, www.msahc.com.au/services/3d-biomechanics, Last accessed on 06/24/2022

ACL Injury, www.mayoclinic.org/diseases-conditions/acl-injury/symptoms-causes/syc-20350738, Last accessed on 06/24/2022

ACL Tears in Female Athletes: Q&A with a Sports Medicine Expert, www.hopkinsmedicine.org/health/conditions-and-diseases/acl-injury-or-tear/acl-tears-in-female-athletes-qa-with-a-sports-medicine-expert, Last accessed on 06/24/2022

Agel, Julie, David E. Olson, Randall Dick, Elizabeth A. Arendt, Stephen W. Marshall, and Robby S. Sikka. "Descriptive epidemiology of collegiate women's basketball injuries:

National Collegiate Athletic Association injury surveillance system, 1988–1989 through 2003–2004." *Journal of Athletic Training 42*, no. 2 (2007): 202.

Alamar, Benjamin. "Sports analytics." In *Sports Analytics*. New York: Columbia University Press, 2013.

Bates, Nathaniel A., and Timothy E. Hewett. "Motion analysis and the anterior cruciate ligament: Classification of injury risk." *The Journal of Knee Surgery 29*, no. 2 (2016): 117–125.

Blanchard, Nathaniel, Kyle Skinner, Aden Kemp, Walter Scheirer, and Patrick Flynn. ""Keep Me In, Coach!": A computer vision perspective on assessing ACL injury risk in female athletes." In *2019 IEEE Winter Conference on Applications of Computer Vision (WACV)*, pp. 1366–1374. New York: IEEE, 2019.

Cao, Z., T. Simon, S. E. Wei. and Y. Sheikh. "Realtime multi-person 2d pose estimation using part affinity fields." In *Proceedings of the IEEE Conference on Computer Vision and Pattern Recognition*, pp. 7291–7299.

Chawla, Nitesh V., Kevin W. Bowyer, Lawrence O. Hall, and W. Philip Kegelmeyer. "SMOTE: synthetic minority over-sampling technique." *Journal of Artificial Intelligence Research 16* (2002): 321–357.

Dar, Gali, Alon Yehiel, and Maya Cale'Benzoor. "Concurrent criterion validity of a novel portable motion analysis system for assessing the landing error scoring system (LESS) test." *Sports Biomechanics 18*, no. 4 (2018): 426–436.

De Backer, Maarten, Filip Boen, Stef Van Puyenbroeck, Bart Reynders, Koen Van Meervelt, and Gert Vande Broek. "Should team coaches care about justice? Perceived justice mediates the relation between coaches' autonomy support and athletes' satisfaction and self-rated progression." *International Journal of Sports Science & Coaching 16*, no. 1 (2021): 27–43.

De Backer, Maarten, Stef Van Puyenbroeck, Katrien Fransen, Bart Reynders, Filip Boen, Florian Malisse, and Gert Vande Broek. "Does fair coach behavior predict the quality of athlete leadership among Belgian volleyball and basketball players: The vital role of team identification and task cohesion." *Frontiers in Psychology 12* (2021).

Düking, Peter, Christian Stammel, Billy Sperlich, Shaun Sutehall, Borja Muniz-Pardos, Giscard Lima, Liam Kilduff et al. "Necessary steps to accelerate the integration of wearable sensors into recreation and competitive sports." *Current Sports Medicine Reports 17*, no. 6 (2018): 178–182.

Fagan, Samantha. "Exploring the role of biofeedback in physiological monitoring of alcohol and caffeine consumption in collegiate softball athletes." (2021).

Fu, Xubo, Kun Zhang, Changgang Wang, and Chao Fan. "Multiple player tracking in basketball court videos." *Journal of Real-Time Image Processing 17*, no. 6 (2020): 1811–1828.

Gianotti, Simon M., Stephen W. Marshall, Patria A. Hume, and Lorna Bunt. "Incidence of anterior cruciate ligament injury and other knee ligament injuries: a national population-based study." *Journal of Science and Medicine in Sport 12*, no. 6 (2009): 622–627.

Gowda, Mahanth, Ashutosh Dhekne, Sheng Shen, Romit Roy Choudhury, Lei Yang, Suresh Golwalkar, and Alexander Essanian. "Bringing {IoT} to sports analytics." In *14th USENIX Symposium on Networked Systems Design and Implementation (NSDI 17)*, Boston, MA, pp. 499–513, 2017.

Han, Hui, Wen-Yuan Wang, and Bing-Huan Mao. "Borderline-SMOTE: a new over-sampling method in imbalanced data sets learning." In *International Conference on Intelligent Computing*, pp. 878–887. Berlin and Heidelberg: Springer, 2005.

Hanzlíková, Ivana, Josie Athens, and Kim Hébert-Losier. "Factors influencing the Landing Error Scoring System: Systematic review with meta-analysis." *Journal of Science and Medicine in Sport 24*, no. 3 (2021): 269–280.

Hanzlíková, Ivana, and Kim Hébert-Losier. "Is the Landing Error Scoring System reliable and valid? A systematic review." *Sports Health 12*, no. 2 (2020): 181–188.

Hastie, Trevor, Robert Tibshirani, Jerome H. Friedman, and Jerome H. Friedman. *The Elements of Statistical Learning: Data Mining, Inference, and Prediction*, vol. 2. New York: Springer, 2009.

Hebert-Losier, Kim, Ivana Hanzlikova, Chen Zheng, Lee Streeter, and Michael Mayo. "The 'DEEP' Landing Error Scoring System." *Applied Sciences 10*, no. 3 (2020): 892.

Hollinger, John, and John Hollinger. *Pro Basketball Forecast, 2005–06*. Sterling: Potomac Books, 2005.

Jaccard, James, Robert Turrisi, and Jim Jaccard. *Interaction Effects in Multiple Regression*, No. 72. Thousand Oaks: Sage, 2003.

Kowshalya, A. Meena, R. Madhumathi, and N. Gopika. "Correlation based feature selection algorithms for varying datasets of different dimensionality." *Wireless Personal Communications 108*, no. 3 (2019): 1977–1993.

Leser, Roland, and Karen Roemer. "Motion tracking and analysis systems." In *Computer Science in Sport*, pp. 96–123. London: Routledge, 2014.

Li, Bin, and Xinyang Xu. "Application of artificial intelligence in basketball sport." *Journal of Education, Health and Sport 11*, no. 7 (2021): 54–67.

Li, Hongfei, and Maolin Zhang. "Artificial intelligence and neural network-based shooting accuracy prediction analysis in basketball." *Mobile Information Systems 2021* (2021).

Liu, Long. "Objects detection toward complicated high remote basketball sports by leveraging deep CNN architecture." *Future Generation Computer Systems 119* (2021): 31–36.

Madley-Dowd, Paul, Rachael Hughes, Kate Tilling, and Jon Heron. "The proportion of missing data should not be used to guide decisions on multiple imputation." *Journal of Clinical Epidemiology 110* (2019): 63–73.

Mangan, Shane, Martin Ryan, Simon Devenney, Aidan Shovlin, Jason McGahan, Shane Malone, Cian O'Neill, Con Burns, and Kieran Collins. "The relationship between technical performance indicators and running performance in elite Gaelic football." *International Journal of Performance Analysis in Sport 17*, no. 5 (2017): 706–720.

Marcílio, Wilson E., and Danilo M. Eler. "From explanations to feature selection: assessing SHAP values as feature selection mechanism." In *2020 33rd SIBGRAPI Conference on Graphics, Patterns and Images (SIBGRAPI)*, pp. 340–347. New York: IEEE, 2020.

Miller, Dean J., Michele Lastella, Aaron T. Scanlan, Clint Bellenger, Shona L. Halson, Gregory D. Roach, and Charli Sargent. "A validation study of the WHOOP strap against polysomnography to assess sleep." *Journal of Sports Sciences 38*, no. 22 (2020): 2631–2636.

Myer, Gregory D., Kevin R. Ford, Jane Khoury, Paul Succop, and Timothy E. Hewett. "Development and validation of a clinic-based prediction tool to identify female athletes at high risk for anterior cruciate ligament injury." *The American Journal of Sports Medicine 38*, no. 10 (2010): 2025–2033.

Myklebust, G., and R. Bahr. "Return to play guidelines after anterior cruciate ligament surgery." *British Journal of Sports Medicine 39*, no. 3 (2005): 127–131.

Nagda, Sameer H., Grant G. Altobelli, Kevin A. Bowdry, Clive E. Brewster, and Stephen J. Lombardo. "Cost analysis of outpatient anterior cruciate ligament reconstruction: autograft versus allograft." *Clinical Orthopaedics and Related Research® 468*, no. 5 (2010): 1418–1422.

Naik, Banoth Thulasya, Mohammad Farukh Hashmi, and Neeraj Dhanraj Bokde. "A comprehensive review of computer vision in sports: Open issues, future trends and research directions." *Applied Sciences 12*, no. 9 (2022): 4429.

Padua, Darin A., Stephen W. Marshall, Michelle C. Boling, Charles A. Thigpen, William E. Garrett Jr, and Anthony I. Beutler. "The Landing Error Scoring System (LESS) is a valid and reliable clinical assessment tool of jump-landing biomechanics: The JUMP-ACL study." *The American Journal of Sports Medicine 37*, no. 10 (2009): 1996–2002.

Ramanathan, Vignesh, Jonathan Huang, Sami Abu-El-Haija, Alexander Gorban, Kevin Murphy, and Li Fei-Fei. "Detecting events and key actors in multi-person videos." In *CVF Proceedings of the IEEE Conference on Computer Vision and Pattern Recognition*, pp. 3043–3053, 2016.

Sarlis, Vangelis, and Christos Tjortjis. "Sports analytics – Evaluation of basketball players and team performance." *Information Systems 93* (2020): 101562.

Srishti Sharma, Srikrishnan Divakaran, Tolga Kaya, Mehul S Raval, "A Hybrid Approach for Interpretable Game Performance Prediction in Basketball,"2022 International Joint Conference on Neural Networks (IJCNN 2022), 18th–23rd July 2022, Padova Italy [Accepted for Publication].

Taborri, Juri, Luca Molinaro, Adriano Santospagnuolo, Mario Vetrano, Maria Chiara Vulpiani, and Stefano Rossi. "A machine-learning approach to measure the anterior cruciate ligament injury risk in female basketball players." *Sensors 21*, no. 9 (2021): 3141.

Thomas, Kevin, Blake Schultz, Mark Cinque, Joshua Harris, and Geoffrey Abrams. "Driving tendency is associated with increased risk of anterior cruciate ligament tears in National Basketball Association players (103)." *Orthopaedic Journal of Sports Medicine 9*, no. 10_suppl5 (2021): 2325967121S00253.

Victor, Brandon, Aiden Nibali, ZHen He, and David L. Carey. "Enhancing trajectory prediction using sparse outputs: Application to team sports." *Neural Computing and Applications 33*, no. 18 (2021): 11951–11962.

Wu, Lifang, Zhou Yang, Qi Wang, Meng Jian, Boxuan Zhao, Junchi Yan, and Chang Wen Chen. "Fusing motion patterns and key visual information for semantic event recognition in basketball videos." *Neurocomputing 413* (2020): 217–229.

14 Federated Learning and Explainable AI in Healthcare

Anca Bucur, Francesca Manni, Aleksandr Bukharev, Shiva Moorthy, Nancy Irisarri Mendez, and Anshul Jain

Contents

14.1 Introduction

Good and useful AI in healthcare relies on good data in terms of quality, volume, and diversity. Access to datasets that are large enough and representative of the diversity of the target populations to which the AI model should apply is a significant challenge in medicine. It is rarely the case that such a dataset that would enable one to build models that are accurate, generalizable, and free of local data biases can be collected at a single institute. A major factor that makes data sharing difficult is the risk it poses to patient data privacy and security. Institutions are reluctant to have data leave their firewalls. These challenges may be addressed by a distributed approach, such as federated learning (FL). With FL, models are trained across multiple systems that each have local datasets without sharing the data. Instead of data, models and model parameters are exchanged. The advantage is significant, as protecting patient data is of paramount importance in the healthcare industry. The approach enables organizations to collaborate at scale while incurring lower risks with respect to data privacy and security. Federated learning may also help to build the needed trust in the healthcare industry for engaging with the AI community in

DOI: 10.1201/9781003333425-14

a wide ecosystem facilitating the efficient development, validation, and adoption of novel, high-quality diagnostic and treatment solutions for better patient outcomes. FL helps maximize the value extracted from research data without increasing privacy risks, responding to the concept that "data should be maximally used for the public good" [Heidelberg et al., 2020].

This approach makes it easier to preserve data privacy while enjoying the benefits of collaboration at scale and may reduce the time and cost of innovation. Leveraging the advantage of training on higher volume and more diverse data, enabling cross-site training and validation, may lead to models that are more robust and more representative and reach a higher performance. While successful applications of FL for solving challenging real-world problems are emerging in use cases that showcase the unique advantages of the approach, it continues to be an active research area with many ongoing developments aiming to address recognized open issues [Kairouz et al., 2021], [Dayan et al., 2021]. Once these issues are adequately addressed, the wide adoption of FL in healthcare may lead to higher trust and increased real-world accuracy of AI applications. Scaling up AI development and adoption and enhancing model interoperability are other important future benefits.

Existing literature primarily focuses on exploiting privacy-preserving techniques, communication protocols and design choices in FL systems. However, to fully realize the promise of FL in the medical domain, it is crucial to provide a solution which mitigates the perceived black-box nature of neural networks integrated in the federated learning setting. In this chapter, we bridge the gap between explainability and FL, with an introduction to the state of the art in FL and future research directions towards explainable and robust models with FL.

In Section 14.2, we describe our approach to building a scalable, componentized FL, aiming to address recognized challenges around building and deploying AI in healthcare. The framework can be efficiently adapted and configured to support the specific requirements of a wide range of use cases, both in cross-silo and cross-device settings. The components of the framework and the implementation in several use cases have been described in Rachakonda et al. [2022]. Here we summarize the results and present the key components. Building on this research, we further focus on two specific aspects of FL in healthcare: explainability and privacy impact. Federated learning comes with opportunities to enhance explainability by leveraging the diversity and the specific characteristics of the populations at the worker node sites where the model is being trained. Compared to a model trained with a single centralized dataset, in FL, each worker may see different datasets with their own characteristics which can be leveraged post-deployment for providing better explanations to clinical users when applying the final model. Moreover, explainability models and metrics can help the data scientist while training a model in federated leaning to identify issues in local data quality, find outliers, get an overview on the differences among datasets that each worker sees, and use this information to get more insights into causes and ways to address potential data and model drifts during training. These aspects are discussed in Section 14.5.

While it is recognized that FL reduces data privacy and security risks by keeping data local and only transferring the model parameters (weights and biases), we aim at understanding the remaining data reconstruction risk to assess if there is still a relevant risk that needs to be considered and to identify ways to manage it. This is covered in Section 14.7.

14.2 The Federated Learning Pipeline

In previous work [Rachakonda et al., 2022], we developed a scalable, componentized FL framework aiming at addressing challenges related to implementation of AI in healthcare. The proposed framework is scalable to both cross-silos and cross-devices FL. The overall architecture is illustrated in Figure 14.1. It is developed on the PySyft library, chosen as a building block because of its customizability and license (Apache 2.0). In the cross-silo scenario, the learning process leverages data from different users at each site, while in the cross-device setting, the process involves user devices that have access to data created by a single user.

In an FL infrastructure, participants transfer model artifacts and share knowledge among them coordinated by a central hosting server. The central server is called coordinator and manages the FL framework. The participants in the FL training are the workers, and they carry out the AI tasks at the locations of the data. The coordinator shares the base model and the training configuration with workers. At each site, a worker trains the model on local data and sends the model updates to the coordinator. Then, the coordinator aggregates the model updates from multiple workers and shares the updated model with workers for the next training round. This process continues until a desired level of performance, or a pre-configured number of training rounds, is reached.

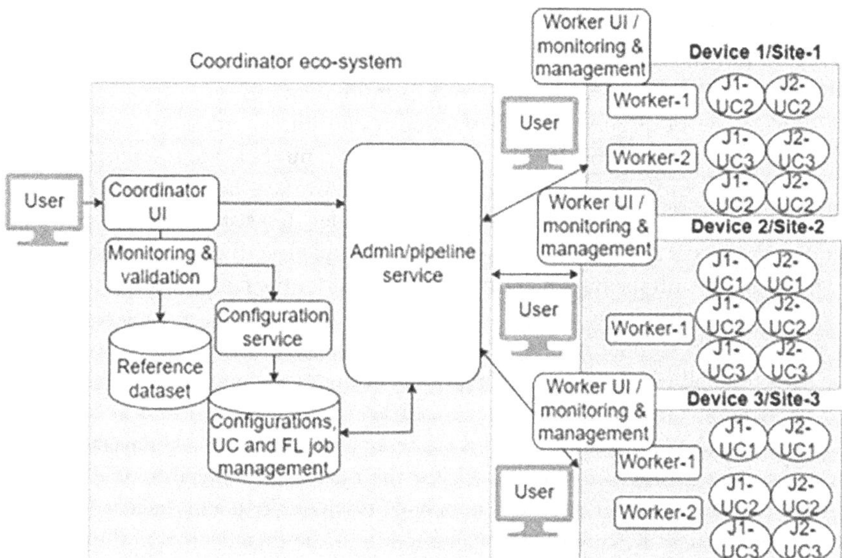

Figure 14.1 The federated learning pipeline.

In the case of multiple use cases that are simultaneously running, the system setup complexity increases. For many simultaneous use cases, this requires a workflow component that keeps track of the state of the system. This is done by the orchestrator component that takes all the responsibility to track the system at the coordinator side, support different use cases that run simultaneously, monitor the pipeline, and handle specific demands related to healthcare. Stringent regulations apply to enable access to hospital networks, mainly due to data privacy concerns.

14.3 Architecture Design

Figure 14.1 depicts the components of our FL framework. These are: (1) the user interface that supports all operations of the framework. The user of the framework has access to an installable Python toolkit to perform operations such as creating use cases, creating and uploading model artifacts by connecting to the coordinator APIs. (2) The coordinator that plays the role of an orchestrator and is responsible for managing the execution of the framework for use cases in a seamless manner. The coordinator consists of admin service hosts which are a set of APIs responsible for use case management, like hosting a new use case, registration of workers, and creating a new configuration. The coordinator executes a job, defined as a single execution of a use case algorithm. Furthermore, it stores the base models for all the hosted use cases, together with their relevant metadata, such as versioning and provenance. These are the models shared with the workers for performing the training during the first round. The coordinator uses a database, which is a Postgres-backed data store responsible for persisting all information and the configuration service. The latter is a set of APIs that allow to configure the training pipeline parameters like the number of training rounds, the optimizer, and the model hyperparameters (learning rate and any other common configurations that need to be shared with the worker). (3) The worker, which is a component that executes tasks at the local sites and contributes to model training in one or more use cases.

During the FL process, at each training round, the coordinator exposes a task for each participating worker. The worker executes this task and submits the results back to the coordinator. Once the participating workers have sent their updates, the coordinator aggregates the results so that the new tasks are available for workers during the next round. Upon training round completion, the worker publishes the weights along with the training round information for the coordinator, which stores in the database the model updates received from the workers. The coordinator waits for the workers to publish their weights and aggregates them once it has received weights from all workers participating in the current training round.

By default, our pipeline uses federated averaging (FedAvg) and also supports FedProx. FedAvg [Sun et al., 2022] is an iterative process for weight averaging, and it is the most common method in FL for the aggregation purpose. At each iteration, FedAvg first performs several epochs of stochastic gradient descent (SGD) on K workers, where K represents a small fraction of the total devices in the network. Then, the workers communicate their model updates to a central server that performs the update averaging. FedProx is another aggregation technique that aims at adding a proximal term to the learning objective and improving the stability of the method. This term enables consideration of data heterogeneity and improves the stability and overall accuracy of FL in heterogeneous networks. After having performed the aggregation, the updated model is available to be executed in the next round by the workers.

14.4 Federated Learning for Cross-Silo and Cross-Device Applications

In cross-silo FL, workers are designed to maintain the state of the model and the training algorithm. This means that workers are stateful and there is no need to iterate the model and the entire configuration during each training round. The coordinator sends the computational graph, initial model state, and training hyperparameters only once. Furthermore, the workers may have persistent memory and the computational resources required to establish the infrastructure for training a deep-learning model. Based on worker persistent memory, we have implemented local optimizers which operate the local model and allow one to upload and unload model updates. Since each worker has its own copy of the model, the user can define global and local model parameters and train local parameters separately for each worker, as well as renewing worker state by submitting a new configuration. Depending on the implementation scenario, the federation may consist of a few workers (such as hospitals or data centers), and each of them might be able to participate in most of the training rounds.

When deploying the framework in a cross-device setting, the main differences are the dataset sizes used for training, the computing performance of the hardware, and the base models. These features must be adapted for edge devices due to the limited support of model operations and the specific hardware accelerators of such devices; therefore, in cross-device FL, the worker is stateless and the coordinator submits the configuration to trigger each training iteration repeatedly. In contrast with the cross-silo setting, in cross-devices, training is triggered according to device constraints (such as idle and charging). For example, in the case of hundreds of devices, aggregation would be triggered according to the minimum number of devices instead of waiting for all participants. Furthermore, edge devices are under the control of the users and the executed processes need to consider user behavior as well as device constraints [Lo et al., 2021].

14.5 Explainability with Federated Learning

While the healthcare domain can greatly benefit from collaboratively training AI models, FL is still under exploration. FL has been applied to electronic health records to predict mortality and ICU stay [Rieke et al., 2020]. Image-based classification and segmentation tasks in the medical field have been explored with FL for segmenting brain tumors in MRI images; classifying disease biomarkers in fMRI; and predicting outcomes in COVID-19 patients, combining lab and vital data with X-ray images [Rieke et al., 2020], [Bonawitz et al., 2019]. However, many challenges are still unsolved. Most research and experiments performed to evaluate FL approaches only simulate privacy-sensitive scenarios [Lo et al., 2021]. Other key challenges investigated are support for scalability, security and reconstruction risk, communication architecture, and system design [Kairouz et al., 2021], [Bonawitz et al., 2019], [Sheller et al., 2020], [Li et al., 2021].

FL aims at helping access high-diversity datasets from many institutions to mitigate the biases in models evaluated on smaller centralized datasets from few sources. It enables exposing a model to diverse inputs (e.g., different demographics, acquisition protocols, and rare cases) [Rieke et al., 2020]. But this means that data from local sites are kept private and cannot be read and analyzed by the other sites, leading to issues related to explainability and interpretation [Haffar et al., 2022].

FL enhances generalization by increasing the diversity of datasets but poses a challenge when data distributions across sites are heterogeneous and non-independently and identically distributed (non-IID). Aggregation techniques, such as FedProx, address issues stemming from data heterogeneity by adding regularization and re-parametrization of the conventional FedAvg. However, key features for a successful model, such as data quality, bias, level of standardization, and related statistics, remain unseen by the central server and remote clients. Local sites cannot retrieve all relevant information such as explanation and interpretability by accessing only the local and global models. The question arises as to whether model updates from local sites are relevant and optimal for each participant. Thus, all participants may decide and agree on whether a certain data population is suitable for training a model in a federated fashion [Rieke et al., 2020]. This is complex in FL because datasets from other parties are private. FL systems should be expanded and re-designed to help explain predictions and mitigate the perceived lack of interpretation which is already present in the inner black-box nature of deep learning models.

In Lahav et al. [2018], attention is shifted away from explainability to methods that are considered simple enough to be human interpretable and outputs that can be linked to sets of steps that are comprehensible and in line with linear human reasoning. The authors focus on trust as an essential component to convince clinical users to use ML/AI models for diagnosing, treating, and managing their patients. The authors present an experiment that shows that technical experts cannot correctly predict which of several alternatives of explaining outputs will maximize clinicians' confidence in the models and that more information does not always lead to more comprehension and increased trust. The hypothesis is that information overload can reduce rather than increase explainability and that interpretability, confidence, and trust are subjective elements. Therefore, explainability methods should be elaborated on and refined in collaboration with the clinical experts through an interactive process. To increase utilization of models, just presenting one or more interpretability modules is not enough. Instead, users should be involved in the definition of the explanations that will be shown to them post-deployment when the model will be used to support clinical decisions.

In Demertzis et al. [2022], an FL model is proposed where explanations are used to suggest retraining those features that are considered important. In this way, the system enables an adaptation of the FL model, by retraining only the necessary features. In this work, Shapley additive explanations (SHAP) and Lipschitz constant (LIPC) methods are applied to generate model explanations. Shapley values have been also integrated in vertical FL to reveal feature importance from the owned features (which remain hidden) and the federated features. The federated features are then used to interpret the model prediction and the contribution from each participant without knowing and exchanging any data. In another study, interpretability is also used to detect misclassification in the federated model, thus preventing security and privacy attacks by local peers or the model coordinator [Haffar et al., 2022].

Nevertheless, extensive research on explainable AI integrated in FL is lacking. FL models should be enhanced with explainable AI methodologies so that explanation by local sites is provided, shared in the federated setting, and used in combination with the global model explanation. This information should be enriched with data quality and statistical measurements that can be used to weight the contribution of each feature based on the local data distribution.

Our preliminary exploration in the context of the collaborative projects SMART-BEAR [www.smart-bear.eu/] and ODIN [https://odin-smarthospitals.eu/] is in line with the previous observations [Lahav et al., 2018]. In these consortia, clinicians find explainability important to increase model use, but the perspectives vary with respect to the kind of explanation that provides most value, and information presentation appears to have an important role in the response to different explainability metrics. Based on discussions with clinical users, our hypothesis is that the specific clinical use case in which the model is developed, the deployment setup, and the perception of and experience with technology and AI of each user are also factors that will influence the feedback on the added value of the provided explanations. SMART-BEAR focuses on multiple clinical domains: hearing loss, cardio-vascular diseases, cognitive impairments, balance disorders, and mental health, in a large study with 5000 patients from five EU countries. We aim to build on the baseline feedback and implement a range of explainability metrics to evaluate in each clinical use case. Hypotheses that we aim to test are that a combination of methods will be perceived as adding more value than one method alone, that the perception to explainabilty is indeed subjective and depends on a variety of factors (clinical use case, experience with AI of the clinician, etc.), that collaboration with clinicians during the development of the interpretations will increase the user satisfaction with results, and that user experience and visualization research can lead to higher user satisfaction with the explanations in the selected explainability methods.

14.6 Explainability Methods: Overview and Challenges

New methods are currently being developed in explainable AI for providing both local and global explanations. Global explanations focus on interpreting model predictions over all data, while local explanations explain the model over a single prediction which might be meaningful when evaluating a model in inference. However, only Shapley values have been employed in federated models and computed locally by the hosts participating to the distributed learning process [Demertzis et al., 2022], [Haffar et al., 2022], [Wang, 2019]. Further research should focus on new design choices of FL systems which include ad-hoc explainability methods in the learning and inference processes.

Shapley values are used to provide the SHAP, which is an importance-based method; SHAP can retrieve the most important input features which contribute to produce a certain prediction. Compared to other approaches in explainability (e.g., LIME, based on locally approximating the model around a given prediction), SHAP values are computationally more efficient and more consistent with human intuition and can be scaled to machine learning and DL models [Manni et al., 2022]. The SHAP values for deep neural networks are called deep SHAP, and they are based on DeepLIFT [Shrikumar et al., 2017], which is a prediction explanation method that attributes the effect of an input set to a reference value. Deep SHAP combines DeepLIFT and Shapley values, and instead of using a single reference value, it uses a background of values and Shapley equations to linearize components such as softmax functions [Lundberg and Su-In, 2017a].

Another group of methods is represented by example-based approaches that explain the prediction using examples. These may add value in healthcare, as they replicate the decision-making process of clinicians, which is based on experience (e.g., previously made observations or diagnoses). One of these methods is based on influence functions [Koh and Liang, 2017]. Influence functions can estimate how the model prediction changes when removing a training data sample from the training set. Thus, from a clinical perspective, the contribution of single training data samples can be explored and used to interpret the model behavior. However, these methods do not provide any visualization, and a combination with SHAP should be explored to visualize the most important features. However, in FL training, data samples cannot be easily shared due to privacy and security issues.

Rule-based methods can use a single prediction to provide a set of rules on input features within which the prediction does not change [Ribeiro et al., 2018]. Other methods, such as counterfactual [Wachter, 2017], provide insight on how the input should change to get a certain model output so that the user can assess whether the model uses the correct decision boundary for making a prediction.

Different explainability methods should be exploited and combined for the workers and coordinator of the FL training process. Local sites may share model interpretation with the central server or to the other participants so that a unified view of each federated contribution is provided. Further, explainability methods in FL should be model agnostic and applicable to conventional ML and DL models to ensure system scalability.

Here we provide an example of explanation with SHAP from a supervised classification task. In this use case, ICU data (from the Philips eICU database [Pollard et al., 2018]), which includes vitals, lab, age, and respiratory data, are used as features to detect hemodynamic instability. In clinical practice, these parameters have crucial importance for monitoring circulatory failure, which is the first consequence and signal of hemodynamic instability [Weil, 2005]. Each sample is labeled either as stable (positive class) or unstable (negative class). When a sample is unstable, an intervention is needed. The dataset of 25 hospitals includes 30,751 samples in the training set (4236 unstable, 26,515 stable) and 12,738 samples in the test set (1942 unstable,

10,796 stable). We tested two models: an eXtreme Gradient Boosting (XGBoost) algorithm and a gradient boosting variant. The latter is an ensemble of differentiable models, such as neural networks and soft decision trees [Frosst and Hinton, 2021]. With soft trees, the decision is learned optimizing a loss function (e.g., cross-entropy loss). By employing neural gradient boosting (NGB) models, we tested a hybrid method which might replace decision-tree based models, the leading and state-of-the-art approach for clinical tabular data, and enable DL-based solutions. We employ SHAP to provide explainability for both models. Deep SHAP was used to provide an explanation of the neural gradient model, while Tree SHAP was used for analyzing the explanation of XGBoost. Tree SHAP is a variant of the model-agnostic SHAP algorithm for a more efficient and faster computation of SHAP values specific to trees and ensembles of trees [Lundberg and Su-In, 2017b].

Figure 7.2 shows the summary plots for the feature importance scores computed for NGB (on the left) and XGBoost (on the right). From top to bottom, the plots show the most significant features. The features on top contribute more to the prediction compared to those at the bottom. For both models, hematocrit and glucose values have the highest impact, followed by other features that are present in both plots for most cases. In general, features related to the circulatory system, such as blood pressure, heart rate, hematocrit, and hemoglobin levels, as well as SpO2 and PaCo2, have an impact on the final prediction. This result leads to the conclusion that by using SHAP values, we can provide reliable model explainability for the neural boosting model as well as for XGBoost, emphasizing features with the highest impact on the final prediction that can potentially reveal a higher risk to develop hemodynamic instability. Although SHAP is one of the most common and preferred methods, it is based on feature importance used to train a model, which in inference can be biased with the testing dataset.

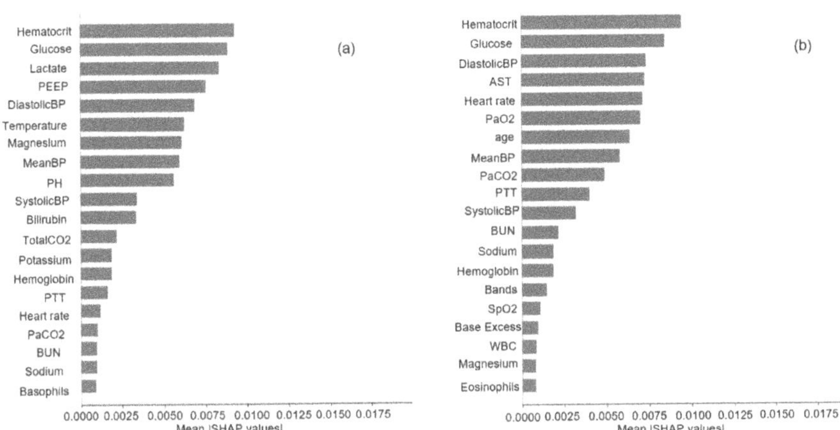

Figure 14.2 On the left and right are the summary plots for SHAP values computed on the test set for the neural gradient boosting and the XGBoost trained models, respectively.

14.7 Data Reconstruction Risk in Federated Learning

Person de-identification (de-ID) is an essential step toward accessing data by a DL practitioner. Practically, it is time-consuming and requires resources that scale with size of the dataset. Moreover, sensitive data, such as face photos and images, could not be de-identified efficiently.

Focusing on DL applications, re-identification (re-ID) risk could be reduced if the data owner keeps training data locally and releases only the trained model or its intermediate updates. In such a scenario, to recognize the identities from the training data, a potential adversary should reconstruct training data from the updates first, meaning that the de-ID procedure could be relaxed if the data are used only for DL applications and if it is proven that the reconstruction risk is negligible.

Reconstruction attacks aim to disclose the training samples based on updates of the DL model. Recent work [Zhu et al., 2019] describes approaches for generating a training sample (or batch of samples) from DL gradients. More precisely, knowing the released update U_θ and training artifacts, such as configuration h, loss function l, architecture and weights θ of the model M_θ, an adversary can reproduce the training algorithm T_{h,l,M_θ} and optimize the distance L_{xy}.

$$L_{xy}\left(h,l,M_\theta,U_\theta\right)=d\left(T_{h,l,M_\theta}\left(x_{rec},y_{rec}\right),U_\theta\left(x_{true},y_{true}\right)\right)+\textit{(constraints)}$$

$L_{xy}\left(h,l,M_\theta,U_\theta\right)$ reaches a minimum when the reconstruction (x_{rec},y_{rec}) is equal to the actual training data $\left(x_{true},y_{true}\right)$. In order to solve the optimization problem, any modifications of the stochastic gradient descent algorithm could be applied. The possibility to reconstruct training data are demonstrated for different DL problems, model architectures, and environment setups [Huang et al., 2021].

In the following, we consider two specific scenarios under which a reconstruction attack is a real threat.

1. Prior knowledge. A potential adversary who knows a lot about the training pipeline may also have some prior knowledge about the training data. This knowledge could be used as constraints during reconstruction to simplify the optimization and achieve better results. Here, we describe a possible way to formalize and utilize prior knowledge that makes possible the reconstruction of relatively large batches of training samples. Our main idea is that an adversary may incorporate prior knowledge to reduce the complexity of the reconstruction problem. As an example, learnt compression could be used to optimize the latent representation of the data samples instead of the samples themselves.
2. Custom training artefacts is a second method to steal private data from data owners during federated (or distributed) training. An adversary who has full control of the training process can define a model architecture, objective, and configuration and copy training samples directly to released updates. Aiming to copy a sample $\left(x^k,y^k\right)$ (here, it is a vector with size n) from a batch of samples $\left\{\left(x^1,y^1\right),\ldots,\left(x^n,y^n\right)\right\}$, one can choose a specific DL model M and a loss function l:

$$M(x) = xW^T, shape(W) = (1,n), W_{0,j} = 1,$$

$$l(y, M(x)) = M(x).$$

Executing a standard backpropagation procedure to compute an update of the model M, a training algorithm $T_{i,m}$ (such as those implemented by PyTorch) copies a training sample x into the update ξ :

$$\xi = \nabla_W \left(l(y, M(x))\right) = \nabla_W \left(M(x)\right) = \nabla_W \left(xW^T\right)$$
$$= \frac{\partial(x_1 w_1)}{\partial w_1} \cdots \frac{\partial(x_n w_n)}{\partial w_n} = (x_1 \ldots x_n) = x.$$

The aforementioned examples illustrate a potential risk of the attack. The risk could be reduced by varying hyperparameters, such as batch size, number of training iterations, or size of the model [Wei et al., 2020].

Basic risk estimation methods focus on simulation of the reconstruction attack [Wei et al., 2020]. Even though these methods may visualize data leakage well, they have several drawbacks. Since optimization in high-dimensional space (up to 10^6 parameters for high-resolution or three-dimensional train images) is an essential part of the attack, there is no guarantee that it converges to the optimum solution. The success of the attack depends on multiple factors. It was shown that initialization and hyperparameters may drastically affect convergence [Wei et al., 2020]. Also, it tends to get stuck in local minima or skip over the right minima. As a result, optimization requires frequent human interventions in the process. In addition, there is lack of research aiming to design proper distance metrics for evaluating data leakage. Therefore, currently only a human can reliably and accurately recognize leaked information on reconstructed data.

14.8 Definition of the Reconstruction Risk

There is limited research and no adequate solution proposing a general definition of the reconstruction risk that could be estimated for every sample and training algorithm. Herein, we open a discussion on possible variants of the definitions. We propose a set of assumptions required for defining reconstruction risk. The assumptions are supplemented with descriptions.

1. The approach should be able to validate any "extracting knowledge from data" algorithms without modifications in the algorithms themselves. The accuracy of DL models is sensitive to any changes in the optimization pipeline for most DL applications. Any modifications in optimization may lead to accuracy deterioration. This means that a risk estimation algorithm could be embedded, but it must not affect the training results.
2. The risk should be computed for every training sample separately. In some cases, the success of the reconstruction varies between training samples [Geiping

et al., 2020]. For instance, if a training example is an edge hard case, it is more likely that the model will memorize it during training rather than memorizing a common one. So reconstruction risk should be computed for every training sample.

3. The algorithm should consider the stochastic nature of the updates. Stochastic sampling from the training subset is an essential part of any training algorithm. Data preparation can also involve some non-deterministic steps, such as online data augmentation or online hard example mining [https://github.com/aleju/imgaug]. This means that even the same training example may result in different updates.
4. The algorithm should also estimate the computational power of a potential adversary for obtaining statistically reasonable results. The methods for estimating hidden parameters based on observed data, such as maximum likelihood estimation, are iterative and require multiple experiments. It implies that the adversary may need to collect a set of updates to successfully reconstruct the training data. Practically it may require a lot of time and make reconstruction infeasible. So it is vital to evaluate the possibility of collecting required data by a protentional adversary.
5. Training data have not been published previously. We do not consider other types of privacy attacks such as membership attacks. The only available prior knowledge is general information about the nature of training data. As we show, this information could be used by an adversary to enhance reconstruction attacks.
6. Computed risk should be in the range [0, 1]. Herein, we provide an example of the edge case where the risk is equal to 0. For a given training sample, the reconstruction risk is equal to zero if there exists at least one similar sample such that the corresponding updates are indistinguishable. At the same time, the risk reaches its maximum if the number of training iterations and the batch size are equal to 1. Any other scenario lies somewhere between the first two.

We provide a new definition of the reconstruction risk. The proposed approach is loosely based on *empirical differential privacy* (eDP) [Burchard et al., 2019]. Avoiding interventions in the training procedure (see Assumption 1), we do not provide any theoretical guarantees of privacy before the calculations. However, our goal is to estimate privacy leaks post factum. Considering collaborative (such as federated or sequential) learning, at every iteration *t*, a client *k* draws a batch B_t of identically distributed data samples $\{d_{t1},\dots,d_{tn}\}$ from a training dataset D_k, $d_i \sim \zeta$. A preprocessing framework $P_k(\star)$ randomly divides the batch into minibatches $\{b_{t1},\dots,b_{tm}\}$ $\left(b_{ti} = \{d_{ti1},\dots,d_{til}\}, l = \frac{n}{m}\right)$, stochastically augments each sample d_{ti}, and prepares it for training. A training framework $T_k(\star)$ iteratively computes parameter gradients for each minibatch b_{ti} and updates the model parameters w_{ii} after every *s*th step (commonly used, *s* is equal to 1). Finally, the client releases the update $\Delta_t^k = w_{tm} - w_{t0}$. A client executes this procedure *N* times, until the convergence of the objective. According to the stochastic nature of the function $P_k(\star)$, we may receive different updates for the same training batch (see Assumption 3), meaning that the update $\Delta_t^k(d_{t1},\dots, d_{tn})$ is a random variable drawn from the distribution χ_k.

14.8.1 Definition 1

Knowing an update Δ_t^k, parameters w_{to}, algorithms $P_k(\star)$ and $T_k(\star)$, possible results of the training for a given sample $P_{T_k P_k}\left(\Delta_t^k\right) = P\left(d_{ti}\right)$, and nature of training data *P(d)*, a *reconstruction attack* aims to find samples $d_{ti} \in D_k$ that maximize the function

$$P_k\left(D_k\right) = P\left(\Delta_1^k,\ldots,\Delta_N^k\right).$$

The probability $P_{T_k P_k}\left(\Delta_t^k\right)$ is vital for risk estimation, and it could be computed by the data owner. One can collect a set of values $\left\{\left(\Delta_t^k\right)_1,\ldots,\left(\Delta_t^k\right)_R\right\}$ by computing updates Δ_t^k for samples $\left\{d_{t1},\ldots,d_{tm}\right\}$ with various random seeds. Then, the kernel density estimation algorithm could be applied to approximate the density function $p_{T_k P_k}\left(\Delta_t^k\right)$. We ignore the problem of estimating the probabilities $P_k(D_k)$ and *P(d)* since it is not required to estimate the risk.

14.8.2 Definition 2

Let *B*, *B*★ be training batches that differ in one sample on the position n : $d_n, d_n^* \sim \zeta$. Let denote the probability measure of the training results $\Delta \sim \chi$ (and $\Delta^* \sim \chi^*$) for *B* (and *B*★) as function *P* (and *P*★). A reconstruction risk δ for a sample d_n is defined as a probability to identify the difference between the updates computed for similar batches *B* and *B*★ for any potential update :Δ_o.

$$P\left(\Delta_o\right) \le e^{\grave{o}} P^*\left(\Delta_o\right) + \delta,$$

$$P^*\left(\Delta_o\right) \le e^{\grave{o}} P\left(\Delta_o\right) + \delta,$$

$$d_n^* = \delta\left(P, P^*\right).$$

Herein, we use the notions of empirical (ϵ, δ) – differential privacy, such as threshold e^{ϵ}, failure probability, δ and "adjacent" batches *B* and *B*★. Nevertheless, we rely on the idea that reconstruction is impossible if a bijection from the samples to the updates is broken (see Assumption 6). Proving that, we aim to find at least one *nearest* (or *similar*) sample (or group of samples) which could replace the target one without considerable consequences. That is the reason to search for the *infimum* among possible candidates. It is not necessary that the distribution ζ be known for the training data; as a result, candidates could be searched among the other training samples $\delta\left(d_n^*\right)$. If the risk is negligible for every sample d_i from batch *B*, we claim that the batch could not be reconstructed.

To compute the risk for the sample d_n, the definition is rewritten with density estimation functions p_n and $p\star n$; see proof of Theorem 1 [Burchard et al., 2019]:

$$\delta_n = \left(\int_A \left(1 - e^{\grave{o}}\frac{p_n^*(x)}{p_n(x)}\right)_+ p_n(x)dx, \int_A \left(\frac{p_n^*(x)}{p_n(x)} - e^{\grave{o}}\right) p_n(x)dx\right),$$

$$x \in A : p_n\left(x\right) \ge e^{\grave{o}} p_n^*\left(x\right) or\ p_n^*\left(x\right) \ge e^{\grave{o}} p_n\left(x\right) for\ all\ x \in A.$$

Assuming that the density estimation $p_n(x)$ and corresponding distribution are known, Monte Carlo integration could be applied to approximate the integrals. Practically, the update Δ is a vector in multidimensional space (up to millions of dimensions). That makes density estimation challenging. As a possible solution, one can sample each component of the update Δ independently.

14.9 Conclusions

This chapter explored federated learning and the value of implementing explainability methods in this setting both to enhance interpretability and trust in AI models and to provide valuable insights to the modeler during model training with unseen data across multiple sites. In our future work, we aim to evaluate in specific use cases provided by the two large-scale projects ODIN and SMART BEAR whether the information provided by explainability methods is sufficient to enable the assessment of key aspects of the datasets such as quality, diversity, bias, and outlier detection when training with distributed data in federated learning. We will also investigate how to enhance the added value of explainability in these use cases by combining methods and customizing the information presentation to the requirements of the clinical users in the specific clinical domains represented in the projects.

Next to the many potential benefits of federated learning, we have also summarized a range of challenges and discussed in more detail the open research question of defining and measuring the risk of data reconstruction.

Acknowledgments

This work was supported by the European Union's Horizon 2020 program and is partially funded under grant agreements No 101017331, ODIN and No 857172, SMART BEAR.

References

Bonawitz, K., et al. "Towards federated learning at scale: System design." *Proceedings of Machine Learning and Systems* 1 (2019): 374–388.

Burchard, P., Daoud, A., and Dotterrer, D. "Empirical differential privacy." *arXiv Preprint arXiv:1910.12820* (2019), pp. 1–20.

Dayan, I., Roth, H. R., Aoxiao, Z., Ahmed, H., Amilcare, G., Anas Z. Abidin, Andrew, L., et al. "Federated learning for predicting clinical outcomes in patients with COVID-19." *Nature News* (Nature Publishing Group), September 15, 2021. www.nature.com/articles/s41591-021-01506-3.

Demertzis, K., Iliadis, L., Kikiras, P., and Pimenidis, E. "An explainable semi-personalized federated learning model". *Integrated Computer-Aided Engineering* (2022): 1–16.

Frosst, N., and Hinton, G. "Distilling a neural network into a soft decision tree". *arXiv.org* (2021), pp. 1–8. https://arxiv.org/abs/1711.09784v1

Geiping, J., et al. "Inverting gradients – How easy is it to break privacy in federated learning?" *Advances in Neural Information Processing Systems* 33 (2020): 16937–16947.

Haffar, R., Sánchez, D., and Domingo-Ferrer, J. "Explaining predictions and attacks in federated learning via random forests." *Applied Intelligence* (2022): 1–17.

Heidelberg, M., Kelman, A., Hopkins, J., and Allen, M. E. "The evolution of data ethics in clinical research and drug development." *Ethics, Medicine and Public Health* 14 (2020): 100517. https://doi.org/10.1016/j.jemep.2020.100517.

Huang, Y., et al. "Evaluating gradient inversion attacks and defenses in federated learning." *Advances in Neural Information Processing Systems* 34 (2021): 7232–7241.

Kairouz, P., et al. "Advances and open problems in federated learning." *Foundations and Trends® in Machine Learning* 14, no. 1–2 (2021): 1–210.

Koh, P. W., and Liang, P. "Understanding black-box predictions via influence functions". *In International Conference on Machine Learning. PMLR* (2017): 1885–1894.

Lahav, O., Mastronarde, N., and van der Schaar, M. "What is interpretable? Using machine learning to design interpretable decision-support systems." *arXiv Preprint arXiv: 1811.10799* (2018), pp. 1–15.

Li, Q., Wen, Z., Wu, Z., Hu, S., Wang, N., Li, Y., . . . and He, B. "A survey on federated learning systems: Vision, hype and reality for data privacy and protection." *IEEE Transactions on Knowledge and Data Engineering* 35, no. 4 (2021): 3347–3366.

Lo, S. K., et al. "A systematic literature review on federated machine learning: From a software engineering perspective." *ACM Computing Surveys (CSUR)* 54, no. 5 (2021): 1–39.

Lundberg, S. M., and Su-In L. "A unified approach to interpreting model predictions." *Advances in Neural Information Processing Systems* (2017a), pp. 4768–4777.

Lundberg, S. M., and Su-In, L. "Consistent feature attribution for tree ensembles." *arXiv preprint arXiv: 1706.06060* (2017b), pp. 1–7.

Manni, F., Buckharev, A., Jain, A., Moorthy, S., Rahaman, A., and Bucur, A. "Neural gradient boosting in federated learning for hemodynamic instability prediction: Towards a distributed and scalable deep learning-based solution." *In Proceedings AMIA Annual Symposium 2022, 5–9 November,* Washington DC, USA.

Pollard, T. J., Johnson, A. E., Raffa, J. D., Celi, L. A., Mark, R. G., and Badawi, O. "The eICU Collaborative Research Database, a freely available multi-center database for critical care research." *Scientific Data* 5, no. 1 (2018): 1–13.

Rachakonda, A. S., Moorthy, B. S., Jain, C. A., Bukharev, D. A., Bucur, E. A., Manni, F. F., . . . and Mendez, I. N. I. "Privacy enhancing and scalable federated learning to accelerate AI implementation in cross-silo and IoMT environments." *IEEE Journal of Biomedical and Health Informatics* (2022): 1–12.

Ribeiro, M. T., Singh, S., and Guestrin, C. "Anchors: High-precision model agnostic explanations.", *AAAI* (2018), 32, no. 1 (2018): 777–780.

Rieke, N., Hancox, J., Li, W., Milletari, F., Roth, H. R., Albarqouni, S., . . . & Cardoso, M. J. "The future of digital health with federated learning." *NPJ Digital Medicine* 3, no. 1 (2020): 1–7.

Sheller, M. J., Edwards, B., Reina, G. A., Martin, J., Pati, S., Kotrotsou, A., et al. "Federated learning in medicine: Facilitating multi-institutional collaborations without sharing patient data." *Scientific Reports* 10, no. 1 (2020): 12598. www.nature.com/articles/s41598-020-69250-1.

Shrikumar, A., Greenside, P., and Kundaje, A. "Learning important features through propagating activation differences." *In International Conference on Machine Learning PMLR* (2017): 3145–3153.

Sun, T., Dongsheng, L., and Bao, W. "Decentralized federated averaging." *IEEE Transactions on Pattern Analysis and Machine Intelligence* 45, no. 4 (2022), 4289–4301.

Wachter, S., Brent, M., and Chris, R. "Counterfactual explanations without opening the black box: Automated decisions and the GDPR." *Harvard Journal of Law & Technology* 31 (2017): 841.

Wang, G. "Interpret federated learning with shapley values." *arXiv preprint* (2019): 1905.04519.

Wei, W., et al. "A framework for evaluating gradient leakage attacks in federated learning." *arXiv preprint arXiv:2004.10397* (2020), pp. 1–21.

Weil, M. H. *Defining Hemodynamic Instability. Functional Hemodynamic Monitoring*. Berlin: Springer, 9–17, 2005.

Zhu, L., Liu, Z., and Han, S. "Deep leakage from gradients." *Advances in Neural Information Processing Systems* 32 (2019).

Glossary

Alzheimer's disease – Progressive mental deterioration that can occur in middle or old age, due to generalized degeneration of the brain.

Artificial intelligence – The ability of a neural network model to intelligently perform a task like humans.

Batch normalization – An algorithmic method applied to stabilize a deep neural network and increase the training speed.

Bayesian deep learning – It is a posterior inference applied on a neural network model.

Binary image – An image where pixels have only two values, generally 0 and 1.

Chromophores – Molecules that absorb a particular wavelength of light.

Clustering – The concept of grouping data in classes based upon the similarity of the data.

Computed tomography – A type of medical imaging technique that produces a detailed image of the part scanned using X-rays.

Contrast – The amount of gray level variation within an image.

Convolution neural network – Series of algorithms put together to extract and analyze the features inherent in the given input.

Coronavirus disease – A life-threatening pandemic caused by SARS-CoV-2 virus.

Deep learning – A subset of artificial intelligence, where the neural network model consists of five or more layers to efficiently perform the task assigned.

Deep residual network – A deep neural network model with additional skip connections among the layers in order to stabilize the training of deeper networks without going into vanishing or exploding or shattered gradients' problem.

Dermoscopy – The examination of the skin using skin surface microscopy.

Diabetic retinopathy – A medical complication caused in eyes due to diabetes.

Digital imaging and communications in medicine – A typical data format to store image data in medical imaging.

Displacement vector field – A field that indicates positional vectors in an image with respect to given coordinates.

Explainable AI – It is a set of framework that explains or interprets the working of neural network and its decisions.

Feature – Any of the properties that are characteristic of an image, from which a description, interpretation, or understanding of the scene can be provided by a machine.

Functional Near-Infrared Spectroscopy (fNIRS) – A neuroimaging technique for measuring the blood oxygenation level in brain regions to infer region-specific brain activity.

Generative adversarial network – Two networks, generator and discriminator, compete against each other in zero-sum game form in such a way that one network's gain is other network's loss.

Glaucoma – A condition of increased pressure within the eyeball, causing a gradual loss of sight.

Glioblastoma – A highly invasive glioma in the brain.

Glycosylated hemoglobin – Three-to-four month-long average blood glucose level is called glycosylated hemoglobin.

Ground glass opacity – The air blockages formed in the chest due to lung-related infections.

Ground truth – It is a true or real information with direct observation.

Heatmap – A visual or image representation of data in such a way that the data values are shown as different colors. Often, the colors used range from "hotter" red to cooler "green" making the image look like a temperature or heat distribution map.

Hemodynamics – Changes in the blood flow.

Hemoglobin – An oxygen carrier in the blood.

High performance computing – The system that can run complex computations and process data at high speed.

High-resolution CT – The type of CT that uses high radiation dose (10 times normal dose) to form a detailed internal structure scan of a human body.

Histogram – Distribution of pixel gray level values. A graph of number of pixels at each gray level possible in an image.

Hyperglycemia – The condition in which blood glucose level is high compared to standard level.

Hypoglycemia – The condition in which blood glucose (BG) level is low compared to standard level.

Image biomarker – A radiomic feature extracted from medical images that represent genetic, molecular, histologic, radiographic, or physiologic characteristic.

Low-dose CT – It is a type of CT that uses low radiation dose (1/10th of normal dose) to form internal human body scan.

Low-resolution ULDCT – A type of CT in which less numbers of detector arrays and ultra-low radiation are used to form the scan.

Magnetic resonance imaging – A type of scan formed in k-space by imparting high magnetic and radio waves.

Mammography – A technique using X-rays to diagnose and locate tumors of the breasts.

Matrix – An image representation using M × N matrix and a 90° clockwise rotation of the conventional two-dimensional Cartesian coordinate representation.

Mean – The average of a set of data values.

Mean-squared error – It calculates the average of squares of the absolute errors.

Morphology – Originally comes from the study of forms of plants or animals. Image morphology represents the study of topology or structure of objects from their images. Morphological processing refers to certain operations where an object is "hit" with a structuring element and thereby reduced to a more revealing shape.

Near-Infrared Light – Light with a wavelength between 700 and 900 nm.

Neuroimaging – Producing images of the brain by noninvasive techniques.

Oncology – Study and treatment of tumors.

Out of distribution data – Data that has characteristics that are significantly different from the data used to train an AI model. It is usually data that comes from different sources and was collected in different environments or is the data from different types of subjects than were included in the training set.

Patch-based dictionary learning – A type of neural network that forms the sparse representations of the input data using patches of an image.

Peak signal-to-noise ratio – It is a ratio of the maximum power of an image to the power of corrupting noise that affects the quality of its representation.

Perception-based image quality evaluator – A type of nonreference evaluation measure to quantify the quality of image.

Pixel – Picture element.

Pointset – A set of connected pixels which can be represented in an efficient way, allowing very fast access to the data they represent.

Positron-emission tomography 0 – Type of medical imaging that uses radiotracers to visualize the internal human structures.

Radiogenomics – The relationship between the image feature of a disease and genetic or molecular characteristic.

Radiomics features – Radiomics features are quantitative features extracted from medical images.

Rectified linear activation unit – A type of nonlinearity introduced in neural network models, which squashes negative values to zero and linearly maps the positive values.

Resolution – Smallest feature (spatial) or gray level value (quantization) that an image system can resolve.

Root mean-squared error – It is a quantitative measure that is square root of the average of squares of the absolute errors.

Schizophrenia – A mentality or approach characterized by inconsistent or contradictory elements.

Segmentation – The act of demarcating different regions in a 2D or 3D image dataset and giving it a label – for example, outlining an organ on a 2D image acquired using Magnetic Resonance Imaging.

Sensitivity – The ability of a system to detect a condition, for example, the presence of a disease, when it is truly present.

Slice – 2D image often described as part of a 3D volume.

Specificity – The ability of a system to detect the absence of a condition, for example, absence of a disease, when it is truly absent.

Structural similarity index – It is a measure that evaluates how much the estimated image is similar to the original image.

Super-resolution – It is an algorithmic technique that increases the spatial resolution of the image.

Threshold – A value used to segment the gray level values of an image into two different regions. Also called the binarization of an image.

Ultra-LDCT – It is a type of CT that uses a very low radiation dose compared to the LDCT.

Voxel – 3D-pixel.

Index